booksonline

Read this book online today:

With SAP PRESS BooksOnline we offer you online access to knowledge from the leading SAP experts. Whether you use it as a beneficial supplement or as an alternative to the printed book, with SAP PRESS BooksOnline you can:

- Access your book anywhere, at any time. All you need is an Internet connection.
- Perform full text searches on your book and on the entire SAP PRESS library.
- Build your own personalized SAP library.

The SAP PRESS customer advantage:

Register this book today at *www.sap-press.com* and obtain exclusive free trial access to its online version. If you like it (and we think you will), you can choose to purchase permanent, unrestricted access to the online edition at a very special price!

Here's how to get started:

1. Visit *www.sap-press.com*.
2. Click on the link for SAP PRESS BooksOnline and login (or create an account).
3. Enter your free trial license key, shown below in the corner of the page.
4. Try out your online book with full, unrestricted access for a limited time!

Your personal free trial **license key**
for this online book is:

qnse-5vdf-rwym-uk2g

ABAP™ Basics

PRESS

SAP PRESS is a joint initiative of SAP and Galileo Press. The know-how offered by SAP specialists combined with the expertise of the Galileo Press publishing house offers the reader expert books in the field. SAP PRESS features first-hand information and expert advice, and provides useful skills for professional decision-making.

SAP PRESS offers a variety of books on technical and business related topics for the SAP user. For further information, please visit our website: *www.sap-press.com*.

Horst Keller, Sascha Krüger
ABAP Objects
2nd ed. 2007, app. 1,059 pp., with DVD
978-1-59229-079-6

Horst Keller
The Official ABAP Reference
2nd ed. 2005, app. 1,213 pp., with 3 CDs
978-1-59229-039-0

Horst Keller
The ABAP Quick Reference
2005, app. 213 pp.
978-1-59229-057-4

Karl-Heinz Kühnhauser
Discover ABAP
2007, app. 503 pp.
978-1-59229-152-6

Günther Färber and Julia Kirchner

ABAP™ Basics

Galileo Press

Bonn • Boston

Galileo Press is named after the Italian physicist, mathematician and philosopher Galileo Galilei (1564–1642). He is known as one of the founders of modern science and an advocate of our contemporary, heliocentric worldview. His words *Eppur si muove* (And yet it moves) have become legendary. The Galileo Press logo depicts Jupiter orbited by the four Galilean moons, which were discovered by Galileo in 1610.

Editor Stefan Proksch
English Edition Editor Laura Korslund
Translation Lemoine International, Inc., Salt Lake City, UT
Copyeditor Pamela Siska
Cover Design Graham Geary
Photo Credit Getty Images/Jeffrey Coolidge
Layout Design Vera Brauner
Production Manager Kelly O'Callaghan
Production Editor Graham Geary
Typesetting Publishers' Design and Production Services, Inc.
Printed and bound in Canada

ISBN 978-1-59229-369-8

© 2011 by Galileo Press Inc., Boston (MA)
2nd Edition, updated and revised, 2011
4th German Edition published 2008 by Galileo Press, Bonn, Germany

Library of Congress Cataloging-in-Publication Data
Färber, Günther, 1971–
   [ABAP -Grundkurs. English]
   ABAP basics / Günther Färber, Julia Kirchner. — 2nd ed.
      p. cm.
   Includes bibliographical references.
   ISBN-13: 978-1-59229-369-8
   ISBN-10: 1-59229-369-7
   1. ABAP/4 (Computer program language) I. Kirchner, Julia. II. Title.
   QA76.73.A12F3713 2011
   005.1'17--dc22
2010040721

Contents at a Glance

1 Technical Overview and Getting Started in the System 19

2 Working with the Development Environment: SAP Object Navigator 55

3 Procedural Language Elements 117

4 Defining and Managing Database Tables 205

5 Screen Input and Output 243

6 Object-Oriented Language Elements 343

7 Practice Scenario—Automated Accounting for Corporate Subsidiaries 421

A Programming Guidelines and Tools 479

B Glossary 491

C Sources and Literature Recommendations 495

D The Authors 497

Dear Reader,

Welcome to the world of ABAP programming! If you have just begun your first journey with SAP programming, I'm confident that this book will meet all of your beginning needs. In this second updated and expanded version for ABAP 7.0, authors Günther Färber and Julia Kirchner will introduce and orient you to this complex language. Using a hands-on approach for comprehensive understanding, they introduce you to the most important commands at the beginning of each sub-chapter, and use numerous screenshots and a real-life scenario to guide you. Upon completion of this book, you will be able to write your first functional application. I'm delighted that you have started your journey with us, and wish you success in your first steps in ABAP.

We welcome you to share any praise or critical comments that will help us improve our books. Our number one goal is to provide accurate and useful information to benefit you, the reader, and to improve and expand your skills. We encourage you to visit our website at *www.sap-press.com* and share your feedback about this work.

Thank you for purchasing a book from SAP PRESS!

Laura Korslund
Editor, SAP PRESS

Galileo Press
100 Grossman Drive, Suite 205
Braintree, MA 02184

Laura.Korslund@galileo-press.com
www.sap-press.com

Contents

Preface 11

Introduction 13

1 Technical Overview and Getting Started in the System 19

1.1 Overview of SAP Software and Architecture 19
1.2 Notes for Setting Up Access to SAP Software 24
    1.2.1 Regular System 25
    1.2.2 Test Systems 26
1.3 Programmer's Checklist for Getting Started 27
1.4 Logon, Getting Started, and System Setup 32

2 Working with the Development Environment: SAP Object Navigator 55

2.1 Getting Started with the SAP Object Navigator 59
2.2 Development Classes and Packages 68
2.3 Namespaces 72
2.4 First Program: "Hello World"—REPORT, INCLUDE, and Application Menu 78
2.5 Online Help, help.sap.com, service.sap.com, and SAP Notes 105

3 Procedural Language Elements 117

3.1 Basic Commands and Fields—WRITE, PARAMETERS, MOVE, SY Fields 120
3.2 Data and Data Types—DATA, PARAMETERS, CONSTANTS, FIELD SYMBOLS, TYPE, CREATE, Text Elements 127
3.3 Structures and Internal Tables—TABLE, MOVE-CORRESPONDING, INSERT, APPEND, READ, MODIFY, DELETE, LOOP 151

3.4 Subprograms and Functions—FORM, FUNCTION,
EXCEPTIONS 163
3.5 Branches and Logical Expressions—IF, CASE 183
3.6 Loops—WHILE, DO 198

4 Defining and Managing Database Tables 205

4.1 Field Properties—DATA ELEMENT, DOMAIN 207
4.2 Defining and Processing Database Tables—SELECT,
INSERT, UPDATE, DELETE 222

5 Screen Input and Output 243

5.1 Simple Input and Output Interfaces—SELECTION
SCREEN, SELECT-OPTIONS, CALL SELECTION SCREEN,
SAP List Viewer 245
5.2 Complex Input and Output Interfaces—Dynpros 278

6 Object-Oriented Language Elements 343

6.1 Classes and Objects—CLASS, CREATE OBJECT,
METHOD 345
6.2 Inheritance and Polymorphism—INHERITING FROM,
REDEFINITION 377
6.3 EVENTS 396

7 Practice Scenario—Automated Accounting for Corporate Subsidiaries 421

7.1 Defining the Requirements and a List of Functions for
the Application 422
7.1.1 List of Functions 424
7.1.2 Selection List 425
7.2 Software Architecture 427
7.3 Software Design 430
7.3.1 Rough Design 431
7.3.2 Detailed Design 435
7.4 Implementation 445

7.4.1   Dictionary Objects 445
7.4.2   Programs 451
7.4.3   Function Groups 453

Appendices **477**

A   Programming Guidelines and Tools 479
    A.1   Programming guideline 479
    A.2   Program Check Tools 489
B   Glossary 491
C   Sources and Literature Recommendations 495
D   The Authors 497

Index 501

Preface

ABAP has transformed itself from a programming language, which was used internally only at SAP, into a development platform for business applications on application servers from SAP—a platform used by over a million programmers. Consequently, the need for more information on ABAP and its object-oriented extensions and tools has grown exponentially; for example, the need to address the following questions: What's the best way to start to use ABAP Objects? What are the typical tasks that an ABAP programmer must perform? What basic concepts are the underpinnings for the programming of SAP applications with ABAP Objects, and how does ABAP differ from other programming languages? What goes on behind the scenes in transactions of the ABAP development environment, and which transactions are important to you? These are only some of the questions that we address in this book.

In this book, we'll introduce you to the most important components, concepts, and ideas regarding SAP programming; namely, the information you'll need to answer the above questions. This book is intended for readers who are looking for an up-to-date and quick tutorial on programming with ABAP Objects—an introduction based on solving real-world tasks. The title of this book, ABAP Basics, says it all. We offer a basic course on the ABAP Objects programming language. This book is based on application scenarios that discuss typical, everyday problems and solutions on the basis of comprehensive SAP systems and applications. The focus is always on practical matters: Actual procedures are shown screenshot by screenshot. The comments on the language elements are by no means complete. They simply convey popular options for usage, and thereby maximize the success of your learning experience.

The groundwork for this book was laid incrementally; it involved many years of training and practical experience, with topics that today would come under the overarching terms *SAP* and *ABAP programming*. Ongoing and intense collaboration with the development departments at SAP in

Walldorf, Germany, has enabled us to learn a great deal about the SAP way of solving problems and what must be considered in the process. A practice scenario that uses the knowledge gained in individual chapters demonstrates how to create a comprehensive and professional application. This shared expertise will enable you to become more familiar with the source code from SAP and ultimately work to your advantage.

We are especially grateful to Horst Keller (SAP), who reviewed the individual chapters and was always ready to advise and help us, and to Florian Zimniak and Stefan Proksch (SAP PRESS), whose editorial work ensured the publication of this book. Moreover, we'd like to thank Sandro Marini, Frank Wierichs, and Dr. Harald Junghans for their support in reviewing and revising the new or international editions.

We hope that this book will provide all readers with a quick and easy-to-understand introduction to ABAP and SAP application programming.

Julia Kirchner and **Günther Färber**
NEXONTIS IT GmbH

The ABAP Objects programming language has become one of the most important languages for the development of enterprise applications. This kind of software must run stably, meet the simultaneous needs of many users, and offer rapid processing. ABAP Objects is the first choice among programming languages to meet all of these requirements.

Introduction

The rapid proliferation of standard business software has fundamentally changed the programming landscape in enterprises. The range of applications used in such software today goes far beyond accounting and managing production. It extends to the furthest areas of an enterprise, and includes the computerization of relationships among vendors, customers, and business partners.

At the cost of in-house development in languages specific to an industry (COBOL, Visual Basic, Delphi, C++, and Java), the number of modifications and enhancements made to the standard business software in use is growing increasingly. Use of the proprietary language from SAP, ABAP Objects, prevails wherever SAP software is being used—in more than 50,000 large and midsize enterprises around the world. This language is not only the foundation of more than 40 application components of SAP ERP (for instance, Financials (FI) and Materials Management (MM)), but also of all SAP solutions that enhance SAP ERP in vital areas such as SAP Customer Relationship Management (SAP CRM) and SAP Supply Chain Management (SAP SCM).

Consequently, there has been such a growth in the popularity of the ABAP Objects language, which many analysts would have found inconceivable just some time ago.

This book introduces you to the programming of efficient business applications with ABAP Objects. It offers beginning programmers and those familiar with other languages practical assistance in getting started. All chapters have the same structure: The tasks and questions that arise are introduced against the background of business and technological problems. Step-by-step directions lead to concrete applications and solutions. Special attention is given to the basics and to showing how professional ABAP programmers, even those at SAP, use individual language elements to solve complex problems. After reading this book, you should be able to deal quickly with real projects and programs.

What's in This Book?

This book introduces you to software development with ABAP Objects and to the SAP NetWeaver Application Server (SAP NetWeaver AS). Based on an outline of the most important topics in SAP development, it enables you to begin working with ABAP Objects. Each section begins with the most important ABAP commands that apply to the topic. These theoretical sections show you the effects of keywords and how to use them correctly. A practice scenario is built piece by piece, extending across individual chapters and throughout the entire book. It shows you how to use your new knowledge in functional ABAP programs. Screenshots and step-by-step instructions help the reader to perform the actual tasks and resolve typical problems that a programmer in the SAP environment might encounter.

The chapters cover the following subjects:

System access, architecture, and check list for programmers

Chapter 1, Technical Overview and Getting Started in the System, outlines the most important basic data on the history of SAP software and the most important concepts and architecture of Releases 7.0 and higher. It offers notes on obtaining access to an SAP system, to a normal system in your enterprise, or to a thin system (without business applications) set up especially for training purposes by SAP and SAP PRESS. It guides you through your first steps in an SAP system, starting with a logon and the initial configuration changes.

Procedural and object-oriented programming

Along with a brief introduction to the Object Navigator (see **Chapter 2**, Working with the Development Environment: SAP Object Navigator), a development environment from SAP, the main part of the book gives you practical knowledge based on business-oriented sample programs from the very beginning. Because its foundation rests on the programming model of a fourth generation programming language, the ABAP Objects language has far more elements than most of the other programming languages. **Chapter 3**, Procedural Language Elements, and **Chapter 6**, Object-Oriented Language Elements, speak to this situation. They address using essentially procedural language elements and demonstrate how to use object-oriented language extensions.

Chapter 4, Defining and Managing Database Tables, examines the significance of databases and data access with several procedural and program examples. **Chapter 5**, Screen Input and Output, describes how to work much as a large SAP application does to retrieve data from the database, display it on a user's screen, and then return the data entered by users to the database. **Chapter 7**, Practice Scenario—Automated Accounting for Corporate Subsidiaries, presents sample programs for selected functions and classes of the system and applications. Both are indispensable for professional development.

Data management and additional functions

The **Appendix** contains a description of important programming guidelines and naming conventions that SAP uses, as do all the sample programs in the book. It also features a comprehensive glossary that contains all the technical terms used in the book, a bibliography for further information, and an index that can be used to look up occurrences of keywords throughout the book.

Appendix with glossary and index

Most chapters deal with specific aspects of a large practical scenario, putting you into a professional development team right away. Within the development team, you work just as an SAP programmer would, handling one actual task after another and learning current approaches to solving problems, as well as getting valuable background information. The exercises at the end of each chapter vary according to the material discussed, and give you the flexibility you need to understand the programming language and development environment, as would a tool or building blocks for your own applications. We hope that you will continue to learn by doing these tasks and exercises intensively over the long term.

Practice scenarios, tasks, and exercises

Tips for those
familiar with other
programming
languages The "Tips for those familiar with other programming languages" in the margins indicate that the text here delves somewhat more deeply into the material. These sections draw comparisons with other programming languages for users who have experience with those languages and help you work with professional software development. If you do not yet have experience with programming and are primarily interested only in writing your first executable programs, you can overlook these sections.

Font Conventions

To give the book a clear design and distinguish specific elements graphically, some terms are highlighted with special fonts:

▶ *Italics*
Italics are used wherever an important term requires highlighting or is used for the first time. It is also used for the names of files and directories, file-system paths, and hyperlinks.

▶ SMALL CAPS
Small caps are used wherever the text speaks directly of screen elements of the SAP system. Menu paths, buttons, tabs, and so on appear in small caps.

▶ `Non-proportional`
A non-proportional font is used for all code samples, all ABAP keywords, and parameters. Within parameters, ABAP keywords are always shown in UPPERCASE.

▶ "Quotation marks"
If you're asked to enter specific values in the screens of the SAP system, the values are placed within quotations marks, except when ABAP commands are involved.

▶ Transparent triangle (▷)
This symbol is followed by specific directions.

System Requirements

There is no prerequisite minimum release level that you must use to work with the content of this book; it covers the different ways of working with Releases 6.10 to 7.0, and on.

The applications, customizing interfaces, and source code can run on the most popular releases of SAP software:

▶ SAP Web Application Server, Release 6.10, 6.20, and 6.40

▶ SAP NetWeaver Application Server, Release 7.0

You don't have to install any application components or SAP software to complete the exercises and sample programs in the book. It deals with only the common application base (AB) or all releases that provide application-specific or cross-application functionalities, such as globally unique identifiers (GUID).

The text highlights enhancements that have appeared in Release 7.0 and higher, so you can also use the book without any limitations for older releases. The following changes to the book have appeared since Release 6.10. The text addresses them in detail.

▶ As of Release 6.10, SAP Application Server is known as *SAP Web Application Server* and since Release 7.0 *SAP NetWeaver Application Server*. This book uses the latest name for the sake of clarity.

▶ The development environment, SAP Object Navigator, features buttons in the upper-left area of the screen that you can use to call five specialized browsers, such as one to search for development objects. The required menu entries and editors have been enhanced for the development of Web applications.

▶ A large number of system functions and the AB are now enabled for Unicode: You can work with all the character sets in the world and enable the ABAP programs you write yourself for Unicode.

▶ ABAP Objects contains enhancements for easily working with reference to data.

Since Release 6.10, SAP has made limited enhancements to the scope of the ABAP Objects language and the part of SAP NetWeaver Application

Releases 6.10 to 7.0

Server that relates to it, namely, the ABAP personality. Instead, SAP has concentrated on integrating external applications with Internet technology and giving Java equal place next to ABAP Objects as a programming language. Given SAP's existing customer base with more than 50,000 installations, as well as new developments and enhancements at SAP, you need not worry about whether the knowledge gained from this book is important and up-to-date. However, readers who want to know more about SAP programming with Java or newer ABAP releases will find worthwhile literature providing more information in the appendix.

Further Information and Downloading the Source Code

This book presents a *basic course* in ABAP Objects. Because of the scope of the language, you must look at more than 500 commands and select those that are indispensable for getting started. You cannot find documentation of every keyword and certainly not of all usage options in this book. If you require more information after reading our book, please refer to the Website *http://help.sap.com*. There you will be provided with comprehensive reference material on all keywords also on ABAP Objects. It is the ideal reference book for a programmer's daily work.

This chapter gives you an overview of the architecture of an SAP system. It shows you how to set up your own training system to complete the examples in this book.

1 Technical Overview and Getting Started in the System

Founded in 1972 as "Systems, Applications, and Products in Data Processing" by five former employees of IBM, SAP AG is headquartered near Heidelberg, Germany, in Walldorf. SAP concentrates on the development and sale of software solutions that map and integrate business processes within and across enterprises. Worldwide, SAP is the third largest software vendor, after Microsoft and Oracle. More than 50,000 employees in over 50 countries work for the enterprise. More than 50,000 large customers use SAP software and are assisted by more than 1,000 partner enterprises and SAP. For more information on the company, please go to *www.sap.com/company/index.epx*.

SAP can look back at a history that stretches over 35 years. In that time, the company has reinvented its software three times. Today it offers an application server as the technical basis for both its own software and non-SAP software. It can easily compete with the best products on the market.

1.1 Overview of SAP Software and Architecture

SAP presented its first accounting software, System RF, in 1973. It used punch cards and served as the foundation for the continuous development of additional software modules for asset accounting and auditing that later became part of an overall product named *SAP R/1* (see Figure 1.1) Mainframe computers and the DOS operating system from IBM (not

From R/1 ...

19

to be confused with MS-DOS) were used as the technical foundation for the software.

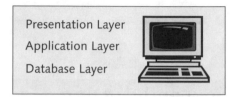

Presentation Layer
Application Layer
Database Layer

Figure 1.1 Overview of the Architecture of SAP R/1

... to SAP R/2 ... At the start of the 1980s, IBM mainframe computers saw increasingly strong competition from more economical UNIX servers. More and more hardware manufacturers (Siemens and DEC are good examples) entered the market, and that was reason enough for SAP to reconsider its software architecture for the first time. Instead of defining an operating system along with the related hardware platform, the software products would become executable on mainframe computers and on UNIX systems. These systems, which could be employed by multiple users, brought SAP and the marked success of the software to preeminence among large enterprises, a position that it holds to this day. Floppy disks and hard drives stored the data, and both users and programmers sat in front of text-based screens and keyboards. The programs themselves and their user interfaces (UIs) were still executed on the central server, which used a *hierarchical database*. These two layers—the server and the database—led to the name of the software that SAP introduced in 1981, SAP R/2 (see Figure 1.2).

The core component of the architecture of SAP R/2 was *SAP Basis*, which provided the runtime environment for the actual applications on the central server and protected them from variations among individual operating systems and hardware platforms. Programming in this environment was performed with a language that approximated machine language for write access to the database. It also used a high-level language that was interpreted by a general report-formatting processor, or ABAP in its German abbreviation. ABAP permitted read-access to data and flexible formatting of list-like reports. This high-level language primarily served customers on site, helping them customize screen output to meet their particular needs.

Figure 1.2 Overview of the Architecture of SAP R/2

At the beginning of the 1990s, SAP started to move to a new architec-   ... **to SAP R/3** ...
ture that had limited compatibility with SAP R/2. The steadily growing
numbers of users of SAP software in large enterprises, the ubiquity of
networked PCs, and the proliferation of graphical user interfaces (GUIs)
required a redistribution of the overall load of business software. A
user's workplace computer, also known as a *client*, could now independently and easily display GUIs and check keyboard and mouse entries.
Therefore, it had to be considered an equally important component of
the architecture. The three software layers of client, server, and database
gave the new architecture its name: SAP R/3 (see Figure 1.3). The name
also applied to all the business applications of SAP, commonly known
as *business modules*. Over the course of time, the number of R/3 business
modules grew to over 40 and therefore supported almost every conceivable process in an enterprise. *Enterprise Resource Planning* (ERP) is the
general term used to describe the use of a single software package for
the planning and management of all resources (money, personnel, and
goods) in an enterprise. The most common modules of SAP include Sales
& Distribution (SD), Finance (FI), Controlling (CO), Human Resources
(HR), and Production Planning (PP).

Figure 1.3 Overview of the Architecture of SAP R/3 1.0 to SAP R/3 4.6D

The core component of the architecture of SAP R/3 is the SAP Application Server, also called the SAP Basis system. It is implemented in the C language, can run on a variety of UNIX derivatives, OS/400, and Windows operating systems, and can manage and run applications written in ABAP/4 in a database. All source code, every program interface, all customizing settings for customers, and even the development environment, are stored in the database.

In 1993, the pressure of internationalization led SAP to change the name of ABAP to Advanced Business Application Programming Language/4 (ABAP/4). The number four is an abbreviation for Fourth-Generation Language (4GL). ABAP/4 is a language that approximates natural human speech and that is designed for special tasks. As the name suggests, ABAP/4 is based on the ABAP language of SAP R/2, but it has been enhanced with various features and expanded into a comprehensive programming language. As proof of its capabilities, note that SAP programmed all business modules in SAP R/3 in the programming language and realized the development environment in ABAP/4.

... to SAP NetWeaver Between 1999 and 2002, SAP undertook its most recent architectural change, a change that is 100 percent compatible with the architecture of SAP R/3 and that should be understood as an extension that supports important Internet technologies and Java. Since then, it has been possible to access all business applications from SAP over a typical Web browser. A proprietary SAP Web server supports important Internet protocols and is also the foundation for new portal and middleware components used to integrate the applications of various manufacturers with a uniform, Web-based user interface. With mySAP.com, SAP created yet another new name for this architecture. Due to the unrestricted compatibility of the more recent SAP solutions, such as SAP Customer Relationship Management (CRM), SAP Supply Chain Management (SCM), or SAP Product Lifecycle Management (PLM), for the R/3 architecture, they all use the functionality of one or more R/3 business modules; for instance, SAP PLM uses the functionality of the PP und MM modules (Material Management).

Since November 2001, SAP has officially entered the market of technology providers and has also marketed its SAP architecture separately, first under the name mySAP Technology, and then under SAP NetWeaver since 2005 (see Figure 1.4). In early 2003, SAP changed the name yet again and replaced mySAP.com with mySAP Business Suite before this name changed to SAP ERP in 2006.

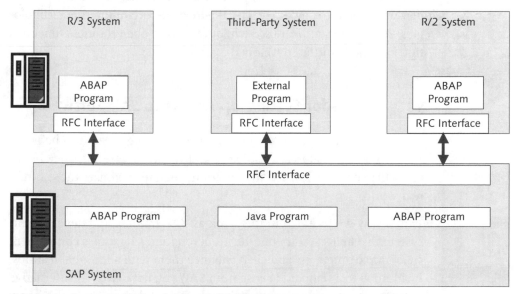

Figure 1.4 Overview of the Architecture of SAP NetWeaver (Release 6.10 to 7.0)

In 2000, the core component of SAP NetWeaver was called the *SAP Web Application Server,* to indicate enhancements related to Internet technology. In the meantime, another renaming, to SAP NetWeaver Application Server, took place. The name of the proprietary SAP programming language was changed to *ABAP Objects* because of object-related enhancements. This change is a tremendous simplification for users of other languages. Although the design of ABAP/4 can be compared to that of familiar programming languages only with difficulty, the object-oriented enhancements of ABAP Objects are clearly oriented toward C++ and Java. Even today, these enhancements have not changed some important basic principles. ABAP Objects continues to be an interpreter language: Source code is translated into an intermediate code that is interpreted and executed by a special area within SAP NetWeaver Application Server, the *ABAP runtime environment*. For reasons of compatibility, ABAP Objects also includes all previously implemented commands from ABAP and ABAP/4, so that in actual programming practice, you have several options that lead to the same goal. By now, most proprietary program code at SAP uses the object-oriented enhancements of ABAP Objects.

Conclusion | Conclusively, it can be said that SAP NetWeaver and ABAP Objects were developed as cross-enterprise applications that can be used across platforms and are compatible with the most important Internet technologies—you don't start from scratch, but revert to open business functions that have been further developed over decades.

1.2   Notes for Setting Up Access to SAP Software

You cannot learn a programming language simply by reading a book. To understand the material completely and retain it, you must be able to use what you have learned in conditions that approximate those of the real world.

This is why we included in this book an SAP training and development system that helps you try out the numerous and sometimes comprehensive sample programs, and even enhance them with additional features. In addition to a standard license from SAP, you have two free alternative options that you can use to complete the practical exercises in this book. The following section presents these options.

1.2.1 Regular System

If your enterprise already uses SAP software, you can speak with your system administrator, who can grant you access to an existing SAP system. The standard license agreement with SAP explicitly permits the setup of up to four completely separate systems. One system can be used for production; the other systems can be used for evaluation and training, implementation, and quality assurance. To avoid harming the production system and endangering a business-critical system for your enterprise, you should avoid using it and instead use one of the other systems for practice.

SAP offers its software for a variety of operating systems and hardware platform, such as Windows, OS/400, and various UNIX derivatives (see Figure 1.5). The platform that the database runs on is unimportant, as long as you use a database that SAP has found to be compatible, such as a database from IBM, Oracle, or Microsoft.

Hardware

Presentation	Web Browser		Java				MS Windows		Mobile Devices	
Communication Environment	Web Services (UDDI/HTTP/XML/SOAP)				.NET				J2EE	
Programming Languages	ABAP Objects				Java				C/C++	
Database	IBM DB2 UDB for			Informix		Microsoft SQL Server		Oracle		SAP DB
	UNIX & Windows	OS/390 and z/OS	iSeries							
		UNIX					Windows	Midrange	Mainframe	
Operating System	Linux	Compac Tru64 UNIX	IBM AIX	HP UX	FSC Reliant UNIX	SUN Solaris	Microsoft Windows	OS OS/400	IBM OS/390/ z/OS	
Architecture/ System	Intel/ zSeries	Alpha	pSeries	PA	MIPS	SPARC	Intel	iSeries	zSeries	

* Not all combinations are supported on all platforms. You can find more detailed information on this in the /platforms alias in SAP Service Marketplace.

Figure 1.5 Overview of Platforms Supported by SAP

Back end SAP NetWeaver Application Server (SAP NetWeaver AS) handles the required abstraction to the operating system, the database, and the hardware. It provides identical functionality on each platform. As an ABAP programmer, it is immaterial to you what operating system and hardware platform your enterprise uses.

Front end The complete SAP GUI for Windows or for Java should be installed on your workplace computer. Access to a Web browser (Internet Explorer or Netscape) over the SAP GUI for HTML is sufficient. Nevertheless, it doesn't have all key combinations, and the screen painter from SAP for creating program interfaces (see Chapter 5, Screen Input and Output) is much more user-friendly. There are also small differences in the display of windows and dialogs that unnecessarily complicate the directions given in the book.

Developer key In a regular SAP system, you also need a developer key registered to your system and your user name for the development tools, not only to look at programs but also for some development or modifications of existing programs (write access). Your system administrator can request the developer key from SAP at *http://service.sap.com*. You will be asked for the developer key when you first create or change an ABAP program and must enter the key.

1.2.2 Test Systems

Since 1999, SAP NetWeaver Application Server has been officially available in a Linux variant. SAP NetWeaver Application Server for Windows has been available since 1994. SAP therefore guarantees availability for test purposes on what has become the most popular server operating system for small and midsize requirements. This version includes all the functions necessary for system administrators and programmers to become familiar with the system. At *https://www.sdn.sap.com/irj/sdn/ nw-downloads*, you can download the latest versions of SAP NetWeaver, including the application server, at no extra costs after registration. In this book, the screenshots were created on the basis of Version SAP NetWeaver 2007 (2004s) – ABAP Trial Version.

Hardware The recommended hardware is a modern workplace computer with 1 GB of RAM, even when the back end (database and SAP NetWeaver Application Server) and the front end (SAP GUI) are installed on the same computer.

SAP NetWeaver for Linux has long had a reputation for being difficult to install. This cannot be confirmed as such; however, Linux configuration has a series of prerequisites that must be met and that undoubtedly will create significant problems for Linux novices. That's why Linux distributors offer specially certified versions of their operating systems that save you from the difficulties of configuration, but they are also expensive. The setup routine installs the database directly and usually doesn't require any special preparation.

In general, you can readily install the versions for Windows; only the (official) support of the installation routines for Windows Vista is still somewhat difficult at the time this book went to press. For this reason, there are various Internet forums on this topic.

The SAP GUI works quickly and reliably, and is well suited to complete all the examples, tasks, and exercises in this book.

Front end

The developer or test versions mentioned contain two predefined user names, *BCUSER* and *DDIC*, with *"minisap"* as the password, and authorizes development and modification of database tables, so that you don't need to request a developer key to get started.

Developer key

1.3   Programmer's Checklist for Getting Started

All members of an SAP project team always work together in a central system. This differs from program development in the C or Basic languages and has far-reaching consequences for collaboration and cross-departmental workflow.

When using the ABAP programming language, development in a team always occurs in an SAP system that is used in common. The system provides a variety of applications that support the work of all participants in the project: product management, quality management, documentation, and translation (see Figure 1.6). SAP combines all the applications needed for these purposes into the *ABAP Workbench*. As you see in the next chapter, the applications are all located within the related menu entry (for instance, ABAP Workbench) of the SAP application menu.

Development in a team

Figure 1.6 Support for the Entire Development Process—From Product Management to Translation

This type of close collaboration among all members of the project team demands technical guidelines and organizational policies that all participants must adhere to during development.

Particularly for programmers, the goal is to have the application appear as though it were cast from one mold in order to enable each programmer to read the source code of other programmers easily, and to ensure that the texts and documentation can be translated. The project lead defines the guidelines and all team members must follow them. It is often a good idea to ask questions of project management. If managers don't come to you, you should approach new team members directly. To simplify your conversation, a checklist for programmers was created, which contains some of the most important points (see Table 1.1).

Getting Started Checklist for Programmers	
1. In which system and clients are the programs to be developed or modified (development system and client)?	Example: FND(500)
2. In which system and clients will the programs be tested (test system and client)?	Example: FND(540)
3. In which systems and clients will the programs be used in production (production system and clients)?	Example: FND(300)
4. In which language will the comments in the source code be composed (comment language)?	Example: English
5. In which language will the program interface, print forms, notifications, and texts be composed (interface language)?	Example: English
6. In which language will the technical documentation in the system be composed (development language)?	Example: English
7. Has SAP reserved its own namespace and, if so, what is it (customer or project namespace)?	Example: /BA1/
8. What programming guidelines and conventions exist for naming development objects and data in the project (programming guidelines)?	See the Appendix
9. Which data and interfaces of existing SAP R/3 business modules, solutions, or individual developments will be used?	Example: the BAPIs in FDB

Table 1.1 Getting Started Checklist for Programmers

To minimize downtimes and maximize availability, SAP strongly recommends that its customers use separate, independent, and executable SAP systems for the development, quality assurance, and productive operation of applications. For this purpose, the commonly used SAP license agreements contain a passage of text that permits the use of a user license not only in the production system but also explicitly in up to four additional systems that serve the needs of evaluation, implementation, and quality assurance.

Points 1-3: Development, test, and production systems

Development occurs in a common *client* (see Section 1.4, Logon, Getting Started, and System Setup), an organizational criterion that combines important settings and configuration. As a rule, each developer has developer rights in only one of several clients.

Point 4:
Comment
language

Comments are absolutely required for a sound and long-term understanding of code. ABAP programmers write comments into the code that they create (see Section 2.4, First Program: "Hello World"—REPORT, INCLUDE, and Application Menu). From the viewpoint of the overall development process, comments usually involve texts that are not reworked by the documentation department and that are not translated. So that the entire team can work with the comments, they should be written in a common language. For small, local teams, it is usually the national language; for large, international teams, it is usually English. If you want SAP or one of your implementation partners to support the project, the question of the common language usually arises. At least for organizations that work internationally, English is the language that ensures smooth support in international project teams that work around the clock. The sample programs in this book use English as the common language.

Points 5-6:
Interface and
development
language

When you create development objects such as notifications, program interfaces, and so on, the SAP system automatically notes the language you used when you logged on. It uses that language as the original language for development objects (see Section 3.2, Data and Data Types—DATA, PARAMETERS, CONSTANTS, FIELD SYMBOLS, TYPE, CREATE, Text Elements). You can imagine how happy the documentation or translation departments would be if they received program and interface texts in English, German, or Turkish, and all because you and your colleagues could not agree on a uniform logon language for all programming members of the project team. As with the comment language, the interface and development language is usually the national language of the project team, or, for large international teams, English.

The same applies to the development language that you use to compose supplemental technical documentation on every function, global class, and other development objects (see Section 3.4, Subprograms and Functions—FORM, FUNCTION, EXCEPTIONS). The documentation and translation departments can also rework these texts. To avoid making the development process any more difficult for employees, projects generally use the same language that has been defined for program and interface texts.

It has become standard practice for development teams (those from SAP or another enterprise) to reserve a *namespace* at SAP Service Marketplace (*http://service.sap.com*) before undertaking any significant new developments. The namespace involves an abbreviation that must preface the name during creation of new development objects. If you don't reserve a namespace, all development objects must begin with the letters Y or Z (free namespace for customers). Only SAP is permitted to create development objects that start with other letters. But if you reserve a namespace (such as "/BA1/" for the SAP Bank Analyzer software project), you can use that abbreviation and be certain that no other programmer in the world can create a development object with the same name. You wouldn't have the same security about using X, Y, and Z as the initial letters for customer projects. Conflicts can arise when two applications have been imported into an SAP system, each of which expects a database table named ZACCOUNT—one to store accounts in financials and the other to store bank accounts. Section, 2.1, Getting Started with the Object Navigator, discusses this topic in more detail.

Point 7:
Namespace

Good programming guidelines are the "be all and end all" of smooth collaboration among programmers. The project team must ask a variety of questions: "Are we using BAPI or BADI techniques for program interfaces?" "Do we have suggestions about uniform names of variables?" The project lead must answer these questions. This is the only way that all programmers can trace the source code and produce an application whose parts work harmoniously and seamlessly. The contents of the programming guidelines given in the appendix are largely based on those of the financial service business area at SAP, where some of the largest new developments are occurring. If you decide to use the guidelines we have provided, you not only save the effort of creating your own guidelines, but you also have an amazing advantage that cannot be underestimated. Right from the start, you will be familiar with a good portion of source code from SAP.

Point 8:
Programming
guidelines

Hardly any ABAP programs work in isolation. They are an enhancement of an existing (SAP) software landscape and must communicate with one or more other applications via an *interface*. Several technical options for communication are often available. For example, SAP software can exchange information with files and database tables, (BAPI) functions, or

Point 9: Interfaces

by enhancing an SAP application with a *Business Add-In* (BAdI). Uniform rules for the project team are critical for the effective flow of information. Every interface to be used must be identified explicitly.

1.4 Logon, Getting Started, and System Setup

Software from SAP undoubtedly meets the contemporary ergonomic requirements of a user interface. Nevertheless, the first time that users familiar with Windows, Linux, or Mac software sit in front of an SAP application, they will notice some important differences in operation. Special directions and setup notes for programmers help shorten the learning curve.

Basics   The apparent differences in operation between SAP and Windows applications arise from the interface technology at SAP. *Dynpro* (see Section 5.2, Complex Input and Output Interfaces—Dynpros), which goes back some twenty years to the days of mainframe computers, defines or limits the flexibility available when designing program interfaces (see Figure 1.7).

▶ **Little Support for Multidocument Interface (MDI) Windows**
  SAP applications rarely employ the widely used window technology of Windows. MDI lets you organize and cascade several non-modal child windows in the main window of an application. Examples include Workbook windows in Microsoft Excel or graphic windows in CorelDRAW. One of the most familiar exceptions is the builder in SAP Business Workflow for creating workflow applications. Instead, SAP applications tend to use forward and backward navigation to move from one window to the next and back again.

▶ **Little Support for Drag-and-Drop**
  As introduced with the Apple Macintosh, drag-and-drop supports intuitive work with programs: Users can highlight, move, and store items in folders or programs just as they would on a real desktop. SAP applications support drag-and-drop only in the rarest of cases, but they do support cutting and pasting text with the keyboard.

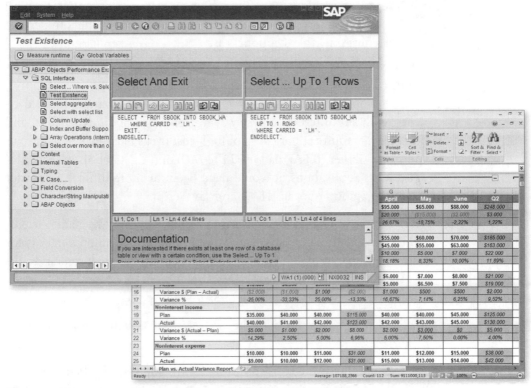

Figure 1.7 Comparison of the Look and Feel of ABAP and Windows Programs

▶ **Little Front-End Integration That the User Can Control**

If you look at contemporary Windows programs like Microsoft Office, you will see that programs for different purposes can work very closely with each other. OLE2 and ActiveX techniques enable you to link an Excel table with address data from Outlook and embed a PowerPoint slide in a Word document. And a Word document can be a complete element of the Outlook Today window. This close collaboration, which users can control, is called *integration*. Because it runs via mechanisms on the workplace computer, the term here is *front-end integration*. With ABAP programs, you will rarely have this kind of integration of programs with other (Windows) programs that users can control. SAP applications run in isolation on SAP NetWeaver Application Server. The SAP GUI displays a window to users that shows exactly what the program is doing on the server in real time.

Integration would have to involve the workplace computer, the SAP GUI, and the server. SAP and its implementation partners undertake this effort only in exceptional cases.

However, every coin has two sides. In 1999, SAP turned these limitations into a competitive advantage. As the first large ERP manufacturer, SAP was able to introduce a Web version of its software that could be used with any Internet browser, even from any cafe in New York, and that didn't require either cheap or high-cost tricks like Citrix or Windows Terminal Server. If SAP had used the MDI and drag-and-drop technologies in its applications, it would have been far more difficult to render the program interface in HTML and JavaScript.

Web Dynpro   *Web Dynpro* is related to the Dynpro technology only by name. It provides much better performance and offers significant improvements for the points mentioned. It also supports the newest Internet standards like XML and Web services. This new development environment has been available since the introduction of SAP Web Application Server 6.30.

Let's take a closer look at the SAP system and its programs' user interfaces.

▷ Execute the SAP GUI logon program by going to the logon website specified by your system administrator, or by starting your locally installed version of Windows or Java.

Figure 1.8 SAP Logon Window

After a brief loading period, a window appears on your screen (see Figure 1.8). The window lists all the SAP systems for which you currently have access.

▷ Now select the first entry under DESCRIPTION and click the PROPERTIES button to see the settings behind the access that has been set up.

A single physical server, with an installation of SAP NetWeaver AS, suffices for SAP systems intended for a small number of users with limited requirements for high availability. In this case, the IP address of the DNS address of the server appears in the Application Server field.

Single server

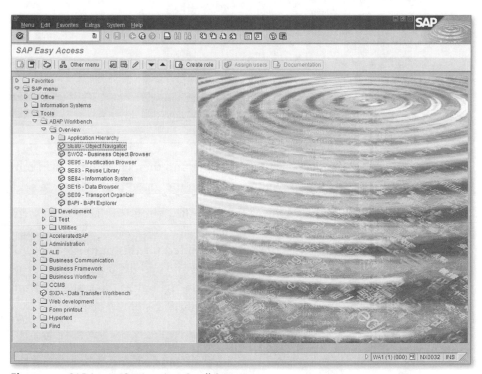

Figure 1.9 SAP Logon Settings in a Small System

If you're using the training system described in Section 1.2, Notes for Setting Up Access to SAP Software, the IP address is actually the IP address of your own computer. The SAP GUI, database, and SAP NetWeaver AS are all installed on your computer. However, SAP systems intended for many users with significant requirements for high availability need servers that run SAP Web AS. A hardware failure would then cripple only

Server cluster

part of the overall system. All installations of SAP NetWeaver AS access a single, common database and appear to the user as a single system.

This constellation is generally called a *server cluster*. You can recognize it by the entry for an IP address or DNS address beneath SAP ROUTER STRING, which uses a special SAP program (*message server*) to assign a server within the cluster to a user to balance the load (see Figure 1.10).

Figure 1.10   SAP Logon Settings in a Large System

▷ Now close the dialog with the setting and then click the LOGON button in the SAP logon window to begin the logon transaction.

Authentication   The logon transaction involves the first ABAP program that you've seen. It runs on SAP NetWeaver AS and in a separate task within the ABAP runtime environment, a task that was generated for this purpose. The SAP GUI displays the program running there and accepts user entries for it. SAP software executes the logon program right after the system startup and prohibits unauthorized access to the SAP system (see Figure 1.11).

> **Tip**
>
> Your success as a programmer is ensured if you look at the SAP system as an operating system with its own concepts, requirements, and rules, rather than as an application. Section 1.1, Overview of SAP Software and Architecture, discussed the architecture of the SAP system and the use of relational databases. The databases store and manage everything, so that you're not working with files, directories, and drive names in the traditional sense. If you consider this odd: Microsoft intended to use a relational database as the basis of the file system for Windows Server 2008; however, this plan has been delayed because of its complexity.

Figure 1.11 Authentication to SAP NetWeaver AS

Authentication to SAP NetWeaver AS is dependent on your entering the necessary input for the following three fields:

▶ **Client**

With the client concept, users from several enterprises could theoretically use the same SAP system without being able to view or modify the data of other enterprises. With rare exceptions (that is, by various small enterprises over the Internet), the client is generally used to separate the subsidiaries or affiliated enterprises of a large corporate group. Technically, the client is nothing more than a value entered by users when they log on. It is a three-digit number that is updated to the primary key of most database tables (see Chapter 4, Defining and Managing Database Tables) so that the data of individual clients can be distinguished.

▶ **Username**

A name of up to twelve characters that uniquely identifies a user within a client. The name must begin with a letter and cannot contain any special characters. Uppercase and lowercase are not distinguished.

▶ **Password**

A string of up to thirty characters and numbers that authenticates the user. Unlike the user name, the password permits the use of special characters and distinguishes between uppercase and lowercase.

Here you can see the first difference from the world of Windows, Mac, and UNIX, where you log on only with a user name and password—entering a client as a distinguishing characteristic is not required there.

▷ Complete the input fields as follows: Windows test version—CLIENT "000", USER "bcuser", and PASSWORD "minisap"; Linux test version—CLIENT "000", USER "developer", and PASSWORD "default".

You can also enter a code to specify the language you want to use when working with the SAP system; for example, "en" for English or "de" for German. Otherwise, the default settings apply.

▷ Use the ENTER key or click the green checkmark in the upper-left corner.

Single Sign-On   Large enterprises often use *Single Sign-On* (SSO) to authenticate users only once. This can occur during the Windows logon. Logging on to other (SAP) system occurs automatically with the same user name and password. But if an enterprise uses more than one client per SAP system, the assignment of a user to an SAP user account might not be unique. There are more than enough examples: Administrators with maintenance rights in every client, developers of application tests that must be executed in all clients, and auditors performing consolidations and audits of several subsidiaries.

In this case, SAP NetWeaver AS must ask what client the user wants to log on to. The window displayed in Figure 1.12 appears. You can click on a line to select the appropriate client and trigger authentication.

SAP Easy Access   After a successful logon, the SAP menu SAP Easy Access is displayed. You can use it to start all the programs in the system (see Figure 1.13). It is, of course, an ABAP program, just like all of the applications that we deal with in this book.

As displayed in Figure 1.13, the structure of the entries is similar to a directory tree. It simply lists the programs, with all entries marked with a small white block. This is the second difference from Windows and other systems: A file window appears where there are no files in the traditional sense.

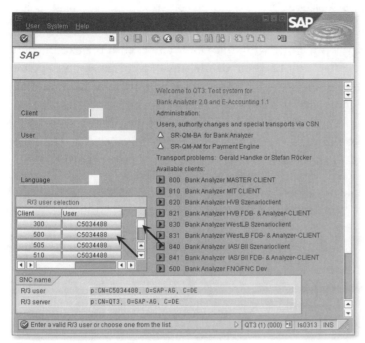

Figure 1.12 Client Selection with Single Sign-On

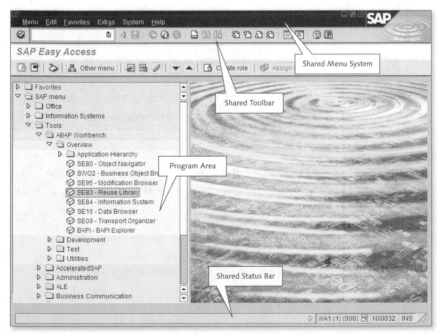

Figure 1.13 Menu System, Standard Toolbar, Program Area, and Status Line

Common menu
system To some extent, SAP defines the common menu system. For example, the entries beneath HELP are always visible. Programs can enrich some menu or submenus, as is the case with Mac OS. If you click at the extreme left of the menu entry, you find one of the most important menu entries for ABAP programmers (see Figure 1.14). If nothing else helps and an ABAP program no longer responds (this can happen with SAP software, but outside of development, it happens less frequently than it does in Windows), you can use the menu option STOP TRANSACTION to end the current program and return to the last program that was executed.

Figure 1.14   SAP Menu: Stop Transaction

Common standard
toolbar Unlike the menu system, all the buttons on the standard toolbar are defined by SAP. You cannot use program-specific buttons to enhance the common standard toolbar (see Figure 1.15). An ABAP program can turn off only some of the buttons if they are not required. It must handle the functionality behind the buttons itself. SAP publishes a style guide with samples of source code (see Chapter 2, Working with the Development Environment: SAP Object Navigator, for more information) that programmers should use as a reference to ensure that the buttons work properly in their applications.

The following is an overview of the functionality of the common standard toolbar:

▶ **Enter and Command Line**

SAP sets the functionality of both these interface elements. Programmers cannot change it. The ENTER button starts commands that have been entered in the command line on the right. In SAP software, commands generally begin with a right slash (/), followed by an ID letter and a command. This will be discussed later on, starting in Chapter 2, Section 3. Here we want to mention only that professional programmers use this line quite often because it enables direct and quick access to many programs and functionalities. You can switch the display of the command line on and off with the arrow to its right.

▶ **Save**

The SAVE button tells the system to save the data that has been entered in the database. The SAVE button is deactivated in Figure 1.15 because no data is entered here. This is the *most important* button for ABAP programmers. Only applications for read-only access can do without it.

Figure 1.15 Common Standard Toolbar

▶ **Back, Finish, Cancel**

The BACK button works as it does in a browser: It returns to the last screen. If the user is at the initial screen of an application, it works like the EXIT button: It ends a program and returns to the previous program. If you've entered data but not yet saved it, a query asks you whether that is your intention. You can use the CANCEL button to leave an input screen, even if you haven't finished entering the data.

▶ **Print**

The PRINT button sends the content of the current program window to a printer set up in the SAP system. In Figure 1.13, the printer would print the contents of the hierarchy on the left side.

▶ **Find, Replace**

The SEARCH button lets you call a search dialog. Its appearance can differ substantially depending on the program that is running and the data that you are working with. The REPLACE button is usually employed only in editor windows. You would most often modify data in a separate entry screen.

▶ **First Page, Previous Page, Next Page, Last Page**

If a program interface displays tabular data that cannot fit on one screen, you can use these buttons to scroll through the display.

▶ **Create New Session, Create Desktop Link**

SAP defines the functionality of both of these buttons; programmers cannot make any changes. You can use the CREATE NEW SESSION button to open additional main SAP GUI windows without having to go through the logon procedure. That's why the term "session" is still used. ABAP programmers often work with several sessions so that they can quickly switch between various program windows. The button to create a link is only occasionally important to SAP users. It enables execution of a specific ABAP program without prior display of SAP Easy Access menu.

▶ **Help, Customize Local Layout**

SAP defines the functionality of both of these buttons; programmers cannot make any changes. When you click the HELP button, a popup window opens that displays help and tips. You can use the CUSTOMIZE LOCAL LAYOUT button to define settings for the appearance of the screen and behavior of the user interface.

Common status line and selected system information

Via the status line (see Figure 1.16), an ABAP program can output messages to the users at any time and display a running clock for program steps that run longer. You can use the arrow at the right side of the status line to display and hide some system information, but SAP defines what can and cannot be displayed.

By default, the status line displays the system you are working in, how many sessions you have opened for a client, the client under which you logged on, the name of the server running the ABAP task, and whether the keyboard is set to insert or overwrite mode. Figure 1.16 shows several elements that clarify the display:

▶ The first screen excerpt shows the context menu that appears when you right-click the small menu icon. You can select various display variants from the context menu. This option shows that the user is working with SAP system FNO, has opened the first session in client 500, is running an ABAP task on server PWDF0665, and that insert mode (INS) is active on the keyboard.

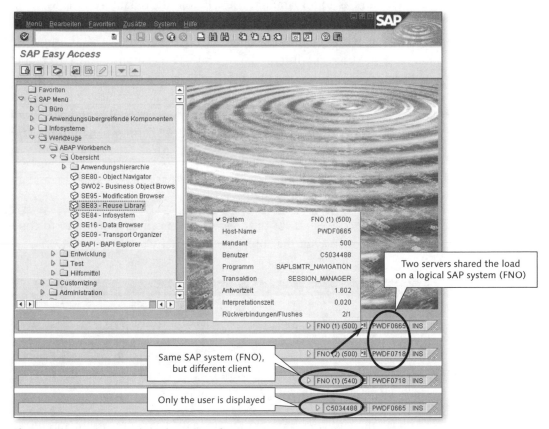

Figure 1.16 Status Bar: Selected System Information

▶ The second excerpt shows that a second session was opened in client 500 and is running on server PWDF0718. You can assume that you're working with a large SAP system with at least two servers for load distribution.

▶ The third excerpt shows that SAP system FNO has at least two clients, because the first session has been opened in client 540.

▶ The fourth excerpt shows an example of the system information that displays only the USER.

In your work as a programmer, you will find the default setting, System, most helpful. When you switch sessions, you can see the system and client you are working with at a glance. A useful feature is the information on response time and interpretation time. The response time covers the entire period from reading the program from the database, to executing the program in the ABAP runtime environment, to being available for the user's next entry. The interpretation time covers only the period in which the application is executed by the ABAP runtime environment.

Technical name After this discussion of the influence of ABAP programs on the user interface, let's take another look at the SAP Easy Access program and at important information that has so far been hidden.

▷ Select EXTRAS • SETTINGS in the menu. You can use this entry to configure the display of the application hierarchy (see Figure 1.17).

Figure 1.17 Selecting Settings

▷ Check the DISPLAY TECHNICAL NAMES checkbox and quit the modification with the OK button (see Figure 1.18).

The hierarchy now displays Transaction SE80 (SE83, SE84, and so on) next to the name of the program. You can execute the program directly by entering the transaction in the command line (see Figure 1.19).

Figure 1.18 SAP Easy Access Settings

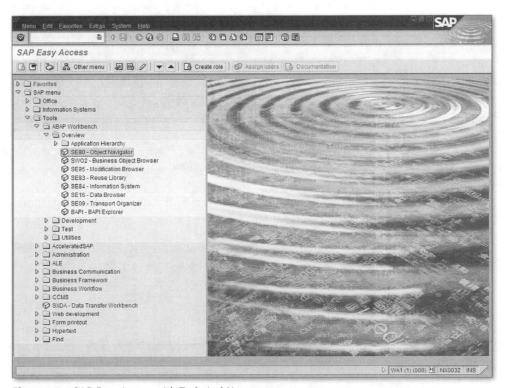

Figure 1.19 SAP Easy Access with Technical Names

Think of a transaction simply as a link or a short command, and don't confuse this long-standing SAP term with a database transaction. Section 2.2, Development Classes and Packages, covers program transactions in detail. Chapter 4, Defining and Managing Database Tables, describes database transactions. Professional ABAP programmers often enter transactions in the command line rather than executing a program by clicking in the SAP Easy Access menu.

But before you try it out, you should get some more status information from the system: Information that can be important to you as a programmer.

▷ Select SYSTEM • STATUS in the menu (see Figure 1.20).

Figure 1.20 Selecting SYSTEM • STATUS in the Menu

This dialog displays an overview of users and data on the SAP systems, operating systems, and databases.

▷ Select the button with the yellow arrow to display kernel information on the server, database, and SAP GUI (see Figure 1.21).

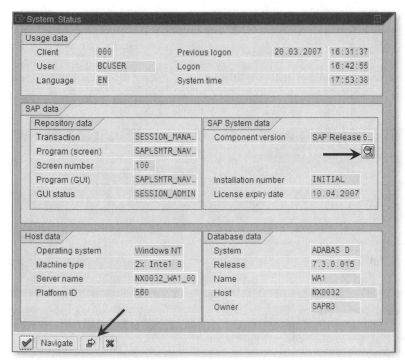

Figure 1.21 System Status

▷ Close the dialog (Figure 1.22).

Figure 1.22 System: Kernel Information

▷ Now select the magnifying glass in the SAP SYSTEM DATA section to display information on the SAP software that has been imported and its release levels.

A new dialog displays information on the installed SAP software (see Figure 1.23).

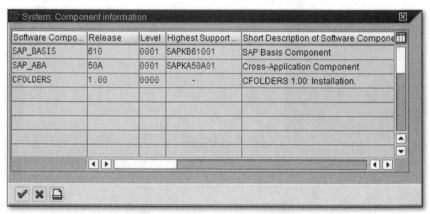

Figure 1.23   System: Component Information

▷ Close the dialog.

The release levels are important when you undertake larger modifications or significantly enhance SAP software. Low-level interfaces can change from one release to the next. Patches (corrections) must also be imported according to release levels.

Starting programs · The SAP system offers various options for starting a program. Here's an overview (see Figure 1.24):

▸ In SAP Easy Access: Double-click a transaction or program name.

▸ In SAP Easy Access: Use the context menu (right-click a transaction or program name) and then select EXECUTE from the menu.

▸ In the command line: Enter "/n" and, for example, the transaction "/nSE83". The advantage of starting the program in this manner is that it always works and it works from every application. You are not limited to SAP Easy Access. You should note, however, that it replaces the currently running program without asking for a confirmation. It doesn't ask if you want to save the data, for example.

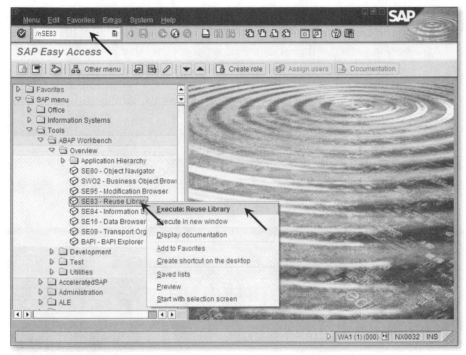

Figure 1.24 SAP Easy Access Context Menu

▷ Now close any open dialogs so that you return to the main window. Try to start the *Reuse Library* with the various options.

▷ To test all the starting options, you can exit the Reuse Library at any time by clicking the green BACK button.

You have even more options for starting programs. For example, when you start a program, you can define whether it should be executed in a new session (main window) rather than replacing the currently running program. You can open a total of up to six sessions at one time. Here's another brief overview:

Starting programs in new sessions

▶ In SAP Easy Access: Use the context menu (right-click a transaction or program name) and then select EXECUTE IN NEW WINDOW.

▶ In the command line: Enter "/o" and, for example, the transaction "/oSE83". The advantage of starting the program in this manner is that it always works, works from every application, and doesn't affect the program that is running.

▶ In the toolbar: Click the CREATE NEW SESSION button and then use the options described to start the program in the new window.

▷ Try to start the Reuse Library application with the various options.

▷ After you have tested all the starting options, simply close the new window.

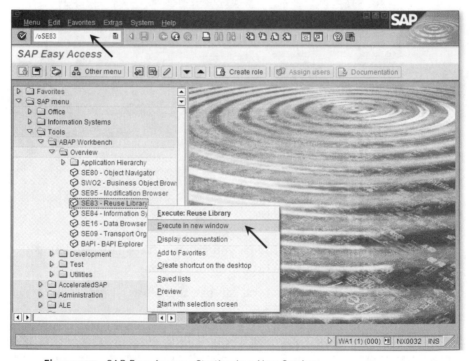

Figure 1.25 SAP Easy Access—Starting in a New Session

When you start new sessions in this manner, the new sessions always access the same server as the current session. New ABAP tasks are never directed to a different server—even when working with clusters. ABAP programmers appreciate this feature. During debugging (testing and error correction), it enables them to let the debugger run in one window while they can simultaneously set or delete breakpoints in the other window. If you were to create each session by logging on to the SAP system, the individual sessions would run on different servers if clusters were operating.

Finally, you can also start an application with *forward navigation*. SAP provides ample support for this option in applications related to development and administration. There you can double-click almost every input field, every label, and even every word in the source code and go to a different program. And the opposite is also true. You can use the green BACK button in the toolbar to jump to the previous program location. To give you a brief idea, the following example demonstrates forward navigation with the Reuse Library (see Figure 1.26):

Forward and backward navigation

▷ Restart the Reuse Library.

▷ Double-click the ALV GRID CONTROL beneath SAP TECHNOLOGY • CONTROLS.

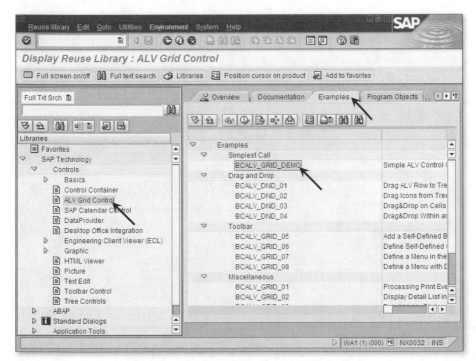

Figure 1.26 Reuse Library with a Sample Program (for ALV Grid Control)

▷ Select the EXAMPLES tab.

▷ Then double-click the demo program: BCALV_GRID_DEMO.

The active program changes so that you now see the ABAP Editor, which displays the source code of the demo program (see Figure 1.27). You have started a new program with forward navigation.

▷ Now you can double-click SFLIGHT in the source code to move to the next program and so on with forward navigation.

▷ You can use the BACK button at any time to return to your starting position.

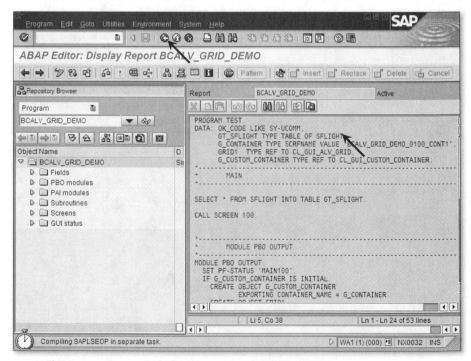

Figure 1.27 Source Code for Program BCALV_GRID_DEMO

Just-In-Time Compiler — During this excursion into the SAP system, you might have encountered the stopwatch in the status line (see Figure 1.27). In the first few hours of working with a brand-new SAP system (such as the training version described in Section 1.2, Notes for Setting Up Access to SAP Software), the stopwatch can truly test your patience. It appears at the start of every program. Section 1.1, Overview of SAP Software and Architecture, already mentioned that ABAP programs are delivered exclusively in source code. At the start, programs must be read from the database and compiled before the ABAP runtime environment can execute them. This accounts for the long wait times in a newly installed system.

*You develop some ABAP programs with the integrated develop-
ment environment, the SAP Object Navigator. This software
contains the most important tools to create and maintain the
source code, program interfaces, and database tables that ABAP
programmers need for their daily work.*

2   Working with the Development Environment: SAP Object Navigator

The SAP Object Navigator is itself an ABAP program, so any users with
SAP access can use it as long as they have the appropriate authorizations.
In the SAP Object Navigator, applications are always created in the same
way and involve the following steps (see Figure 2.1):

▶ **Select Existing Development Object or Create a New One**
Working with the SAP Object Navigator is quite visual. It involves
many secondary windows, dialogs, and confirmation requests. That's
because of the various types of development objects that exist in addition to the actual source code and that, taken together, produce an
ABAP program. Examples include data and table definition, to name
a few. You'll learn about all these development objects in the following chapters.

▶ **Complete Information, Write Code, and so on**
In actual practice, you spend half of your time writing ABAP source
code and the other half creating development objects, such as database tables and function groups.

▶ **Check Development Object**
Every development object must undergo a manually started or automatic check—something akin to the system check of a source code.
Penetration is a typical issue in general and in the SAP Object Navigator in particular, which focuses primarily on avoiding having incorrect

or incomplete entries in the database. The great deal of work that you must perform here is the main reason for the excellent runtime stability of ABAP programs. That kind of stability is required in SAP systems that may have hundreds of thousands of users.

Figure 2.1 From a Development Object to a Finished Application

► **Activate Development Object**

Before one development object (for instance, source code) can use another development object (for instance, table definition), it must be activated. The entire development environment and the transport system for copying ABAP programs are embedded in a version control system. The system not only monitors versions, but also distinguishes between an active and inactive status for every development object. While other development objects use the active variant, you can modify the inactive variant as you wish. Unless you activate the other development systems, the changes will not affect them or team members working with them.

► **Debug and Perform Isolated Tests**

The SAP Object Navigator contains a debugger for testing ABAP programs. You can work through a program you have developed not only as a whole but also line by line. These are features you'd expect. What's unexpected is that the Object Navigator also has a test environment for individual functions, classes, and methods. You can execute functional tests at the lowest level, even when the entire program is not ready for execution. This is a helpful feature, especially in large development teams. It means that you don't have to wait for the work of other team members. Another user-friendly feature lets you move the command cursor almost as you do in Visual Basic to affect the flow of the program directly. You'll try out this feature later.

▶ **Release and Transport Development Object**
Once a development object has passed the individual tests, you usually transport the object into a second, independent SAP system that is dedicated to quality assurance. The object and other components create a copy of the ABAP program in that system.

▶ **Perform Integration Tests**
Testers and quality assurance personnel perform additional tests and integration tests with other applications. They might also check the behavior of various customizing settings that your program uses.

▶ **Release and Transport Application**
Finally, the whole application can be copied to one or more production systems or burned to a CD for sale.

In his book, *The Road Ahead*, Bill Gates relates that each individual development department at Microsoft has a *build master*. That person must organize and monitor the compiler run that combines all the source code into a common product. For a large product like the Windows operating system, preparation for and execution of the build can last overnight. It's no surprise that the job is unpopular. The last developer whose source code caused a termination or error in the compiler is always named the next build master. Because of the problem, the testers would have nothing to test the next day, which would delay the entire development process. The poor developer has to keep at this job until the work of another developer causes a problem, and that developer becomes the next build master. Similar procedures are known in

Decentralized builds

enterprises with automation technology, where the operating systems for programmable monitoring are also developed in C.

The situation differs with ABAP programs because they are not centrally compiled and linked. The ABAP runtime environment works with a *decentralized build*. That means that each individual development object is activated in isolation, translated into intermediate code if necessary, and then exchanged with the previous version, regardless of the size and complexity of the overall application (see Figure 2.2).

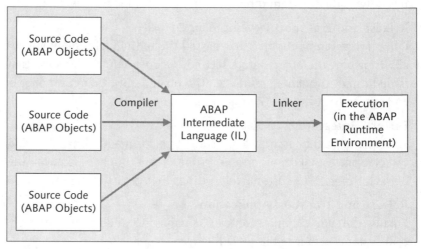

Figure 2.2 Decentralized Builds in ABAP Objects

Those familiar with other programming languages can imagine that C, Basic, and Delphi would pack every method, every function, and even every data type into its own DLL; compile each one separately; and place them into a program directory for execution. Users who start a program in the directory would automatically work with the most recent version of all program components stored in the directory. You can update ABAP programs with that fine level of granularity. The new development objects simply replace the old ones; the next user to call a program automatically works with the updated version. SAP calls the technology behind all these features the *transport system*. We'll encounter this term again later in this book.

2.1   Getting Started with the SAP Object Navigator

Let's take a closer look at the SAP Object Navigator (see Figure 2.3).

▷ You can execute Transaction SE80 (Object Navigator) by entering "/nSE80" or clicking that entry in SAP Easy Access.

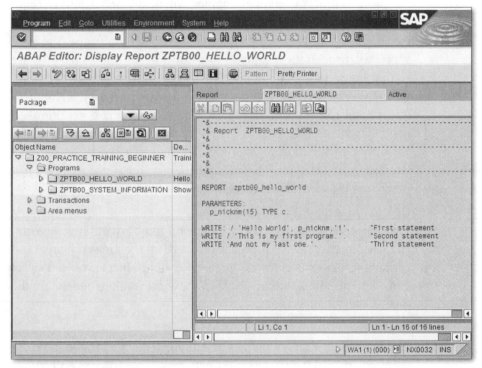

Figure 2.3 SAP Object Navigator

The program interface of the Object Navigator has generally remained   Interface in detail
unchanged over the years, so its appearance in the program versions is
quite similar. Improvements in new releases primarily occur behind the
scenes. You might notice a new menu entry here, or a new option for
forward navigation there. The new browsers in the browser area are the
most striking difference between the releases:

- ▶ **Browser Area**

  You can enter, search for, and select development objects in the browser area, located in the upper left of the screen. You can see that the browser area includes four other browsers besides the Repository Browser. Both the MIME Repository and the tag library support development of Web applications based on *Business Server Pages (BSP)*. The pages are akin to the similarly named Microsoft Active Server Pages (ASP) and JavaServer Pages (JSP) from Sun. You can use this technology to place ABAP source code directly into HTML pages. The Web server will process the text just before transmitting it to a Web browser so that you can supplement the HTML page with program-driven content. The repository info system lets you search for all development objects and can support use of a wildcard (*) or text descriptions. It combines the individual tools in the *ABAP Workbench* directory of SAP Easy Access into a single interface. This is discussed in more detail later on in this chapter. The Transport Organizer is not new; it's just integrated into the Object Navigator.

- ▶ **Object List Area**

  The object list area fills the space beneath the browser area. It corresponds directly to the browser selected in the browser area and contains a hierarchical list of the development objects you can select and edit. The commands available in the context menu depend on the type of entry in the list.

- ▶ **Tools Area**

  The tools area displays the actual editing window for the development object selected in the object lists area. Here you can edit source code, define tables, and manage data types.

Examples
The menus of the Object Navigator house additional functions. The comprehensive programmer examples that SAP provides are especially interesting (see Figure 2.4).

▷ Try selecting ENVIRONMENT • EXAMPLES in the menu.

The examples provide a comprehensive collection of source codes on subjects like ergonomics, performance and controls, and (as of Release 6.20) every ABAP command (ABAP EXAMPLES in the menu). In releases prior to

6.20, you can reach this documentation (with examples) with [F1] help and the DOCUMENTATION button, or use Transaction /nABAPDOCU. Take a closer look at the entry for PERFORMANCE EXAMPLES in the menu.

Figure 2.4 Programmer Examples on Various Topics

▷ You can do this by selecting ENVIRONMENT • EXAMPLES • PERFORMANCE EXAMPLES in the menu.

The object list area displays a structured list that contains all the performance examples. Most relate to a comparison of two ABAP commands. The content covers a specific aspect of optimizing performance.

▷ Now double-click SELECT ... WHERE VS. SELECT + CHECK in the list. Two source codes are loaded into the tool area to compare their performance in terms of time.

▷ Click the MEASURE RUNTIME button (see Figure 2.5). As you can see, the runtime of the SELECT-WHERE construction is significantly lower than that of the SELECT + CHECK statement.

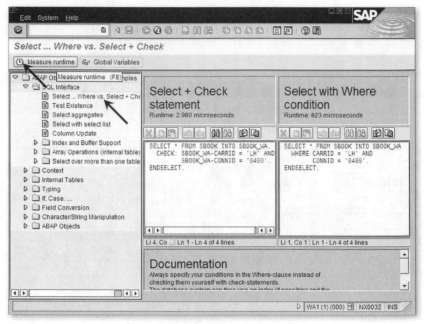

Figure 2.5 Tips and Tricks for the Performance of ABAP Objects

Repository info
system and ABAP
Workbench

As of Release 6.10, the repository information system is a feature of the Object Navigator and permits direct access to all development objects. For this purpose, it provides a high performance search system that you can use to search for names and descriptions with and without place-holders. Try it out by starting a search query for transaction codes that contain "SE8" in their names. You expect Transaction SE80 to appear in the results. You execute the query as follows (see Figure 2.6):

▷ In the browser area, click the REPOSITORY INFORMATION SYSTEM button or select ENVIRONMENT • REPOSITORY INFORMATION SYSTEM in the menu.

▷ Select OTHER OBJECTS/TRANSACTIONS in the object list area.

▷ Enter "*SE8*" as the transaction code: You want to see if the query also works well with wildcards.

▷ Click the EXECUTE button or press the ⌈F8⌉ key.

The result is a list of all hits that meet the criterion of the search string.

▷ Now double-click Transaction code SE80 to display details on this development object.

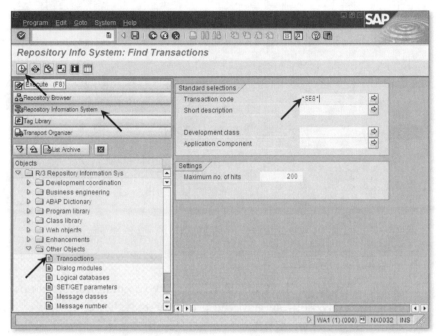

Figure 2.6 Searching for Transactions in the Repository Information System

As you can see, the repository info system then displays the program in the tool area of the window so that you can edit transactions (see Figure 2.7).

You could modify the transaction here or by forward navigation. For example, you could query additional information on the name of the package.

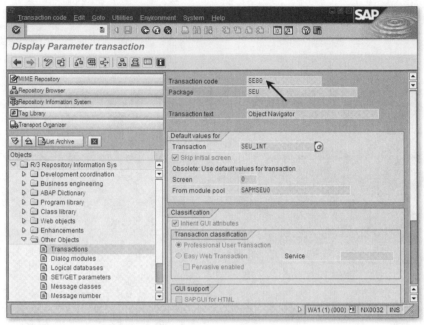

Figure 2.7 Detailed Information for the Parameter Transaction

Here we want to show how the search for development objects is possible alternatively. You can start the programs that the repository info system calls to display detailed information on a development object individually and use wildcards by following these steps:

▷ Click the CANCEL button until you return to SAP Easy Access menu.

▷ Under TOOLS • ABAP WORKBENCH • DEVELOPMENT in the application menu, you'll find all the individual programs controlled by the repository info system.

▷ Execute Program SE93 (Transactions), which you can find under TOOLS • ABAP WORKBENCH • DEVELOPMENT • OTHER TOOLS in the application menu (see Figure 2.8).

Figure 2.8 Application SE93—Transactions

The program interface is displayed. Now do the following:

▷ Enter "*SE8*" in the input field as the search string.

▷ Click the SELECT button to the right of the input field or use the [F4] key to call the *value help*. Value help is also called selection, or [F4] help. You can use it in ABAP programs that call for user input. When users open this help, they see the values that are permissible for a specific input field (see Figure 2.9).

The hit list for our search query appears. It contains Transaction SE80 (see Figure 2.10).

▷ Now select Transaction SE80 and confirm your selection with the OK button. You can also simply double-click the transaction.

Figure 2.9 Initial Screen of the Transaction Interface

Transaction code	Short text
SE80	Object Navigator
SE81	Application Hierarchy
SE82	Application Hierarchy
SE83	Reuse Library
SE83_START	Start Reuse Library
SE84	R/3 Repository Information System
SE85	ABAP/4 Repository Information System
SE89	Maintain Trees in Information System
SE8I	Lists in Repository Infosystem

Figure 2.10 Selection Dialog for the Transaction Code

The selection dialog closes and the transaction code is transferred to the input field.

▷ Now click the DISPLAY button.

You will come to the same detailed display that is controlled from the repository info system (see Figure 2.7).

By now, it should be apparent that you can go to the same program from the repository info system and that the functionality here is identical. Theoretically, you could repeat this demonstration for all other development objects. As a developer working with Release 4.6, you have all the functions described here at your disposal. In exceptional cases, however, operating Release 4.6 may differ slightly from the procedures described here.

The Transport Organizer has been a component of the Object Navigator since Release 6.10. It resides as a separate application in the application menu of SAP Easy Access under TOOLS • ABAP WORKBENCH • OVERVIEW • TRANSPORT ORGANIZER. You can also reach it with Transaction SE09. The Transport Organizer will be important to you as a programmer when you have a complete or partial development and want to copy your results to a different SAP system. The transport occurs in four steps. The first two steps are important to programmers; the last two steps are important to administrators:

Transport Organizer

1. Before you can create a new development object or modify an existing one, a dialog asks you which request you want to record your work in. The project lead or administrator can create such a request, or you have permission to create one yourself. Each request automatically creates a task for each programmer so that the work of individuals can be distinguished. Section 2.3, Namespaces, demonstrates the procedure.

2. As soon as you have completed your development or the program is able to function, you can release your task with the Transport Organizer. In Release 4.6, you call Transaction SE09, enter your login name as the selection criterion for display, and select the appropriate request with the task to be released in the list. As of Release 6.10, the Transport Organizer is integrated with the Object Navigator. You can display an overview of your requests and tasks by selecting the appropriate button in the browser area. In any case, you can right-click to display the context menu that also contains an entry for RELEASE TASK. If you created the request yourself, you can also display it from the context menu as soon as all tasks have been released. The transport system then takes over all the modified and newly created development elements and writes them to a file that is stored on the server in the export directory.

3. From the directory, administrators can do what they like with the file. The development is usually tested again in a separate SAP system. The file is copied to the import directory of that SAP system. The administrator imports the file with the *transport management system*, a tool for configuring, executing, and monitoring modifications of an SAP system.

4. After a successful test, SAP, SAP implementation partners, and customers with widely distributed system landscapes burn the file to a CD so that it can be distributed as a product.

2.2 Development Classes and Packages

Packages and development classes help create a structure for large development projects. You can use them to organize and combine development objects thematically (see Figure 2.11). You can reserve namespaces at SAP. They are a precondition for copying ABAP programs to any external SAP systems with ease.

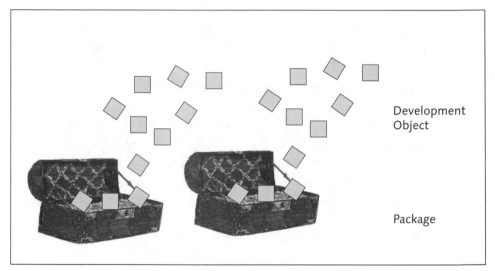

Figure 2.11 Packages and Development Classes Improve Organization

Basics   In Release 4.6, development of ABAP programs is structured with *development classes*. Development classes have nothing to do with classes in an object-oriented sense. Instead, you should think of them as a directory that you can use to store other development objects. And just as storing files in subject-oriented directories creates organization, assigning development objects to a development class increases the manageability of large programs.

As of Release 6.10, development classes have a new name: *packages*. The new name indicates the new properties available that enhance your ability to organize development objects. The design of the properties is similar to the package concepts in Java, Microsoft .NET, and Borland Delphi. Because of compatibility issues (package A running with versions 1.0 to 1.3 of package B), ABAP does not permit the coexistence of different versions of a package in an SAP system, unlike the case of Borland Delphi.

As an example of how packages and development classes are used, imagine a large application. All its database-related functions are in one package, the functionality for application logic is in another package, the user dialogs and windows are in yet another package, and so on. The core of a large SAP application, like SAP Bank Analyzer, consists of more than 190 packages that can access 20 additional packages containing related developments and basic functionalities.

You can nest packages within other packages. The higher-level packages are called *structure packages*, which eventually form a *main package* that generally constitutes the entire application. Figure 2.12 shows an example of a structure package.

Structure package

Figure 2.12 Nested Packages of an Application

Searching
for packages
and following
their nested
relationships To get a better feeling for working with packages and development classes, take a more detailed look at some existing packages and how they nest within each other. You can do this by following these steps:

▷ Start the Object Navigator and select the REPOSITORY INFORMATION SYSTEM browser.

▷ Select DEVELOPMENT COORDINATION/PACKAGES in the Object List area.

▷ Enter "S*" as the package name and then click the EXECUTE button or F8 (see Figure 2.13).

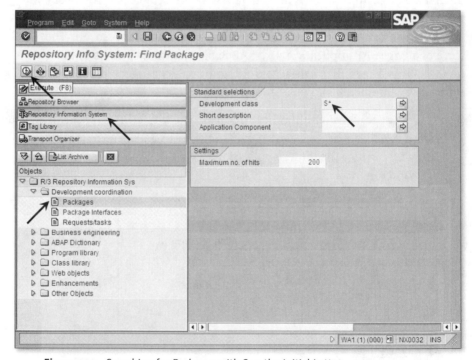

Figure 2.13 Searching for Packages with S as the Initial Letter

The result is a list of all hits that meet the criterion of the search string.

▷ Double-click the SABA package to display details on this development object.

A detailed view of the SABA package appears in the tool area and shows that SABA has a direct relationship with the BASIS package. Of course, you could double-click the BASIS to view more information about that package. But there is another approach that you might prefer:

▷ Check the name SABA and use the key combination Ctrl + C to copy the same to the clipboard.

▷ Click the REPOSITORY BROWSER button in the browser area.

▷ Insert the name of the package into the input field with Ctrl + V .

▷ Press the Enter key or click the DISPLAY button (eyeglasses icon) to load the package into the Object Navigator.

▷ Click the DISPLAY SUPERORD. OBJECT LIST to display the hierarchy of the packages.

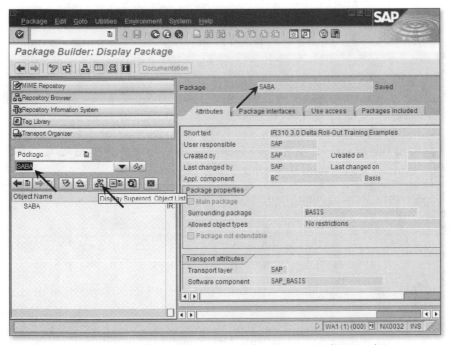

Figure 2.14 Moving the Package Name to the Object List Area with Cut and Paste

Now you can see that the SABA package, along with many others, is a component of the BASIS package and part of a very large hierarchy of packages. You can use the hierarchy for easy navigation between topically related packages.

2.3   Namespaces

Everyone has run into the problem of trying to store two files with different content, but the same name, in one directory. You have to rename one of the files unless you want to lose its content. A similar problem occurs when creating and copying development objects because development objects must always have a unique name. The challenge becomes even greater because the requirement for a unique name also applies across packages and development classes. In ABAP, almost every development object is global. Each is known to the entire SAP system. Names can occur more than once only in development objects.

Avoiding name conflicts

In addition to SAP, hundreds of implementation partners develop applications in ABAP. Do they all consult with each other? How do they avoid naming conflicts when the applications of two different manufactures are installed at one customer? The solution is the namespace that customers and partners can exclusively reserve at SAP. The namespace is actually a prefix placed at the beginning of the name of all development objects. The namespace begins and ends with a right slash (/) as a delimiter and can consist of up to ten characters. For example, the namespace "BA1" has been reserved at SAP for SAP Bank Analyzer, so that every development object related to the product (/BA1/B1_API_FP_TOTALS_GET, for example) begins with the prefix.

Listing and enhancing the namespace

Perform the following steps to look at the namespace in your SAP system.

▷ First, go to the SAP Easy Access menu and select TOOLS • ABAP WORK-BENCH • OVERVIEW • WORKBENCH ORGANIZER or Transaction SE09.

The Transport Organizer starts and displays the initial interface of the program.

▷ Now click the TRANSPORT ORGANIZER TOOLS button or press Shift + F6 (see Figure 2.15).

The program interface that appears is similar to the SAP Easy Access menu, but it contains only utility programs for organizing transports. Now select ADMINISTRATION • DISPLAY/CHANGE NAMESPACES.

Depending on the SAP systems you work with, one or more registered namespaces are displayed (see Figure 2.16).

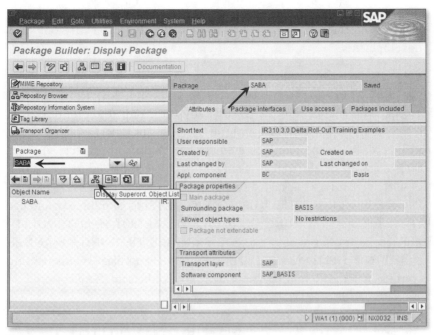

Figure 2.15 Calling the Transport Organizer Tools

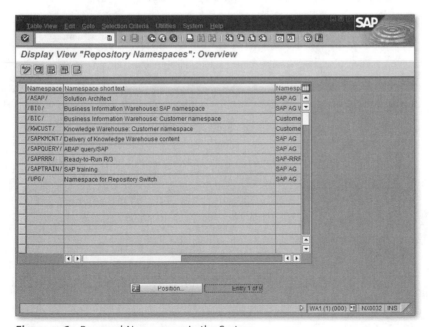

Figure 2.16 Reserved Namespaces in the System

If you have reserved a namespace for your project at SAP, you can use this interface to enter it. It is then available to you for your own developments.

Before you continue with the creation of your first development object, consider the naming convention for this book. It helps individuals and groups work with the book. Particularly for group training, note that every participant receives a unique two-digit number, which is used instead of 00 in the name element of a development object. Number 00 is reserved for the trainer (see Figure 2.17). For example, if the book describes creating a package or program named Z00_PRACTICE_TRAINING_BEGINNER or ZPTB00_HELLO_WORLD, the first trainee would use Z01_PRACTICE_TRAINING_BEGINNER and ZPTB01_HELLO_WORLD, the second trainee would use Z02_PRACTICE_TRAINING_BEGINNER and ZPTB02_HELLO_WORLD, and so on. This approach avoids naming conflicts when different users are working on the same SAP system.

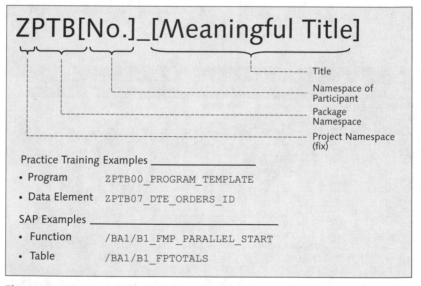

Figure 2.17 Names and Their Use for Group Training

If you have reserved something other than the generic "Z" for a customer namespace, make the necessary adjustments to the names of the objects created here.

Exercise 2.1

Create a development class or a package named Z00_PRACTICE_TRAINING_ BEGINNER.

▷ To create a package or development class, select the OTHER OBJECT button, or press ⎡Shift⎤ + ⎡F5⎤ (see Figure 2.18).

Creating a package or development class

A dialog opens in which you can select and create development objects according to the specifications of various tabs:

▷ Select the DEVELOPMENT COORDINATION tab and enter "Z00_PRAC-TICE_TRAINING_BEGINNER" in the PACKAGE or DEVELOPMENT CLASS input field.

▷ Select the CREATE button or press ⎡F5⎤.

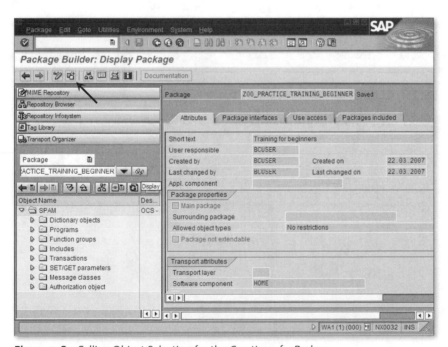

Figure 2.18 Calling Object Selection for the Creation of a Package

Another dialog appears in which you must enter more information on the package or development class:

▷ Enter a short description of the package or development class, such as "practical training for users of other languages and beginners."

▷ Enter "HOME" as the software.

▷ Select the SAVE button or press the ⌈Enter⌋ key.

The last dialog asks for the transport request that logs your development and that will later copy it from one system to the next.

Your administrator will allow you to create requests yourself or will assign you an existing request that you can use to create the package.

▷ Enter the name of the request set up by your administrator and confirm your entry with OK or click the NEW button.

▷ If you have to create a new transport request, you must enter a short description of the transport request ("Training for Beginners") and confirm your entry with SAVE (see Figure 2.19).

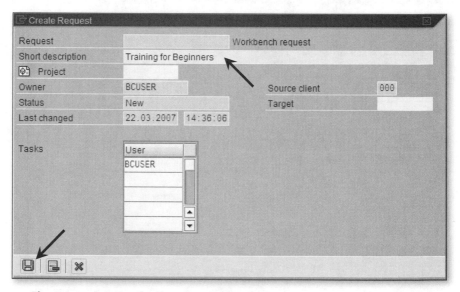

Figure 2.19 Entering the Short Description of a Request

After the request has been created, the dialog displays it with its number and description.

▷ You need to confirm your entries with OK until all the dialogs are closed (see Figure 2.20).

Figure 2.20 Confirming the Request Number

The tool area displays the detailed information that you entered. You now want to have the object list area display the package for easy creation and selection of additional development objects. You can do this by following these steps:

▷ Check the name of the package and copy the text to the clipboard with [Ctrl] + [C].

▷ Select PACKAGE or DEVELOPMENT CLASS as the object type.

▷ Copy the text into the input field with [Ctrl] + [V] and confirm with the DISPLAY button or ENTER (see Figure 2.21).

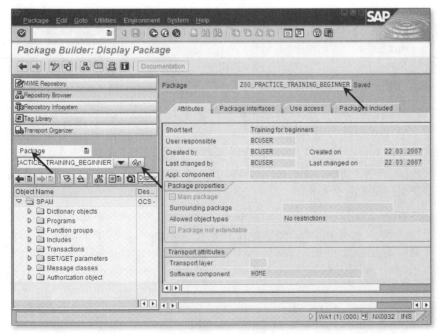

Figure 2.21 Loading a Package or Development Class into the Object List Area

You've completed all the preparatory steps to create your first program. The Object List area displays your (empty) package and you can add additional development objects to it.

2.4 First Program: "Hello World"—REPORT, INCLUDE, and Application Menu

The word "program" is now part of the vocabulary of every school-age child and is most commonly associated with terms like computer, software, and Internet. But what's special about an ABAP program? How do you create one? How do end users work with programs?

Basics No other programming language has experienced the kind of checkered history that ABAP has had over the past 30 years. From its conception to the advent of SAP R/3, ABAP was designed solely for the creation of *reports*, such as a listing of all liabilities to customers or a company balance sheet at the end of a fiscal year. ABAP programs could read data in the database and output it to the screen in table-based texts, or *lists*. Customers who use SAP software could modify the ABAP source code of these reports or design new reports to meet their needs. At that time (SAP R/2), programs with write access to the database had to be programmed in Assembler (directly in machine language). You can imagine the complexity and effort involved, and you can certainly understand that the task was reserved solely for SAP itself.

With the introduction of SAP R/3 at the beginning of the 1990s, the ABAP programming language had expanded to the point where it could be used to implement write access to the database. That enabled writing all SAP R/3 application completely in ABAP—without the help of other programming languages.

Module pool and report ABAP generally offers several options for writing an executable program. The *module pool* and the *report* are the most important. Originally, it was clear which alternative could be used at any given time. Complex input screens that had to be realized with the Dynpro interface technique (see Section 5.2, Complex Input and Output Interfaces—Dynpros) required a module pool. Creation of a posting document in accounting is a good example. Simple input templates, like the selection criteria for year and period in a period-end balance sheet, were programmed as reports. There have not been any technical limitations on the use of either technology since Release 3.0. Nevertheless, SAP continues to offer only a few programs that have been realized as module pools. In other words, reports have been in the forefront. Accordingly, this book focuses on programs of the report type and doesn't cover programming with module pools. For special cases, ABAP also offers a variety of other program types that cannot be covered here.

Because of the history involved, those familiar with SAP might use the term report to describe a program. Technically, a report is just one of several options that can generate a program.

Anyone who has ever started Word or Excel in Windows is already familiar with large programs that take up several megabytes on the hard drive and that are completely loaded into main memory. But SAP applications (like the Object Navigator or SAP CRM) consist of a large number (often more than 100) of individual programs. The user often doesn't even notice the switch from one program to the next. An individual ABAP program is often designed for a very specific task. For example, one program might handle the creation of a sales order, another the creation of a delivery note, and yet another the printing of an invoice. The organization of programs on one topic into one directory in the application menu (SAP Easy Access) and forward navigation give the user the impression that he is working with one large application.

ABAP programs: Cut Small

This concept reflects an essential difference between ABAP and other programming languages, such as C, Basic, and Pascal. The difference arises from ABAP's historical background. Every operation that writes to the database used to have its own assembler program, and the same idea still exists and has proven itself in ABAP.

Includes allow you to modularize source code, that is, to split it into small, manageable parts. The approach in ABAP is similar to that of include files in other programming languages, such as C or Pascal. You can store any size sections of source code in units that you load with `INCLUDE name`, where `name` contains the name of the include that stores that part of the source code. For example, you use includes to store constants that are supposed to be used in several applications. Each program

Includes

then links parts of the source code to the correct location in the program with an INCLUDE statement and can then use that part at will. The following excerpt of code clarifies this process. The code calculates a gross price from the net price entered by the user. It accesses a constant, CON_SALES_TAX , defined in an INCLUDE named ZPTB00_CONSTANTS for the sales tax rate:

```
REPORT zptb00_business_transaction.
INCLUDE zptb00_constants.
PARAMETERS:
  net_price TYPE p DECIMALS 2.
DATA:
  gross_price TYPE p DECIMALS 2.
* con_sales_tax is in include zptb00_constants defined.
  Gross_price = net_price + net_price * con_sales_tax.
```

Listing 2.1 Code Excerpt for Integrating an Include

Include programs perform nothing more than a library function for ABAP source code and cannot be executed as independent programs.

Making a program available

To make your own ABAP program available to end users, perform the following steps:

1. **Create program**
   Executable programs are created as source code within the Object Navigator and introduced with the keywords REPORT or PROGRAM.

2. **Write program code**
   The program code, which consists of individual ABAP commands, is inserted after the keyword REPORT.

3. **Create a transaction for the program**
   Once the program is complete, a transaction code is assigned to it. You can enter the transaction code in the command line to start the program directly.

4. **Assign rights for starting the transaction**
   As an option, the administrator can limit execution of a transaction to a specific user or user groups.

5. **Record transaction in the application menu**
   The transaction is ultimately recorded in the application menu of SAP Easy Access, where end users can easily find and execute it.

Create a program, ZPTB00_Hello_World, which queries your name and then displays it on the screen.

Test the program with the debugger.

Assign a transaction code to the program so that end users can call it.

Enhance the SAP application with an entry that calls the transaction.

You now have the knowledge you need to develop your first program in ABAP. The program is the typical example used by beginning programmers. It displays "Hello World" on the screen. You'll have the opportunity to become more familiar with the Object Navigator. To get started, follow these steps:

First program "Hello World"

▷ Go to the Repository Browser of the Object Navigator. The fastest way is to enter "/nSE80" in the command line.

▷ Select PACKAGE as the object type (DEVELOPMENT CLASS in Release 4.6).

▷ Enter the name of your development class or package (Z00_PRACTICE_TRAINING_BEGINNER) and click the DISPLAY button or press Enter.

▷ In the context menu for your package or development class, select CREATE • PROGRAM (see Figure 2.22).

A dialog appears: you can enter the name of the program in it by doing the following:

▷ Enter "ZPTB00_Hello_World" as the name of your program.

▷ Deactivate the checkbox WITH TOP INCLUDE and confirm your entry with OK.

Another dialog appears: you can enter additional information about the program (see Figure 2.23). As you can see, the implicit assumption is that the program will reside in the package Z00_PRACTICE_TRAINING_BEGINNER.

▷ Enter "Hello World" as the title of the program. Leave the other default entries alone.

▷ Confirm your input with SAVE.

Figure 2.22 Creating a Program with the Context Menu

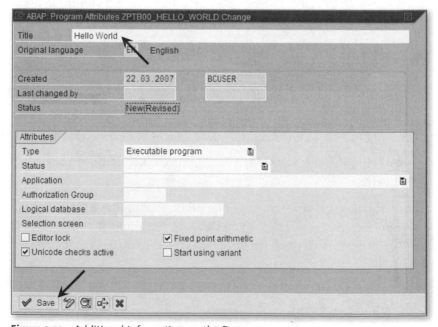

Figure 2.23 Additional Information on the Program

The last dialog asks for the transport request that logs your development and that will later copy it from one system to the next. Because you've already created a package, the entry given there for the package appears here as a suggestion (see Figure 2.24).

▷ Confirm the transport request set by default. If none appears, use F4 to select a transport request that has already been created.

Figure 2.24 Entering the Transport Request for the Program

The new program has now been created, and the first lines of source code and some comments have already been inserted automatically as a framework for the program. As discussed in Section 1.3, Programmer's Checklist for Getting Started, good comments are extremely important so that developers who have not helped write the program can easily understand what it does or should do. Comments can occupy an entire line or appear at the end of a line of code. If comments occupy an entire line, they begin with an asterisk (*). If they appear at the end of a line of code, they begin with quotation marks ("). The compiler regards everything after these characters in a line as non-ABAP text and ignores it.

Program framework and comments

▷ Type the following lines as an additional program framework beneath the comment lines:

```
WRITE: / 'Hello World', '!'.
WRITE / 'This is my first program.'.
WRITE 'And not my last one.'.
```

The WRITE command displays the text that follows on the screen. This is discussed in more detail later on.

▷ Now click the CHECK button or use Ctrl + F2.

If the line does not contain any syntax errors, a message to that effect appears in the status line.

▷ Next click the ACTIVATE button or use `Ctrl` + `F3`.

If no other program checks and activations produce an error, a message to that effect appears in the status line. The text next to the program name in the Tool area changes from INACTIVE to ACTIVE.

▷ Now click the DIRECT button or use `F8`.

The program is started and displays the desired text on the screen (see Figure 2.25). The title of the program, "Hello World," appears again, twice: In the title of the program and again in the output area. In the output area, it appears as a headline and is separated from the actual output by a horizontal line.

Figure 2.25 Program ZPTB00_Hello_World in Action

▷ Now click the BACK button to return to the Object Navigator and its source display.

As you can see, our program already has working BACK, EXIT, and CANCEL buttons.

Now you can modify the title of the program.

▷ Select GOTO • PROPERTIES in the menu.

▷ Enter "Hello my friend" in the TITLE field and confirm with the SAVE button.

Note that the source code provided in this book may contain line breaks due to the layout of this book. You need to copy them only if a period is visible at the end of the line. Otherwise, syntax errors could occur during execution. In this case, you can combine the corresponding statement in one line.

In the next step, you set the formatting of the source code to reflect the most common usage.

▷ Select UTILITIES • SETTINGS in the menu.

A dialog appears: You can change a number of settings of the ABAP Editor by doing the following:

▷ Select the PRETTY PRINTER tab.

▷ Activate the checkbox CONVERT UPPER-/LOWERCASE.

▷ Select the KEYWORD UPPERCASE radio button and confirm the settings (see Figure 2.26).

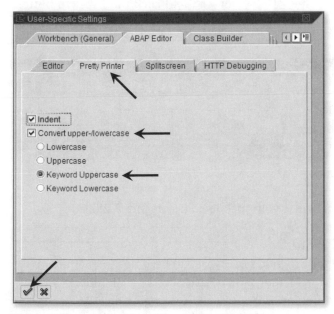

Figure 2.26 User-Specific Settings of the ABAP Editor

You also want to enhance the program somewhat so that it asks the users for a nickname and then greets them with their nicknames.

▷ Insert the following source code:

```
PARAMETERS:
  p_nicknm(15) TYPE c.
WRITE: / 'Hello World', p_nicknm, '!'.   "First statement
```

You will receive more detailed information on the PARAMETERS command later on. Here, it's enough to note that it can accept user entries at the start of a program and make them available for further processing.

▷ Next click the PRETTY PRINTER button.

▷ Activate the source code with ⌨Ctrl⌨ + ⌨F3⌨ and start the program with ⌨F8⌨.

The program then appears with a modified title and an input field (see Figure 2.27).

▷ Enter your nickname, "Heidelberger", and click the EXECUTE button or ⌨F8⌨.

Figure 2.27 Entering a Nickname

The display now includes your nickname (see Figure 2.28).

▷ Now select the BACK button or ⌨F3⌨.

Debugging Now you execute the program step by step to become more familiar with the debugger. Users of Delphi, Visual Basic, and Java (JBuilder) will have to get used to a different user interface. Debugging an ABAP program occurs in a separate program rather than in the editor, but the familiar functionality of other programming languages is still available.

Figure 2.28 Output of Program ZPTB00_Hello_World

The ABAP debugger offers the following essential features:

▶ **Single-step button**
Executes a program line by line. After execution of the statement in one line, the processing arrow is placed on the next statement. If the current statement involves a subprogram, function, or method, the debugger looks for the next complete statement and places the processing arrow there.

▶ **Execute button**
Executes a program line by line, but also executes the statements of subprograms, functions, and methods as a whole (in a single step). The processing arrow is then placed on the next statement in the same part of the program.

▶ **Return button**
Executes all the lines of the current program at one time, so you can use it to execute the remaining statements of a subprogram, function, or method. Your sample program contains only a main program portion, so it is executed right up to its end.

▶ **Continue (to cursor) button**
Execute the program as a whole rather than step by step, as is typical without debugging. But if you previously marked a statement in the debugger by double-clicking, execution stops and the processing arrow remains on that statement.

▶ **Debugging/Goto statement**
If you marked a statement by clicking it, the processing arrow moves to that statement, whether the statement is ahead of or behind the

processing arrow and whether doing so makes sense in terms of the program logic.

▶ **Debugging/Restart**
This menu entry stops the program at the current statement and returns to the Object Navigator. You can restart the program from there.

▶ **Create/Delete context menu/breakpoint**
You can create a stop, a *breakpoint*, on almost any statement. Execution of the program will stop at the point, regardless of what buttons you've already clicked. If you then click the SAVE button, breakpoints remain in effect until you close the session. If you reselect the menu entry, the breakpoint is deleted. You can also create and delete a breakpoint by double-clicking to the left of a statement.

▶ **Breakpoint/Breakpoint at**
In this menu, you can set breakpoints at specific locations within the program, even when the processing arrow is not located close by. You often need BREAKPOINT AT FUNCTION MODULE and BREAKPOINT AT STATEMENT.

▶ **Examine field content**
Double-clicking a field (such as parameter p_nicknm in our source code) displays the content under the source code.

▶ **Change field content button**
You can even change field content during debugging. Perform the same steps you do when you examine field content. You can enter new content where the previous content is displayed and then keep the modification by clicking the CHANGE FIELD CONTENT button.

▶ **Calls button**
When debugging large programs that contain subprograms, function modules, or methods, it's important to know where those items are called in the source code. That information is provided by the *stack list*, which is displayed when you click the CALLS button. You can also return to the source-text display of the debugger with the BACK button.

▶ **Settings button**
You can change the behavior of the debugger. You can use the SET-
TINGS button to display and change all configuration options.

Let's look at the ABAP debugger in the real world.

▷ First, select EXECUTE • DEBUGGING in the context menu of the program (see Figure 2.29).

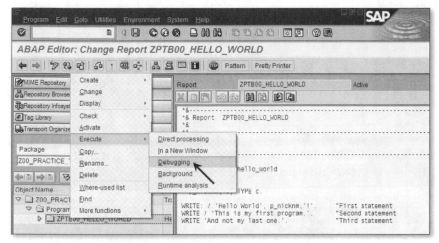

Figure 2.29 Context Menu: EXECUTE • DEBUGGING

An input field is displayed. You can enter your nickname here.

▷ Now enter your nickname and confirm your entry with F8 .

After entering all the parameters, you move to the debugger. The processing arrow points to the first statement, the REPORT statement in this
case (see Figure 2.30).

▷ Select the SINGLE STEP button or F5 .

The processing arrow moves from the REPORT statement to the first
WRITE statement.

▷ Double-click parameter p_nicknm.

The current content of the parameter is displayed in the list next to the
source code (see Figure 2.31).

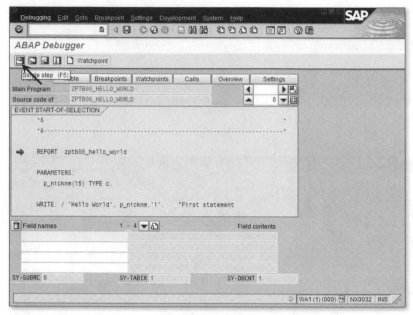

Figure 2.30 The Debugger on the REPORT Statement

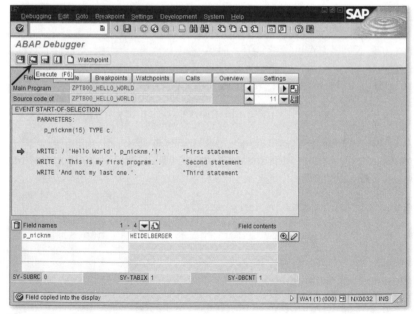

Figure 2.31 The Debugger Displays the Content of a Parameter

▷ Now select the EXECUTE button or F6 .

The processing arrow is now at the second WRITE statement. Perform the following steps:

▷ Change the content of the input field from "Heidelberger" to "Berliner".

▷ Click the CHANGE button.

▷ Click the first WRITE statement (see Figure 2.32).

The processing arrow is still at the second statement.

▷ Select DEBUGGING • GOTO STATEMENT in the menu.

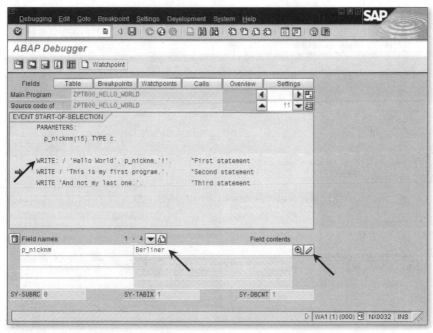

Figure 2.32 The Debugger Displays the Modified Content of the Parameter

The processing arrow returns to a position in front of the first WRITE statement. Perform the following steps:

▷ Click the last WRITE statement.

▷ Select the CONTINUE (TO CURSOR) button or F8 (see Figure 2.33).

The processing arrow then moves to the last WRITE statement.

▷ Select the RETURN button or ⌗F7⌗.

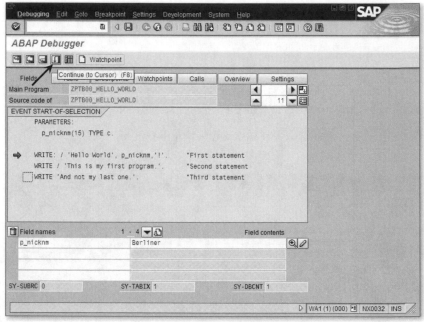

Figure 2.33 Navigating in the Debugging for the Statement

That executes all the statements of your main program (the last state-ment); the screen displays the results (see Figure 2.34).

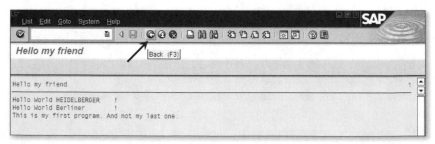

Figure 2.34 All Program Outputs Are Displayed

As you can see, you have twisted the logic of your program by modifying the parameters and executing the WRITE statement again. Now it outputs two nicknames instead of one. Ultimately, the example shows the powerful features of the debugger, especially its ability to modify and move the processing arrow deliberately. During debugging, you can force the program to behave in ways that would never occur in real operations.

Now let's make your program available to end users who normally don't have access to development tools. You would normally create a *transaction* here, that is, a link that enables starting the program from the command line.

Transaction

Given this history at SAP, the term "transaction" often replaces "program." In technical terms, however, a transaction is a link to a program, as described below. To explain the multiple meanings of the term thoroughly, Chapter 4, Defining and Managing Database Tables, covers database transactions.

▷ To create a transaction, first select CREATE • TRANSACTION from the context menu of your package or development class (see Figure 2.35).

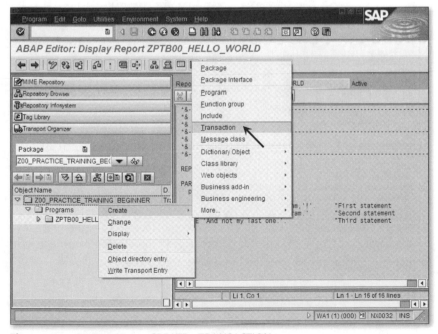

Figure 2.35 Context Menu: CREATE • TRANSACTION

A dialog appears in which you can specify additional detailed information on the transaction and a transaction code that is as short as possible.

▷ Now enter "ZPTB00_HW" as the transaction and "Hello World and Nickname" as the short text.

▷ Next you need to define the transaction of type PROGRAM AND SELECTION SCREEN (REPORT TRANSACTION) and confirm it with OK (see Figure 2.36).

Figure 2.36   Create Transaction

The tool area then displays additional information that you can specify:

▷ Enter "ZPTB00_HELLO_WORLD" as the program.

▷ Define the GUI ABILITY as appropriate for HTML, Java, and Windows; click the SAVE button or Ctrl + S.

As is always the case when you create a new development object, you must specify a transport request that will log your actions.

▷ Then confirm the usual transport number with OK.

The transaction has now been created and you can try it out.

▷ Enter the transaction code (preceded by "/n") in the command line and confirm with ⎡Enter⎤ (see Figure 2.37).

Figure 2.37 Testing the New Transaction

The program you have written, ZPTB00_HELLO_WORLD, then starts.

▷ Use the ⎡F3⎤ key to return to the Object Navigator.

As you can see, it's simple to make a program available to end users. But end users learn a transaction code only for programs they use frequently, so let's make access to the program more user-friendly, and include it in the application menu in SAP Easy Access. The application menu is a large menu tree that consists of individual area menus. The area menus contain topically related applications and organize them into menus and submenus (see Figure 2.38).

Area menu

Accordingly, the application menu is really an area menu that's particularly large, is connected with many other area menus, and is displayed by SAP Easy Access.

Your task here is to create an area menu you can use to store your transaction and a menu text. You then add it to a specific location in the application menu, making it available to all users.

Creating an area menu

▷ To begin, select CREATE • ADDITIONAL • AREA MENU in the context menu of the package or development class.

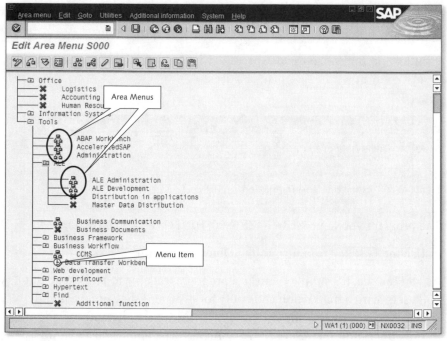

Figure 2.38 Application Menu of SAP Easy Access Consists of Several Area Menus

A dialog appears: you can enter a unique name and short text as a description:

▷ Enter "ZPTB00" as the name of the transaction.

▷ Enter "Training for beginners" and confirm your entries (see Figure 2.39).

Figure 2.39 Creating an Area Menu

A program appears that fills the entire work area.

▷ Check the entry for TRAINING FOR BEGINNERS.

▷ Then select the ADD ENTRY AS SUBNODE button or Shift + F7 (see Figure 2.40).

Figure 2.40 Editing the Area Menu

A dialog appears: You can make entries for the area menu.

▷ Now enter "Hello World and Nickname" and Transaction code "ZPTB00_HW" and confirm with OK (see Figure 2.41).

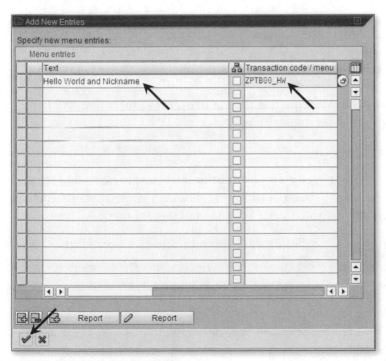

Figure 2.41 Creating a New Menu Entry

The main window reappears and you can save the area menu.

▷ Click the SAVE button or ⌜Ctrl⌝ + ⌜S⌝.

A dialog appears that requests the name of the package or development class that will store the area menu.

▷ Enter "Z00_Practice_Training_Beginner" as the package and save the entry (see Figure 2.42).

Figure 2.42 Package That Will Store the Area Menu

As always, the last request is for the transport request that will log the changes to this development object.

▷ Confirm with OK.

Adding to the application menu

You have now created a small submenu for your programs and transactions. But you still have not added the submenu to the application menu provided by SAP. You do this by following these steps:

▷ Select the CANCEL button until you return to SAP Easy Access.

▷ Start SAP MENU • TOOLS • ABAP WORKBENCH • DEVELOPMENT • ADDITIONAL TOOLS • AREA MENUS or Transaction SE43.

A window appears: You can enter the area menu you want to work with. You want to enhance the SAP application menu that is stored under the name "S000." Next:

▷ Enter the name of SAP application menu "S000" or select it with F4 help.

▷ Select the DISPLAY AREA MENU button or F7 (see Figure 2.43).

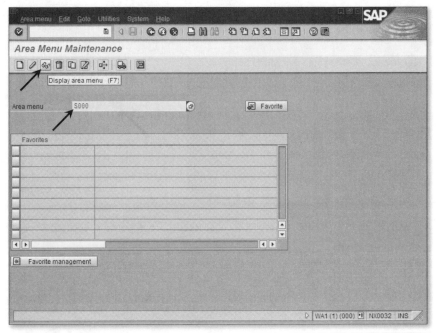

Figure 2.43 Selecting Area Menu S000

The area menu then appears; you're already familiar with it from SAP Easy Access.

▷ Check the entry for SAP R/3 SYSTEM.

▷ The select the DISPLAY <-> CHANGE button or Ctrl + F1 (see Figure 2.44).

A security query appears: Enter the editing mode.

▷ Click the ENHANCE button.

Figure 2.44 Displaying Area Menu S000

Enhancement ID | A dialog opens. Enter the *Enhancement ID* that you want to use to store your modification. Put simply, your changes are made not to the original but to a copy that will later be blended with the original. If you have not yet created an enhancement ID, you must do so now. You can use this ID for all later modifications of the menu.

▷ Click the CREATE ENHANCEMENT ID button.

Another dialog opens, prompting you to enter a text that describes your enhancement ID.

▷ Now enter "ZPTB00" as the Enhancement ID, "Enhancement for own area menu" as the Explanatory text, and confirm with Enter (see Figure 2.45).

Figure 2.45 Creating an Enhancement ID

Your enhancement ID appears under ENHANCEMENT ID: ORIGINAL, and you can now begin the modification.

▷ Click Enhancement ID ZPTB00.

▷ Then click the SELECT button (magnifying glass) (see Figure 2.46).

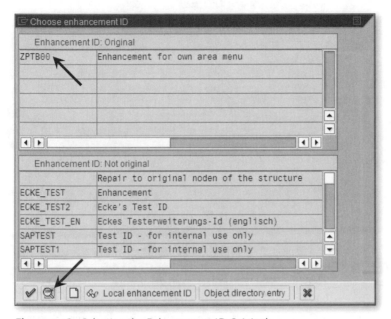

Figure 2.46 Selecting the Enhancement ID Originals

You are now in editing mode for the menu and want to insert your area menu into the second level.

▷ Click the uppermost entry in the list (usually SAP R/3 SYSTEM—see Figure 2.47).

▷ Then select INSERT AS SUBNODE from the context menu.

In the next dialog (see Figure 2.48), you can enter your menu entries directly or add them to an area menu. You've already created an area menu, so let's use it here:

▷ Enter "Practice Training Beginner" as the text.

▷ Check the checkbox to identify your entry as an area menu.

▷ In the TRANSACTION CODE/MENU column, use the [F4] key to select your area menu easily.

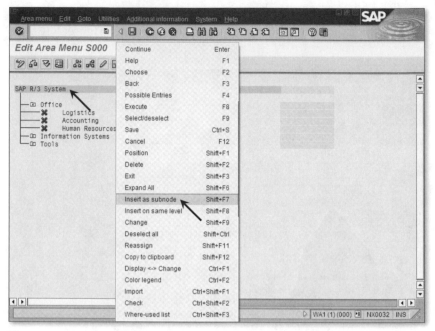

Figure 2.47 Inserting the Area Menu One Level Deeper

Your area menu appears at the bottom of the suggested values. Now do the following:

▷ Check area menu ZPTB00 and click the OK button to include your area menu as an input field.

▷ Click the OK button again to place your area menu in the application menu.

▷ Click the SAVE button to save your changes (see Figure 2.49).

The familiar dialog that asks for the transport request appears.

▷ Confirm with ⌑Enter⌑ to use the suggested request.

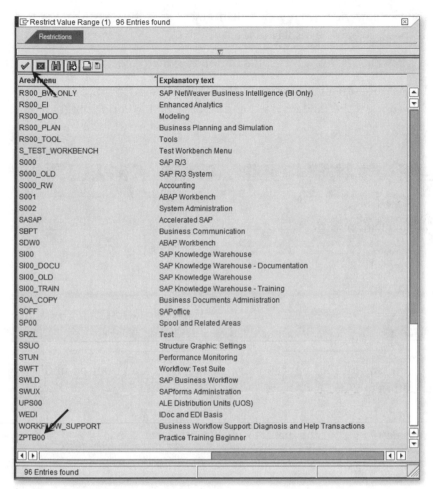

Figure 2.48 Creating New Entries

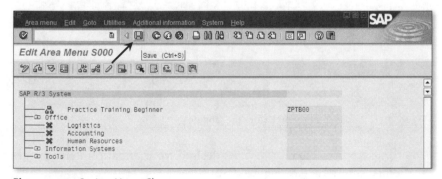

Figure 2.49 Saving Menu Changes

You can now view what your enhancement actually looks like. For this purpose, go back to display mode.

▷ Click the DISPLAY <-> CHANGE button to switch to display mode.

The application menu has now been enhanced with your area menu and contains the new transaction for your "Hello World" program (see Figure 2.50).

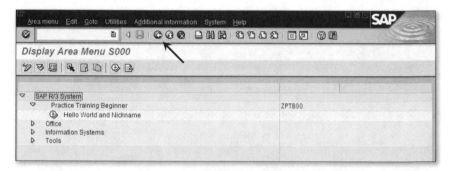

Figure 2.50 Application Menu with New Area Menu and Transaction

▷ You can quit the application by clicking the CANCEL button until you return to SAP Easy Access.

In SAP Easy Access, you'll see that your changes are not (yet) displayed. You have to restart the menu to see your changes.

▷ Do this by clicking the SAP MENU button (see Figure 2.51).

Figure 2.51 Application Menu Before the Update

The complete menu is reloaded. As desired, your enhancement appears as the first submenu (see Figure 2.52).

Figure 2.52 Application Menu After the Update

2.5 Online Help, help.sap.com, service.sap.com, and SAP Notes

Help and support are your primary needs when learning a new programming language. Doing everything yourself and making sense of it requires a great deal of time. That's the reason behind this book, and SAP offers a variety of other information.

In addition to traditional training and support from consultants, SAP and its partners offer a large number of sources of electronic information to different target groups. This chapter introduces some of the most important sources of information.

Basics

- ► **Online help**
  These days, almost every application offers online help and SAP applications are no exception. Note the distinction between online help for various applications (Object Navigator, reuse library, and so on) and online help for ABAP, along with its statements (WRITE, PARAMETER, and so on) and development objects (programs, tables, and so on). Local installation of the Web-based knowledge warehouse from SAP covers the first kind of online help; the database manages documentation on ABAP keywords.

- ► **SAP Help Portal** *(help.sap.com)*
  This information source is designed for SAP users and developers. It is available to all free of charge over the Internet, and is comparable

to the help portals of other manufacturers, such as *MSDN.microsoft. com*. In addition to online help for various releases of SAP software, it contains comprehensive, cross-application documentation on all development and administrative tools, ABAP statements, and ABAP development objects.

▶ **SAP Service Marketplace** *(service.sap.com)*
This information source is primarily intended for SAP administrators and consultants. It's accessible to SAP customers and partners on the Internet. In addition to technical installation and configuration guidelines, it offers lists of business functions, business scenarios, and descriptions of best practices for individual SAP applications.

▶ **SAP Notes**
SAP calls its replies to support questions from customers and partners "SAP Notes." The term applies to questions that might well have general interest. The replies are made anonymously and are understandable to a general audience. They are then given a unique number, categorized by applications, and published. This channel provides tips, solutions to problems, and even patches.

Exercise 2.3

Use the online help on the ABAP editor to display information on the use of the ABAP keyword REPORT.

Surf to the SAP Help Portal at *help.sap.com*, and read the information on executing a report.

Surf to SAP Service Marketplace at *service.sap.com*, and download the most recent problem reports and patches on activating data elements.

Online help   Here you start with online help, which you can call with F1 from every program. Regardless of a focus on an input field, tab, or window, online help displays specialized help for applications and parts of applications. Here's a brief example:

▷ Place the cursor on the keyword REPORT in the source code of your program and press F1 to call online help for this command.

A new window, ABAP KEYWORD DOCUMENTATION, is displayed. It explains the REPORT command in a variety of forms. The left side displays the navigation tree: A list of individual documentation that is organized by topic (see Figure 2.53).

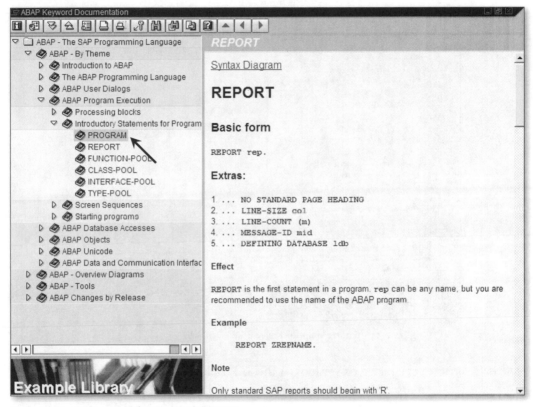

Figure 2.53 Online Help for Keyword REPORT

The documentation on the keyword PROGRAM is interesting; you're already familiar with it from other programming languages as the introduction to a source code.

▷ Double-click the keyword PROGRAM in the navigation tree of online help.

The description on the right side changes and explains that the PROGRAM command is a synonym for the REPORT command (see Figure 2.54).

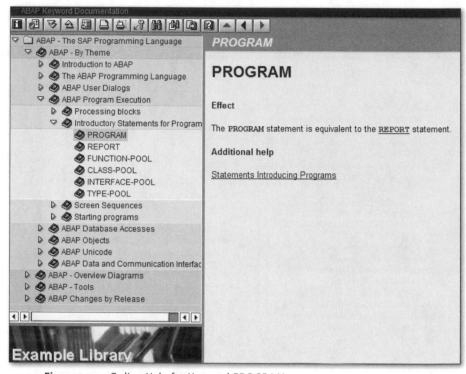

Figure 2.54 Online Help for Keyword PROGRAM

SAP Help Portal Let's take a closer look at the SAP Help Portal, which supplies programmers with information on ABAP development. As an example, search for the information on reports by doing the following:

▷ Start your browser and enter "help.sap.com" as the URL.

▷ Click SAP NETWEAVER in the navigation bar on the left side. If you're working with SAP Application Server 4.6, you must click SAP R/3 AND R/3 ENTERPRISE instead.

▷ A list of all available releases is displayed. Select the latest release that you use. The right side of the help screen lets you select help for the latest support package (including all previous support packages for the release) and an entire help offering.

▷ Click your preferred language from the entire help offering (see Figure 2.55).

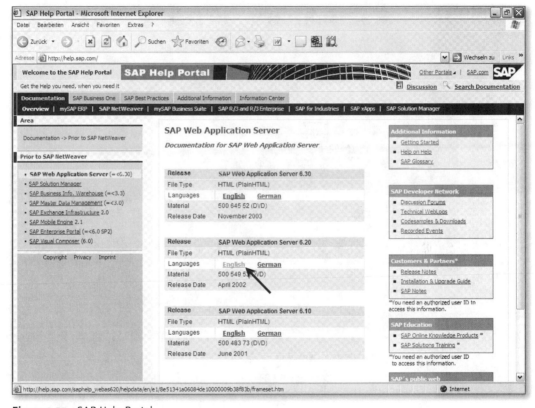

Figure 2.55 SAP Help Portal

The knowledge warehouse from SAP appears. It displays the entire subject area on the left side and the contents on the right side. You can scroll by topic title or use the full-text search:

▷ Click SEARCH in the menu.

▷ Enter "execute report" as the search string and confirm your selection with the SEARCH button (see Figure 2.56).

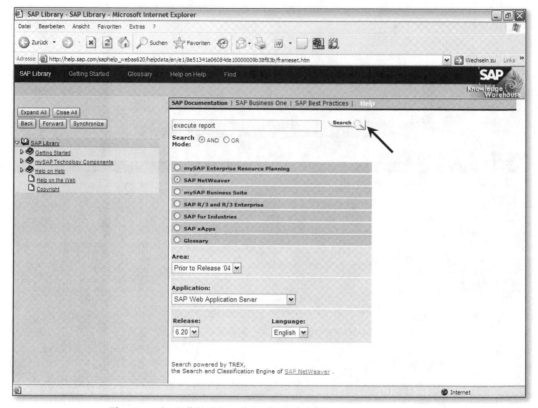

Figure 2.56 Full-Text Search in the SAP Library

The screen then displays a hit list based on the search string (see Figure 2.57).

▷ Click EXECUTE REPORT in the hit list.

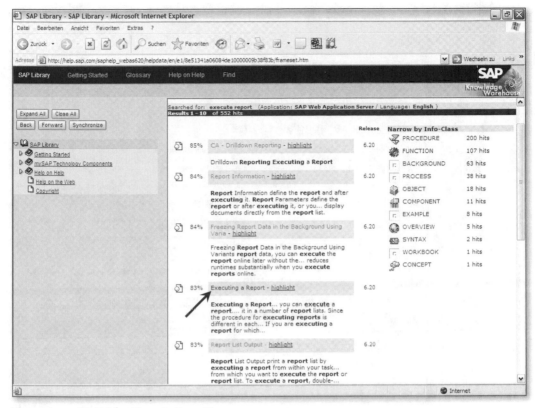

Figure 2.57 Hit List for "Execute Report"

The help document on "Executing a Report" is displayed (see Figure 2.58).

The SAP Help Portal is preferable even when the information (for instance, help for an ABAP statement) you are looking for is available in online help. That's because the high-performance search engine displays a list of results in a few seconds, offering you quick access to the information.

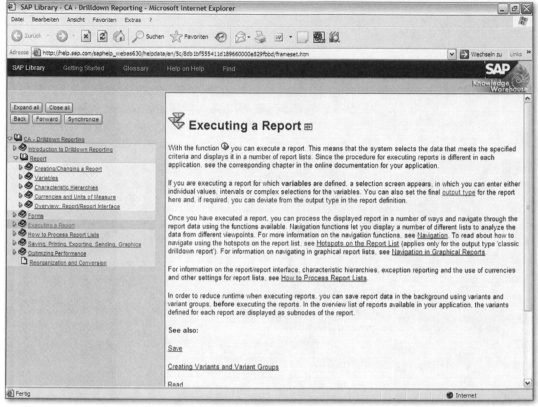

Figure 2.58 Help on "Executing a Report"

SAP Service
Marketplace

You can visit SAP Service Marketplace from the help menu of every SAP application and via a Web browser. A few pages from the comprehensive help portal are presented here as examples.

▷ Select HELP • SAP SERVICE MARKETPLACE or open *service.sap.com* in your web browser.

The home page of SAP Service Marketplace appears. Your SAP administrator can supply you with the information you need to log on.

▷ Click the LOGIN NOW button and log on (see Figure 2.59).

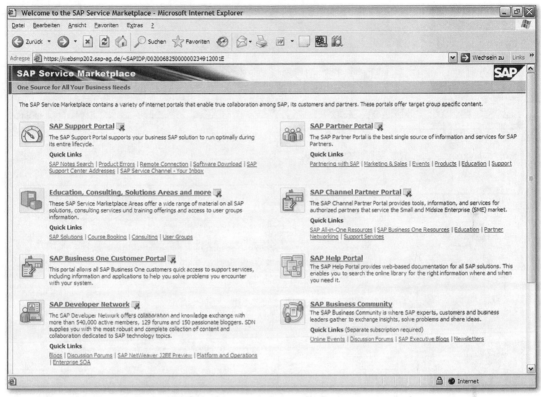

Figure 2.59 SAP Service Marketplace—Login Page

After you have logged on, you reach the home page of SAP Service Marketplace (see Figure 2.60). Here you'll find very interesting "solutions in detail" and information on consulting, training, and support.

▷ Click SUPPORT in the menu.

This area is the most comprehensive part of SAP Service Marketplace. The right side has a menu area from which you can control all further information on the support site.

SAP Notes are by far the most important element for administrators and developers. You can call them via the SEARCH FOR SAP NOTES link on the SAP Service Marketplace. As a practical example, search for SAP Notes in activating development objects.

SAP Notes

▷ Click the SEARCH FOR SAP NOTES link.

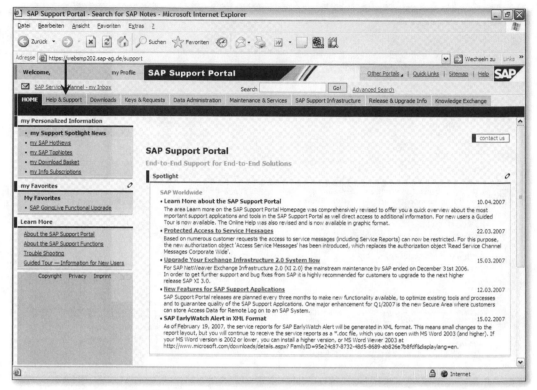

Figure 2.60 Support Page of SAP Service Marketplace

A search screen appears: you can search for SAP Notes on a specific application directly by entering keywords and numbers or by entering a topic (*see* Figure 2.61).

▷ Now click the magnifying glass icon next to TOPIC.

A selection dialog appears. It displays all SAP applications in a hierarchical list. Search for notes on activating development objects.

▷ Navigate to the application components in the tree and click BC-DWB-DIC-AC (*see* Figure 2.62).

Figure 2.61 Searching for SAP Notes on Activation

Figure 2.62 Selecting Application Components

The selection dialog closes and your entry is copied to the search screen.

▷ Next click the SEARCH button.

A hit list is displayed with all matches for the selected application component.

▷ Navigate through the hit list and click the SAP Note you were looking for.

The SAP note is displayed (see Figure 2.63).

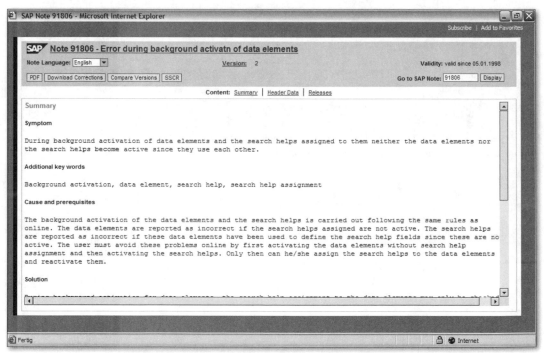

Figure 2.63 Selected SAP Note

ABAP has over 500 different language elements, far more than other popular programming languages, like C, Java, Pascal, or Visual Basic, which have 30 to 50 language elements. Fortunately, most of these language elements can be seen as variations of a few main elements, and can therefore be sorted by topic.

3   Procedural Language Elements

For every purpose, there's a separate command. This is how we could describe the original concept of the ABAP programming language. The result is a list of commands, which, comprising 500 different language elements, is probably the longest of any popular programming language when the numerous variants are considered.

Basics

Technically, the reason for this is the declarative concept behind ABAP, which is better compared to Natural or another mainframe or 4GL language than to typical 3GL languages like C, Java, Pascal, or Visual Basic. Indeed, ABAP has its own commands for communication between processes using a shared memory range, which is typical with mainframes (e.g., SET, GET, and so on, instead of using the application programming interface (API) functions of the system such as on Windows or UNIX) and has a series of language elements for set processing of tabular (database) data, such as those provided by 4GL languages (e.g., LOOP or SELECT), instead of using FOR loops and complex object-oriented classes like those in C++ or Delphi. Furthermore, the few commands that are similar to those in 3GL languages (e.g., IF/THEN/ELSE, CASE, and WHILE) are less significant in terms of quantity. But it is precisely those commands that make ABAP what it is—a full-fledged programming language.

4GL language
ABAP Objects

Instead of just writing ABAP off as a special case among programming languages, it can often help newcomers to think of ABAP as a standard 3GL language like C, Java, Pascal, or Visual Basic, that also has a series of special and very powerful language elements for working with tables in main memory (instead of arrays) and for accessing the database

Tips for those familiar with other programming languages

directly (instead of using complicated ADO, JDBC, or BDE classes). Here is another tip for newcomers: You may have worked with pointers or variant data types (for instance, `Variant` under Visual Basis or Delphi) in other languages. These, and a few other things, don't exist in ABAP because SAP considers them as endangering type safety. You also need to get used to a lot more data declarations (for instance, of variables) for a given amount of code, on average about five times as much as in other programming languages. Nesting of functions, multiple dereferencing in methods, and formula calculation within branch statements (for instance, `Write(Time(Now))`, `Application.Workbooks('Sheet1'). Caption, IF (A>=3*B) THEN`) are not permitted, so the result of each intermediate step must first be stored in a variable, and only then can the next operation be carried out.

Figure 3.1 Grouping of the Many Language Elements of ABAP Objects

Here's an example. The Pascal statement

```
Write(TimeToString(date-1))
```

is expressed as follows in ABAP:

```
DATA: yesterday TYPE d.
yesterday = sy-datum - 1.
WRITE yesterday.
```

From the Visual Basic statement

```
Application.Workbooks('Sheet1').Caption,
```

we might derive the following ABAP statement:

```
DATA: WB TYPE Workbook.
Call method application->Workbook
  Exporting
     Name = 'Sheet1'
   receiving
     result = wb.
```

ABAP uses a period to separate multiple statements. Within a statement, spaces are used to separate required parameters, even though most languages use a comma for this purpose. Another special feature of ABAP is that commands such as CALL FUNCTION can be used with a colon so that multiple commands in sequence can be listed without specifying that keyword, all separated by commas. The basic notation therefore looks like this:

Basic notation rules

```
CALL FUNCTION   'first_function'
CALL FUNCTION   'second_function'
CALL FUNCTION   'third_function'
```

The following notation is also possible as an alternative:

```
CALL FUNCTION:  ' first_function ',
                ' second_function ',
                ' third_function '.
```

ABAP isn't always just ABAP. While most of the chapters in this book cover the ABAP Objects programming language, Section 5.2, Complex Input and Output Interfaces—Dynpros, deals with the presentation of complex user interfaces whose programming is done using so-called *Dynpro flow logic*. Here, different conditions apply, and there is a different set of commands. The new *Web Dynpro technology* makes Dynpro flow logic superfluous, instead using normal ABAP (that is, ABAP without Dynpro flow logic) for the programming of the user interface. But as long as customers still have applications in use based on the SAP NetWeaver Application Server at releases prior to Release 6.30—and this will definitely continue to be the case for years to come—this new technology cannot be used.

ABAP versus Dynpro flow logic

3.1 Basic Commands and Fields — WRITE, PARAMETERS, MOVE, SY Fields

The basic commands of ABAP provide functionality such as the output of text and numbers on the screen, the entry of user input on the keyboard, or the retrieval of general information about the system and the user.

Basics   The basic commands and fields learned when beginning a new programming language are among the most important and are most often used in the whole language. Over time, however, hundreds of more convenient and more powerful function or class libraries are added by software manufacturers, increasingly replacing the older commands and fields. This development has also taken place in ABAP, and, for that reason, the following description only selectively covers a few important aspects.

Basic commands   The following commands are still among the most often used today:

▶ WRITE — **Output to the Screen or into a Text Variable**
The WRITE command is actually a component of an extremely powerful list concept, which was SAP's preferred method of screen output for many years. Basically, this command allows the output of text, numbers, and data to the screen, taking into consideration position and formatting instructions, such as the language-specific output of date values, and can output both symbols or lines and even include tooltips, which are displayed when the mouse passes over the text. Nowadays, the WRITE command is largely used to format data, which is then passed on to complicated input and output controls for display on the screen and to receive mouse and keyboard input (see Section 5.2, Complex Input and Output Interfaces — Dynpros). And just in case you're wondering: A READ system command, used in other programming languages for the receipt of keyboard input, does not exist in ABAP. The PARAMETERS command, which assumes this task in ABAP, is discussed in Section 3.2, Data and Data Types — DATA, PARAMETERS, CONSTANTS, FIELD SYMBOLS, TYPE, CREATE, Text Elements.

▶ GET — **Reading Values**
Depending on the keywords also supplied, the GET command may read the system time (GET TIME), the current cursor position on the

screen (`GET CURSOR`), or other information. There are 12 such basic forms of the `GET` command, each with entirely different tasks. However, the most important basic form is used for the administration of data references (`GET REFERENCE OF`) and is explained in detail in Section 3.2, Data and Data Types—DATA, PARAMETERS, CONSTANTS, FIELD SYMBOLS, TYPE, CREATE, Text Elements. This chapter presents the `GET` command in the context of reading the current time.

▶ `SET`—**Setting Values**
This chapter presents the `SET` command in the context of setting value in global memory. It has no fewer than 21 basic forms in all. The most commonly used forms are undoubtedly `SET PARAMETER` to set a value in global memory and `SET EXTENDED CHECK ON/OFF` to turn extended syntax checking on or off.

▶ `MOVE`—**Assignment of Data, Copying of Substrings**
The `MOVE` in its basic form is identical to the assignment operator =; that is, the command `MOVE a TO b` has the same effect as `b = a`, namely that it copies the content of `a` into `b` (assignment). The `MOVE` command has other variants, however, such as the copying of parts from a character string, which is also possible with any other character-based operands in ABAP. Here, the specification of the *offset* is needed; that is, you must specify the character at which the copy should start (`MOVE f+[offset]([count]) TO g`).

Besides its predefined selection of basic commands, the ABAP language also has, nicely arranged in a structure called `SY` (see Section 3.3, Structures and Internal Tables—TABLE, MOVE-CORRESPONDING, INSERT, APPEND, READ, MODIFY, DELETE, LOOP), no fewer than 171 fields called *system fields* in which the system stores certain information about its status (for instance, the current date, the release version, and the login name of the user). The information in these system fields can be retrieved and used at any time from your own code. Some of these fields are meaningful only for the ABAP runtime environment, and others are also valuable for programmers, so the following briefly describes a few of the most important system fields:

System field

▶ `sy-subrc`—**Return Value After ABAP Commands and Functions**
This is by far the most commonly used system field. After the call of ABAP commands and functions, it contains the so-called *return value*

(subprogram return code). This indicates whether the command or function called was executed without error (content has value 0) or an error occurred (content has a value <> 0). In the online help, you can find a description of the possible return values for each ABAP command, for instance, "4=record not found," "2=field symbol not assigned," and so on.

▶ `sy-uname`—**Login Name of the User**
An ABAP program can easily use this system field to determine the login name of the user who executed the program. When printing or checking permissions, this information is very useful. Instructions in the code such as the following are very popular with programmers for testing:

```
IF sy-uname = 'JOHNSON'.
  BREAK-POINT.
ENDIF.
```

Here, Johnson is the login name of the programmer, and when he runs the problem, the program enters the debugger at that point and stops so that the following program steps can be traced individually.

▶ `sy-host`—**Name of the SAP NetWeaver Application Server**
This system field gives information about the name of the SAP NetWeaver Application Server that is running the actual program. For SAP systems with many users, which often consist of multiple SAP NetWeaver Application Servers for the purpose of load distribution, this information may well vary, and, using this field, you can easily determine which SAP NetWeaver AS is currently running the program.

Over the course of reading this book, you will get to know a few system fields that have valid values only in certain situations, such as `sy-index` (number of times through the current loop), `sy-tabix` (index of the current record when accessing an internal table), and `sy-dbcnt` (number of records in a database table processed by an SQL statement).

A brief practical example presents the functioning of these basic commands and fields, even though some of the details about the processing of data are explained only in the next few chapters.

Exercise 3.1

Create a program called ZPTB00_System_Information, which prints as many items of information as possible from the following categories:

▶ Date and time information

▶ Login information

▶ System and program information

Use the selected SY fields and system commands to do this.

▷ First, in the context menu of the package or the development class, select the point CREATE • PROGRAM.

Then the familiar dialog appears to ask for the name of the program:

▷ Enter "ZPTB00_System_Information" as the name of the program.

▷ Uncheck the WITH TOP INCLUDE checkbox and confirm your entry with the OK button.

The next dialog asks you for the program properties (see Figure 3.2).

Figure 3.2 Specifying Program Properties for ZPTB00_System_Information

Now do the following:

▷ Enter "Show system information" as the title.

▷ Leave all the other settings unchanged, and confirm with the SAVE button.

The SAP Object Navigator finally asks for the transport request.

▷ The number of the transport request used previously is set by default. Simply confirm it with the OK button.

As usual, the SAP Object Navigator creates a program structure (see Figure 3.3), which you can now fill in.

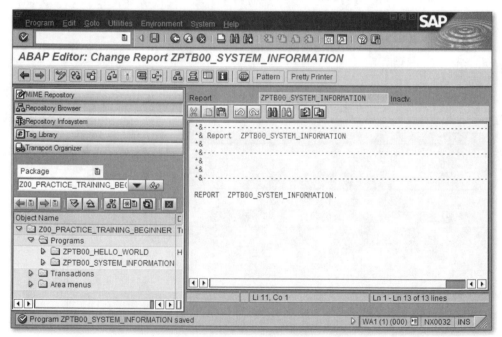

Figure 3.3 Program Structure for ZPTB00_System_Information

▷ Now type the following source code under the comment lines:

```
REPORT zptb00_system_information.

DATA:
* Date & time information variables
```

```
    l_timestamp TYPE timestampl,
    l_string(30) TYPE c.

* R         efresh all internal date & time fields like
* sy-uzeit, etc.
GET TIME.

* Get exact time stamp up to nanoseconds and convert
* to string
GET TIME STAMP FIELD l_timestamp.
WRITE l_timestamp TIME ZONE sy-zonlo TO l_string.

* Write information to screen
WRITE: /, / 'Date & Time Information',
       / 'System Date: ', 30 sy-datum,
       / 'System Time: ', 30 sy-uzeit,
       / 'Exact System Time Stamp:', 30 l_string,
       / 'Daylight Saving Time: ', 30 sy-dayst AS
         CHECKBOX INPUT OFF,
       / 'Local Date: ', 30 sy-datlo,
       / 'Local Time: ', 30 sy-timlo,
       / 'Local Time Zone: ', 30 sy-zonlo.
WRITE: /, / 'Login Information',
       / 'Logical SAP System: ', 30 sy-sysid,
       / 'Client: ', 30 sy-mandt,
       / 'user_name: ', 30 sy-uname.
WRITE: /, / 'System & Program Information',
       / 'SAP WebAS Name: ', 30 sy-host,
       / 'Database Name: ', 30 sy-dbsys,
       / 'Operating System Name: ', 30 sy-opsys,
       / 'Program Transaction: ', 30 sy-tcode,
       / 'Program Name: ', 30 sy-repid.
```

Listing 3.1 Program ZTPB00_System_Information for Querying System Information

How to declare your own variables using the DATA instruction is explained in detail in Section 3.2. These variables are needed to be able to receive the timestamp from the GET TIME STAMP instruction, and to convert it to a string data type (text) to prepare it for output to the screen. The subsequent screen outputs using the WRITE read a number of data items from the sy structure and print it to the screen together with explanatory text.

Explanation of the source code

The frequent use of the slash (/) forces output on a separate line, increasing its clarity for the end user.

▷ Activate the program with $\boxed{\text{Ctrl}}$ + $\boxed{\text{F3}}$ and start the program with $\boxed{\text{F8}}$.

As you see in Figure 3.4, the WRITE command has no problems writing the different system information; only for the timestamp, with its accuracy up to within 100 nanoseconds, is special handling required using the additional format specifications after the TIME ZONE keyword. To demonstrate that the WRITE command cannot write text only to the screen but also into a variable (see Section 3.2), the TO clause was used once.

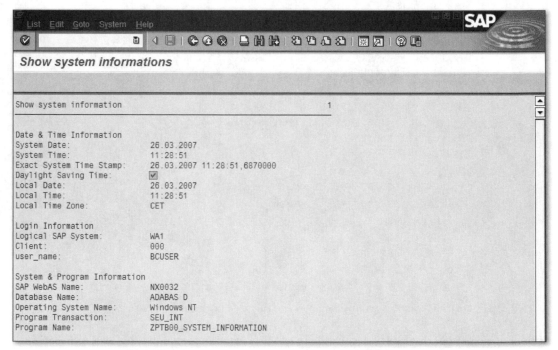

Figure 3.4 Program ZPTB00_System_Information During Execution

Naturally, you can extend the program and print even more information to the screen.

3.2   Data and Data Types—DATA, PARAMETERS, CONSTANTS, FIELD SYMBOLS, TYPE, CREATE, Text Elements

Data and data types form the basic framework of any modern programming language. Under the control of the commands in your program, the ABAP runtime environment can perform calculations and manipulations on the data in main memory (RAM) and then store the data permanently on the hard drive. This process results in the creation of information and permanently retrievable knowledge.

When it starts, every ABAP program is assigned an exclusive part of main memory (RAM) by the ABAP runtime environment, where it can temporarily store whatever data it needs. An "artificial" order is applied to the bits and bytes there, in which names are assigned to individual storage locations, and special interpretation rules apply to their content. By using instructions in the source code, you determine what names (data) and interpretation rules (data types) are required. For instance, the command

Basics

```
DATA: l_pieces TYPE i.
```

tells the ABAP runtime environment to reserve a storage area 4 bytes in length (defined by the data type i) under the name of l_pieces when the program runs, in which only whole numbers between -2,147,483,648 and +2,147,483,647 will be stored.

From that point on, the content of that memory range will be interpreted as a whole number, and your program can access it for reading and writing under the name l_pieces, that is, to process it in any way.

To simplify the processing of data in main memory even further, they are broken down by topic in ABAP according to their use (see Figure 3.5). A series of keywords is available, which you can place before the first appearance (the declaration) of data in the source code:

Data

▸ DATA—**Declaration of Variables and Reference Variables**
  Variables are data ranges in main memory whose content can be changed by the program at runtime using instructions; their content is therefore variable. Variables are declared using the DATA keyword

and may have a name of at most 30 characters in length, which must start with a letter and can then have Roman letters, digits, and underscores. The maximum length of variables can be given in parentheses after the variable name.

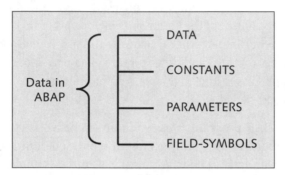

Figure 3.5 Topical Subdivision of Data in ABAP

ABAP distinguishes between so-called *static variables* and *reference variables*. A static variable always automatically reserves a data range in main memory, which can be used immediately by the program with no other effort. It is declared using the keyword TYPE, and an initial value can be specified after the optional keyword VALUE. In contrast, a reference variable does not reserve a data range in main memory; this can be done as needed in the program using the CRE-ATE DATA, so this is also referred to as dynamic data. Of course, this process saves main memory space because data ranges are reserved only when they are actually used, but it takes more effort to program. Alternatively, a data range can also be assigned to the reference variable using the GET REFERENCE OF command if the data range has been reserved previously using a variable. A reference variable is declared using the keyword TYPE REF TO. Unlike other programming languages, such as C, in ABAP prior to Release 4.6, you cannot directly change the content of a reference variable; you can only assign it to a field symbol. As of Release 6.10, however, this limitation has been eliminated, and access to references is possible using the ->* operator (for instance, l_ref_consumer->*).

Examples:

```
DATA:
```

```
l_amount TYPE REF TO f,
l_consumer(30) TYPE c.
```

▶ CONSTANTS—**Declaration of Fixed Values**

Constants are data ranges in main memory whose content *cannot* be changed by the program at runtime using instructions; that is, their content is constant. The only valid content is already specified in the declaration in the source code, and this value cannot be overwritten by an incorrectly coded instruction. Constants are declared using the CONSTANTS keyword and may have a name of at most 30 characters in length, which must start with a letter and may then have Roman letters, digits, and underscores. Constants are always static; that is, once the ABAP runtime environment executes a command to declare a constant, the memory range is reserved in main memory and the value is set according to your specification.

Examples:

```
CONSTANTS:
  con_pi TYPE f VALUE '3.41',
  con_eacc_fld_fiscyear TYPE string VALUE 'FISCYEAR'.
```

▶ PARAMETERS—**Declaration of Input Elements**

The PARAMETERS command is actually a component of a powerful screen input process called "selection screen"; however, the options of this method for designing input and output interfaces are not described in detail until Section 5.1, Simple Input and Output Interfaces—SELECTION SCREEN, SELECT-OPTIONS, CALL SELECTION SCREEN, SAP List Viewer. In this chapter, the PARAMETERS command is used to receive inputs from users in a simple way. Here, you first need to specify the input element that the user should use to perform the input—that is, an input field, checkbox, or list field. You also need to define the data type to which the content of the input should correspond. At runtime, then, the input from the user is stored in the data range of the parameter, and you can access it and process it in the same way as for a static variable. ABAP imposes strict rules regarding the possible combination of input elements and data types, which you can find in the online help. The name of the parameter, in contrast to that of a variable or a constant, may be only a maximum of eight characters long. Parameters have no direct counterpart in other familiar programming languages, which tend to use READ commands instead to listen for user input. Nevertheless, newcomers to ABAP can learn how to use parameters very quickly because they can be used to make input forms very easily. The power of the PARAMETERS command is augmented by the fact that it understands a whole series of optional commands. For instance, a parameter can be marked as required using OBLIGATORY, or AS CHECKBOX can be used to specify how it can appear on the screen.

Examples:

```
PARAMETERS:
  p_date TYPE d OBLIGATORY,
  p_save TYPE c AS CHECKBOX.
```

► FIELD-SYMBOLS—**Declaration of References to Data**
Field symbols can be used very flexibly to access the data objects of reference variables, static variables, constants, or parameters—in short, any other variables—and the type of field symbol can even differ from the original type of the data object (*casting*, see also Section 6.1, Classes and Objects—CLASS, CREATE OBJECT, METHOD). Up until Release 4.6, using field symbols was the only way to access the content of reference variables. The names of field symbols always begin and end with angle brackets, and can be up to 30 characters in length. Between the angle brackets, the same naming conventions apply as for variables and constants. There is no direct counterpart to ABAP Objects field symbols in C, Basic, Java, Pascal, or any other familiar programming languages. Therefore, it is often difficult for the programming newcomer to see why field symbols make sense. The easiest way to think of them is that you need data declared using the REF TO instruction to create and store dynamic variables in the program, and field symbols to be able to work with their contents. Before the introduction of true references in Release 4.6, field symbols were the only way to access data objects dynamically.

Examples:

```
FIELD-SYMBOLS:
  <l_amount> TYPE f,
  <l_fiscyear> TYPE string.
```

The examples above already used a few basic data types implicitly (i, f, d, c, and string), which will now be explained. In general, data types influence how a storage area is interpreted by the program and the CPU, and what operations are possible with its contents. The basic data types, i.e., interpretation options, shown in Table 3.1 are provided in ABAP.

Data types

Data type	Character	Length	Example	Sample Declaration
c	Character	1-65,535 characters	'S'	DATA: l_customer (35) TYPE c.
n	Numeric text	1-65,535 characters	'069'	DATA: number TYPE n.
d	Date	8 characters	'20021231'	PARAMETERS: P_year TYPE d.
t	Time	6 characters	'233059'	DATA: l_booking_time TYPE t.
x	Byte	1-65,535 bytes	'F7'	PARAMETERS: l_guid(16) TYPE x.
i	Whole number	4 bytes	8846	CONSTANTS: con_mount_everst TYPE i VALUE 8846
p	Packed number	1-16 bytes	319	PARAMETERS: P_roomno(3) TYPE n DEFAULT '319'.
f	Floating point number	8 bytes	'1,2345'	DATA: l_amount TYPE ref to f.
string	Character string	Variable	'Hello'	DATA: con_aecc_fld_fiscyear TYPE string VALUE 'Fiscyear'.
xstring	Byte sequence	Variable	'F7A3'	DATA: l_header TYPE xstring

Table 3.1 Basic ABAP Data Types

▶ c—**Character or Text with Defined Maximum Length (Character)**
The character data type is needed when individual characters or strings with a defined length between 1 and 65,535 characters will be

131

processed in the program. For instance, to process individual letters and numbers like "A", "z", or "3", only a single character is needed, while for the text "Manual posting" a character string with a length of at least 14 characters is required. The declaration of the corresponding data might look like this:

```
CONSTANTS:
  l_character TYPE c VALUE 'A'.
DATA:
  l_text(14) TYPE c VALUE 'Manual Posting'.
```

▶ n — **Numeric Text with Defined Maximum Length (Numeric)**
The numeric data type should always be used when the program needs to work with a sequence of digits but when calculations would not make sense because the data is not a number but simple numeric text. For instance, room number "319" in a hotel is definitely a sequence of digits, but adding up room numbers would not be useful. The same applies to deposit number "397293" at a bank, the number of a drawer, and so on. The maximum length of a numeric text is 65,535 digits. The declaration of the corresponding data might look like this:

```
PARAMETERS:
  p_roomno(3) TYPE n DEFAULT '319'.
DATA:
  l_depotno(10) TYPE n VALUE '397293'.
```

▶ i — **Whole Number (Integer)**
The integer data type is well suited for the fast processing of whole numbers because it is supported directly by the CPU and therefore does not first need to be converted by the ABAP runtime environment for processing. Data can store whole numbers between -2,147,483,648 and +2,147,483,647, and is therefore suitable for the calculation of large quantities. Integer values are used, for instance, for the calculation of unit quantities or when it is sufficient to measure lengths to a meter's accuracy. The declaration of the corresponding data might look like this:

```
CONSTANTS:
  con_mount_everest TYPE i VALUE 8846.
```

```
DATA:
  l_pieces TYPE i.
```

▶ f—**Floating Point (Number)**
The float data type is to numbers with decimal points what the integer is to whole numbers. Thanks to direct support in the CPU, calculations are performed very quickly, the precision of 15 to 16 significant digits is high, and the resulting numeric range that can be represented is very large, ranging from 2.2250738585072014E-308 to 1.7976931348623157E+308, negative or positive, and including zero. Floating point numbers are the standard when representing scientific formulas, and are also used in risk management at banks. The declaration of the corresponding data might look like this:

```
CONSTANTS:
  con_pi TYPE f VALUE '3.14159265358979323846'.
DATA:
  l_radius TYPE f.
```

▶ x—**Byte (Hexadecimal)**
The hexadecimal data type was originally intended for the processing of small files with a length between 1 and 65,536 bytes where the program didn't need any more detailed information about the content of these files. The declaration of the corresponding data might look like this:

```
PARAMETERS:
  l_guid(16) TYPE x.
CONSTANTS:
  con_mime_header(2) TYPE x VALUE '3FB1'.
```

▶ p—**Packed Number**
The packed data type is the standard for calculating with lengths, weights, and monetary amounts. Calculations with this data type are performed by the ABAP runtime environment using correct decimal arithmetic, in the same way as you use pencil and paper. You must also always use this data type when whole numbers will be used in calculations exceeding the value range of the integer data type (for instance, greater than two billion), or when a higher accuracy is needed than that provided by the floating point data type (more than

15 significant digits). The packed data type can store numbers with a maximum of 31 digits (plus a sign), of which at most 16 can be declared as decimal places using the DECIMALS keyword. Calculation with packed numbers is comparatively slow because the data type is not supported directly by the CPU and must run through extensive internal conversions and intermediate steps. The declaration of corresponding data takes some getting used to because the total length results from the number of decimal places used and must be specified divided by two minus the sign. A declaration might look like this:

```
PARAMETERS:
  p_price(16) TYPE p DECIMALS 2.
* 2*16-1=31 digits including 2 decimals
DATA:
  l_kgweight(3) TYPE p DECIMALS 3.
* 2*3-1=5 digits including 3 decimals
```

▶ d — **Date**

There is a separate data type for the storage of date information, which can store eight digits in the form YYYYMMDD: the first four digits specify the year, the next two the month, and the last two the day. Comparisons between dates are performed by comparing the digits. Calculation with dates (for instance, April 30, 2003 + 3 days) works, too. The declaration of the corresponding data might look like this:

```
PARAMETERS:
  l_date TYPE d DEFAULT sy-datum.   " Default: today
DATA:
  l_booking_date TYPE d.
```

▶ t — **Time**

Analogous to the date, there also exists a date type for the storage of times. This is six digits long and storage times in the format HHMMSS, that is, the first two digits are the hour, the next two the minutes, and the last two the seconds. Comparisons between two times can be performed very quickly, and calculations are also supported by the ABAP runtime environment. The declaration of the corresponding data might look like this:

```
CONSTANTS:
  l_early_morning TYPE t VALUE '010000'. " 1 o'clock
DATA:
  l_booking_time TYPE t.
```

▶ `string`—**Character String with Indeterminate Total Length**
The string data type is used for the processing of very long strings of characters (larger than 65,535 bytes, up to a maximum of 2GB) or when the maximum length of the string cannot be predicted and the reservation of a storage location with a defined length with c would not be efficient. The string data type cannot be directly requested with the PARAMETERS instruction. Instead, the c data type must be used or the more complicated Dynpro interface technique in combination with the EnjoySAP controls (see Section 5.2). The declaration of the corresponding data might look like this:

```
CONSTANTS:
  l_question TYPE string VALUE 'What is your name?'.
DATA:
  l_name TYPE string.
```

▶ `xstring`—**Byte Sequence of Indeterminate Total Length**
The xstring data type works for the processing of longer binary data in the same way that the string data type is used for the processing of longer text documents. It is therefore suitable for the storage of files with unknown content and unknown length, although this is rarely useful in business applications. Data of type xstring cannot be requested using the PARAMETERS instruction (that is, it cannot be used as constants), and the specification of an initial value is not allowed during the data's declaration. A declaration might look as follows:

```
DATA:
  l_header TYPE xstring,
  l_body TYPE xstring.
```

If you know another programming language, you will already have noticed one thing: There is no Boolean data type to store the values *true* or *false*. Instead, it is customary to use the c data type, which is then assigned the value "X" for *true* or a " " (blank) for *false*.

Metadata

All other data types, which we will discuss in this book, are based on the basic elemental datatypes (e.g., structures, tables). In particular, outside of ABAP programs, there are reusable data types defined that are stored in the ABAP Dictionary (see Section 4.1, Field Properties—DATA ELEMENT, DOMAIN). There, additional metadata can be defined: Additional descriptive information and particular limitations on their content. This metadata is used automatically by the programming interface during execution to test content, to prepare value selection help, or to display descriptive texts. In a professional SAP development, it is therefore only in exceptional cases that ABAP data types are used directly (as seen in the above examples) because this additional metadata is then missing.

Managing dynamic data

Although the dynamic reservation of data ranges in memory via a reference variable is possible in ABAP using the CREATE DATA command, the ABAP runtime environment handles its release automatically. To do this, the so-called *garbage collector* continually monitors all data ranges and releases them automatically once no reference variables point to them.

In information science over the years, certain types of tasks have crystallized in which the dynamic processing of data should always be considered for reasons of efficiency:

► **Working with Variables That Consume a Significant Portion of Main Memory**
When working with many variables (for instance, many texts), performance bottlenecks can arise if data is swapped out to the hard drive by the operating system due to a lack of main memory. It is true that memory is always getting cheaper, but in ABAP programs you must consider that many users are generally working with a program on a single server, thus multiplying the total storage requirements. The use of reference variables can help save memory in this case because the programmer can specify precisely when each storage area should be reserved, used, and finally released.

► **Working with Variables Whose Data Types Are Only Known When the Program Executes**
This case can lead to very unreadable source code if only static variables are used because data areas must be provided for all plausible data types and then the code must always keep track of which variable

actually has the content and must therefore be processed. Here, the use of a single dynamic variable is simpler; the data range is reserved only during program execution after its data type is known (for instance, after a selection is made by the user).

▸ **Working with Variables That Are Chained Together**
In information science, there are algorithms that work particularly efficiently and elegantly with reference variables, for instance, the processing of doubly linked lists, hierarchies, and networks. The use of reference variables or pointers has been well researched by generations of programmers and in all possible programming languages so that for many applications there is even ready-made code.

If you look at the use of different programming languages over the past few years, working with reference variables has always gained importance, and if you look at object-oriented programming (see Chapter 6, Object-Oriented Language Elements), there is not a single programming language that doesn't implement that concept on the basis of reference variables or pointers.

In contrast to other familiar programming languages, ABAP has explicit support for multilingual applications, that is, for programs that can be used by users in several languages simultaneously on a single SAP system. For this purpose, all the *text elements* are managed in a table, which you can reference by both source code and constants (see Figure 3.6). In the source code, then, there are only references to the text elements to be used but no text. Translators need only to translate the texts in this table into a different language and store it there. Depending on the local language configured at login, the ABAP runtime environment selects the correct version when each program starts.

Text elements

Figure 3.6 Text Elements for Multilingual Programs

ABAP differentiates between three types of text elements:

▶ **List Headers**

List headers are rarely used today. List and column headings can be defined, which are then used for list output with the `WRITE` command. Now, the ALV Grid display is used instead (see Chapter 5, Screen Input and Output).

▶ **Selection Texts**

Selection texts are powerful names for the parameters of a program. Instead of shocking the user with cryptic names limited to eight characters and having to adhere to certain conventions from the programming guidelines, you can simply define an appropriate long text for each parameter.

▶ **Text Symbols**

Text symbols are suitable for storing program texts and are used in `WRITE` instructions instead of having to specify the text there directly in quotation marks. But text symbols should also be used for all the other texts specified in the source code (for instance, for pop-up dialogs).

The corresponding tables can be reached in the SAP Object Navigator through the menu item GOTO • TEXT ELEMENTS.

Tip
This book still specifies texts explicitly in source code, even though it is a poorer programming style than using the methods we described above. Because the clarity of the source code is so much higher, we decided to make this compromise in the book.

Exercise 3.2
Implement the program ZPTB00_SALES_ORDER to create a sales order, such as might be used when purchasing a product or a service. As an entry, the item number, item name, unit price and currency, value-added tax (VAT) rate, and the quantity are expected, and the result should include the subtotal and total quantities and the usual value-added tax information.
In addition, the monthly payment of the amount should still be possible, whereby the payoff period should additionally be entered in months, and the monthly gross charge and total charge should additionally be displayed.

▷ First, in the context menu of the package or the development class, select the point CREATE • PROGRAM.

Then the familiar dialog appears to ask for the name of the program:

▷ Enter "ZPTB00_SALES_ORDER" as the name of the program.

▷ Uncheck the WITH TOP INCLUDE checkbox and confirm your entry with the OK button.

The next dialog asks you for the program properties:

▷ Enter "Create outgoing invoice" as the title.

▷ Leave all the other settings unchanged, and confirm with the SAVE button.

The SAP Object Navigator finally asks for the transport request. The number of the transport request used previously is set by default.

▷ Simply confirm it with the OK button.

As usual, the SAP Object Navigator creates the program framework, and you can then complete it. You now do that in order to take into account the item number, item name, unit price, currency, VAT rate, and quantity input, and to derive the subtotal and total amount plus the usual VAT information.

▷ Type the following source code beneath the comment lines:

```
REPORT  zptb00_sales_order.
PARAMETERS:
* Article data
  p_ano(10) TYPE n OBLIGATORY,
  p_aname(40) TYPE c OBLIGATORY,
  p_aprice TYPE p DECIMALS 2 OBLIGATORY,
  p_curr TYPE currencysap OBLIGATORY DEFAULT 'EUR',
  p_aquant TYPE i OBLIGATORY DEFAULT 1,
* Tax
  p_tax TYPE p DECIMALS 2 DEFAULT '19' OBLIGATORY,
* Terms of payment
  p_cash TYPE c RADIOBUTTON GROUP 0001 DEFAULT 'X',
  p_credit TYPE c RADIOBUTTON GROUP 0001,
  p_months TYPE i OBLIGATORY DEFAULT '24'.
```

```
CONSTANTS:
* Interest per year in percent
  con_annual_interest TYPE p DECIMALS 2 VALUE '6.75'.

DATA:
* Temporary data
  l_net_amount TYPE p DECIMALS 2,
  l_tax_factor TYPE f,
  l_credit_amount TYPE p DECIMALS 2,
  l_monthly_interest_factor TYPE f,
* Result data
  l_monthly_vat_amount TYPE p DECIMALS 2,
  l_monthly_amount TYPE p DECIMALS 2,
  l_vat_amount TYPE p DECIMALS 2,
  l_total_amount LIKE l_net_amount.


* Temporary calculations
l_net_amount = p_aprice * p_aquant.
l_tax_factor = p_tax / 100.
* Write article information to screen
WRITE: /, / 'Article information',
       / 'Article number: ', 30 p_ano,
       / 'Article name: ', 30 p_aname,
       / 'Article net price: ', 30 p_aprice, p_curr,
       / 'Quantity: ', 30 p_aquant.


* Write conditions to screen
WRITE: /, / 'Conditions',
       / 'Tax rate: ', 30 p_tax,
       / 'Quantity: ', 30 p_aquant.

WRITE: /, / 'Result'.
IF p_cash = 'X'.
* Calculate cash results
  l_vat_amount = l_net_amount * l_tax_factor.
  l_total_amount = l_net_amount + l_vat_amount.
* Write results to screen
  WRITE: / 'Total VAT amount: ', 30 l_vat_amount,
           p_curr,
         / 'Total amount: ', 30 l_total_amount, p_curr.
ELSE.
* Calculate interest results
```

```
      l_monthly_interest_factor = con_annual_interest / 100
      / 12.
      l_credit_amount = l_net_amount + l_net_amount *
      l_monthly_interest_factor * p_months.
      l_vat_amount = l_credit_amount * l_tax_factor.
      l_total_amount = l_credit_amount + l_vat_amount.
      l_monthly_vat_amount = l_vat_amount / p_months.
      l_monthly_amount = l_total_amount / p_months.
  * Write results to screen
      WRITE: / 'Month: ', 30 p_months,
             / 'Monthly VAT amount: ', 30
               l_monthly_vat_amount, p_curr,
             / 'Monthly amount: ', 30 l_monthly_amount,
               p_curr,
             / '(VAT amount: ', 30 l_vat_amount, p_curr,
               ')',
             / '(Total amount: ', 30 l_total_amount,
               p_curr, ')'.
  ENDIF.
```

Listing 3.2 Source Code for the Program ZPTB00_Sales_Order

First, you declare all your parameters that you use to receive the input from the user. Then program the algorithms needed to calculate the total amount and the total VAT amount. In this case, you only need to multiply the unit price p_aprice by the quantity of product ordered p_aquan, then calculate the VAT amount l_vat_amount, and then finally add the net amount l_net_amount to the VAT amount to get the total amount l_total_amount for a cash sale.

Explanation of the source code

If a payment plan is needed, then the internal interest rate of 6.75% per year must always be taken into account, and it must appear in the calculation. Because the customer can determine the number of monthly payments, you first need to convert the yearly interest rate into a monthly rate. Then the total net credit amount to be paid l_credit_amount is easy to calculate from the cash net amount (l_net_amount) plus the monthly interest rate (l_net_amount times l_monthly_interest) multiplied by the number of months (p_month). You can now easily use that value to calculate the other output data such as l_monthly_amount, and so on by dividing by the number of months.

As a special feature, you aren't using a basic data type for the declaration of the parameter p_curr (for instance, character string of length 3), but an SAP-defined data element behind which there is an entire table with possible currencies from which the user can select at runtime. This is a preview of Section 4.1, Field Properties—DATA ELEMENT, DOMAIN, but it gives you the advantage of content checking during input and a selection help that allows the user to select the currency conveniently. You've also "smuggled in" an IF branch, which won't be covered until Section 3.5, Branches and Logical Expressions—IF, CASE. Faced with the decision of whether to demonstrate the function of the radio button properly, you decide on a little premature use of the IF branch.

You are now supposed to test the functionality of your program by doing the following:

▷ Click the CHECK button to check the syntactic correctness of the code.

▷ Click the ACTIVATE button to generate a program from the code.

▷ Click the DIRECT button to start the program directly (see Figure 3.7).

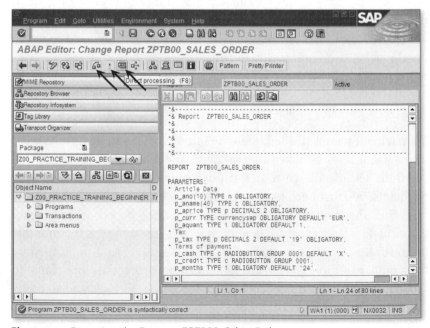

Figure 3.7 Executing the Program ZPTB00_Sales_Order

The program starts, showing its user interface on the screen. Now perform the following steps:

▷ As an example, enter item number "4711", the name "Microsoft Office SBE", the price "549", the currency "EUR", and the quantity "7".

▷ Select cash payment (parameter P_CASH) and click the EXECUTE button (see Figure 3.8).

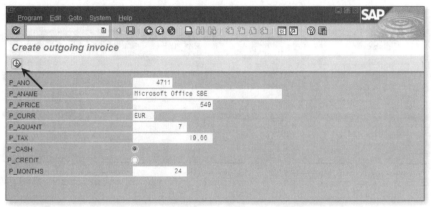

Figure 3.8 Program ZPTB00_Sales_Order in Action

The program performs the calculation of the total price and outputs the result (see Figure 3.9).

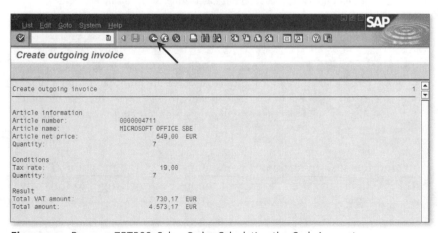

Figure 3.9 Program ZPTB00_Sales_Order Calculating the Cash Amount

Now, instead of the cash amount, you want to calculate the monthly credit amount, and so you return to the input screen and do the following:

▷ Click the BACK button.

▷ Select monthly payments (parameter P_CREDIT) and click the EXECUTE button again.

Now your program uses the predefined 6.75% interest and outputs the monthly payment in parentheses next to a correspondingly increased total amount (see Figure 3.10).

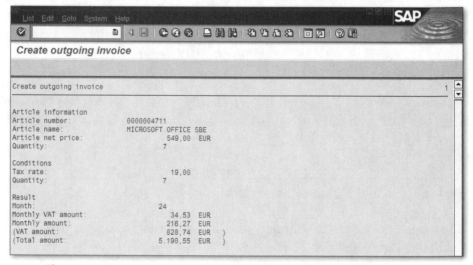

Figure 3.10 Program ZPTB00_Sales_Order Calculating the Monthly Payment

Exercise 3.3

Create the program ZPTB00_SALES_ORDER_DYNAMIC, in which you store only the variables required for the calculation of the monthly payment when they are actually needed. In this case, work with reference variables and field symbols. Also use text elements to prepare your program for translation into other languages.

You start this task by making a complete copy of the program ZPTB00_SALES_ORDER and then making all the necessary changes to the copy.

▷ Call up the context menu for the program ZPTB00_SALES_ORDER, and select the COPY menu item there.

A dialog appears in which the source name of the program to be copied is shown, along with a field for entry of the target name.

▷ As the name for the target program, enter ZPTB00_SALES_ORDER_ DYNAMIC, and click the COPY button (see Figure 3.11).

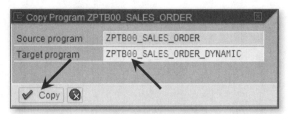

Figure 3.11   Copying the Program ZPTB00_Sales_Order_Dynamic

Another dialog appears where you can exclude or include individual development objects from the copy process.

▷ Because your program doesn't need separate development objects, you can accept the standard settings.

▷ Click the COPY button again (see Figure 3.12).

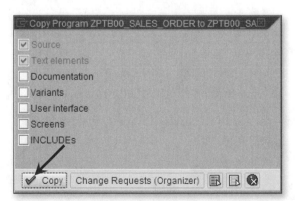

Figure 3.12   Specifying the Development Objects to Be Copied

Next, you need to specify the package or development class in which the program should appear, and to select the responsible programmer.

▷ As the package/development class, enter Z00_PRACTICE_TRAINING_
BEGINNER, and click the SAVE button (see Figure 3.13).

Figure 3.13 Specifying the Package for the Program Z00_Sales_Order_Dynamic

Finally, as always, the development environment needs a transport request in which it can log the changes.

▷ Leave the preset from your previously created transport request, and click the CONTINUE button.

The source code of the program has now been copied, and you can start with the adaptation by:

▷ Double-clicking the program ZPTB00_SALES_ORDER_DYNAMIC. This is important, because during the copy process, the copy is not automatically loaded into the editor.

▷ Clicking the button DISPLAY<->EDIT to switch to edit mode.

The source code is now exclusively reserved for you; no other team member can make changes to it until you leave the edit mode by clicking the DISPLAY<->EDIT button again.

▷ Now make the following changes to the code:

```
REPORT  zptb00_sales_order_dynamic.
PARAMETERS:
* Article data
  p_ano(10) TYPE n OBLIGATORY,
```

```
    p_aname(40) TYPE c OBLIGATORY,
    p_aprice TYPE p DECIMALS 2 OBLIGATORY,
    p_curr TYPE currencysap, " OBLIGATORY DEFAULT 'EUR',
    p_aquant TYPE i OBLIGATORY DEFAULT 1,
* Tax
    p_tax TYPE p DECIMALS 2 DEFAULT '16' OBLIGATORY,
* Terms of payment
    p_cash TYPE c RADIOBUTTON GROUP 0001 DEFAULT 'X',
    p_credit TYPE c RADIOBUTTON GROUP 0001,
    p_months TYPE i OBLIGATORY DEFAULT '24'.
CONSTANTS:
* Interest per year in percent
    con_annual_interest TYPE p DECIMALS 2 VALUE '6.75'.
TYPES:
    currency TYPE p DECIMALS 2.
DATA:
* Temporary data
    l_net_amount TYPE p DECIMALS 2,
    l_tax_factor TYPE f,
* Result data
    l_vat_amount TYPE p DECIMALS 2,
    l_total_amount LIKE l_net_amount,
* Dynamic variables
    l_rda_credit_amount TYPE REF TO currency,
    l_rda_monthly_interest_factor TYPE REF TO f,
    l_rda_monthly_vat_amount TYPE REF TO currency,
    l_rda_monthly_amount TYPE REF TO currency.
FIELD-SYMBOLS:
* Access to reference variables
    <l_credit_amount> TYPE currency,
    <l_monthly_interest_factor> TYPE f,
    <l_monthly_vat_amount> TYPE any,
    <l_monthly_amount> TYPE currency.
* Temporary calculations
l_net_amount = p_aprice * p_aquant.
l_tax_factor = p_tax / 100.
* Write article information to screen
WRITE: /, / 'Article information',
       / 'Article number: ', 30 p_ano,
       / 'Article name: ', 30 p_aname,
       / 'Article net price: ', 30 p_aprice, p_curr,
       / 'Quantity: ', 30 p_aquant.
```

```
* Write conditions to screen
WRITE: /, / 'Conditions',
       / 'Tax rate: ', 30 p_tax,
       / 'Quantity: ', 30 p_aquant.
WRITE: /, / 'Result'.
IF p_cash = 'X'.
* Calculate results
  l_vat_amount = l_net_amount * l_tax_factor.
  l_total_amount = l_net_amount + l_vat_amount.
* Write results to screen
  WRITE: / 'Total VAT amount: ', 30 l_vat_amount,
  p_curr,
         / 'Total amount: ', 30 l_total_amount, p_curr.
ELSE.
* Calculate results
  CREATE DATA l_rda_monthly_interest_factor.
  ASSIGN l_rda_monthly_interest_factor->* TO
    <l_monthly_interest_factor>.
  CREATE DATA l_rda_credit_amount.
  ASSIGN l_rda_credit_amount->* TO <l_credit_amount>.
  CREATE DATA l_rda_monthly_vat_amount.
  ASSIGN l_rda_monthly_vat_amount->* TO
    <l_monthly_vat_amount>.
  CREATE DATA l_rda_monthly_amount.
  ASSIGN l_rda_monthly_amount->* TO <l_monthly_amount>.
  <l_monthly_interest_factor> = con_annual_interest /
  100 / 12.
  <l_credit_amount> = l_net_amount + l_net_amount *
  <l_monthly_interest_factor> * p_months.
  l_vat_amount = <l_credit_amount> * l_tax_factor.
  l_total_amount = <l_credit_amount> + l_vat_amount.
  <l_monthly_vat_amount> = l_vat_amount / p_months.
  <l_monthly_amount> = l_total_amount / p_months.
* Write results to screen
  WRITE: / 'Month: ', 30 p_months,
         / 'Monthly VAT amount: ', 30
           <l_monthly_vat_amount>, p_curr,
         / 'Monthly amount: ', 30 <l_monthly_amount>,
           p_curr,
         / '(VAT amount: ', 30 l_vat_amount, p_curr,
           ')',
         / '(Total amount: ', 30 l_total_amount,
```

```
        p_curr, ')'.
ENDIF.
```

Listing 3.3 Source Code for the Program ZPTB00_SALES_ORDER_DYNAMIC

First you define your own data type named `currency`, which you need for the declaration of the reference variables. If you were to use `p DECI-MALS 2` as a data type instead, you would get an error message.

Explanation of the source code

Next you change the variables that are required only during the calculation of the credit rates to reference variables, for which you need the keyword `TYPE REF TO`. These are the variables `l_rda_credit_amount`, `l_rda_monthly_interest_factor`, `l_rda_monthly_vat_amount`, and `l_rda_monthly_amount`. Some variables that are needed later in the `ELSE` branch (see Section 3.5, Branches and Logical Expressions—IF, CASE, for details) are also used in the calculation of the cash amount, and you don't change those.

Now you define a field symbol for each reference variable, which you use later on to access the stored content of the reference variables. These are the field symbols `<l_credit_amount>`, `<l_monthly_interest_factor>`, `<l_monthly_vat_amount>`, and `<l_monthly_amount>`. Note that the field symbol doesn't have the same data type as the reference variable but it still needs to have a compatible data type. The most flexible alternative is the special data type `any`, which is only allowed for field symbols and which automatically assumes the data type of the reference variable after assignment. You use it here as an example; otherwise, you can simply take the data type of the reference variables, such as `currency` or `f`. All preparations are now complete to reserve the storage spaced needed for the calculation dynamically if the calculation of the monthly rate is needed. This calculation takes place within the `ELSE/ENDIF` part, and therefore you reserve the storage only for the reference variables there.

To reserve the storage space, you need to use the command `CREATE DATA` on each reference variable. Next you access the storage space using field symbols, which have no counterpart in other familiar programming languages. Using the `ASSIGN` command, you assign each field symbol to the storage space of a reference variable. Then you can work with the field symbols in exactly the same way as with normal variables, so the code from this point forward looks very similar to the original version.

149

The conversion to reference variables to calculate the monthly payments is now complete, and you can test the program by doing the following:

▷ Click the CHECK button to check the syntactic correctness of the code.

▷ Click the ACTIVATE button to generate a program from the code.

▷ Click the DIRECT button to start the program immediately.

To make sure that your program is working correctly, you provided it with the same data as you did with the program ZPTB00_SALES_ORDER.

▷ As an example, enter item number "4711", the name "Microsoft Office SBE", the price "549", the currency "EUR", and the quantity "7".

▷ Select monthly payments (parameter P_CREDIT) and click the EXECUTE button.

The program now calculates using the predefined 6.75% interest rate and should produce the same result as the version with static variables (see Figure 3.14).

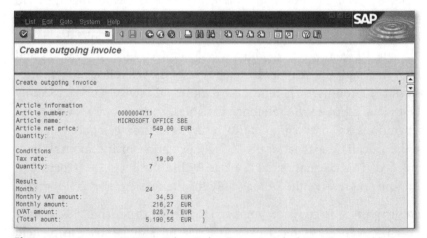

Figure 3.14 Program ZPTB00_Sales_Order_Dynamic Calculating the Monthly Payment

Working with reference variables *and* field symbols certainly takes a little getting used to. However, once you understand how to use reference variables to reserve space and as interface parameters (see Section 3.4,

Subprograms and Functions—FORM, FUNCTION, EXCEPTIONS) and how to work with field symbols, you can use them easily.

> **Tip**
>
> Another tip for larger projects: In professional ABAP development, it is customary to create shared parameters, variables, and particularly constants in includes (see Section 2.4, First Program: "Hello World"—REPORT, INCLUDE, and Application Menu) so that they can be reused in several programs and ensure a common look and feel as well as a uniform data basis. In your example program, the constant `con_annual_interest` would be a perfect candidate because an interest rate used internally within the enterprise should be identical for all programs.

3.3 Structures and Internal Tables—TABLE, MOVE-CORRESPONDING, INSERT, APPEND, READ, MODIFY, DELETE, LOOP

Structures and internal tables in ABAP are the perfect basis for working with mass data in main memory. Mass data occurs in nearly all business applications, is entered by users (for instance, invoices, parts lists) or mechanical sensors (for instance, photosensors used as production counters, or warehouse scanners), and processed by ABAP programs.

Basics

Mass data in business applications can be best characterized as follows. It has a uniform structure, and it comes neatly packaged in a long list of rows (see Figure 3.15). There are plenty of examples, like a list of customers with names and addresses, a list of posts for a day with credits and debits, or a list of all warehouse inventory, with names, quantities, and storage locations.

Anyone who has worked with long lists of uniform data (for instance, in Microsoft Excel) knows how they are best stored in the computer. You define column headings for each individual datum, like first name, last name, street, house number, city, zip code, and country, and under that, for each row, you enter the data corresponding to the column header. Exactly the same concept is used in ABAP, except that a line with its uniform data in main memory is called a *structure* or a *record*, and multiple lines with uniform data in memory is called an *internal table*.

Country	Capital	Continent	Acreage	Alphabetization	Export
Nigeria	Abuja	Africa	4,923,768	51	cacao, peanuts, crude oil
Egypt	Cairo	Africa	1,001,449	48	crude oil, cotton, onions
Ethiopia	Addis Abeba	Africa	1,097,000		coffee, vegetables
Zaire	Kinshasa	Africa	2,345,095	72	copper, cobalt, coffee
South Africa	Pretoria	Africa	1,221,037	61	gold, diamonds, ores
Sudan	Khartum	Africa	2,505,813	27	cotton
Algeria	Algiers	Africa	2,381,741	57	crude oil, iron ore, vegetables, wine
Kenya	Nairobi	Africa	582,646	69	coffee, tea, sisal
Marocco	Rabat	Africa	458,730	65	phosphate, fruit, ores
Tanzania	Dodoma	Africa	945,087	85	cotton, coffee, sisal
Uganda	Kampala	Africa	235,880	48	coffee, cotton, ores
Ghana	Accra	Africa	238,537	60	cacao, real wood, bauxite
Mozambique	Maputo	Africa	799,380	33	sugar, cotton, sisal
Ivory Coast	Yamoussoukro	Africa	322,463	54	coffee, cacao, wood
Madagascar	Antananarivo	Africa	587,041	80	coffee, vanilla, rice
Cameroon	Jaunde	Africa	475,442	54	cacao, coffee, aluminum
Angola	Luanda	Africa	1,246,700	42	crude oil, coffee, diamonds
Zimbabwe	Harare	Africa	390,580	67	asbestos, copper
Burkina Faso	Ouagadougou	Africa	274,200	18	nuts
Malawi	Lilongwe	Africa	118,484	41	tobacco, tea, peanuts, corn
Zambia	Lusaka	Africa	752,614	73	copper, lead, cobalt, tobacco
Tunisia	Tunis	Africa	163,610	65	phosphate, iron ore, crude oil
Mali	Bamaku	Africa	1,240,142	32	cotton, agriculture
Nigeria	Niamey	Africa	1,267,000	28	peanuts, brute, cotton
Somalia	Mogadischu	Africa	637,657	24	brute, banana
Senegal	Dakar	Africa	196,192	38	peanuts, phosphate
Ruanda	Kigali	Africa	26,338	50	coffee, tin, tea
Guinea	Conakry	Africa	245,857	24	bauxite, fruit, coffee
Chad	Ndschamena	Africa	1,284,000	30	cotton
Burundi	Bujumbura	Africa	27,834	50	coffee, cotton

Figure 3.15 Mass Data—Long Lists of Uniform Data

Structures

A structure groups data together in an ABAP program. It is therefore a tool to organize data in memory, and it can also help make program code clearer. Instead of declaring dozens of individual data items, you can use a *type definition* (keyword TYPES) using the keywords BEGIN OF structurename and END OF structurename to group them into a structure and then you can declare them all together. Accessing the individual fields of a structure in the code is done using the declared name followed by a dash (-) and the name of the individual datum, that is, structurename-fieldname. Of course, structures can contain other structures, so you can have a whole series of *nested structures*. Here is a small code fragment as an example:

```
* Definition
TYPES:
  BEGIN OF str_address,
    street_and_number(40) TYPE c,
```

```
    zipcode_and_city(40) TYPE c,
  END OF str_address,
  BEGIN OF str_customer,
    name(80) TYPE c,
    address TYPE str_address,
  END OF str_customer.
* Declaration
DATA:
  l_str_customer TYPE str_customer.
FIELD-SYMBOLS:
  <l_str_customer> TYPE str_customer.
* Implementation
l_str_customer-name = 'Georg Meiers'.
l_str_customer-address-street_and_number = 'Goethe Strasse 24'.
l_str_customer-address-zipcode_and_city = '69120 Heidelberg'.
```

Listing 3.4 Code Fragment to Demonstrate Flat and Nested Structure

In the code fragment above, after the TYPES instruction, you define two structures, str_customer and str_address, using the keywords BEGIN OF and END OF. The structure str_customer, using field name address, includes the str_address structure in its own definition. Thus, str_customer represents a nested structure because it contains another structure. In contrast, str_address is called a *flat structure*. Those familiar with other programming languages will recognize ABAP structures as record or struct types as used in Delphi, C, and Visual Basic. ABAP also has the concept of a *deep structure*. A deep structure is a structure that contains an internal table, a string, or an object.

The convenient processing of structures, some with different field names and some with the same, is provided by ABAP in the MOVE-CORRESPONDING command. This command goes through a structure field name by field name and searches for a field of the same name in the target structure. If successful, the content is moved; otherwise, it isn't. The syntax of the command is as follows:

MOVE-CORRESPONDING

```
MOVE-CORRESPONDING struc1 TO struc2
```

where struc1 is the source structure and struc2 the target. The instruction also works with nested structures, automatically performing a MOVE-CORRESPONDING on each common level. The following code fragment demonstrates the use of the command:

```
* Definition
TYPES:
  BEGIN OF str_address,
    street_and_number(40) TYPE c,
    zipcode_and_city(40) TYPE c,
  END OF str_address,
  BEGIN OF str_customer,
    name(80) TYPE c,
    address TYPE str_address,
  END OF str_customer.
  BEGIN OF str_address2,
    street_and_number(40) TYPE c,
    zipcode_and_city2(40) TYPE c,
  END OF str_address2,
  BEGIN OF str_customer2,
    name(80) TYPE c,
    address TYPE str_address2,
  END OF str_customer2.
* Declaration
DATA:
  l_str_customer TYPE str_customer,
  l_str_customer2 TYPE str_customer2.
* Implementation
l_str_customer-name = 'Georg Meiers'.
l_str_customer-address-street_and_number = 'Goethe Strasse 24'.
l_str_customer-address-zipcode_and_city = '69120 Heidelberg'.
MOVE-CORRESPONDIG l_str_customer TO l_str_customer2.
```

Listing 3.5 MOVE-CORRESPONDING in Use for Flat and Nested Structures

The only difference between the str_customer and str_customer2 structures is within the nested field address, with the fields zipcode_and_address and zipcode_and_address2. When assigning l_str_customer to l_str_customer2, the content of all the other fields is moved, and the field zipcode_and_address2 remains empty after the MOVE-CORRESPONDING command.

Internal tables

Once you've defined a structure, you're not far from using internal tables in memory. The ABAP programming language includes special support for the efficient processing of uniform mass data. This is a significant difference from other familiar programming languages. Many developers consider the concept of internal tables the best and outstanding feature in the ABAP programming language. The declaration of an internal table is very easy: Simply use the keyword `TABLE OF`. Accessing the table in a program, on the other hand, requires a little getting used to because it doesn't use square brackets and indices like arrays, but uses ABAP commands instead, such as `INSERT`, `MODIFY`, `READ`, or `DELETE`. Here is a small code fragment as an example:

```
* Declaration
DATA:
  l_tab_customer TYPE STANDARD TABLE OF str_customer.
```

In this example, an internal table is created based on the structure information of `str_customer`. It's apparent that ABAP isn't afraid of tables based on nested structures, so you can use either flat or deep structures to declare tables. The newcomer will probably find it easiest to compare internal tables with the `Variant` data type from Delphi, C#, or Visual Basic, whose content can be constructed using structures and open arrays so that it comes very close to the structure of an internal table. But when it comes to finding a counterpart for the special ABAP commands for fast read and write access to internal tables (for instance, `READ`, `MODIFY`, and `DELETE`), other languages have to pass.

ABAP offers three different types of internal table, each of which has different features. One of these table types must always be specified in each declaration.

Internal table types

- ▶ STANDARD TABLE—**Good for tables that will be processed sequentially or using a row index**
  Standard tables are internally managed by the ABAP runtime environment like an array, using a logical row index. Non-unique keys can also be defined. All the ABAP access commands are supported: `INSERT`, `MODIFY`, `READ`, `DELETE`, `APPEND`, `COLLECT`, and `LOOP`.

  Example:

  ```
  DATA:
    l_tab_customer TYPE STANDARD TABLE OF str_customer.
  ```

- ▶ SORTED TABLE—**Can be used for tables whose records are to be sorted on certain columns**
  Sorted tables, like standard tables, are managed using a logical row

155

index but also have a *table key* specified by the programmer using the keywords NON-UNIQUE KEY or UNIQUE KEY, defining the columns to be used to sort the table. During insertion, a record is automatically placed into the correct row. The following ABAP access commands are supported: INSERT, MODIFY, READ, DELETE, and LOOP.

Example:

```
DATA:
  l_tab_customer TYPE SORTED TABLE OF str_customer
                 WITH NON-UNIQUE KEY name.
```

▶ HASHED TABLE—**Can be used for tables where records are searched for very frequently**
Hash tables are internally administered using a *hash algorithm* and have no logical row index, just a table key. All the rows in the table are stored in random order in memory, and the position of a row is calculated by a hash function from the specification of the key columns. The implicit result is that the table key must be unique for each record. The fascinating thing about hash tables is that access to a record through the table key always takes the same amount of time, regardless of whether you have 100 or 100 million records in the internal table. The following ABAP access commands are supported: INSERT, MODIFY, READ, DELETE, and LOOP.

Example:

```
DATA:
  l_tab_customer TYPE HASHED TABLE OF str_customer
                 WITH UNIQUE KEY name.
```

ABAP also defines two *generic internal table types*, which can be used only when declaring field symbols (see Section 3.2) or call parameters for functions, subprograms (see Section 3.4, Subprograms and Functions— FORM, FUNCTION, EXCEPTIONS), and methods. They are useful when you aren't sure or can't determine in advance which table types might be used by a field symbol or a routine. Therefore, generic internal table types declared using the keyword ANY TABLE include all the internal table types (STANDARD, SORTED, and HASHED), while those declared using INDEX TABLE can refer only to tables of type SORTED or HASHED. Approximately 80 percent of all cases use standard tables, while sorted and hash tables account for the other 20 percent.

ABAP has a whole series of commands for working with internal tables or the records in them. These can be broken down into four areas: Filling (INSERT, APPEND, and COLLECT), reading (READ and LOOP), changing (MODIFY), deleting (DELETE) of records in an internal table.

ABAP commands for access to internal tables

▶ INSERT—**Inserting records into an internal table**
This command inserts one or more records into an internal table starting in a certain position. Depending on whether the position is specified using a row index or a table key, whether the data to be inserted is one record (structure) or several records (internal table), and the table type of the target table, slightly different variants of the command are used.

Example:

```
INSERT l_str_customer INTO l_tab_customer.
INSERT l_str_customer INTO l_tab_customer INDEX 1.
```

▶ APPEND—**Appending a record to an internal table**
This command adds one or more records to the end of an internal table. Depending on the table type of the target table, the record may be added only if it fits the sort order or if it won't result in two records with the same table key.

Example:

```
APPEND l_str_customer TO l_tab_customer.
APPEND LINES OF l_tas_customer TO l_tab_customer.
```

▶ COLLECT—**Inserting or adding a record to an internal table**
This command either inserts the contents of a record into an internal table or adds the content of all numerical columns to the content of an already existing record with the same table key. This procedure, called *aggregation*, is often used to create reports to calculate subtotals. The command can only be used with flat tables, that is, those without deep structures.

Example:

```
COLLECT l_str_seats INTO l_tab_seats.
```

▶ READ—**Reading a record from an internal table**
This command reads a record from an internal table. If the record to be read is not specified uniquely, the first matching record will be read. Depending on whether the record to be read is specified using a row index or a table key, and on where the record to be read should be returned (into a structure, an internal table, or not at all), different variants of the command are used.

Example:

```
READ TABLE l_tah_customer WITH TABLE KEY name =
    'Georg Meiers' INTO l_str_customer.
READ TABLE l_tab_customer INDEX 1 INTO l_str_customer.
```

▶ LOOP—**Reading several records in a row from an internal table**
This command defines a loop using the keywords LOOP and ENDLOOP. On each run through the loop, a record is read from the internal table specified, and can be processed by the commands within the loop. The records that should be read can be limited using conditions. The order in which the records are read out depends on the table type.

Example:

```
LOOP AT l_tas_customer ASSIGNING <l_str_customer>.
  <l_str_customer>-address-street_and_number =
      ' Neurottstraße 16'.
ENDLOOP.
LOOP AT l_tah_customer INTO l_str_customer.
  WRITE: / l_str_customer.
ENDLOOP.
```

▶ MODIFY—**Changing records in an internal table**
This command changes the content of one or more records in an internal table. Depending on whether the position of the row to be changed is specified using a row index or a table key, whether the changes are given in one record (structure) or several records (internal table), and the table type of the target table, slightly different variants of the command are used. The optional keyword TRANSPORTING can also be used to limit the overwriting process to selected columns.

Example:

```
MODIFY l_tab_customer FROM l_str_customer
    TRANSPORTING name WHERE name = 'Georg Meiers'.
MODIFY l_tas_customer FROM l_str_customer INDEX 1.
```

▶ DELETE—**Deleting Records from an Internal Table**

This command deletes one or more rows from an internal table and is capable of deleting duplicated neighboring rows when the optional keyword DUPLICATES is used. Depending on whether the records to be deleted are specified by row index or table key, and the type of the target table, slightly different variants of the command are used.

Example:

```
DELETE l_tab_customer WHERE name ='Georg Meiers'.
DELETE l_tas_customer INDEX 2.
```

Exercise 3.4

Create a program ZPTB00_INTERNAL_TABLE_JUGGLER. Use the structures str_customer and str_address from Listing 3.5 to create an internal table (STANDARD TABLE) in memory and fill the table with three example entries. Use the APPEND command to do this. Then output the contents of the internal table to the screen using the LOOP command.

Then use the MODIFY command to change the customer name of the first record to one that starts with "Z". Use the SORT command to sort the internal table on the name of the customers. Output the contents of the table to the screen again, and use the READ command to read the data from the table.

Finally, delete the contents of the internal table.

This exercise requires you to perform the following steps:

▷ Create a program called "ZPTB00_INTERNAL_TABLE_JUGGLER" in the usual way, without a TOP include.

▷ In the program properties, assign the title "Internal Table Juggler", and keep the same transport request.

▷ Type the following source code under the comment lines:

```
REPORT zptb00_internal_table_juggler.
* Definition
TYPES:
  BEGIN OF str_address,
    street_and_number(40) TYPE c,
    zipcode_and_city(40) TYPE c,
  END OF str_address,
  BEGIN OF str_customer,
    name(80) TYPE c,
    address TYPE str_address,
  END OF str_customer.
DATA:
* Customer
  l_tab_customer TYPE STANDARD TABLE OF str_customer,
  l_str_customer TYPE str_customer.
* Fill some data
l_str_customer-name = 'John Miller'.
l_str_customer-address-street_and_number = 'Yorkstr. 3'.
l_str_customer-address-zipcode_and_city = '69120 Heidelberg'.
APPEND l_str_customer TO l_tab_customer.
l_str_customer-name = 'Linda Evens'.
l_str_customer-address-street_and_number = 'Yorkstr. 4'.
APPEND l_str_customer TO l_tab_customer.
l_str_customer-name = 'Robbie Bush'.
l_str_customer-address-street_and_number = 'Yorkstr. 5'.
APPEND l_str_customer TO l_tab_customer.
* Use loop to write all data to screen
LOOP AT l_tab_customer INTO l_str_customer.
  WRITE: l_str_customer-name, l_str_customer-
address-    street_and_number.
ENDLOOP.
* Read data of first customer into structure
READ TABLE l_tab_customer INDEX 1 INTO l_str_customer.
* Modify name
l_str_customer-name = 'Zeta Jones'.
* Write it back to first line of internal table
MODIFY l_tab_customer INDEX 1 FROM l_str_customer.
* Sort the table by the content of name column
SORT l_tab_customer BY name.
* Just to train the read statement
```

```
WRITE sy-uline AS LINE.
READ TABLE l_tab_customer INDEX 1 INTO l_str_customer.
WRITE: l_str_customer-name, l_str_customer-address-street_
and_number.
READ TABLE l_tab_customer INDEX 2 INTO l_str_customer.
  WRITE: l_str_customer-name, l_str_customer-
address-    street_and_number.
READ TABLE l_tab_customer INDEX 3 INTO l_str_customer.
  WRITE: l_str_customer-name,
        l_str_customer-address-street_and_number.
* Actually, clearing l_tab_customer would be better
DELETE l_tab_customer FROM 1 TO 3.
```

Listing 3.6 Source Code for the Program ZPTB00_INTERNAL_TABLE_JUGGLER

First you define the two structures str_address and str_customer and declare the internal table l_tab_customer as well as the structure l_str_customer, which you will need later for access to the data in the internal table. Then you start assigning values to the individual fields in the l_str_customer structure, using the APPEND command to add them to the end of the internal table l_tab_customer. To simplify your programming work a little, you change only the house number in the demo data, allowing everybody to live in Heidelberg.

Explanation of the source code

Now you can output the data row by row using the LOOP, limiting your output to just the name, street number, and house number of the customers.

To modify the first record, you first have to use the READ command to read it from the table into the structure. Here, you can perform the change you want, then use MODIFY to write the record back into the same place in the table.

Just for practice, the next output isn't done using LOOP, but with the READ command, even though in this case it's a much poorer choice.

Now test the functionality of your program:

▷ Click the TEST button, then click the ACTIVATE button and the DIRECT button to start the program immediately (see Figure 3.16).

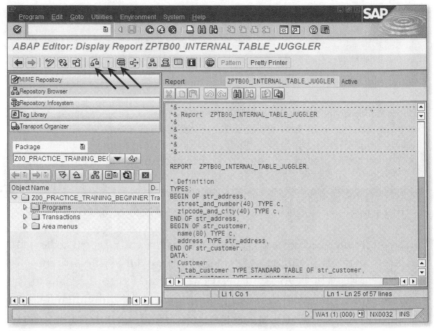

Figure 3.16 Executing the Program PTB00_INTERNAL_TABLE_JUGGLER

The program starts and immediately shows the results of processing without waiting for input (see Figure 3.17).

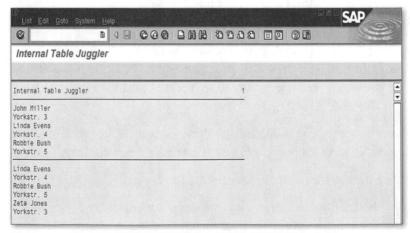

Figure 3.17 Program ZPTB00_INTERNAL_TABLE_JUGGLER in Action

3.4 Subprograms and Functions—FORM, FUNCTION, EXCEPTIONS

Just as multiple rooms in an office building allow for the separation of different departments and project groups, subprograms and functions (collectively known as *procedures*) are used to structure and specialize program parts. A well organized office building supports workflows by placing closely collaborating employees close together, ensuring short, clear communication. In the same way, a well organized program also helps in organizing the workflow, determining clear responsibilities, and creating clearer interfaces between different parts of the program. This is the origin of the term *procedural programming*.

Main programs today generally consist of no more than two to three calls to subprograms, functions, or methods. Delphi and Microsoft. NET developers, for instance, know the instructions `Application.Init`, `Application.Run`, and `Application.Done` as the only parts of the main program. In Java or Visual Basic, it's not that different. Under the main program, developers attach the individual areas of functionality in a well thought out, orderly fashion, ensuring an easily understood program structure.

Basics

A well-developed ABAP program looks similar and subdivides its functionality into main areas, subareas, and so on, making the program look like a system of boxes and:

Subprograms and functions

▶ Dividing the program text into logical units, which each executes precisely defined tasks (structure).

▶ Enabling repeated calls to the same program parts from different locations in the program (avoidance of redundancy).

▶ Allowing the use of program parts in other programs or even from other systems (modularization).

For this reason, ABAP provides not only extensive options for object-oriented programming (see Chapter 6, Object-Oriented Language Elements) but also *subprograms* and *functions*, which can each use its own local data and data types and can also use *interface parameters* to obtain data from calling program areas and to return their (possibly intermediate) results (see Figure 3.18).

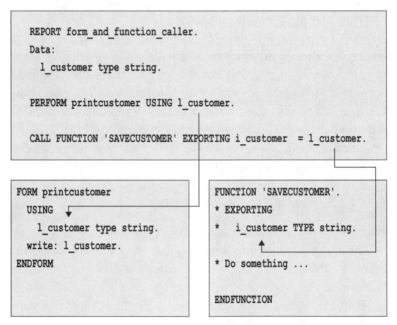

```
REPORT form_and_function_caller.
Data:
  l_customer type string.


PERFORM printcustomer USING l_customer.


CALL FUNCTION 'SAVECUSTOMER' EXPORTING i_customer = l_customer.
```

```
FORM printcustomer
  USING
    l_customer type string.
  write: l_customer.
ENDFORM
```

```
FUNCTION 'SAVECUSTOMER'.
* EXPORTING
*    i_customer TYPE string.

* Do something ...

ENDFUNCTION
```

Figure 3.18 Organization of a Program Using Subprograms and Functions

Subprograms and functions differ in their capabilities to a certain extent, as well as in the way they are called from other parts of the program:

▶ FORM—**Subprogram**
Subprograms are defined using the FORM and ENDFORM keywords, and programmers give each one a name that must be unique within the program. The code between the two keywords is a subprogram, and

can be called using the PERFORM keyword, followed by the name of the subprogram and any call parameters. If a subprogram needs to signal an error to its caller, either you need to provide a special interface parameter (because in contrast to functions, there is no ability to return errors or exceptions), or you can use the RAISING clause available as of Release 6.10. Documentation of subprograms with the SAP Object Navigator tools is possible only using comments in the source code. Of course, subprograms can also be moved out into separate source code and included in different programs using the INCLUDE command. The syntax for calling a subprogram is:

```
PERFORM [Name] [Interface parameters].
Example:
DATA:
 l_timestamp TYPE timestampl.
GET TIME STAMP FIELD l_timestamp.
* Call the subprogram
PERFORM write_timestamp_to_screen USING l_timestamp.
* Implement the subprogram
FORM write_timestamp_to_screen
  USING
    i_timestamp TYPE timestampl.
  WRITE i_timestamp TIME ZONE sy-zonlo.
ENDFORM.
```

▶ FUNCTION—**Function**

Functions, often called *function modules* in the SAP world, are created using a convenient user interface within the SAP Object Navigator, which automatically creates a source code structure. The name of the function, which must be unique throughout the system, along with all the interface parameters and return values for errors and exceptions, are entered through dialogs and then appear in the source code. For each function, programmers can create a separate documentation, which can refer to other documents, example code, programs, and even Websites, and is automatically placed on the work queue for translation; the documentation of a function into different local languages is easy. Functions can also very easily be released for remote call, and can thus be addressed from other SAP systems, and all current programming languages and operating systems, such as Java, Windows, or UNIX. Functions are always grouped into *function groups*, in which variables can be defined between functions and under which, as in other program types, a whole series of development objects can be created (for instance, user interfaces). The syntax for calling a function is somewhat extensive due to the different types of interfaces for data and looks like this:

```
CALL FUNCTION 'name' [EXPORTING par1 = var1]
[IMPORTING par2 = var2] [CHANGING par3 = var3]
[TABLES par4 = var4] [EXCEPTIONS exc1 = 1, others = 2]
[DESTINATION dest].
```

It is worth noting that the clause DESTINATION dest can be used to call a function on other SAP systems. Here is a simple example, in which a global ID, important for database operations, is transmitted:

```
DATA:
 l_guid TYPE guid_32.
CALL FUNCTION 'GUID_CREATE'
  IMPORTING
*    EV_GUID_16      =
*    EV_GUID_22      =
     ev_guid_32      = l_guid.
```

Interfaces   Passed parameters, passed data, passed variables, signatures, interfaces, interface parameters, and so on—all of these terms are really just different names for data that is passed between the calling program on the one hand and the subprogram or function on the other. This data transfer in both directions must be well thought out because it not only influences the general functionality of the entire program but also ensures an uncomplicated data flow and the reusability of program sections. The more complicated programs become, the greater the need for and the significance of these requirements:

▶ **Functionality**
A plug that doesn't fit into the socket is something that can confound anyone. If the data that a program passes doesn't match the data that a function or subprogram expects, it's no different. Even the wrong sequence or an incorrect data type can result in the function's performance no longer being guaranteed.

▶ **Uncomplicated data flow**

Anybody who has reregistered a car already knows what a complicated data flow is. You first have to find the title, the registration, and your driver's license; then sign an insurance contract and request a duplicate insurance card; then have a current exhaust gas measurement and inspection done in a garage; and then wait in line for a few hours before the clerk at the registration office will write the new name on the title. A program that processed its data in this difficult and time-consuming manner would certainly never be popular with the public. "Keep it simple, stupid" is the motto, or in other words, "In simplicity lies genius."

▶ **Reusability**

Reusability cuts both ways. For example, consider the function `Gross_To_Net_Amount`, which takes a gross amount passed in, automatically calculates the value-added tax (VAT) amount and subtracts it, and then returns the resulting net amount. The reusability of this function could be increased if the VAT rate were defined as another parameter and used in the calculation. Then the function could also be used in an international context and with different VAT rates, and could handle the VAT unification of the European Union without a hitch. But from the point of view of the calling program, there would now be the problem that the valid VAT rate would need to be determined there before the function could be called. Complexity arises as a result. This classical dilemma between reusability and complexity must be decided anew for every function. You are the only person who can decide, from case to case.

From an organizational standpoint, you distinguish between interface parameters that are passed in during a call to the subprogram or function (*input parameters*), that are passed back to the caller from the subprogram or function immediately after the call (*output parameters*), and that are passed in both directions (*changing parameters*). Functions also have special data that can transfer error or exceptional conditions back to the caller (*exceptions*) (see Figure 3.19). Unfortunately, some of the corresponding keywords differ between subprograms and functions, which makes learning them a little harder. The following keywords are used in declarations:

Input, output, and changing parameters and exceptions

▶ USING **(for subprograms) and** IMPORTING **(for functions)—Input Parameters**
These keywords are placed before data that are passed from the calling program into the subprogram or function. Because functions are conveniently defined using an input form, we provide only an example for subprograms:

```
FORM mult USING a TYPE i b TYPE i
```

▶ EXPORTING—**Output Parameters (functions only)**
This keyword is placed before data that are passed from the function back to the caller.

▶ CHANGING—**Changing Parameters**
This keyword is placed before data that are passed from the calling program section to the subprogram or function, and that are passed back from the function to the caller (perhaps with changed values) after execution.

▶ TABLES—**Changing Parameters**
This keyword used to be placed before data that were passed between callers and functions in the form of internal tables. Now, the keywords listed can also be used. In a few, generally older, functions, you can still find parameters declared in this way for compatibility reasons.

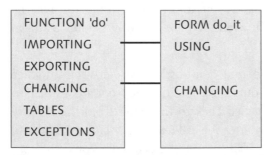

Figure 3.19 Categorization of Interface Parameters by Input, Output, Changing, and Exception

▶ EXCEPTIONS—**Exceptions (functions only)**
This keyword is used to declare exception and error states, which may occur within the function and which should be passed back to the caller. After the function is called, the caller can check the sy-subrc system field, obtaining information as to whether an exception was raised, and, if so, what it was. Exceptions provide a standardized way for functions to transmit these exceptional situations and enjoy great popularity. Since Release 6.10, you can also define error classes using the RAISING clause. These exceptions are not covered here in any more detail.

It is also important to know that the calling program section *reverses* the keywords; that is, an interface parameter that is passed from the caller to the function is an EXPORTING parameter from the caller's perspective, but an IMPORTING parameter for the function, and vice versa.

There is another distinction that the programmer must make when creating subprograms and functions: this aspect is clearly technical in nature and can therefore have an effect on the way you program. The basic question is whether a subprogram or function should work with a copy of the data passed, or with the original data.

Working with copies or with original data

▶ **Call by Reference—Works with original data**
This is the standard configuration for both subprograms and functions; therefore, the actual keyword to categorize the individual interface parameters can be omitted. As the programmer, you need to be aware that changes passed to the data (regardless of the direction) will also be seen by the calling program section. With functions, the compiler checks whether the code in a function attempts to write to importing parameters, and it will give you an error message. A call is faster if it has more parameters or only Call by Reference parameters, and it also uses less memory in comparison to Call by Value (see Figure 3.20).

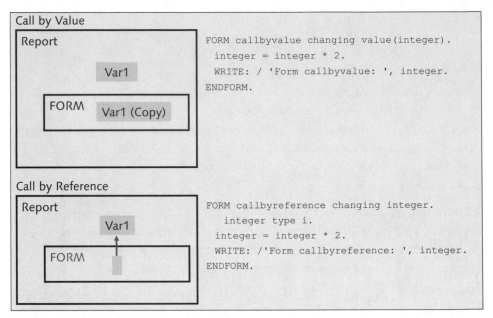

Figure 3.20 Passing Interface Parameters by Value or by Reference

▶ **Call by Value—Passing of Values**

For subprograms, every parameter must be enclosed with the `VALUE([Parameter])` keyword. For functions, checking the appropriate box in the user interface will suffice. The ABAP runtime environment will automatically create a copy of the data in memory during execution before every call to a subprogram or function (of course, this costs extra memory and time) so that the code only works with the copy and not with the original data. The same applies in the reverse case for output parameters. If this is a remotely callable function, all interface parameters must always be declared as Call by Value.

Fortunately, the SAP Object Navigator provides some mechanisms that make it easier to work with subprograms and functions, particularly supporting the programmer with the correct call and retrieval of exceptions. Let's take a practical look at working with subprograms and functions in this way.

Exercise 3.5

Create the program ZPTB00_PERFORMANCE_TESTER. Create a subprogram and a function to calculate trip costs to be reimbursed given the distances passed in kilometers. Use 0.3 Euros as the kilometer rate.

Call the subprogram five times in a row with different distances, then the function five times, and then the function five times by remote call. The name of the function should be ZPTB00_CALCULATE_TRAVEL_EXPENSE, and the function group should be ZPTB00_PRACTICE_TRAINING_B.

Compare the call times using the command GET RUN TIME FIELD f.

This time, start by writing the function that you want to use later in your program. Because a function can only exist in a function group, you have to create that first.

▷ Do this by selecting the CREATE • FUNCTION GROUP menu option in the context menu of the package or development class (see Figure 3.21).

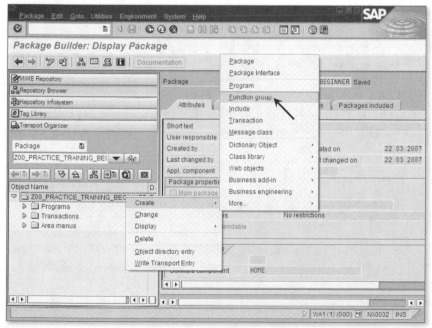

Figure 3.21 CONTEXT MENU • CREATE • FUNCTION GROUP

A dialog opens, prompting you to enter the name of the function group and a brief description of it:

▷ As the name of the function group, enter "ZPTB00_PRACTICE_ TRAINING_B", and for the brief description enter "Practice Training Beginner" (see Figure 3.22).

▷ Click the SAVE button.

Figure 3.22   Adding the Function Group ZPTB00_PRACTICE_TRAINING_B

Next, the transport dialog appears to query the transport request.

▷ Leave the predefined transport request unchanged, and click the CON- TINUE button.

Finally, the new function group appears in the object list area of the SAP Object Navigator. You can now continue with the creation of the function.

▷ From the context menu of the function group ZPTB00_PRACTICE_ TRAINING_B, select CREATE • FUNCTION MODULE (see Figure 3.23).

A dialog opens, prompting you for the name and a brief description of the function being created:

▷ As the name of the function module, enter "ZPTB00_CALCULATE_ TRAVEL_EXPENS", and enter "Calculate Travel Expense" as the brief text.

▷ Click the SAVE button.

Figure 3.23 Function Group ZPTB00_ PRACTICE_TRAINING_B Has Been Inserted

In the tool area of the SAP Object Navigator, an extensive dialog is now shown, which can be used to determine the properties of the function and to write the source code. Do this by following these steps:

▷ Select the IMPORT tab.

▷ As the Parameter name, enter "I_KM"; as the Type spec., enter "Type"; as the Reference type, enter "i"; and then select the checkbox PASS VALUE (see Figure 3.24).

▷ Switch to the EXPORT tab.

The properties on the EXPORT tab appear.

▷ As the Parameter name, enter "E_AMOUNT"; as the Type spec., enter "Type"; as the Reference type, enter "f"; and then select the checkbox PASS VALUE (see Figure 3.25). Switch to the EXCEPTIONS tab.

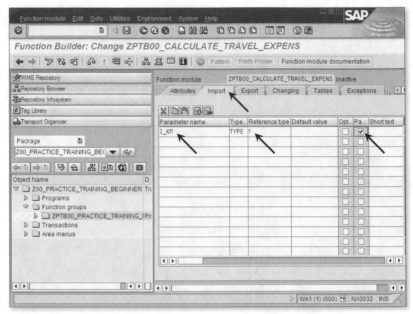

Figure 3.24 Editing the Import Parameters for ZPTB00_CALCULATE_
TRAVEL_EXPENS

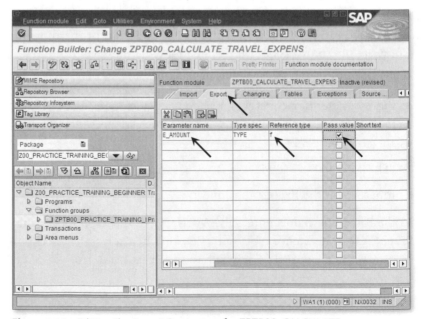

Figure 3.25 Editing the Export Parameters for ZPTB00_CALCULATE_
TRAVEL_EXPENS

The EXCEPTIONS tab is displayed, and you define one exception. You want to end the function with an exception if an error occurs in the calculation:

▷ For the Exception, enter "FAILED", and type "Function failed" for the Short text (see Figure 3.26).

▷ Switch to the SOURCE CODE tab.

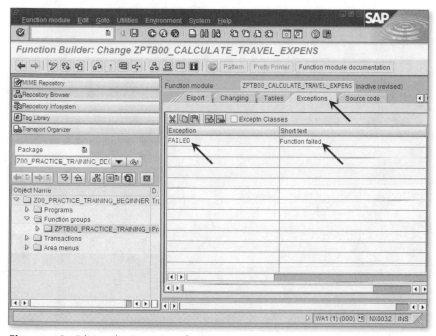

Figure 3.26 Editing the Exceptions for ZPTB00_CALCULATE_TRAVEL_EXPENS

The source code of the function is shown. This is a skeleton function with documentation of the interface parameters.

▷ Enter the following source code, in which you perform the calculation and throw in an exception in case of error:

```
FUNCTION zptb00_calculate_travel_expens.
*"----------------------------------------------------------------------
*"*"Local interface:
*"  IMPORTING
*"     VALUE(i_km) TYPE i
```

```
*"    EXPORTING
*"        VALUE(e_amount) TYPE f
*"    EXCEPTIONS
*"        FAILED
*"--------------------------------------------------------

   e_amount = i_km * '0.3'.
   IF sy-subrc <> 0.
      RAISE failed.
   ENDIF.
ENDFUNCTION
```

▷ Now click the SAVE button, then the CHECK button, and finally the ACTIVATE button.

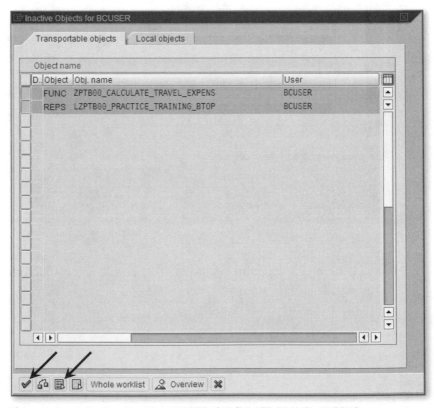

Figure 3.27 Activating Function ZPTB00_CALCULATE_TRAVEL_EXPENS

A dialog appears in which all the development objects to be activated, in this case, the function group as well as the function, are provided.

▷ Click the SELECT ALL button and then CONTINUE.

Now you are supposed to execute the ZPTB00_CALCULATE_TRAVEL_EXPENS function.

▷ Click the DIRECT button.

A very useful feature of ABAP is to be able to test functions individually. A test interface is automatically provided in which you can enter all the import parameters, execute the function, and view the export parameters.

▷ Enter "768" for the kilometer input and click EXECUTE.

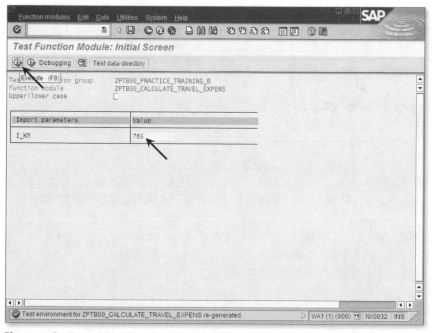

Figure 3.28 Testing Function ZPTB00_CALCULATE_TRAVEL_EXPENS

Alternatively, you can even go through each program line individually in the debugger. However, you have executed the function as a whole this time, and now you see the result screen listing all the values of the return parameters. The return value 230.39 Euros is correct, and it is safe to integrate this function with the program (see Figure 3.29).

▷ Click the BACK button.

Now you return to the SAP Object Navigator, and you can create the main program from there:

▷ Create a new program in the usual way, named "ZPTB00_PERFOR-MANCE_TESTER," without a TOP include.

▷ In the program properties, title it "Performance Tester"; otherwise, leave all the other settings unchanged. Keep the transport request, too.

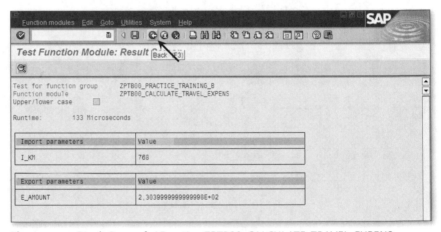

Figure 3.29 Result Screen for Function ZPTB00_CALCULATE_TRAVEL_EXPENS

Now you need to fill in the new program structure in order to calculate the trip reimbursement from the entry of the kilometers drive, and measure performance while doing so.

▷ Type the following source code beneath the comment lines:

```
REPORT  zptb00_performance_tester.
PARAMETERS:
* KM of last travel
  p_km TYPE i.
DATA:
* Amount and runtime for form and function
```

```
    l_amount_form TYPE f,
    l_runtime_form TYPE i,
    l_amount_function TYPE f,
    l_runtime_function TYPE i.
* First initialize l_runtime_form, then measure
* performance
GET RUN TIME FIELD l_runtime_form.
PERFORM calculate_travel_expens USING p_km CHANGING
l_amount_form.
PERFORM calculate_travel_expens USING p_km CHANGING
l_amount_form.
PERFORM calculate_travel_expens USING p_km CHANGING
l_amount_form.
PERFORM calculate_travel_expens USING p_km CHANGING
l_amount_form.
PERFORM calculate_travel_expens USING p_km CHANGING
l_amount_form.
GET RUN TIME FIELD l_runtime_form.
* First initialize l_runtime_function, then measure
* performance
GET RUN TIME FIELD l_runtime_function.

GET RUN TIME FIELD l_runtime_function.
* Write performance results to screen
WRITE: /'Runtime of form      :', l_runtime_form,
       /'Runtime of function :', l_runtime_function.
WRITE: /'Result of form       :', l_amount_form,
       /'Result of function  :', l_amount_function.
FORM calculate_travel_expens
  USING
    i_km TYPE i
  CHANGING
    e_amount TYPE f.

  e_amount = i_km * '0.3'.
ENDFORM.                        "calculate_travel_expens
```

Listing 3.7 Source Code of the Program ZPTB00_PERFORMANCE_TESTER

First you declare the parameter for input of the kilometers driven, along with the variables for receiving the results of the computation and measurement of the runtimes.

Explanation of the source code

Now you can start with the performance measurement of the subprogram by calling the `GET RUN TIME FIELD` command once at the start and once at the end.

Prepare the same call to measure the performance of the function. You insert the call to the function using a dialog.

Then you use the `WRITE` command to output the runtime and computation results to the screen.

The subprogram comes at the end of the source code, and includes the declaration of the interface parameters, plus a single line in which the result is calculated.

Inserting function calls by pattern

A very powerful tool is the automatic creation of pattern source code by the SAP Object Navigator. You use this capability for the completion of the function call in the source code.

▷ Place the cursor on the line where the function call should be inserted, and click the PATTERN button (see Figure 3.30).

Figure 3.30 Calling the Pattern Button in the SAP Object Navigator

A dialog opens and displays patterns for an entire series of ABAP commands.

▷ Enter the function name "ZPTB00_CALCULATE_TRAVEL_EXPENS" and click the CONTINUE button (see Figure 3.31).

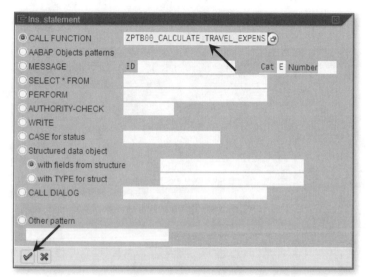

Figure 3.31 Generating a Pattern for ZPTB00_CALCULATE_TRAVEL_EXPENS

A prototype for the function call is inserted into the source code, which you can now complete with your own calling parameters and error handlers.

▷ Change the source code as shown in Figure 3.32 by typing the following code into the selected section:

```
CALL FUNCTION 'ZPTB00_CALCULATE_TRAVEL_EXPENS'
   EXPORTING
     i_km        = p_km
   IMPORTING
     e_amount    = l_amount_function
   EXCEPTIONS
     failed      = 1
     OTHERS      = 2.
IF sy-subrc <> 0.
   RETURN.
```

> **Tip**
>
> If you're working with Release 4.6, replace the RETURN in the code with the
> STOP keyword.

▷ Click the SAVE button, then the CHECK button, ACTIVATE, and finally
  the EXECUTE button.

Figure 3.32 Inserted Function Call to ZPTB00_CALCULATE_TRAVEL_EXPENS

The program starts showing the input interface, where you're prompted
to enter the number of kilometers.

▷ Enter "768", and then click the EXECUTE button (see Figure 3.33).

The result screen of the program appears and you can see that calls to
subprograms take about 53 microseconds on your computer, about twice
as fast as functions, with 125 microseconds (see Figure 3.34).

Figure 3.33 Program ZPTB00_Performance_Tester in Action

Figure 3.34 Result Screen for ZPTB00_PERFORMANCE_TESTER

The calculation command itself hardly counts in the execution and delivers the same result of 230.39 Euros.

Tip

Don't restrict the functionality of subprograms and functions too much. The call itself could cost more time than the entire program code to be executed. In professional ABAP programming, a good average is around 100 to 1000 source code lines for each subprogram or function.

3.5   Branches and Logical Expressions—IF, CASE

Programs and people are very different when it comes to making decisions. While a program always makes the same decision for identical facts, for people the result of a decision depends heavily on emotional situations and character. The *nonhuman* behavior of programs is desirable because they can be used to handle tasks where innumerable decisions must be made, a fixed legal or enterprise regulation must always be followed, and the making of the decision must always be possible to track in all details.

Making decisions is one of the most important tasks of a program. For this reason, *branching instructions*, which compute a result based on comparisons and then can execute certain commands and skip others based on that result, belong to the standard repertoire of any programming language (see Figure 3.35).

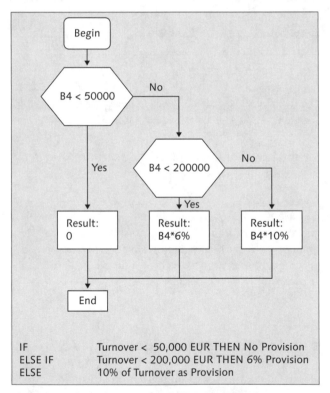

IF   Turnover < 50,000 EUR THEN No Provision
ELSE IF   Turnover < 200,000 EUR THEN 6% Provision
ELSE   10% of Turnover as Provision

Figure 3.35 Branches Execute Code Only Under Certain Circumstances

Logical expressions The basis of a comparison, from a technical standpoint, is a *logical expression* whose result is either true or false and which is determined during the runtime of the program. The keywords provided by ABAP for the construction of logical expressions (*operators*) are particularly numerous, because on the one hand, there are many substitutes, and on the other hand, complex comparisons are possible for character data, which are only supported in other programming languages using functions (for instance, pattern recognition in character strings). For better clarity, you therefore have to explain the structure and effect of logical expressions.

You can use the following comparison operators in a logical expression together with any data types:

▶ [a] = [b] (or EQ)—**Equality test**
Example in which the logical expression is true:

```
DATA:
  a TYPE i VALUE 4,
  b TYPE i VALUE 4.
IF a = b.
  WRITE: / 'a equals b'.
ENDIF.
```

▶ [a] < [b] (or LE)—**Less-than test**
Example in which the logical expression is true:

```
DATA:
  a TYPE i VALUE 3,
  b TYPE i VALUE 4.
IF a LT b.
  WRITE: / 'a is less than b'.
ENDIF.
```

▶ [a] > [b] (or GT)—**Greater-than test**
Example in which the logical expression is true:

```
DATA:
  a TYPE i VALUE 5,
  b TYPE i VALUE 4.
IF a > b.
  WRITE: / 'a is greater than b'.
ENDIF.
```

▶ [a] <= [b] (or LE)—**Less-than or equals test**
Example in which the logical expression is true:

```
DATA:
  a TYPE i VALUE 3,
  b TYPE i VALUE 4.
IF a <= b.
  WRITE: / 'a is less equal than b'.
ENDIF.
```

▶ **[a] >= [b] (or GE)—Greater-than or equals test**
Example in which the logical expression is true:

```
DATA:
  a TYPE i VALUE 4,
  b TYPE i VALUE 4.
IF a GE b.
  WRITE: / 'a is greater equal than b'.
ENDIF.
```

▶ **[a] <> [b] (or NE)—Inequality test**
Example in which the logical expression is true:

```
DATA:
  a TYPE i VALUE 3,
  b TYPE i VALUE 4.
IF a <> b.
  WRITE: / 'a is not equal b'.
ENDIF.
```

▶ **[a] BETWEEN [b] AND [c]—Interval test**
Example in which the logical expression is true:

```
DATA:
  a TYPE i VALUE 4,
  b TYPE i VALUE 3,
  c TYPE I VALUE 5.
IF a BETWEEN b AND c.
  WRITE: / 'a is between b and c'.
ENDIF.
```

As you can see, the comparison operators can also be specified as text abbreviations (for instance, EQ for equals), which was common for many years in database programming and is still very popular in ABAP programs today. For ABAP, it's immaterial whether you write A >= B or A GE B to determine whether "A" is larger than or equal to "B."

The following comparison operators may be used only for character and byte data. For all comparisons, uppercase versus lowercase and trailing blank spaces are taken into consideration. Exceptions are mentioned explicitly.

▶ [a] CO [b]—**Contains only**
Checks whether "a" contains only characters from "b." Example in which the logical expression is true:

```
DATA:
  a(10) TYPE c VALUE 'ACE',
  b(10) TYPE c VALUE 'ABCDEF'.
IF a CO b.
  WRITE: / 'a contains only characters of b'.
ENDIF.
```

▶ [a] CN [b]—**Contains not only**
Checks whether "a" contains characters not only from "b." Example in which the logical expression is true:

```
DATA:
  a(10) TYPE c VALUE 'ACEX',
  b(10) TYPE c VALUE 'ABCDEF'.
 IF a CN b.
  WRITE: / 'a contains not only characters of b'.
ENDIF.
```

▶ [a] CA [b]—**Contains any**
Checks whether "a" contains at least one character from "b." Example in which the logical expression is true:

```
DATA:
  a(10) TYPE c VALUE 'AX',
  b(10) TYPE c VALUE 'ABCDEF'.
IF a CA b.
  WRITE: / 'a contains at least one character of b'.
ENDIF.
```

▶ [a] NA [b]—**Contains not any**
Checks whether "a" doesn't contain any characters from "b." Example in which the logical expression is true:

```
DATA:
  a(10) TYPE c VALUE 'GXYYYYYYYY',
  b(10) TYPE c VALUE 'ABCDEF'.
 IF a NA b.
  WRITE: / 'a contains no character of b'.
ENDIF.
```

▶ **[a] CS [b]—Contains string**
Checks whether "b" is completely contained in "a." Example in which the logical expression is true:

```
DATA:
  a(10) TYPE c VALUE 'AABCDEFF',
  b(10) TYPE c VALUE 'ABCDEF'.
IF a CS b.
  WRITE: / 'String b found in a'.
ENDIF.
```

▶ **[a] NS [b]—Contains no string**
Checks whether "b" is completely contained in "a." Example in which the logical expression is true:

```
DATA:
  a(10) TYPE c VALUE 'AABCDEFF',
  b(10) TYPE c VALUE 'ABCDF'.
IF a NS b.
  WRITE: / 'String b not found in a'.
ENDIF.
```

▶ **[a] CP [b]—Contains pattern**
Checks whether the pattern in "a" matches the content in "b." This operator cannot be used for byte-type data. You can use the wildcard (*) for any character string and the plus sign (+) for any single character. Case and trailing spaces are not significant. Example in which the logical expression is true:

```
DATA:
  a(10) TYPE c VALUE 'ABCDEF',
  b(10) TYPE c VALUE '*A*D+F'.
IF a CP b.
  WRITE: / 'Pattern b found in a'.
ENDIF.
```

▶ **[a] NP [b]—Contains no pattern**
Checks whether the pattern in "a" doesn't match the content in "b."
Otherwise, the same wildcards and rules as *Contains pattern* (CP) apply.
Example in which the logical expression is true:

```
DATA:
  a(10) TYPE c VALUE 'ABCDEF',
  b(10) TYPE c VALUE '*A*DF'.
IF a NP b.
  WRITE: / 'Pattern b not found in a'.
ENDIF.
```

This type of text comparison is used when end users are searching for certain names or designations in data inventories because they allow *fuzzy* searching, which is possible only in other programming languages using additional function libraries. At this point, you should note that ABAP also provides a FIND command that can be used to search for character strings.

Another operator for logical expressions is IS, which occurs in several variants to check the status of data.

▶ **<l_a> IS [NOT] ASSIGNED—Field symbol assigned**
Checks whether a field symbol has been assigned to a data location using the ASSIGN command. Example in which the logical expression is true:

```
DATA:
  l_a TYPE i VALUE 1234.
FIELD-SYMBOLS:
  <l_a> TYPE i.
ASSIGN l_a TO <l_a>.
IF <l_a> IS ASSIGNED.
  WRITE: / '<l_a> is assigned'.
ENDIF.
```

▶ **l_rda_a IS [NOT] BOUND—Reference variable valid**
Checks whether a reference variable is valid. Before you assign a storage location to a reference variable using CREATE DATA or

GET REFERENCE OF, it is considered invalid because in that state you cannot work with it. Example in which the logical expression is true:

```
DATA:
  l_a TYPE i VALUE 1234,
  l_rda_a TYPE REF TO i.
GET REFERENCE OF l_a INTO l_rda_a.
IF l_rda_a IS BOUND.
  WRITE: / 'l_rda_a is bound'.
ENDIF.
```

▶ l_a IS [NOT] INITIAL—**Has initial value**
Checks whether the content of a variable is its initial value. When declaring a variable, it is automatically assigned its initial value if no VALUE clause is used. Example in which the logical expression is true:

```
DATA:
  l_a TYPE i.
IF l_a IS INITIAL.
  WRITE: / 'l_a is initial'.
ENDIF.
```

▶ i_a IS [NOT] SUPPLIED—**Input parameter filled in**
Checks whether an input parameter has actually been passed. Because optional input parameters are supported in ABAP, which are filled in by the caller only when needed (generally when the caller doesn't agree with the default value for the parameter), this test is very helpful in a function. Example in which a text is printed when the optional input parameter i_tax is supplied by the caller:

```
FUNCTION calculate_sales_tax.
*"*"Local interface:
*"  IMPORTING
*"    REFERENCE(I_TAX) TYPE f OPTIONAL
  IF i_tax IS SUPPLIED.
    WRITE: / I_tax is supplied.
  ENDIF.
```

▶ e_a IS [NOT] REQUESTED **or** e_a IS [NOT] SUPPLIED—**Output parameter used**
Checks whether an output parameter is actually used by the caller. Because ABAP allows an output parameter not to be received by the

caller (in this case, its content is simply discarded), it can be useful for the processing within a function to know that. This could make it possible for the code to skip some sections that are concerned with the calculation of this output parameter. As of Release 6.20, the REQUESTED clause is obsolete and is replaced by SUPPLIED.

An example in which the VAT amount is calculated when the output parameter E_TAX_AMOUNT is requested by the caller:

```
FUNCTION calculate_sales_tax.
*"*"Local interface:
*"  IMPORTING
*"     REFERENCE(I_GROSS_AMOUNT) TYPE  AMOUNTSAP
*"     REFERENCE(I_TAX) TYPE  F OPTIONAL
*"  EXPORTING
*"     REFERENCE(E_NET_AMOUNT) TYPE  AMOUNTSAP
*"     REFERENCE(E_TAX_AMOUNT) TYPE  AMOUNTSAP
  DATA:
   l_tax_factor TYPE f.
  IF i_tax IS SUPPLIED.
    l_tax_factor = ( i_tax / 100 ) + 1.
  ELSE.
    l_tax_factor = '1.16'.
  ENDIF.
  e_net_amount = i_gross_amount / l_tax_factor.
  IF e_tax_amount IS REQUESTED.
    e_tax_amount = i_gross_amount - e_net_amount.
  ENDIF.
ENDFUNCTION.
```

The operators mentioned are used quite often in today's ABAP programs because they provide valuable services for the optimization and securing of the code, and therefore support high-quality code.

There are also comparison operators for bit patterns, although they rarely are used in business applications, along with the IN operator, which is explained in more detail in Section 4.2, Defining and Processing Database Tables—SELECT, INSERT, UPDATE, DELETE. Nesting, combination, or negation of logical expressions is simple using parentheses ( ) and the Boolean operators AND, OR, and NOT.

ABAP provides the two usual branching instructions IF ... ELSE and CASE ... WHEN that are available in nearly every programming language. As usual, the IF instruction is more powerful than the CASE instruction, and you can actually use it to cover all application cases. In some cases with a large number of different decisions, however, the CASE instruction can be clearer. Both instructions are subject to a limitation, which is particularly difficult for newcomers to embrace. Comparisons are supported only between data without computation (that is, it is possible to test A<=B, but A<=3*B is already too much for the compiler to handle). Instead, you must first perform the computation in a separate instructions, for instance C=3*B, and then run the comparison as A<=C. This "formula weakness" in ABAP is, besides the need for field symbols, a significant reason that programming in ABAP needs so many data declarations. The syntax of the two instructions, as you can imagine, is quite simple.

▶ IF ... ELSE—If ... then ... else

The IF instruction is suitable for all types of data comparisons (texts, numbers, equality, inequality, and so on) with subsequent branching. The complete syntax is:

```
IF [comparison is true]
  [statements]
ELSEIF [comparison is true]
  [statements]
ELSE [statements]
```

The ELSEIF branch can be inserted as often as needed, and like the ELSE branch, it can be omitted entirely. All the operators mentioned can be used within a logical expression.

Example:

```
READ TABLE l_tab_customers INDEX 1 INTO l_str_customer.
IF ( sy-subrc = 0 ) OR ( sy-subrc = 2 ).
  WRITE: / 'Entry found'.
ELSEIF sy-subrc = 4.
  WRITE: / 'Entry not found. sy-tabix undefined'.
ELSE.
```

```
   WRITE: / 'Entry not found. sy-tabix defined'.
ENDIF.
```

▶ **CASE ... WHEN—In case ... then ... else**

The CASE instructions are only provided for simple "equals" and "not equal" decisions, and are therefore primarily used when comparing data with discrete (that is, predetermined) values. The syntax is:

```
CASE [Variable] WHEN [values]
  [statements]
WHEN OTHERS [statements]
```

There can be any number of WHEN branches and then an optional final WHEN OTHERS branch.

Example:

```
READ TABLE l_tab_customers INDEX 1 INTO l_str_customer.
CASE sy-subrc.
  WHEN 0 OR 2.
    WRITE: / 'Entry found'.
  WHEN 4.
    WRITE: / 'Entry not found. sy-tabix undefined'.
  WHEN OTHERS.
    WRITE: / 'Entry not found. sy-tabix defined'.
ENDCASE.
```

Both instructions get complicated when they are combined or nested in one another, and when the IF condition uses complex NOT, AND, or OR combinations, so that even difficult decisions can be made.

Exercise 3.6

Create the program ZPTB00_PROVISION_CALCULATOR. It calculates the setup and commission fees, which are charged by familiar Internet auction sites like QXL or eBay. Implement a calculation program, which calculates the expected costs of setup fees, sales commissions, and so on for the sale of an item. To keep this exercise simple, ignore special rules for certain product groups, like automobiles and motorcycles. For the example solution, assume a VAT rate of 19% and the following rates:

Setup Fee:	
Starting Price	**Offer Fee**
$1.00	$0.25
$1.01 – $9.99	$0.40
$10.00 – $24.99	$0.60
$25.00 – $99.99	$1.20
$100,00 and higher	$2.40
Provision:	
Sales Price	**Sales Provision**
$0.00 – $50.00	4% of the sale price
$50.01 – $500.00	$2.00 plus 3% of the price above $50.00
$500.01 and more	$15.50 plus 1.5 % of the price above $500.00

Start by doing the following:

▷ Create a new program with the name "ZPTB00_PROVISION_CALCU-LATOR" and without a TOP include.

▷ Title it "Commission calculator" and use the number of the transport request used before.

As usual, the SAP Object Navigator creates the program framework, and you can then complete it. You now do this in order to calculate the total and net costs for the seller from the start price and sale price entered.

▷ Type the following source code beneath the comment lines:

```
REPORT  zptb00_provision_calculator.
PARAMETERS:
* Start price and sales price
  p_astart TYPE p DECIMALS 2,
  p_asales TYPE p DECIMALS 2.
DATA:
* Net fee, net provision, cost and total cost
  l_fee TYPE p DECIMALS 2,
  l_provision TYPE p DECIMALS 2,
  l_net_cost TYPE p DECIMALS 2,
```

```
    l_total_cost TYPE p DECIMALS 2.
* Calculate fee by start price
IF p_astart <= 0.
  WRITE: /'Please enter a valid start price'.
  RETURN.
ELSEIF p_astart <= 1.
  l_fee = '0.25'.
ELSEIF p_astart <= '9.99'.
  l_fee = '0.40'.
ELSEIF p_astart <= '24.99'.
  l_fee = '0.60'.
ELSEIF p_astart <= '99.99'.
  l_fee = '1.20'.
ELSE.
  l_fee = '2.40'.
ENDIF.
* Calculate provision by sales price
IF p_asales < p_astart.
  WRITE: /'Please enter a valid sales price'.
  RETURN.
ELSEIF p_asales <= 50.
  l_provision = p_asales * '0.04'.
ELSEIF p_asales <= 500.
  l_provision = 2 + ( p_asales - 50 ) * '0.03'.
ELSE.
  l_provision = '15.50' + ( p_asales - 500 ) * '0.015'.
ENDIF.
* Calculate total cost and write them to screen
l_net_cost = l_fee + l_provision.
l_total_cost = l_net_cost + ( l_net_cost * '0.16' ).
WRITE: /'Start price  : ', p_astart,
       /'Sales price  : ', p_asales,
       /'Net cost     : ', l_net_cost,
       /'total cost   : ', l_total_cost.
```

Listing 3.8 Source Code for the Program ZPTB00_PROVISION_CALCULATOR

For the conversion, the IF instruction is attractive because the commission rules work with from-to ranges. Besides the two parameters for input of the starting price and the sales price, you also need a few variables for the storage of intermediate and final results.

Explanation of the source code

Begin by calculating the starting fee l_fee, which is higher the higher the starting price is. A lower starting price increases the attractiveness of the offer and thus the entire auction offering, but also results in a higher risk to the seller, who may have to part with the product at a price far below its value. To implement the from-to framework, we also use the ELSEIF clause of the IF branch.

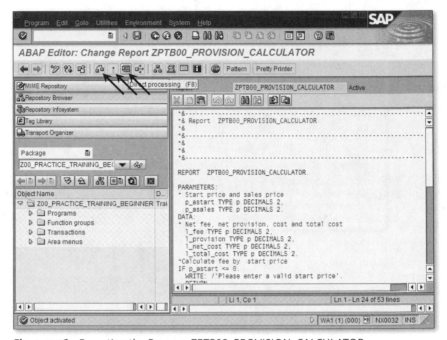

Figure 3.36 Executing the Program ZPTB00_PROVISION_CALCULATOR

Next is the calculation of the sales commission l_provision, which increases with the amount of the sales price from an absolute standpoint, but decreases from a relative point of view, because the percentage is lower for larger sales prices. We use the ELSEIF clause here, too, in order to implement the commission brackets quickly and without redundancy.

Finally, calculate the required 19% value-added tax and print the result on the screen using the WRITE command.

Let's look at the program flow in a little more detail.

Testing the program

▷ Click the TEST button, then click the ACTIVATE button, and lastly, click the DIRECT button to start the program immediately.

The program starts, asking you for the starting and sales prices:

▷ Enter "1" as the Start price and enter "124" as the Sales price (see Figure 3.37).

▷ Click the EXECUTE button.

Figure 3.37   Program ZPTB00_PROVISION_CALCULATOR in Action

The program calculates the total costs according to the fee and commission model, and prints them on the screen both with and without the value-added tax (see Figure 3.38).

Figure 3.38   Results of the Program ZPTB00_PROVISION_CALCULATOR

> **Tip**
>
> In professional ABAP development, you see a lot of `IF` statements and not many `CASE` statements because business applications often have more complicated conditions; therefore, the `CASE` statement cannot model them well. There are programmers who refuse to use `CASE` statements for this very reason.

3.6   Loops—WHILE, DO

Loops are very well suited for the execution of instructions more than once, and on varying data. Besides simple loops, ABAP also has an entire series of special commands for the processing of tabular mass data, which were already discussed in Section 3.3, Structures and Internal Tables—TABLE, MOVE-CORRESPONDING, INSERT, APPEND, READ, MODIFY, DELETE, LOOP. The statement for single-line processing, `LOOP ... END-LOOP`, is used very often.

Basics   As long as the main processors of your computer don't consist of massively parallel units, you require loop instructions to process similar data at the same time. Special commands for the control of statements that can be executed in parallel, such as those that exist in COBOL, will continue to be the exception for a long time to come.

Loops   ABAP offers the programmer two different loops, although thanks to the availability of powerful commands for the processing of tabular mass data (see Section 3.3), they are usually needed only for mathematical algorithms. Suitable applications might be the approximation of integrals or infinite elements. These loops are the `DO` loop, which is comparable to the `FOR` loops that you might be familiar with from other programming languages, and the `WHILE` loop, which is included in all other similar programming languages.

▶ `DO [n TIMES] ENDDO`—**Unconditional (numerical) loop**
   The `DO` loop can be used in ABAP either with or without the `[n TIMES]` clause. Without the clause, the statements between the two keywords are executed infinitely (at least in theory). Because this can't be the actual intent of the program, of course, you would use the `EXIT` command to

exit the loop. You can use the [n TIMES] clause to determine the number of loop executions exactly, whereby an (early) exit can be generated using the EXIT command. The term "counting loops" is sometimes used for this construct. The CONTINUE command is very practical, allowing you to skip all the remaining instructions in the current loop iteration, and start the next loop execution immediately if there is one. Within a loop, the sy-index system field always contains the number of loop executions already run through, including the current one. Because loops can also be nested in one another, in such cases sy-index always refers to the currently innermost loop. The following two examples show usage with and without specification of the number of loops. The first case calculates the number of years that will be needed for a given starting amount (assuming that there is 15% interest per year to save a target amount); the second case simply prints "Hello" ten times in a row:

```
PARAMETERS:
  p_invest TYPE p DECIMALS 2,
  p_profit TYPE p DECIMALS 2.
DO.
  p_invest = p_invest * '1.05'.
  IF p_invest >= p_profit.
    WRITE: / 'You need ', sy-index, ' years to achieve
             this profit.'.
    EXIT.
  ENDIF.
ENDDO.

DO 10 TIMES.
  WRITE: / 'Hello for the ', sy-index, '''th time.'.
ENDDO.
```

▶ **WHILE log_exp ENDWHILE—Conditional loop**
After the keyword WHILE, there must be a logical expression, which is tested at the beginning of each run through the loop. If the result is "true," all statements will be executed until ENDWHILE is encountered; but if the result is "false," the loop ends and program execution resumes with the next statement after the loop. A WHILE loop can also be ended prematurely using the EXIT command, and you can use the CONTINUE statement to skip to the next loop iteration. The global field

sy-index contains the current number of runs through the loop. The two next examples show the use of the WHILE loop in the same application cases as the DO loop:

```
PARAMETERS:
  p_invest TYPE p DECIMALS 2,
  p_profit TYPE p DECIMALS 2.
DATA:
  l_years TYPE i VALUE 0.
WHILE p_invest < p_profit.
  p_invest = p_invest * '1.05'.
  l_years = l_years + 1.
ENDWHILE.
WRITE: / 'You need ', l_
years, ' years to achieve this          profit.'.

WHILE sy-index <= 10.
  WRITE: / 'Hello for the ', sy-index, '''th time.'.
ENDWHILE.
```

In principle, both the WHILE loop and the DO loop can cover all possible application cases for loops, so, actually, you would only need one of them. However, each of them has its advantages and disadvantages. Although a DO loop used as a counting loop is clearer and somewhat faster to execute than the comparable WHILE, an unlimited DO loop and EXIT command within a condition behaves exactly the opposite in comparison with the corresponding WHILE loop. Analogous to decision statements, both loop statements can get quite complex when they are combined or nested in one another and use complex NOT, AND, or OR expressions as conditions for their termination.

Let's take a look at the functionality of the loops in a little more detail in the context of a practical example.

> **Exercise 3.7**
>
> Create the program ZPTB00_SAVINGS_CALCULATOR. For the input parameter, request for the savings target desired, the monthly savings amount, and the bank's current savings interest rate. As a result, the program should provide the number of months you will have to save to reach your goal. As the basis for the calculation, use the WHILE loop and the DO loop once respectively.

▷ First, create a new program with the name "ZPTB00_SAVINGS_CAL-CULATOR" and without a TOP include.

▷ The title should be "Savings Target Calculator", and the transport request stays the same.

As usual, the SAP Object Navigator creates a program structure that you can fill in to take the savings goal, monthly savings amount, and bank interest rate into account and calculate the savings period and the final amount including compounded interest.

▷ Type the following source code beneath the comment lines:

```
REPORT  zptb00_savings_calculator.
PARAMETERS:
* Savings target, monthly savings and yearly interest
* rate
  p_atargt TYPE p DECIMALS 2,
  p_mrate TYPE p DECIMALS 2,
  p_iperc TYPE p DECIMALS 2.
DATA:
* Monthly interest rate, current savings and months
  l_monthly_interest_rate TYPE f,
  l_savings TYPE p DECIMALS 2,
  l_months TYPE i.
* Calculate Months and savings
l_monthly_interest_rate = p_iperc / 12 / 100.
WRITE: /'Savings target : ', p_atargt,
        /'monthly amount : ', p_mrate,
        /'Interest rate %: ', p_iperc.
WRITE sy-uline AS LINE.
* WHILE Version
WHILE l_savings < p_atargt.
  l_savings = l_savings + ( l_savings *
  l_monthly_interest_rate ) + p_mrate.
  l_months = l_months + 1.
ENDWHILE.
WRITE: /'WHILE Statement',
        /'Months needed  : ', l_months,
        /'Saved amount   : ', l_savings.
* DO Version
CLEAR l_savings.
CLEAR l_months.
DO.
```

```
      l_savings = l_savings + ( l_savings *
      l_monthly_interest_rate ) + p_mrate.
      l_months = l_months + 1.
      IF l_savings >= p_atargt.
        EXIT.
      ENDIF.
    ENDDO.
    WRITE: /'DO Statement',
           /'Months needed  : ', l_months,
           /'Saved amount   : ', l_savings.
```

Listing 3.9 Source Code for the Program ZPTB00_SAVINGS_CALCULATOR

Explanation of the source code

First you use the PARAMETERS command to request the input values for the target savings amount p_atargt, the monthly amount saved p_mrate, and the bank's yearly interest rate p_iperc. To calculate the savings amount with interest and the months needed, you also need the variables l_savings and l_months.

The program then first uses the yearly bank interest rate to calculate the monthly bank interest rate, which you need to determine the monthly increase in value of the amount already saved. The values entered are printed on the screen simply for reasons of clarity.

Now the WHILE loop runs until the savings goal is reached or exceeded. Inside the loop, you must first calculate the monthly interest on the amount saved and then the incoming monthly savings deposit. Every iteration through the loop corresponds to the changes to the amount in a month, so you need to count only the iterations in l_month to be able to print the length of the savings plan afterwards. Both the final savings amount and the number of months are finally output to the screen.

With the DO loop, the principle of the calculation is of course identical. However, for a termination condition we use an IF statement, which uses the EXIT command to leave the loop as soon as the savings goal is met or exceeded.

Both loops should produce the same final amount and the same duration.

Testing the program

Test the program now by doing the following:

▷ Click the SAVE button, then click CHECK, ACTIVATE, and the DIRECT button to start the program immediately (see Figure 3.39).

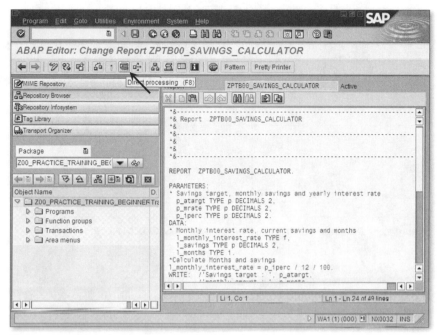

Figure 3.39 Executing the Program ZPTB00_SAVINGS_CALCULATOR

The program starts, asking for the savings target amount, the monthly savings amount, and the yearly interest at the bank.

▷ Enter "10000" as the target savings amount, "300" as the monthly savings amount, and "4.5" (%) as the bank's interest rate (see Figure 3.40).

Figure 3.40 Program ZPTB00_SAVINGS_CALCULATOR in Action

▷ Click EXECUTE (see Figure 3.41).

Figure 3.41 Results of the Program ZPTB00_SAVINGS_CALCULATOR

> **Tip**
>
> In professional ABAP development, you usually work with tabular mass data, which can be processed very efficiently with the LOOP statement (see Section 3.3).

In contrast to traditional programming languages, programs and data in ABAP are always stored in a database, and only in rare exceptions are files used. This concept brings with it comparatively high costs; however, there are also clear advantages to this concept that become apparent, especially during the processing and evaluation of business mass data.

4 Defining and Managing Database Tables

Section 1.1, Overview of SAP Software and Architecture, explained that the SAP NetWeaver Application Server (SAP NetWeaver AS) manages all programs and data in a database, which is responsible for the long-term storage and correct retrieval. The strength of ABAP Objects is the integration of database accesses into the ABAP Objects language (see Figure 4.1), and this option is precisely what this chapter focuses on.

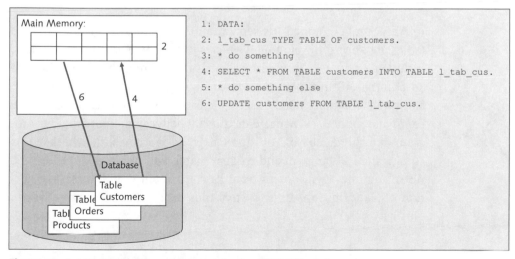

Figure 4.1   Integrating Database Accesses into the ABAP Objects Language

Of course, there are a few necessary conditions that this type of data storage needs to satisfy because, in a (relational) database, data can only be stored in the form of tables. These tables must first be created, and their internal row structure must be determined, in such a way as to meet the requirements of your application. This process is called *database design*, and in some enterprises, there are entire departments devoted to this process. In the world of science, there are academic disciplines that are concerned solely with the question of finding the optimum distribution of data in tables so that the read, processing, and write speed of the application can meet requirements optimally. A detailed excursion in that direction exceeds the scope of this book. Therefore, Section 4.2, Defining and Processing Database Tables—SELECT, INSERT, UPDATE, DELETE, simply limits itself to a few significant and basic aspects of this topic.

Tips for those familiar with other programming languages

In other programming languages, like Delphi or Java, the creation of database applications is normally carried out using two separate tools. On the one hand, the development interface of the programming language is used for the creation of the program; on the other hand, the administrative interface of a database is used to create the tables required. Then you use a database driver to create a connection between the program and the database; you can use special functions to exchange data between the two.

In ABAP programming, this separation doesn't exist. Instead, database tables are normal development objects in the same way that programs, include files, or text symbols are, and, all together, they are treated as an application, transported from one system to another if necessary, and so on. You don't need to set up a driver, and you need to use ABAP commands only to exchange data directly between memory in your program and the database. You don't need to worry about whether this combination of program and database table will run or not because the ABAP runtime environment ensures compatibility with a broad selection of platforms (operating system plus database management system plus hardware).

4.1   Field Properties—DATA ELEMENT, DOMAIN

The most frequently used data types in ABAP development are not the
ABAP data types defined in Section 3.2, Data and Data Types—DATA,
PARAMETERS, CONSTANTS, FIELD SYMBOLS, TYPE, CREATE, Text Elements, such as i, c, or p, but *data elements* based on the data types in
the database. They ensure considerably stricter type checking, defined
value lists, brief descriptions, online help, and other features that far
surpass the options of the ABAP data types (see Figure 4.2). This allows
them to contribute a great deal to operational convenience and runtime
stability.

Figure 4.2   Features of SAP Systems Based on Data Elements

Data elements are not based on the ABAP data types (see Section 3.2, Data   **Basics**
and Data Types—DATA, PARAMETERS, CONSTANTS, FIELD SYMBOLS,
TYPE, CREATE, Text Elements), but on the data types of the underlying

database, the *dictionary data types*. They are used to define the individual columns of a database table; furthermore, they can be used as data types in the ABAP programs. The latter is covered in this chapter; Section 4.2, Defining and Processing Database Tables—SELECT, INSERT, UPDATE, DELETE, and details their use in tables.

Data elements ensure better readability and clarity of the program because the programmer has not only additional descriptions and help, but also a function of the Object Navigator, which can show all uses within source code and tables at the click of a button (the *usage explanation*, a button that is displayed on the toolbar of the SAP Object Navigator). So working with data elements in an ABAP program works entirely to your advantage. In professional ABAP, development data elements are used almost exclusively for the typing of data. The entire concept has become so fundamental that SAP is also porting it for Java development. This is reason enough to look a little more closely at data elements and their possible uses in ABAP programs.

From dictionary data type to data type in a program

The path from the definition of a data element to its use in a program generally includes several steps (see Figure 4.3), each of which will be examined in the following subsections:

1. Selection of a dictionary data type
2. Definition of a domain referring to the dictionary data type
3. Definition of a data element referring to the domain
4. Declaration of data within the program source code, referring to the data element as the data type

SAP supports this path with convenient user interfaces in the SAP Object Navigator for entry of the information required, along with the activation mechanism already familiar from working with source code, which greatly simplifies working in teams.

Figure 4.3 Hierarchy of Data, Data Elements, and Domains

The ABAP programming language provides an entire series of dictionary data types, but they cannot be used directly in a program. Instead, they must serve as basic components. Table 4.1 shows the most important dictionary data types and the *mapping* between the dictionary data type and an ABAP data type.

Selecting a dictionary data type—determining basic properties

Dictionary Data Type	Characters Permitted	Description	ABAP Data Type
CHAR n	1 – 255	Character string	C(n)
CLNT	3	Client	C(3)
CUKY	5	Currency key, referenced by CURR fields	C(5)
CURR n, m, s	1 – 17	Currency field, stored as DEC	P((n + 2) / 2) DECIMALS m [NO-SIGN]
DEC n, m, s	1 – 31, in tables 1 – 17	Computed or amount field with decimal point and sign	P((n + 2) / 2) DECIMALS m [NO-SIGN]
DATS	8	Date field (YYYYMMDD), stored as CHAR(8)	D
FLTP	16	Floating point number with eight bytes precision	F
INT4	10	Four-byte integer, whole number with sign	I

Table 4.1 Built-in Dictionary Data Types

Dictionary Data Type	Characters Permitted	Description	ABAP Data Type
NUMC n	1 – 255	Character string with digits only	N(n)
QUAN n, m, s	1 – 17	Quantity field, shows a unit field with format UNIT	P((n + 2) / 2) DECIMALS m [NO-SIGN]
STRING	256 – ...	Character string with variable length	STRING
TIMS	6	Time field (HHMMSS), stored as CHAR(6)	T
UNIT n	2 – 3	Unit key for QUAN fields	C(n)

Table 4.1 Built-in Dictionary Data Types (Cont.)

Defining a domain— determining technical properties

Dictionary data types serve as the basis for the definition of *domains*. Domains refer to the dictionary data type, thus defining their basic technical suitability as amount field, quantity field, numeric field, text field, and so on. Furthermore, you can also define additional technical properties (for instance, that amounts can only have positive signs, numbers may only take values from a certain range, or values must already be present in a different table, that is, a master data check). Newcomers know these kinds of technical properties as *constraints*, but what you are doing here is nothing more than defining limitations, which are largely automatically checked during execution of the programmer. Once a domain is activated, it can be used as the basis for the definition of data elements.

Defining a data element— determining descriptive properties

Data elements generally refer to a domain and determine their technical characteristics in that way. Moreover, they also define descriptive properties like text labels in different lengths for optimum output in places with little or a lot of room, brief descriptions for output as tooltips, and online help for detailed description with links to related topics. If you look at the richness of the terms used in the departments of today's enterprises and the software to support them, you will quickly realize that this kind of descriptive property is very important. It's important to know, when needed, what a "legal unit," an "accounting metric," or an "inventory conversion component" is and how that information needs to be entered. All the texts in a data element are automatically added to the worklist for the translator, and ABAP is careful when displaying input and output fields to select the proper local language. Once a data element is activated, it can be used in program code as a data type.

Within the program code, data elements are treated in the same way as ABAP data types, and can be used to type constants, variables, field symbols, and interface parameters. For instance, if you've defined a zroom_number data element to store the room number in a hotel, the declaration will hardly be different from that of the corresponding ABAP data type:

Declaring data—using data elements as data types

```
PARAMETERS:
  p_room_number TYPE zroom_number OBLIGATORY VALUE
    CHECK,
  p_room_number2(3) TYPE numc.
```

Assuming that the zroom_number is ultimately based on a dictionary data type numc with three characters, during processing you won't see any difference as long as you don't try to store invalid room numbers in the zroom_number domain. If you do, the user will automatically see an error message during input, but in the second case your program must take care of the checking and output of appropriate messages itself. This data check actually only takes place during input, and is performed by the program user interface. In the program, you can assign both parameters any numeric values with three digits without the check stopping you or even noticing. An example in Section 7.4.3, Function Groups, in Function ZPTB00_OBJ_BTC_CHECK shows how you can implement this kind of checking in the program.

The totality of all technical and descriptive properties of a data element is called its *metadata*, and in this respect ABAP cannot be compared with any other familiar programming language. ABAP easily gets top marks when it comes to data consistency, type safety, and runtime stability, because when only carefully selected and defined data can be input and processed, the probability that you'll also get the right results is much higher.

Metadata, type checking, and type safety

Take a look at the practical aspects of working with domains and data elements, as well as the processing in programs.

Exercise 4.1

Create the program ZPTB00_ROOM_CHECKER. As input parameters, request the arrival and departure dates, as well as the room number desired, and check these against those actually available, namely 001–004, 101–104, and 201–204. Use a data element to perform the check.

If the room number has been entered correctly, print a booking confirmation on the screen.

Creating domains   Let's start by creating the domain.

▷ In the context menu of the package or development class, select the CREATE • DDIC OBJECT • DOMAIN menu option.

A dialog box appears, where you must specify the name of the domain.

▷ Enter "ZPTB00_Room_Number" as the name of the domain.

A window is displayed in the tools area of the SAP Object Navigator where you can maintain the domain properties.

▷ As the brief description, enter "Hotel room number", enter "NUMC" as the data type, and "3" as the number of digits (see Figure 4.4).

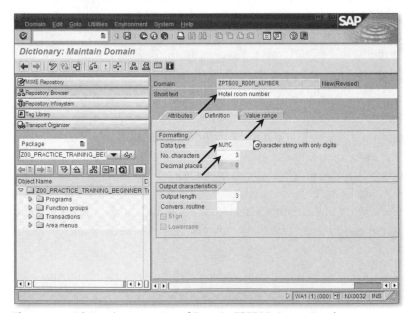

Figure 4.4   Editing the Properties of Domain ZPTB00_Room_Number

▷ Select the VALUE RANGE tab.

The configuration options on the VALUE RANGE tab are displayed (see Figure 4.5). There, use the setting options under SINGLE VALS to ensure that a check is automatically performed on the entered values afterwards.

▷ Under SINGLE VALS, enter the room numbers 001 through 004, 101 through 104, and 201 through 204, together with a brief description, and click SAVE.

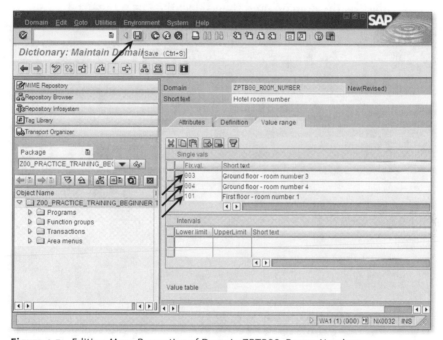

Figure 4.5 Editing More Properties of Domain ZPTB00_Room_Number

A transport dialog box opens, where you must define the request for logging the domain.

▷ Copy the settings unchanged, and click the CONTINUE button.

You can now check and activate the domain.

▷ Click CHECK, and then click ACTIVATE.

Next create a data element based on this domain.

Creating a data
element

▷ Select CREATE • DDIC OBJECT • DATA ELEMENT in the context menu.

A dialog box appears, where you must specify the name of the data element.

▷ Enter "ZPTB00_Room_Number" as the name of the domain.

In the tool area of the SAP Object Navigator, a window appears in which you can edit the properties of the data element (see Figure 4.6).

▷ Enter "Hotel room number" as the brief description, "ZPTB00_Room_Number" as the domain, and then select the FIELD LABEL tab.

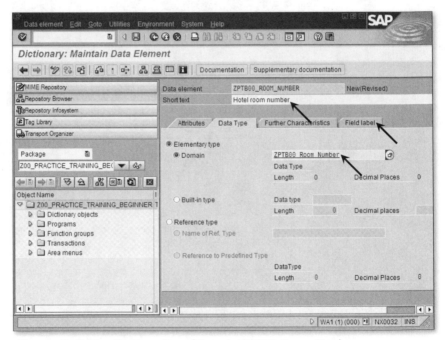

Figure 4.6 Editing the Properties of Domain ZPTB00_Room_Number

The setting options in the FIELD LABEL tab are displayed. Specify field labels of varying lengths for the data element here in order to be able to use the data element in all possible input and output screens.

▷ Under SHORT enter the label "RoomNo", under MEDIUM enter "Room number", under LONG enter "Hotel room number", and under HEADING also enter "Hotel room number". The dialog box fills the length information automatically (see Figure 4.7).

▷ Click the SAVE button.

A transport dialog box opens, where you must define the request for logging the data element.

▷ Copy the settings unchanged, and click the CONTINUE button.

You are now supposed to maintain the documentation for the data element to ensure that the user can call online help for this input field.

▷ Click the DOCUMENTATION button.

A new window appears, where you can enter the documentation for the data element.

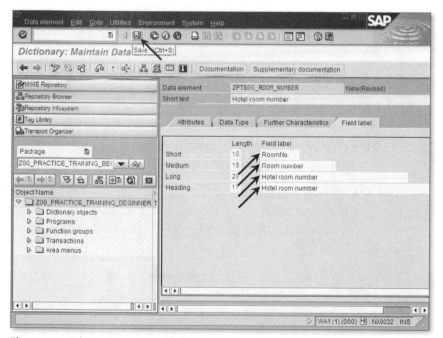

Figure 4.7 Editing More Properties of Data Element ZPTB00_Room_Number

▷ Accept the documentation from Figure 4.8.

▷ Click the SAVE ACTIVE button and then select the BACK button.

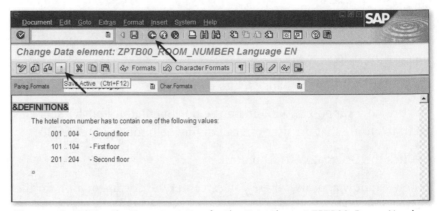

Figure 4.8 Editing the Documentation for the Data Element ZPTB00_Room_Number

You can now check and activate the data element.

▷ Click the CHECK button, then click ACTIVATE.

Creating a program — After this preparation, you can start with the actual program.

▷ Create a new program in the usual way, named "ZPTB00_ROOM_ CHECKER", without a TOP include.

▷ Give it the title "Room checker" and leave all the other program properties unchanged. The transport request is also accepted as preset.

As usual, the SAP Object Navigator creates a skeleton program that you can fill out to check the hotel room number, check-in day, and check-out day entries for correctness, and print the data to the screen if the result is positive.

▷ Type the following code under the comment lines of the program skeleton and save:

```
REPORT  zptb00_room_checker.
PARAMETERS:
  p_room TYPE zptb00_room_number OBLIGATORY
  VALUE CHECK,
  p_chkin TYPE d OBLIGATORY,
  p_chkout TYPE d OBLIGATORY.
WRITE: / 'Room Reservation',
       / 'Hotel room number:', p_room,
```

```
/ 'Check in day     :', p_chkin,
/ 'Check out day    :', p_chkout.
```

Listing 4.1 Source Code for the Program ZPTB00_ROOM_CHECKER

The parameter `p_room` is based on the data element `zptb00_room_number` you've defined. So that a check of the fixed values entered in the domain will take place, you have to use the `OBLIGATORY` and `VALUE CHECK` clauses. At runtime, then, entries are checked and a value help is also available that the user can call up using the F4 key. Of course, the online help for the entry field is also available, and is displayed when the F1 key is pressed. The other parameters accept the check-in and check-out dates, and, because these are date fields, a value help is automatically generated for them.

Explanation of
the source code

Once all the data has been correctly entered, the information collected is shown on the screen.

> **Tip**
>
> After activation of the program, if you still make changes to the individual allowed values in the domains, they won't appear automatically in the value help. Instead, you must provide a little manual help by temporarily renaming the parameter, activating the program again, and then changing the name back. Only then is the compiler forced to redo the generation and take into account the current individual values from the domain.

For the clarity of the program, it makes sense to give the parameters descriptive labels. Let's take care of this important step, which is essential for professional ABAP programming.

Editing the
selection text

▷ From the menu, select GOTO • TEXT ELEMENTS • SELECTION TEXTS.

A dialog box opens, displaying fields in which all the parameters are already entered and only the texts need to be entered.

▷ For the parameter `p_chkin`, enter the text "Check in day", and for `p_chkout`, enter the text "Check out day".

▷ Select the DICTIONARY REFERENCE checkbox for the parameter `p_room`, which will automatically accept the heading already given in the data element, which in this example is "Hotel room number" (see Figure 4.9).

▷ Click the ACTIVATE button, and then click BACK.

Figure 4.9 Editing Selection Texts for the Program ZPTB00_ROOM_CHECKER

Testing the program

Now check the effectiveness of your settings in the running program.

▷ As usual, click the CHECK button, then ACTIVATE, and finally the DIRECT button to start the program immediately.

The program starts, prompting you for the room number and the check-in and check-out dates.

▷ Enter "401" as the room number, 1.1.2014 for the check-in date, and 1.2.2014 for the check-out date (see Figure 4.10).

▷ Confirm your input with ⌐Enter⌐.

Figure 4.10 Entries in the Program ZPTB00_ROOM_CHECKER

The selection form determines the invalid room number, prints an error message in the status line, and locks all the input fields except for the hotel room number.

▷ Call the online help for this input field with the F1 key (see Figure 4.11).

Figure 4.11 Online Help for the Hotel Room Number Input Fields

The user can get information here about the correct input values for this input field. Particularly for developers, it can also be helpful for testing to call up information about the underlying data element.

▷ Click the TECHNICAL INFORMATION button (see Figure 4.12).

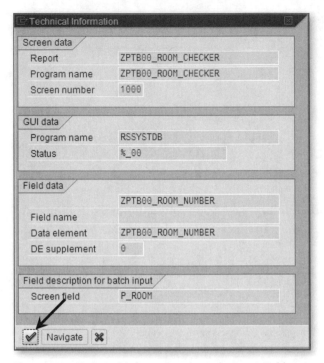

Figure 4.12 Technical Information about the Input Field

From there, you can also navigate to the data element, for instance, to make corrections. However, you want to continue to test your program.

▷ Click the CLOSE button in the Technical Information dialog. This makes the original help window active again.

▷ Close the online help and press the F4 key or click the button to the right of the HOTEL ROOM NUMBER input field.

The value help appears on the screen and offers you the values entered in the domain for selection (see Figure 4.13).

▷ Select the hotel room number "201" and click the COPY button.

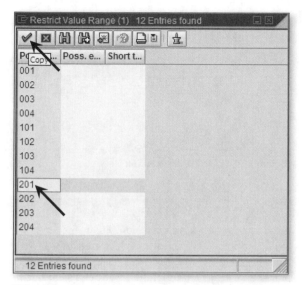

Figure 4.13 Input Help for the Hotel Room Number Field

The selection is copied into the input field.

▷ Click the EXECUTE button (see Figure 4.14).

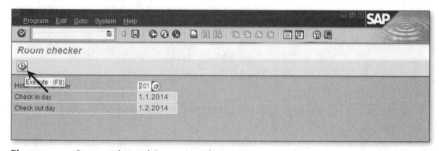

Figure 4.14 Corrected Hotel Room Number

All entries now pass the test perfectly, and the test results are printed on the screen (see Figure 4.15).

Figure 4.15 Results of the Program ZPTB00_ROOM_CHECKER

Tip

In professional ABAP development, the importance of completely maintained data elements, domains, and text elements cannot be overstated. ABAP derives a large part of its runtime stability and flexibility from the metadata edited there. Up to 20 percent of project effort regularly goes toward the maintenance and documentation of data. Two of the most important domains used by all ABAP developers are WAERS and MEINS. The former is of type CUKY and uses a value table to define all the currency units used worldwide (for instance, EUR, USD, YEN, and so on). The latter is of type QUAN and uses a value table to define the most commonly used ISO units, like units and hours, and so on.

4.2 Defining and Processing Database Tables— SELECT, INSERT, UPDATE, DELETE

Relational databases manage information in tables that consist of rows (*records*) and columns (*fields*). Once stored, you can retrieve information quickly, selectively, and by different applications at the same time. They are especially designed for reading and writing access by many users, and far exceed the capabilities of files.

Basics   In the early 1980s, the triumphant success of the computer in the business word would have been impossible without relational databases; enterprises like Oracle owe their success to this very fact. While home computers and PCs stored most data as files, whose data formats were completely different and often not even published, most enterprises bought a database management system and installed it in a central location so they could work with it via the network from their individual workplaces. In the beginning, simple command line scripts and text-based user interfaces for the writing and reading out of data from perhaps a few dozen tables dominated; however, over the years, these gave way to increasingly more refined programs with Graphical User Interfaces (GUIs), which made the greater part of ever more complicated business logic and the consequent necessary multiplication of the tables transparent to the user. Today, a current installation of SAP ERP can reach 109,000 tables, required for the storage and data for over 40 business modules (such as Purchasing, Production, Sales, and so on), and that number doesn't even include the more than 20 new SAP (industry) solutions.

The greater part of the data in these tables is closely related to other parts of the data; that is, the data is *relational*. For instance, one table may store the addresses of customers, the next table the purchase orders for those customers, and another the information about the products ordered (see Figure 4.16).

Figure 4.16 Tables for the Storage of Data and Relations

Relational
database design In custom-developed ABAP programs, which don't use the tables or even the data management functions of existing SAP applications, you still have to think through the same kind of relational network of tables that you'll be using in your program to store and read data. As shown in Figure 4.17, fields with identical content are used to compare data in different tables. The trick of this relational database design is nothing new for the newcomer to ABAP. Every row in a table has one field with a value unique in the table, the *key*. If you want to refer to the data in this row from another table, you only need to include a field in the other table in which this value can be stored, the *foreign key*. If you need the information referenced by the foreign key later on, you only have to look for the row with that value in the original table.

Figure 4.17 Three Types of Relation: 1:n, 1:1, and m:n

This results in relational networks between tables that break down into three types:

▶ **1:n relation**
One row in table A is referenced by 0, 1, or several (n) rows in another table B. Examples are the relation between customers and orders,

between a room in a school and the children in the class taught there, between a schoolchild and the child's books, and so on.

► **1:1 relation**
One row in table A is referenced by exactly one row in another table B. Examples are the relation between the inhabitant of a country and his main place of residence, between the VIN number of a car and its license plate, between a corporation and its trade register entry, and so on.

► **m:n relation**
One row in table A is referenced by 0, 1, or more rows of another table B, while one row in table B can also be referenced by 0, 1, or more rows in table A. To model this relation, you require a third table, C, which has a 1:n relation with both tables A and B, where the n side, that is, the foreign key, is stored in table C. So actually an m:n relation is split up into two 1:n relations in order to model it in a relational database.

These three basic types of relation allow all possible relationships between data in tables, regardless of how complicated the relationships are between the data in the tables. The art of database design consists of solving this task for the data at hand as elegantly as possible, without duplicated data storage (no redundancy) and suitably for fast read or write access.

The individual columns (also called *fields*) of a database table are provided with as descriptive a name as possible, which must adhere to similar rules in ABAP as the names of variables (e.g., only a Roman letter at the start, followed by a sequence of letters, digits, and underscores, with a maximum length of 30 characters). The data type of each column is usually determined by providing a data element that controls all the technical and descriptive properties, except for its use as a key or foreign key. The latter information is added directly by the table (see Figure 4.18). Because the same data elements can also be used in the ABAP program, there is a basic compatibility when transferring values.

Database tables and data elements

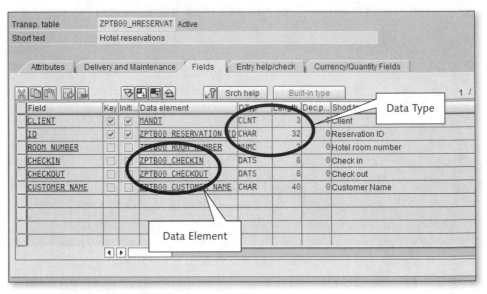

Figure 4.18 Using Data Elements to Determine Technical and Descriptive Properties of Fields

Data transfer between memory and the database

Within an ABAP program, you should prepare your data in the form of suitable internal tables and structures (see Section 3.3, Structures and Internal Tables—TABLE, MOVE-CORRESPONDING, INSERT, APPEND, READ, MODIFY, DELETE, LOOP) because only in this form can the data be written to the database and retrieved again. Ideally, you should use internal tables and structures for this purpose that correspond structurally to the database tables. In ABAP there is nothing easier because you can specify the database table as a data type. A short code fragment makes a good example:

```
DATA:
  l_tab_flight TYPE STANDARD TABLE OF sflight,
  l_str_flight TYPE sflight.
l_str_flight-planetype = 'A320-200'.
* ... more assignments ...
INSERT sflight FROM l_str_flight.
* ... or insert table instead of structure like this ...
l_str_flight-carrid = 'AA'.
APPEND l_str_flight TO l_tab_flight.
INSERT sflight FROM TABLE l_tab_flight.
```

In the first declaration instruction, the variable `l_tab_flight` is defined as an internal table of type `sflight`, so that it can accept multiple rows with the same row structure as the database table `sflight`. This allows you to write multiple records to the table at once, as you do in the two `INSERT` statements. In the second declaration instruction, the variable `l_str_flight` is defined as a structure of type `sflight`, so that it has the same row structure as the database table `sflight`. The fields in the structure only need to be assigned values, and in the next statement their content can already be inserted as a row into the database.

The following commands are the most important for the transfer of data between one or more database tables and data in memory, and are grouped together by SAP under the term *Open SQL* because they provide a common subset of the statements that work under all databases (see Figure 4.19).

Open SQL

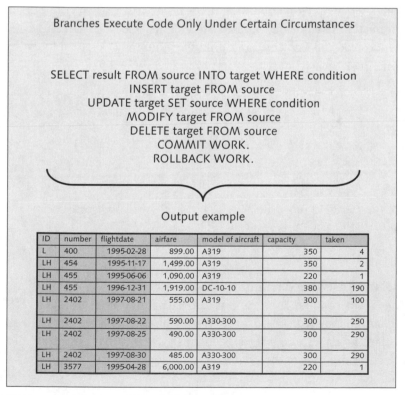

Figure 4.19 Overview of Open SQL Commands

▶ SELECT—**Reading data from database tables**
The SELECT command reads data from a database table into a structure or internal table. Its basic syntax is

```
SELECT result FROM source INTO target WHERE condition.
```

After the WHERE clause, you can define logical expressions that the data to be read in must match, thus limiting the result set. There is also a SELECT ... ENDSELECT form, which works similarly to a LOOP instruction, reading and processing the lines from the database one by one.

Over the years, the SELECT command has grown more and more powerful, and it now supports a whole series of clauses that can also be found in the SQL 92 standard, including nested selects, joins, and aggregation. If you would like to learn more about the functionality of the SELECT command, we recommend looking at *http://help.sap.com*. In the two following examples of SELECT commands, demo tables from SAP (flight data tables) are used, in the first case to read out all information (* wildcard) on Lufthansa flights, and in the second case, only to read the first line, and only the columns CARRID and CONNID from American Airlines:

```
DATA:
  l_tab_sflight TYPE STANDARD TABLE OF sflight,
  l_str_sflight TYPE sflight.
* read potentially more than one line into internal
* table
SELECT * FROM sflight INTO TABLE l_tab_sflight
WHERE carrid = 'LH'.
* read single line and only two fields into structure
SELECT SINGLE carrid connid FROM sflight INTO
    l_str_sflight
WHERE carrid = 'AA'.
```

▶ INSERT—**Inserting data into database tables**
The INSERT command inserts data into a database table without affecting the existing data. Here, you must be absolutely sure that the key field of the data to be inserted contains a value not yet inserted into the table; otherwise, the command will stop with an error message. The INSERT command has the syntax

```
INSERT target FROM source.
```

and inserts into table `target` the data from the internal table or structure `source`. The two following examples show the insertion of values from a structure and an internal table:

```
DATA:
  l_tab_flight TYPE STANDARD TABLE OF sflight,
  l_str_flight TYPE sflight.
l_str_sflight-carrid = 'LH'.
l_str_sflight-connid = '0400'.
l_str_sflight-fldate = '1.8.2003'.
l_str_sflight-planetype = 'A320-200'.
APPEND l_str_sflight TO l_tab_sflight.
* ... more assignments here to fill internal table ...
* insert lines of internal table into database table
INSERT sflight FROM TABLE l_tab_sflight.
* insert structure into database table ...
l_str_sflight-carrid = 'AA'.
INSERT sflight FROM l_str_sflight.
```

▶ **UPDATE—Changing data in database tables**

The UPDATE command changes the content of one or more existing records in the database by overwriting it with data from individual variables, a structure, or an internal table. The syntax of the UPDATE command can correspondingly vary considerably, depending on whether data in the main memory (without considering the key field) should be written to multiple records in the database table or only applies to exactly one row in the database (taking the key field into consideration). In the first case, the syntax is

```
UPDATE target SET source WHERE condition.
```

and in the second case

```
UPDATE target FROM source.
```

The three following examples show the update of records between internal tables in memory and database tables, update between a structure in memory and a row in the database table, and the modification of all records from the carrier Lufthansa where the airplane should be set to "Airbus 320-200."

```
DATA:
  l_tab_flight TYPE STANDARD TABLE OF sflight,
  l_str_flight TYPE sflight.
* ... assignments to fill structure and internal table ...
* update identification by key ...
UPDATE sflight FROM TABLE l_tab_sflight.
UPDATE sflight FROM l_str_sflight.
* update identification by condition ...
UPDATE sflight SET planetype = l_str_sflight-planetype
   WHERE carrid = 'LH'.
```

▶ **MODIFY — Insert or change data in database tables**
The MODIFY command is a combination of the INSERT and UPDATE commands. An attempt is first made to insert the rows from a structure or an internal table into the database. Any rows whose key fields refer to an already existing value in the table are instead modified using an UPDATE command. The data passed is thus always in the database in either case. The MODIFY command has the syntax

```
MODIFY target FROM source.
```

Here, target is the name of the database table and source, as before, is a structure or an internal table. The following two examples show the use of the command in a single database row or multiple database rows:

```
DATA:
  l_tab_flight TYPE STANDARD TABLE OF sflight,
  l_str_flight TYPE sflight.
* ... assignments to fill structure and internal table ...
* modify one line in the database table
MODIFY sflight FROM l_str_sflight.
* modify more lines in the database table
MODIFY sflight FROM TABLE l_tab_sflight.
```

▶ **DELETE — Deleting data from database tables**
The DELETE command is used to delete one or more rows from a database table. The syntax of the DELETE command differs depending on whether a structure or internal table with key values, or a logical expression, is used to identify the rows to be deleted. In the first case, the syntax is

```
DELETE target FROM source.
```

and in the second case

```
DELETE FROM target WHERE condition.
```

The next three examples show the use of the `DELETE` command using a structure, an internal table, and a logical expression:

```
DATA:
  l_tab_flight TYPE STANDARD TABLE OF sflight,
  l_str_flight TYPE sflight.
* fill keys into structure
l_str_sflight-carrid = 'LH'.
l_str_sflight-connid = '0400'.
l_str_sflight-fldate = '1.8.2003'.
* delete line defined in structure
DELETE sflight FROM l_str_sflight.
 * delete lines defined in internal table
APPEND l_str_stlight TO l_tab_sflight.
DELETE sflight FROM TABLE l_tab_sflight.
* delete lines, where carrid is 'LH'
DELETE FROM sflight WHERE carrid = 'LH'.
```

For the sake of completeness, it should be mentioned at this point that besides the Open SQL commands described, SAP also has a few commands with explicit database cursor management (`OPEN CURSOR`, `FETCH`, `CLOSE CURSOR`) as well as *native SQL commands*, with which multiple databases can be used at the same time, and all the SQL commands can be used. These commands are then no longer database-independent, of course, which is why they are not further discussed in this book. SAP itself uses native SQL only in absolutely exceptional cases, for instance, when accessing customer data from other systems in SAP CRM.

Each database table defined in SAP must be equipped with a primary key by marking the columns required for unique access to a row (for instance, the unique postal code, street, and house number for addressing a letter). The other columns in a table (also called *attributes*) can then be found using this primary key.

Primary key and secondary key of database tables

Secondary keys can be defined for database tables in SAP, but they don't have to be. They define alternative sets of columns, which can be used to limit retrieval to a few rows or one row in the database (like a P.O. box), which can be used as an alternative when addressing a letter. And just like a P.O. box, which can be used by a single person or shared by several, secondary keys can reference one row uniquely, but they don't have to.

SAP LUW concept

Another important concept regarding database access, and one of the outstanding features of ABAP, is the SAP LUW concept.

Once an application needs to use more than one database table, there is the basic problem that the data managed in these tables may not be in a consistent state at any given time. For instance, when an amount in accounting is transferred between accounts, it is first debited from one and then credited to the other. Between the two posting steps, the state of the data is inconsistent because the amount to be posted is not in the data inventory: It is "on its way." If the computer were to crash exactly between these two steps, the data would be permanently inconsistent. To avoid this kind of permanent inconsistency, SAP supports the LUW concept (*Logical Unit of Work*), also called the "all-or-nothing" principle. Its goal is to perform logically related write accesses (in actuality, the Open SQL commands INSERT, UPDATE, MODIFY, and DELETE) to tables either completely and successfully, or not at all. Thus, write accesses are largely automatically bundled in ABAP source code and performed at a time determined by the programmer, namely when the COMMIT WORK command is called, or they are discarded when the ROLLBACK WORK command is called. If the user doesn't call these commands and there was no runtime error, the COMMIT WORK command is automatically called at the end of a program or dialog step (see Chapter 5, Screen Input and Output). The rest of the application examples are based on the framework of this automatic mechanism.

Exercise 4.2

Create the program ZPTB00_HOTEL_RESERVATION and use the parameter declarations from the program ZPTB00_RESERVATION_CHECKER. Remove the OBLIGATORY clause from all the parameters. In addition to the parameter p_name to request the customer's name, add three radio buttons that the user can use to decide whether to insert, delete, or display reservations.

Before inserting a reservation, check whether the room is still unused.

To identify a reservation to be deleted, take the input data from the parameters.

Always show all reservations on the screen.

Let's take a practical look at the definition of tables and access using Open SQL commands.

First, the domains and data elements must be created; you need them to create the table. The exact procedure is described in Section 4.1, Field Properties—DATA ELEMENT, DOMAIN, so this description here is limited to the changes, based on which you can perform the steps needed yourself. In Table 4.2, for better orientation, the specifications for the data element and domain ZPTB00_ROOM_NUMBER from Section 4.1 are shown. Create all the other domains and data elements analogously.

Creating the domain and data elements

Data Element or Domain	Dictionary Type	Short Label	Long Label
ZPTB00_Reservation_ID	char 32	ID	Reservation ID
(ZPTB00_Room_Number)	numc 3	Room No.	Hotel room number
ZPTB00_Checkin	dats 8	Check in	Check in
ZPTB00_Checkout	dats 8	Check out	Check out
ZPTB00_Customer_Name	char 40	Name	Customer name

Table 4.2 Data Elements and Domains from the Example

After you have created and activated all the domains and data elements named, you can start creating the table.

Creating the table

▷ In the context menu of the package or development class, select the Create • DDIC Object • Database Table menu option.

A dialog box subsequently opens, prompting you to enter the name of the database table that you want to create.

▷ Enter "ZPTB00_HRESERVAT" as the table name and confirm your entry with the OK button.

In the tool area, a window is displayed where you can maintain all properties of the table.

▷ Enter "Hotel reservations" as the brief description, and "A" as the delivery class (see Figure 4.20).

▷ Switch to the FIELDS tab.

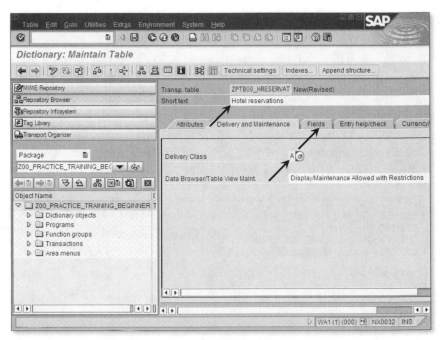

Figure 4.20 Entering Table Properties for ZPTB00_HReservat

Specify the names of all fields here that are supposed to appear as columns in the table.

▷ Enter the fields CLIENT, ID, ROOM_NUMBER, CHECKIN, CHECKOUT, and CUSTOMER_NAME, along with the corresponding data elements. For the CLIENT field, select the predefined data element MANDT.

▷ Check the KEY checkbox for the fields CLIENT and ID, and click the TECHNICAL SETTINGS button. You have now defined the table's primary key (see Figure 4.21).

A dialog box opens, prompting you to confirm whether you want to save the table.

▷ Click YES to confirm the prompt.

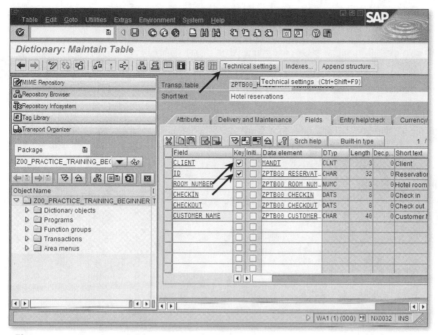

Figure 4.21 Entering Field Properties for ZPTB00 HReservat

You're now asked for the package to which you want to assign the database table.

▷ The package is already preset, so you can simply confirm your entries by clicking the SAVE button.

Next, you're asked for the transport request for the table.

▷ Accept the existing transport request without changing it, and confirm with the YES button.

The usual transport dialog follows.

▷ Accept the existing transport request without changing it and confirm with the CONTINUE button.

The technical settings must be specified before you activate the table and contain information about the data class and size category in particular.

▷ Enter "APPL1" as the data class because this is data that is changed frequently.

▷ Select "0" as the size category (this corresponds to 0 – 3,200 records) because you can hardly expect more than a few hundred reservations at such a small hotel (see Figure 4.22).

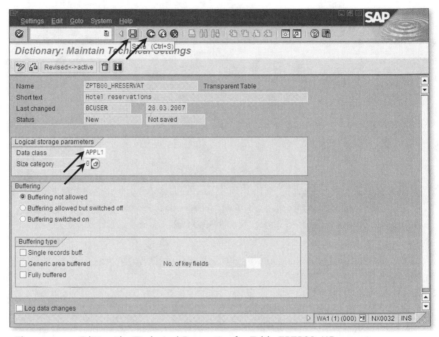

Figure 4.22 Editing the Technical Properties for Table ZPTB00_HReservat

▷ Click the SAVE button and then on BACK.

All the necessary properties for table ZPTB00_HRESERVAT have now been set up, and you can activate it.

▷ Click the BACK button, and then click ACTIVATE.

Creating a program After these preparations, you can begin writing the program.

▷ Create a program called "ZPTB00_HOTEL_RESERVATION" in the usual way, without a TOP include. The title should be "Hotel reservation" and the rest of the program properties can stay unchanged. The transport request is also accepted as preset.

The SAP Object Navigator creates a skeleton program, which you can now fill out in order to take the inputs HOTEL ROOM NUMBER, CHECK-IN, CHECK-OUT, and CUSTOMER NAME, together with the actions ADD, DELETE, and SHOW, to build a little database application.

▷ Type the following code under the comment lines, and save it.

```
REPORT   zptb00_hotel_reservation.
PARAMETERS:
* Reservation data
  p_room TYPE zptb00_room_number VALUE CHECK,
  p_chkin TYPE zptb00_checkin,
  p_chkout TYPE zptb00_checkout,
  p_name TYPE zptb00_customer_name,
* Application menu
  p_add TYPE c RADIOBUTTON GROUP grp1 DEFAULT 'X',
  p_delete TYPE c RADIOBUTTON GROUP grp1,
  p_show TYPE c RADIOBUTTON GROUP grp1.
DATA:
* For working with table zptb00_hreservat
  l_str_reservation TYPE zptb00_hreservat,
  l_tab_reservation TYPE STANDARD TABLE OF
      zptb00_hreservat.

IF p_add = 'X'.
* Check whether period is free
  SELECT * FROM zptb00_hreservat INTO TABLE
      l_tab_reservation
  WHERE ( room_number = p_room )
    AND ( ( checkin BETWEEN p_chkin and p_chkout )
    OR ( checkout BETWEEN p_chkin AND p_chkout ) ).
  IF sy-dbcnt > 0.
    WRITE: / 'Period already reserved'.
  ELSE.
* Make reservation
    CALL FUNCTION 'GUID_CREATE'
      IMPORTING
*       EV_GUID_16       =
*       EV_GUID_22       =
        ev_guid_32       = l_str_reservation-id.
    l_str_reservation-room_number = p_room.
    l_str_reservation-checkin = p_chkin.
```

237

```
            l_str_reservation-checkout = p_chkout.
            l_str_reservation-customer_name = p_name.
            INSERT zptb00_hreservat FROM l_str_reservation.
            WRITE: / 'Reservation made'.
          ENDIF.
        ELSEIF p_delete = 'X'.
        * Delete reservation
          DELETE FROM zptb00_hreservat WHERE room_number =
                p_room
          AND checkin = p_chkin AND checkout = p_chkout.
          WRITE: / 'Reservation deleted'.
        ELSEIF p_show = 'X'.
        * Show reservations
          SELECT * FROM zptb00_hreservat INTO TABLE
                l_tab_reservation
          ORDER BY room_number checkin customer_name.
          WRITE: / 'Room Reservations'.
          LOOP AT l_tab_reservation INTO l_str_reservation.
            WRITE: / 'Room:', l_str_reservation-room_number,
                     'Check in:', l_str_reservation-checkin,
                     'Check out:', l_str_reservation-checkout,
                     'Customer name:', l_str_reservation-
                                       customer_name.
          ENDLOOP.
        ENDIF.
```

Listing 4.2 Source Code for the Program ZPTB00_Hotel_Reservation

Explanation of the source code

The parameters read the information needed to insert or delete records and are only used for the display of reservations. You define the three parameters for the radio buttons in a shared group grp1, so that only one radio button can be selected at any time. The two variables with the structure and the internal table for ZPTB00_HRESERVAT are needed to insert using the INSERT command or to read the data using the SELECT command.

Depending on the content of the radio buttons, use an IF statement to branch to different code segments. First, the insertion of a reservation is processed. For this, as required in the exercise, any possible overlap with other reservations must be ruled out, for which we use a corresponding SELECT statement. Only if no record with overlapping check-in/

check-out dates is found (`sy-dbcnt` is 0) does the insertion of the new reservation take place.

Deletion of a reservation, as a "sanity check," requires at least the specification of the room number and the check-in and check-out dates. Only then can the database be uniquely determined and deleted using the `DELETE` statement.

To display all reservations, they must first be read from the database into an internal table using the `SELECT` command. We use a `LOOP` to copy each record into the `l_str_hreservat` structure, where a `WRITE` command is used to write the content to the screen.

Now you need to test the functional efficiency of your source code in the running program.

Testing the program

▷ Click the CHECK button, then ACTIVATE, and finally the DIRECT button to start the program immediately.

The program starts and asks for the action to be performed. First, you are supposed to insert a record.

▷ Enter "201" as the room number, 1.01.2014 for the check-in date, 1.02.2014 for the check-out date, and "John Smith" as the customer name.

▷ Select the `p_add` parameter and click EXECUTE.

Figure 4.23 Performing a Reservation

The result screen appears, where the reservation is confirmed (see Figure 4.24).

Figure 4.24 Confirming the Reservation

▷ Click the BACK button.

Now check whether duplicates can be detected.

▷ Enter "201" as the room number, 1.31.2014 for the check-in date, 2.11.2014 for the check-out date, and "Roman Herzog" as the customer name.

▷ Select the p_add parameter and click EXECUTE.

The program determines the overlap and prints a corresponding message to the screen (see Figure 4.25).

▷ Click the BACK button.

Figure 4.25 Rejection Notice for the Reservation

To find out more about the overlap, you can have the system display the reservations.

▷ Click the parameter p_show.

The program shows the reservations on the screen (see Figure 4.26).

▷ Click the BACK button.

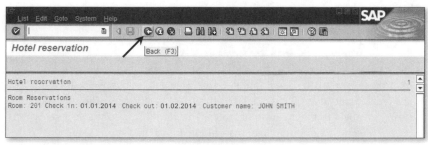

Figure 4.26 All Reservations Are Listed

You now know that you first need to delete this reservation.

▷ Enter "201" as the room number, 1.01.2014 for the check-in date, and 1.02.2014 for the check-out date (see Figure 4.27).

▷ Select the p_delete parameter and click EXECUTE.

Figure 4.27 Deleting the Reservation

You receive a confirmation of the deletion in the form of a message on the screen (see Figure 4.28).

Figure 4.28 Deletion Confirmation for the Reservation

This example program could be tested much more thoroughly. However, this testing is not within the scope of this book.

> **Tip**
>
> In professional ABAP development, not only tables but all possible types are created and managed globally in the ABAP Dictionary. The procedure is nearly identical to the creation of tables. This form is especially popular when used for very generic applications—applications that may determine only which data they must process and store during customization for a particular customer—because it means that the customer can have a direct influence on content

To control the screen input and output, SAP provides several technologies that differ from each other in terms of their complexity and capabilities.

5 Screen Input and Output

"Two hearts, alas, reside within my breast," announces the protagonist in Goethe's masterpiece *Faust*. This quotation could also be used to describe ABAP programmers, who, faced with two completely different processes for creating program interfaces, are torn because of the advantages and disadvantages inherent in both processes. You have a very simple input and output process to be programmed, based on the PARAMETERS command (see Section 3.2, Data and Data Types—DATA, PARAMETERS, CONSTANTS, FIELD SYMBOLS, TYPE, CREATE, Text Elements) with its "related commands" (in particular the SELECT OPTIONS command) and support from the SAP List Viewer control—a technology that nevertheless quickly reaches its limits when more complex screen layouts are involved. Alternatively, you also have a screen technology that is quite complicated to program and is used to create sophisticated screen layouts. This technology challenges even experienced programmers of other development systems, such as Delphi or Visual Basic, due to the transfer of data between interface and program. It also doesn't help that both processes are ultimately based on the same fundamental technology and can actually be used in mixed operating mode. In particular, dynamically creating or adapting interface elements (for instance, providing a new input field as a reaction to a user entry, which is child's play with Visual Basic or C#) are not the strengths of the technology. However, the transformation of ABAP to an all-purpose programming language that can also be used to write Web, portal, and mobile business applications means that requirements change (see Figure 5.1).

Basics

Figure 5.1 Typical Interfaces of Each Interface Technology

Since 2007, SAP has therefore provided the *Web Dynpro* technology for interfaces with special requirements. Only state-of-the-art Internet standards such as XML, HTML and Web services are used in the Web Dynpro. These standards ensure that the program interfaces can be used purely through Web browsers, ranging from cell phones to PDAs to PCs and mainframe computers, for providing extensive compatibility with existing dynpro technology. The replacement of existing dynpro interfaces is planned only for individual cases.

Tips for those familiar with other programming languages

Use the simple input and output process based on the PARAMETERS command with the SAP List Viewer wherever you can and are allowed to because the resulting interface design is not all that unusual for SAP users and everyone can grasp it quickly. You will subsequently be able to carry out a tool-supported conversion into Web Dynpro largely without any problems. You should use the dynpro technology only if you want to create complex input layouts with master/detail views, editable table contents or graphics, or you have to redesign existing SAP user interfaces in the dynpro technology. A subsequent conversion into Web Dynpro can only be partially implemented automatically.

5.1 Simple Input and Output Interfaces— SELECTION SCREEN, SELECT-OPTIONS, CALL SELECTION SCREEN, SAP List Viewer

The ABAP programming language has a number of very simple methods for designing input and output interfaces that convey the typical look and feel of known SAP applications. Because they cover a significant proportion of the requirements for the user interfaces of business applications in this way, these methods support both beginners and experienced programmers through a steep learning curve.

Simple input and output interfaces are used frequently in SAP applications: Customizing interfaces, reports for evaluating and displaying data, and many back-office applications without specific requirements for the user interface use this type of interface creation and form the foundation for the uniform appearance of screens in SAP applications (see Figure 5.2).

Figure 5.2 Examples of Input and Output Interfaces

From a technical perspective, this involves using a range of language elements for the input and some function modules for the output.

Simple input interfaces are based on the PARAMETERS command, which were introduced in Section 3.2, Data and Data Types—DATA, PARAMETERS, CONSTANTS, FIELD SYMBOLS, TYPE, CREATE, Text Elements. They are enhanced by a number of additional commands (for instance, the SELECT OPTIONS command) and events for structuring and checking the input data, the most important of which are discussed in the following:

▸ SELECTION-SCREEN—**Defining selection screens**
The SELECTION-SCREEN ABAP keyword begins the definition of a simple user interface for inputting and outputting values and tables and also finally ends it again. The syntax for the beginning of the definition for a selection screen is

```
BEGIN OF SCREEN screennumber.
```

screennumber in this case must be a four-digit number that must also be restored when the definition is ended with the syntax SELECTION-SCREEN END OF screennumber. As an option, a title description can also be provided using the TITLE addition. Another interesting feature is that you can use the SELECTION-SCREEN COMMENT /col1(len1) comment command to output texts in the selection screen, the SELECTION-SCREEN ULINE command to output a horizontal line, and the SELECTION-SCREEN PUSHBUTTON pushbutton command to output a pushbutton. In addition, you can use the SELECTION-SCREEN BEGIN OF BLOCK block or SELECTION-SCREEN END OF BLOCK block statements to create blocks for thematically related input and output fields. The following two examples define a selection screen—the first with input elements, the second with output elements—although other combinations are, of course, also allowed:

```
* data input dialog
SELECTION-SCREEN BEGIN OF SCREEN 110.
PARAMETERS:
  p_name(80) TYPE c,
  p_addr(80) TYPE c.
SELECTION SCREEN END OF SCREEN 110.
* data output dialog
SELECTION-SCREEN BEGIN OF SCREEN 120.
```

```
SELECTION-SCREEN BEGIN OF BLOCK b120 WITH FRAME
TITLE
text-001.
  SELECTION-SCREEN COMMENT /5(79) c_name.
  SELECTION-SCREEN COMMENT /5(79) c_addr.
 SELECTION-SCREEN END OF BLOCK b120.
SELECTION-SCREEN END OF SCREEN 120.
```

▶ **SELECT-OPTIONS — Defining selection criteria**

Selection criteria are comparable to parameters; however, they automatically provide two input fields and an additional button and dialog box that you can use to specify value ranges and lists of single values as well as exclusions of single values or value ranges. In this context, these are also referred to as *ranges*, and they enable inputs such as from "A" to "E" or also "G," "H" to "M" and not "I," for example, all of which is very practical for selecting data records. The syntax of the command is as follows:

```
SELECT-OPTIONS name FOR data.
```

name here is the maximum eight-digit name of the selection criterion and data is an already declared data field (for instance, a variable or constant), from which the selection criterion copies the data type. The ABAP runtime environment uses this information to automatically create a table invisible to the programmer that has a structure similar to the following and assigns it as the data type for the name field:

```
DATA:
  g_field TYPE i.
TYPES:
BEGIN OF str_seltab,
  sign TYPE c,       " I(nclude), E(xclude)
  option(2) TYPE c, " =, EQ, <>, NE, <, LT, >, GT, <=,
                     " LE, >=, GE, BT, NB, CP, NP
  low LIKE g_field,  " data type like the field
  high LIKE g_field, " only used for BT, NB, CP, NP
END OF str_seltab.
TYPES:
  tab_seltab TYPE STANDARD TABLE OF str_seltab.
```

247

Section 3.5, Branches and Logical Expressions—IF, CASE, contains a detailed description of all comparison operations that the user can input as `option`. Selection criteria are particularly ideal for restricting the database queries controlled by the user. Especially for this purpose, the `SELECT` command (see Section 4.2, Defining and Processing Database Tables—SELECT, INSERT, UPDATE, DELETE) has the optional addition `IN` enables the selection criteria to be used directly when data is imported from a database table. The following example demonstrates this type of scenario and reads the corresponding values from the `SFLIGHT` table using the selection criteria defined by the user for the `CARRID` column:

```
DATA:
  g_carrid TYPE s_carr_id.
SELECT-OPTIONS:
  o_carrid FOR g_carrid. " o_carrid is a table now!
DATA:
  l_tab_sflight TYPE STANDARD TABLE OF sflight.
SELECT * FROM sflight INTO TABLE l_tab_sflight WHERE
carrid IN o_carrid.
```

▶ **PARAMETERS—Defining input/output parameters**
Section 3.2 provides an initial description of the `PARAMETERS` command. If you don't use the `SELECTION-SCREEN` command to introduce `PARAMETERS` declarations, the standard selection screen is used, which is created automatically for each program. Otherwise, the parameter is assigned to the explicitly defined `SELECTION-SCREEN` and is consequently displayed only when you call `SELECTION-SCREEN` using the `CALL SELECTION-SCREEN screennumber` command. The following example declares the `p_name` parameter as part of the standard selection screen, while the `p_addr` parameter is part of selection screen 110.

```
* default selection screen
PARAMETERS:
  p_name(80) TYPE c.
* data input dialog
SELECTION-SCREEN BEGIN OF SCREEN 110.
PARAMETERS:
  p_addr(80) TYPE c.
SELECTION-SCREEN END OF SCREEN 110.
```

▶ `CALL SELECTION-SCREEN [STARTING AT]`—**Displaying a selection screen**
The `CALL SELECTION SCREEN` command calls a selection screen that is defined in the main program or in an integrated include. The syntax of the command is as follows:

```
CALL SELECTION-SCREEN screennumber
```

The command displays the called selection screen in the main window by default. You can also use the `STARTING AT col1 line1` addition to force the screen to be displayed in a separate window, wherein the columns and line specification in `col1` and `line1` can be considered an approximate cursor position and the window size is automatically designed in such a way that as many of the input and output fields as possible are displayed. You can use the `ENDING AT col2 line2` addition to also explicitly specify the size of the window. With a content of 0, the return value in `sy-subrc` signals that the user has subsequently exited the selection screen using the EXECUTE or EXECUTE AND PRINT button. If the content is 4, however, the user exited the selection screen by selecting BACK, EXIT, or CANCEL. The following examples demonstrate how the statement is used to call a selection screen in the same window and in a separate dialog box as of column 5 and line 6:

```
CALL SELECTION-SCREEN 100.
CALL SELECTION-SCREEN 110 STARTING AT 5 6.
```

These simple basic elements enable you to create already impressive user interfaces. Restrictions worth mentioning include the missing option to define your own menu bars and toolbars, and missing tabular input and output fields.

Another interesting feature of the ABAP language is that, with the `MESSAGE` command, ABAP has built-in support for outputting all types of messages on the screen. The call is quite simple because the minimum that is required is merely one text and one classification (error, warning, information, etc.). The following two variants of the `MESSAGE` command are particularly popular:

Outputting messages on the screen

▶ `MESSAGE msg TYPE mtyp`—**Outputting specified text**
This form of `MESSAGE` command is interesting for simple test programs that are not to be translated. The `msg` placeholder in this case is replaced by a string constant and the type of message is replaced by a character constant. The following message types are provided:

- ▶ A (Abort): Termination message
- ▶ E (Error): Error message
- ▶ I (Information): Information message
- ▶ S (Status): Status message
- ▶ W (Warning): Warning message
- ▶ X (Exit): Termination message with a short dump

The program environment determines whether the message is output in the form of a dialog box or whether it is output in the status bar. For more information, refer to the online help. The following example shows the output of a status message:

```
MESSAGE 'Reservation successfully finished' TYPE 'S'.
```

▶ `MESSAGE mtype/mnum (mclass)`—**Copying and outputting text from the message class**
In professional ABAP programming, you use *message classes* where the message texts for a certain topic are stored under a unique number, similar to the text elements. They are consequently transferred to the worklist for translators and are automatically *retrieved*, depending on the current user language. As an option, a maximum of four placeholders are provided in the text by `&1`, `&2`, `&3`, and `&4`, which can be specified when a call is made using the `WITH` addition. As another option, you can divert the output of the message from the screen to a string variable if, for example, all messages are collected and are to be subsequently written into a file or database table as a log. Each message class is identified by a unique `mclass` name and the message itself is still only specified by a three-digit `mnum` number and the preceding message type. The following examples demonstrate the output of the message text with the number 002 from message class ZPTB00_ MESSAGES as an error message, the output of message 003 as a status message where a placeholder is replaced by the contents of a variable,

and the output of a message in a string variable instead of on the screen.

```
* 001 = 'Period is already reservated'
MESSAGE E002(ZPTB00_MESSAGES).
* 003 = '&1 reservations were deleted'
l_count = 2.
MESSAGE S003(ZPTB00_MESSAGES) with l_count.
* 002 = 'Reservation successfully finished'
MESSAGE E002(ZPTB00_MESSAGES) into l_string.
```

The latter variant of the MESSAGE command is extremely useful for ABAP programs because it enables messages to be assigned uniquely to source code positions if each message in the program is only used once (for instance, a message about whether a consistency check has been successful or unsuccessful). If a user contacts support with an output error message, the number and message class of the message can be used to determine the relevant package and therefore the developer group responsible. A where-used list (context menu on the corresponding message) can also be used to find all source code positions automatically where the message is output. Support can now display the relevant parts of the program and determine whether the error message is legitimate or whether it is a programming error.

Tabular inputs and outputs, SAP List Viewer

At the end of 1998, the *EnjoySAP initiative* introduced a number of new interface elements that rapidly multiplied the range of design options. This was because Windows could consist of other panes for the first time, a table display similar to Excel was available, hierarchical structure displays in modern layouts could be displayed, and editors such as graphics that could be manipulated were provided.

One of these interface elements, the table display similar to Excel (called *SAP List Viewer*, ALV for short, based internally on the *ALV Grid Display*), can also be used within simple input and output interfaces and enjoys great popularity there (see Figure 5.3). In this regard, the inwardly complex object-oriented component was packed into a function that was easy to call and it was enhanced with additional functions. Since then, the following call options are available within the CALL FUNCTION statement for each ABAP programmer to use in his own programs:

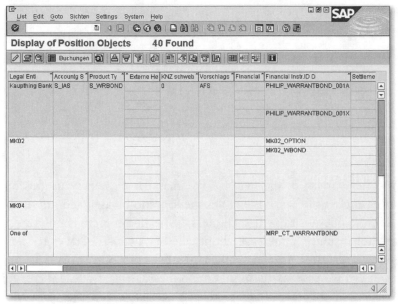

Figure 5.3 SAP List Viewer, Called Using REUSE_ALV_GRID_DISPLAY

▶ **REUSE_ALV_GRID_DISPLAY**—Displaying and editing internal tables

The REUSE_ALV_GRID_DISPLAY function has an abundance of optional interface parameters that you can use to adapt the functions provided to meet your requirements. For example, you can show and hide individual functions such as SORT or FILTER from the toolbar, specify a title, influence the way the table is displayed, and receive relevant information through user actions such as mouse clicks. You can even insert your own buttons in the toolbar, even if this means that you must exceed the limit for programming a screen (see Section 5.2, Complex Input and Output Interfaces—Dynpros) a little. The following example demonstrates the SAP List Viewer call with the interface parameters that must at least be transferred, specifically the name of the structure for the internal table `sflight` and the internal table itself using `l_tab_sflight`:

```
* Contains ALV-Grid structures, needed for variables
TYPE-POOLS slis.
* Define internal table
 DATA:
```

```
  l_tab_sflight TYPE TABLE OF sflight.
* Read data from database table into internal table
SELECT * FROM sflight INTO TABLE l_tab_sflight.
* Display data with SAP List Viewer
CALL FUNCTION 'REUSE_ALV_GRID_DISPLAY'
   EXPORTING
     i_structure_name = 'SFLIGHT'
   TABLES
     t_outtab          = l_tab_sflight
   EXCEPTIONS
     program_error                  = 1
     OTHERS                         = 2.
```

► **REUSE_ALV_GRID_LAYOUT_INFO_GET — Reading the current ALV configuration information**

You should call this function only when editing a user interaction such as the reaction on the double-click event. In this case, this function returns all current settings in the state in which the user is using them. This information can help you in evaluating and editing user events. The current layout and field catalog, sorting information, and filter conditions and information about the current scroll status of the display are returned. The following example demonstrates the reading for the layout and column settings specifically, although all information can of course also be read:

```
  CALL FUNCTION 'REUSE_ALV_GRID_LAYOUT_INFO_GET'
     IMPORTING
        es_layout            = l_str_layout
        et_fieldcat          = l_tab_fieldcat
*        ET_SORT              =
*        ET_FILTER            =
*        ES_GRID_SCROLL       =
*        ES_VARIANT           =
*        ET_MARKED_COLUMNS    =
*        ET_FILTERED_ENTRIES  =
     EXCEPTIONS
        no_infos             = 1
        program_error        = 2
        others               = 3.
```

▶ **REUSE_ALV_GRID_LAYOUT_INFO_SET** — Setting the current ALV list information

Like the _GET function mentioned above, you should use this function only when editing user interactions. A typical procedure involves your first obtaining the current configuration information using REUSE_ALV_LIST_LAYOUT_INFO_GET, changing the required settings, and then transferring the changed configuration to the SAP List Viewer again using REUSE_ALV_LIST_LAYOUT_INFO_SET. Then the list is output again with the changed settings:

```
CALL FUNCTION 'REUSE_ALV_GRID_LAYOUT_INFO_SET'
  EXPORTING
    is_layout          = l_str_layout
    it_fieldcat        = l_tab_fieldcat
*   IT_SORT            =
*   IT_FILTER          =
*   IS_GRID_SCROLL     =
*   IS_PRINT           =
```

Let's now look at how you can use simple input and output interfaces.

Exercise 5.1

Create the ZPTB00_HOTEL_RESERVATION_COOL program. Design a new interface for the ZPTB00_HOTEL_RESERVATION program. Create a main screen to select the user action, an input dialog to insert reservations, a list display to show reservations, and an additional list display to select and delete reservations easily.

▷ Create a program called "ZPTB00_HOTEL_RESERVATION_COOL" and without a TOP include. The title should be "Hotel Reservation Cool". The remaining settings and the transport request should stay unchanged.

Copying a GUI status — Before you complete this new program structure, you first need a *GUI status* that you can use to integrate function keys and pushbuttons into the screen. You first copy a GUI status, which is used by the REUSE_ALV_GRID_DISPLAY function, from the SLVC_FULLSCREEN function group. You need to add another button to this toolbar and the original toolbar should (of course) remain untouched.

▷ Select the FUNCTION GROUP object type in the object list area (see Figure 5.4).

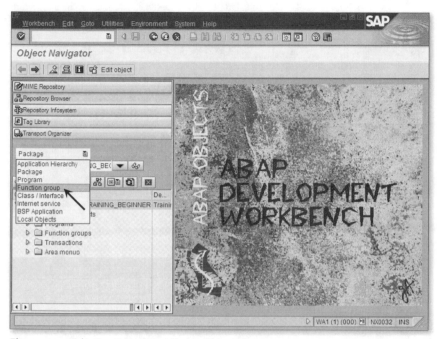

Figure 5.4 Selecting a Function Group Object Type

The function group for the REUSE_ALV_GRID_DISPLAY function is called SLVC_FULLSCREEN and contains the GUI status you require. Now do the following:

▷ Enter "SLVC_FULLSCREEN" as the name of the function group and click the button with the eyeglasses icon.

▷ Expand the GUI STATUS object type in the object list area.

▷ Call the context menu for the STANDARD_FULLSCREEN entry and select the COPY menu option.

A dialog box appears, where you can specify the target program into which you want to copy the GUI status.

▷ Enter "ZPTB00_Hotel_Reservation_Cool" as the target program and click the COPY button.

A confirmation prompt is displayed.

▷ Exit the confirmation prompt by clicking the Copy button (see Figure 5.5).

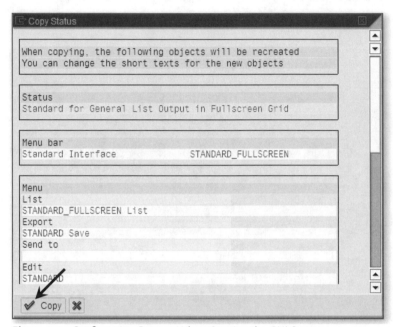

Figure 5.5 Confirmation Prompt When Copying the GUI Status

Adapting the
GUI status

You can now navigate back to the program by doing the following:

▷ Click the Back button of the object list area.

▷ Expand the objects in the ZPTB00_HOTEL_RESERVATION_COOL program and double-click the STANDARD_FULLSCREEN GUI STATUS.

▷ Click the Display <-> Change button.

▷ In the tools area, then click the Application toolbar area by clicking the corresponding green cross.

▷ Select the Insert Entry menu option using the &ETA entry in the context menu (see Figure 5.6).

Figure 5.6 Navigating Back and Selecting the Copied GUI Status

All buttons are now moved one position to the right and there is room for a new entry. You first specify the command that you want to be returned when you select the new buttons.

▷ Enter the "EXECUTE" command and then click the line below it (see Figure 5.7).

You must next specify whether a statically assigned or dynamically assigned text should be made available for the button.

▷ Leave it as the STATIC TEXT default setting and click the CONTINUE button.

Another dialog box is issued, from where you can select the text for the button and the tooltip, and an icon:

▷ Enter "Execute" as the function text.

▷ Enter "ICON_EXECUTE_OBJECT" as the icon or select it using the F4 help.

▷ Enter "Execute delete operation" as the infotext and click the CONTINUE button.

Figure 5.7 Entering the Command to Be Triggered by the Button

The editor automatically notes that you have not yet assigned a function key and provides the corresponding dialog box for this purpose.

▷ Select [Shift] + [F8] as the function key and click the CONTINUE button (see Figure 5.8).

A dialog box opens, displaying a line where you can specify an icon text. The text you specify here is the output in the button next to the icon. Although this means that the button requires considerably more space, it also immediately attracts more attention.

▷ Enter "Execute" as the icon text and click the CONTINUE button again.

The icon for the new button is now displayed in the tools area along with the command and an excerpt of the text.

▷ Click the SAVE button, then click CHECK, and lastly click ACTIVATE (see Figure 5.9).

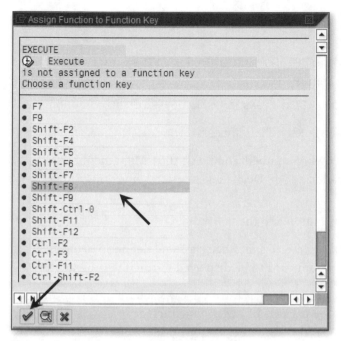

Figure 5.8 Assigning a Function Key to the Button

Figure 5.9 Enhanced GUI Status of ZPTB00_HOTEL_RESERVATION_COOL Program

A couple of significant texts that you can use to structure the selection screens are still missing:

▷ Double-click the ZPTB00_HOTEL_RESERVATION_COOL program to return to the source code.

▷ Select the GOTO • TEXT ELEMENTS • TEXT SYMBOLS menu option.

The editor for the text symbols appears.

▷ Enter the following numbers and texts: "001 Main menu", "002 Insert reservation", "003 Delete reservations", and "004 Show reservations".

▷ Click the SAVE button and then click BACK.

In the next step, you create a message class and define some messages in this class that are supposed to be displayed during the program flow.

▷ Select the CREATE • OTHERS • MESSAGE CLASS menu option in the context menu of the package or development class.

A dialog box opens, requesting the name of the message class.

▷ Enter "ZPTB00_MESSAGES" as the name of the message class and confirm your entries by clicking the OK button.

In the tools area, a window is displayed where you can maintain other properties of the message class and also define individual messages in the MESSAGES tab.

▷ Select the MESSAGES tab (see Figure 5.10).

The usual prompt for the transport request appears:

▷ The number of the transport request used previously is set by default. Simply confirm it with the OK button.

The active tab then switches to MESSAGES and you can enter the required messages.

▷ Enter the following message texts:

  ▷ Message 000: "Period already reserved"

  ▷ Message 001: "Reservation was made"

  ▷ Message 002: "&1 Reservation(s) deleted"

Figure 5.10 Properties of the ZPTB00_MESSAGES Message Class

▷ Click the SAVE button and then click BACK to return to the source code (see Figure 5.11).

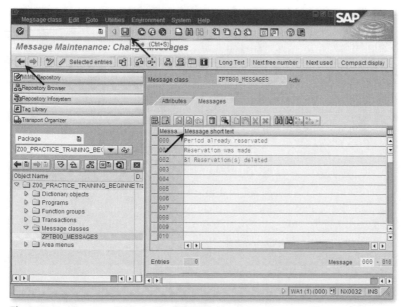

Figure 5.11 Creating Texts in the ZPTB00_Messages Message Class

The only thing still missing now is the source code. This is where you define the two selection screens for the main menu and the input of an additional reservation. In the source code, you also implement the two ALV grids for displaying reservations and selecting reservations for deletion.

▷ Type the following (admittedly not very short) source code:

```
REPORT  zptb00_hotel_reservation_cool.
* Contains ALV-Grid structures, needed for variables
TYPE-POOLS slis .
* Main menu as selection screen
SELECTION-SCREEN BEGIN OF SCREEN 110.
SELECTION-SCREEN BEGIN OF BLOCK b110 WITH FRAME TITLE text-
001.
PARAMETERS:
  p_add TYPE c RADIOBUTTON GROUP grp1 DEFAULT 'X',
  p_delete TYPE c RADIOBUTTON GROUP grp1,
  p_show TYPE c RADIOBUTTON GROUP grp1.
SELECTION-SCREEN END OF BLOCK b110.
SELECTION-SCREEN END OF SCREEN 110.


* Input new reservation as selection screen
SELECTION-SCREEN BEGIN OF SCREEN 120.
SELECTION-SCREEN BEGIN OF BLOCK b120 WITH FRAME TITLE text-
002.
PARAMETERS:
  p_room TYPE zptb00_room_number VALUE CHECK,
  p_chkin TYPE zptb00_checkin,
  p_chkout TYPE zptb00_checkout,
  p_name TYPE zptb00_customer_name.
SELECTION-SCREEN END OF BLOCK b120.
SELECTION-SCREEN END OF SCREEN 120.

* Main program
DO.
  CALL SELECTION-SCREEN 110.
  IF sy-subrc <> 0.
    EXIT.
  ELSEIF p_add = 'X'.
    PERFORM zptb00_hrc_add.
  ELSEIF p_delete = 'X'.
```

```
      PERFORM zptb00_hrc_delete.
    ELSEIF p_show = 'X'.
      PERFORM zptb00_hrc_show.
    ENDIF.
ENDDO.


*--------------------------------------------------------*
*  FORM zptb00_hrc_add
*--------------------------------------------------------*
* Shows an input dialog and adds a new reservation to
* the database table
*--------------------------------------------------------*
FORM zptb00_hrc_add.
  DATA:
* For working with table zptb00_hreservat
      l_str_reservation TYPE zptb00_hreservat,
      l_tab_reservation TYPE STANDARD TABLE OF
      zptb00_hreservat.

* Call input dialog
  CALL SELECTION-SCREEN 120 STARTING AT 5 5.
  IF sy-subrc = 0.
* Check if period is free
      SELECT * FROM zptb00_hreservat INTO TABLE
      l_tab_reservation
      WHERE ( room_number = p_room )
        AND ( ( checkin BETWEEN p_chkin and p_chkout )
        OR ( checkout BETWEEN p_chkin AND p_chkout ) ).
      IF sy-dbcnt > 0.
        MESSAGE S000(ZPTB00_MESSAGES).
      ELSE.
* Make reservation
        CALL FUNCTION 'GUID_CREATE'
          IMPORTING
*           EV_GUID_16      =
*           EV_GUID_22      =
            ev_guid_32      = l_str_reservation-id.
        l_str_reservation-room_number = p_room.
        l_str_reservation-checkin = p_chkin.
        l_str_reservation-checkout = p_chkout.
        l_str_reservation-customer_name = p_name.
        INSERT zptb00_hreservat FROM l_str_reservation.
```

```
      MESSAGE S001(ZPTB00_MESSAGES).
    ENDIF.
  ENDIF.
ENDFORM.                        "zptb00_hrc_add


*-------------------------------------------------------*
*   FORM zptb00_hrc_delete
*-------------------------------------------------------*
* Shows a list of all reservations, where the user can
* pick some and then press the delete button to delete
* the lines out of the database table
*-------------------------------------------------------*
FORM zptb00_hrc_delete.
  TYPES:
* builds a structure named t_str_reservationx,
* containing of the fields MARK, CLIENT, ID,
* ROOM_NUMBER, CHECKIN, CHECKOUT, CUSTOMER_NAME
* Needed for ALV-Grid-Display
    BEGIN OF t_mark,
      mark TYPE c,
    END OF t_mark,
    BEGIN OF t_str_reservationx.
         INCLUDE STRUCTURE zptb00_hreservat.
  INCLUDE TYPE t_mark.
  TYPES:
    END OF t_str_reservationx.
  DATA:
* for ALV-Grid-Display
    l_dis TYPE disvariant,
    l_str_layout TYPE slis_layout_alv,
    l_str_exit_by_user TYPE slis_exit_by_user,
    l_tab_reservationx TYPE STANDARD TABLE OF
      t_str_reservationx,
    l_str_reservationx TYPE t_str_reservationx,
* For working with table zptb00_hreservat
    l_tab_reservation TYPE STANDARD TABLE OF
    zptb00_hreservat,
    l_count TYPE i.
  FIELD-SYMBOLS:
* For working with table zptb00_hreservat
    <l_str_reservation> TYPE zptb00_hreservat,
    <l_str_reservationx> TYPE t_str_reservationx.
```

```
* Load content of reservation table into memory table
* with additional field MARK
  SELECT * FROM zptb00_hreservat INTO TABLE
  l_tab_reservation.
  LOOP AT l_tab_reservation ASSIGNING
  <l_str_reservation>.
    MOVE-CORRESPONDING <l_str_reservation> TO
      l_str_reservationx.
    APPEND l_str_reservationx TO l_tab_reservationx.
  ENDLOOP.
* Make column width as small as possible
  l_str_layout-colwidth_optimize = 'X'.
* This text should be displayed as the window title
  l_str_layout-window_titlebar = text-003.
* This is the name of the field in the table, which
* ALV-Grid can use to store, whether the user has
* marked it or not
  l_str_layout-box_fieldname = 'MARK'.
* Give the name of our report, so that the user can
* save individual configurations of the ALV-Grid-
* Display
  l_dis-report = sy-repid.

* Call the ALV-Grid-Display function
  CALL FUNCTION 'REUSE_ALV_GRID_DISPLAY'
    EXPORTING
*     I_INTERFACE_CHECK                = ' '
*     I_BYPASSING_BUFFER               = ' '
*     I_BUFFER_ACTIVE                  = ' '
      I_CALLBACK_PROGRAM               = l_dis-report
      I_CALLBACK_PF_STATUS_SET         =
                        'CB_ALV_PF_SET_STATUS'
      I_CALLBACK_USER_COMMAND          =
                        'CB_ALV_USER_COMMAND'
*     I_CALLBACK_TOP_OF_PAGE           = ' '
*     I_CALLBACK_HTML_TOP_OF_PAGE      = ' '
*     I_CALLBACK_HTML_END_OF_LIST      = ' '
      i_structure_name                 =
                        'ZPTB00_HRESERVAT'
*     I_BACKGROUND_ID                  = ' '
*     I_GRID_TITLE                     =
```

265

```
*        I_GRID_SETTINGS                  =
         is_layout                        = l_str_layout
*        IT_FIELDCAT                      =
*        IT_EXCLUDING                     =
*        IT_SPECIAL_GROUPS                =
*        IT_SORT                          =
*        IT_FILTER                        =
*        IS_SEL_HIDE                      =
*        I_DEFAULT                        = 'X'
         i_save                           = 'A'
         is_variant                       = l_dis
*        IT_EVENTS                        =
*        IT_EVENT_EXIT                    =
*        IS_PRINT                         =
*        IS_REPREP_ID                     =
*        I_SCREEN_START_COLUMN            = 0
*        I_SCREEN_START_LINE              = 0
*        I_SCREEN_END_COLUMN              = 0
*        I_SCREEN_END_LINE                = 0
*        IT_ALV_GRAPHICS                  =
*        IT_HYPERLINK                     =
*        IT_ADD_FIELDCAT                  =
     IMPORTING
*        E_EXIT_CAUSED_BY_CALLER          =
         es_exit_caused_by_user           =
                          l_str_exit_by_user
     TABLES
       t_outtab                           =
                          l_tab_reservationx
     EXCEPTIONS
       program_error                      = 1
       OTHERS                             = 2.
   IF sy-subrc <> 0.
* Error? -> Show to the user what happened
     MESSAGE ID SY-MSGID TYPE SY-MSGTY NUMBER SY-MSGNO
             WITH SY-MSGV1 SY-MSGV2 SY-MSGV3 SY-MSGV4.
   ENDIF.

* Leave the whole program, if the user pressed exit
* Leave back to the main screen, if the user pressed
* back or cancel
   CASE 'X'.
```

```
      WHEN l_str_exit_by_user-exit.
        LEAVE PROGRAM.
      WHEN l_str_exit_by_user-back OR l_str_exit_by_user-
          cancel.
        RETURN.
    ENDCASE.

* Otherwise the user must have pressed our delete
* button, so delete all lines in the reservation table,
* which are marked with an 'X'
    l_count = 0.
    LOOP AT l_tab_reservationx ASSIGNING
    <l_str_reservationx>.
      IF <l_str_reservationx>-mark = 'X'.
        DELETE FROM zptb00_hreservat WHERE id =
          <l_str_reservationx>-id.
      ENDIF.
    ENDLOOP.
    MESSAGE s002(zptb00_messages) WITH l_count.
ENDFORM.                       "zptb00_hrc_delete


*--------------------------------------------------------*
*   FORM zptb00_hrc_show
*--------------------------------------------------------*
* Shows a list of all reservations. Much easier than an
* interactive deletion list display.
*--------------------------------------------------------*
FORM zptb00_hrc_show.
  DATA:
* for ALV-Grid-Display
    l_dis TYPE disvariant,
    l_rda_table TYPE REF TO data,
    l_str_layout TYPE slis_layout_alv,
* For working with table zptb00_hreservat
    l_tab_reservation TYPE STANDARD TABLE OF
    zptb00_hreservat.

* Load all data of reservation table into memory table
  SELECT * FROM zptb00_hreservat INTO TABLE
  l_tab_reservation.

* Make column width as small as possible
```

```
        l_str_layout-colwidth_optimize = 'X'.
* This text should be displayed as the window title
        l_str_layout-window_titlebar = text-004.
* Give the name of our report, so that the user can
* save individual configurations of the ALV-Grid-
* Display. You could also provide another text here, if
* you want separate configuration of the show and
* deletion display
        l_dis-report = sy-repid.
* Call the ALV-Grid-Display function
        CALL FUNCTION 'REUSE_ALV_GRID_DISPLAY'
          EXPORTING
*           I_INTERFACE_CHECK               = ' '
*           I_BYPASSING_BUFFER              = ' '
*           I_BUFFER_ACTIVE                 = ' '
*           I_CALLBACK_PROGRAM              = ' '
*           I_CALLBACK_PF_STATUS_SET        = ''
*           I_CALLBACK_USER_COMMAND         = ' '
*           I_CALLBACK_TOP_OF_PAGE          = ' '
*           I_CALLBACK_HTML_TOP_OF_PAGE     = ' '
*           I_CALLBACK_HTML_END_OF_LIST     = ' '
            i_structure_name = 'ZPTB00_HRESERVAT'
*           I_BACKGROUND_ID                 = ' '
*           I_GRID_TITLE                    =
*           I_GRID_SETTINGS                 =
            is_layout                       = l_str_layout
*           IT_FIELDCAT                     =
*           IT_EXCLUDING                    =
*           IT_SPECIAL_GROUPS               =
*           IT_SORT                         =
*           IT_FILTER                       =
*           IS_SEL_HIDE                     =
*           I_DEFAULT                       = 'X'
            i_save                          = 'A'
            is_variant                      = l_dis
*           IT_EVENTS                       =
*           IT_EVENT_EXIT                   =
*           IS_PRINT                        =
*           IS_REPREP_ID                    =
*           I_SCREEN_START_COLUMN           = 0
*           I_SCREEN_START_LINE             = 0
*           I_SCREEN_END_COLUMN             = 0
```

```
*        I_SCREEN_END_LINE                 = 0
*        IT_ALV_GRAPHICS                   =
*        IT_HYPERLINK                      =
*        IT_ADD_FIELDCAT                   =
*     IMPORTING
*        E_EXIT_CAUSED_BY_CALLER           =
*        ES_EXIT_CAUSED_BY_USER            =
      TABLES
         t_outtab                          =
                        l_tab_reservation
      EXCEPTIONS
         program_error                     = 1
         OTHERS                            = 2.
   IF sy-subrc <> 0.
* Error? -> Show to the user what happened
      MESSAGE ID sy-msgid TYPE sy-msgty NUMBER sy-msgno
            WITH sy-msgv1 sy-msgv2 sy-msgv3 sy-msgv4.
   ENDIF.
ENDFORM.                        "zptb00_hrc_show


*&---------------------------------------------------*
*& FORM cb_alv_user_command
*&---------------------------------------------------*
* Is called, whenever the user presses a button. Then
* we check if the delete button was pressed
*----------------------------------------------------*
FORM cb_alv_user_command
  USING
    r_ucomm LIKE sy-ucomm
    rs_selfield TYPE slis_selfield.        "#EC CALLED

* Delete button pressed? -> then force to leave the
* grid display now by switching on the exit button
  IF r_ucomm = 'EXECUTE'.
    rs_selfield-exit = 'X'.
  ENDIF.
ENDFORM. " cb_alv_user_command


*&-------------------------------------- ------------*
*& FORM cb_alv_pf_set_status
*&---------------------------------------------------*
* Sets a new Dialog status, needed because of
```

269

```
* additional execute (F8) functionality.
*-------------------------------------------------------*
FORM cb_alv_pf_set_status
  USING
    rt_extab TYPE slis_t_extab.              "#EC CALLED
* Take our pf-status instead of your own
  SET pf-status 'STANDARD_FULLSCREEN' EXCLUDING
    rt_extab.
ENDFORM. " cb_alv_pf_set_status
```

Listing 5.1 Source Code of the ZPTB00_HOTEL_RESERVATION_COOL Program

Explanation of the source code

The source code begins with the inclusion of the TYPE-POOLS slis. This contains all the required data types that you need to communicate with the ALV grid functions. Similar to using an include file, you can display the contents of slis by double-clicking the name.

The first selection screen contains the main menu of the program. The number 110 is intended for it and, to improve its appearance, you define a block (frame) for which you have specified the text "Main menu." The three parameters p_add, p_delete, and p_show are defined as radio buttons of the grp1 common group, which means that the user can select only one of them at a time.

Save the second selection screen under the number 120. This selection screen is used to receive the input data for a new reservation and is given its own frame and title, as usual. Define p_room, p_chkin, p_chkout, and p_name as parameters, which all refer to separate data elements and therefore, for the most part, automate the check for the input data.

Main loop

The main loop of your program then follows, where you can call the main menu either until sy-subrc doesn't equal 0 (that is, the user has pressed one of the BACK, EXIT, or CANCEL buttons) or until the user has selected one of the parameters and pressed F8. In this case, you execute one of three prepared subroutines that is to copy the additional processing.

The content of the first subroutine zptb00_hrc_add is copied from the previous version of the reservation program (see Section 4.2, Defining and Processing Database Tables—SELECT, INSERT, UPDATE, DELETE). Next a check is carried out to verify whether the selected space is already occupied in the specified period. In this case, a status message is issued on the screen, informing the user of the current situation. Otherwise, the reservation persists on the database and a success message is issued.

The content of the second subroutine `zptb00_hrc_delete` is already more complex there because the ALV grid display must be called in such a way that the user can select one or more of the displayed reservation lines. To do this, you must first define a new structure that comprises all fields of the `zptb00_hreservat` database table and also receives a character field named `Mark`. This field can use the ALV grid display at a later stage to inform the program of the marking status of each individual line. You also need some variables that you can use to transfer the configuration settings and database data that you require to the ALV grid display, as well as a variable to access the database table with all reservations and two field symbols for copying table data.

The `SELECT` command imports all the data from the database table into the internal `l_tab_reservation` table. From there, copy the content line by line via a loop into the `l_tab_reservationx` table to which the `Mark` column has been added.

You can adapt the ALV grid display extensively to meet your requirements using structure settings. You should note that you are merely scratching the surface of possibilities here when you change some settings of the `l_str_layout` and `l_dis` variables, such as automatically optimizing the column width, transferring a window title, specifying the column for line markings, or assigning a program name to save user-defined layouts. You will discover even more functions if you refer to the function module documentation and the examples in the Reuse Library (Transaction SE83). The best way to create the function module call is to use the PATTERN button in the tools area. The optional specifications that you can use to influence the display to meet the requirements of the individual program are very extensive. While the list display is being executed, you change the GUI status and react to mouse clicks to ensure that you specify your own subroutines as callbacks. The responsibility in this case is to specify the program or function group where the individual subroutines are located; this is the only way that the subroutines can be called correctly by the ALV grid display. The next relevant transfer parameter is `i_structure_name`, which expects the name of the table or structure that you can use to learn about the fields to be displayed and

ALV grid display

their texts. Use `is_layout` to transfer the layout settings you require; the `i_save` transfer parameter uses the value "A" to release the storing of user-specific layouts; and `is_variant` determines the ID under which you can find the user-specific settings again. To find out which button the user pressed to exit the ALV grid display, return the `l_str_exit_by_user` structure. Transfer the table to be displayed to `t_outtab`. If errors occur while you're displaying the table, the function module returns a corresponding `sy-subrc`. As a precaution, issue the last part of the message on the screen using the `MESSAGE` command.

Exiting a program   Lastly, you evaluate the content of the `l_str_exit_by_user` structure and exit the program using LEAVE PROGRAM, provided you click the EXIT button. If you click the BACK or CANCEL button, the program immediately returns to the main menu via RETURN. If the user didn't click any of these buttons, the only button in question is the additional EXECUTE button in the GUI status, and you begin with the LOOP by the `l_tab_reservationx` table to delete all the lines selected with 'X' in the database table using the DELETE command.

The `zptb00_hrc_show` subroutine, however, is structured in a much simpler way, because you're not trying to communicate with the ALV grid functions here. You merely want to display the content of the table. After the table content is imported using the SELECT command, only a few more layout settings follow and the REUSE_ALV_GRID_DISPLAY is then called.

In the subroutine for deleting reservations, you have already specified two subroutines that are to be set by the ALV grid display at the time of the GUI status and must be called by the user's mouse clicks. You must implement this now.

The `cb_alv_user_command` subroutine only checks whether the button that is clicked corresponds to the EXECUTE command. In this case, you set the exit flag of the `rs_selfield` structure. As a result, you exit immediately from the function module. Alternatively, you could have also placed the SQL statement DELETE for deletion directly here. If you had left the exit field blank in the `rs_selfield` structure and updated the changes in the internal `l_tab_reservationx` table, the deletion would proceed without having to exit the display. However, it was important here to demonstrate the behavior with a set exit field.

The cl_alv_pf_set_status subroutine is also quite short. The only command it contains is the SET PF-STATUS statement for setting the GUI status stored in the program. This enables the ALV grid display to display the additional DELETE button.

You have now completed the program implementation and want to test it.

Testing the program

▷ Click the SAVE button, then CHECK, ACTIVATE, and finally DIRECT to start the program immediately.

The program starts and prompts you for the next action in the main menu.

▷ Select the INSERT RESERVATION radio button and click the EXECUTE button (see Figure 5.12).

Figure 5.12 ZPTB00_HOTEL_RESERVATION_COOL Program in Action

The program now displays a dialog box where you can enter all the data required for reserving a room.

▷ Enter the values shown in Figure 5.13 and click EXECUTE.

Figure 5.13 Inserting a Reservation Using the ZPTB00_HOTEL_RESERVATION_COOL Program

273

The program then switches back to the main menu and confirms the reservation in the status bar. You are supposed to make another reservation.

▷ Select the INSERT RESERVATION radio button again and click EXECUTE (see Figure 5.14).

Figure 5.14 Confirming the Successful Reservation in the Status Bar

The input dialog box for new reservations appears again.

▷ Now enter "2" as the room number, "01.01.2014" as the check-in date, "01.03.2014" as the check-out date, and "Mr. Johnson" as the name of the customer, and click EXECUTE.

Deleting the first reservation

Because you have changed the room, this reservation will also be completed successfully. You are now supposed to delete the first reservation.

▷ Select the DELETE RESERVATIONS radio button and then EXECUTE.

The ALV grid display appears; additional selection buttons are now available on the left margin of the list. You can use these buttons to select and deselect individual lines.

▷ Select the data record for the customer "Mr. Twister" and click the EXECUTE button (see Figure 5.15).

The display switches back to the main menu and a note appears in the status bar, indicating that the reservation was deleted successfully. Check this message by selecting the menu option for displaying the reservations.

Figure 5.15 Deleting the Reservation for Mr. Twister

▷ Select the SHOW RESERVATIONS radio button and click the EXECUTE button one last time.

The ALV grid display appears again. This time, however, it doesn't contain any selection options and the data record you just deleted is no longer displayed. You are now supposed to make the output a little more user-friendly. To do this, use the end user functions from the toolbar of the ALV grid display.

▷ Use the mouse to increase the column that displays the customer name and then select the CHANGE LAYOUT button (see Figure 5.16).

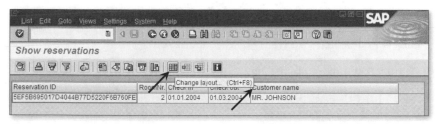

Figure 5.16 Adjusting the Column Width of the Display for Hotel Reservations

Among the many actions you can perform in this dialog box, you can individually select the columns to be displayed and determine their sequence. Because the ID is primarily needed by the system and not necessary for the end user to view, remove it from the display and make it the default setting for future calls of the display.

Determining the sequence of columns

▷ Select the RESERVATION ID column name.

▷ Click the HIDE SELECTED FIELDS button. The column name then switches to the right-hand listbox.

▷ Click the SAVE LAYOUT button.

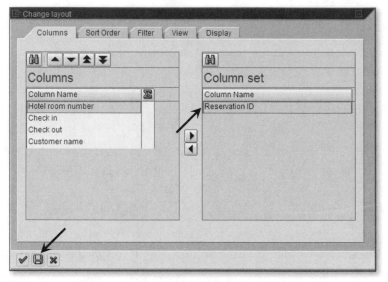

Figure 5.17 Adjusting the Layout of the Display for Hotel Reservations

Name of the layout Another dialog box is displayed, where you are prompted to enter the name under which you want to store the layout.

▷ Enter "/Standard" as the name and "Standard layout" as the description.

▷ Check the DEFAULT SETTING checkbox and confirm your entries by clicking OK (see Figure 5.18).

You return to the previous dialog box and copy the settings for the current display there.

▷ Click the COPY button.

The layout now appears, as required, without specifying the ID. Because you assign the same `dis-repid` value to the REUSE_ALV_GRID_DIS-PLAY function module in the source code for both deletion and display purposes, the layout settings are applicable to both displays (see Figure 5.19). This means that the functions of the program are fully utilized.

Figure 5.18 Saving the Layout of the Display for Hotel Reservations

Figure 5.19 Display of Hotel Reservations with a New Layout

Tip

The ALV grid display is used quite often in professional ABAP development because it supports practically every conceivable feature that is convenient for displaying data in tables. If you take just a little time to experiment with the toolbar functions, you'll be amazed by the settings that you can actually make: the capabilities range from hiding and sorting columns to creating subtotals and filtering out lines to displaying data graphically and transferring it to Excel, Word, or Crystal Reports (if installed). Additional fields of the l_str_layout structure even provide you with functions to edit fields:

```
* l_str_layout-edit = 'X'.
* l_str_layout-edit_mode = 'X'.
```

Furthermore, if you really want to use all the functions of the ALV grid display (for instance, let's say that you want to define your own context menus), you can use the underlying object-oriented CL_ALV_GRID_DISPLAY class directly.

5.2   Complex Input and Output Interfaces—Dynpros

Elaborately designed program interfaces are mainly used in SAP applications for inputting tabular or hierarchical data for purchase orders with several individual items, for example, or for the headers, debit and credit items of an accounting document, or for material Bill of Materials (BOMs) of a machine. These types of program interfaces usually consist of a large number of windows and dialog boxes. It therefore makes sense for SAP to provide a GUI editor—the *SAP Screen Painter*—and a special menu editor—the *SAP Menu Painter*—to make it easier to create the interfaces. These two tools will enable you to arrange all the interface elements of a window, such as the buttons, input fields, tables, and menus graphically and to set them up to look like dialogs.

Components of a screen window

The SAP Screen Painter and the SAP Menu Painter enable you to graphically design complex input and output interfaces and are very similar to the visual interface design in other known programming languages and their development environments. Apart from that, the similarities are limited because a special programming language called *screen flow logic* is used for communication between the interface and the program (for instance, to transfer data to be displayed or to accept inputs).

Each screen consists of different areas where you, as the programmer, can exert your influence in varying degrees (see Figure 5.20). Section 1.4, Logon, Getting Started, and System Setup, already described the individual areas of the window; therefore, this section focuses on how the corresponding interface tools are allocated.

▶ **Menu Bar**
You can design your own menus, submenus, and menu options, and assign a *code* to the latter. The ABAP program is notified of this code by the sy-ucomm system variable when the user selects the menu option. You use the SAP Menu Painter to create the menu bar, which becomes part of the GUI status of an application.

▶ **Standard Toolbar**
You can also assign a code to some buttons using the SAP Menu Painter. The ABAP program is notified of this code by the sy-ucomm system variable when the user selects the buttons. You edit the prop-

erties of the standard toolbar using the SAP Menu Painter, which makes them part of the GUI status of an application.

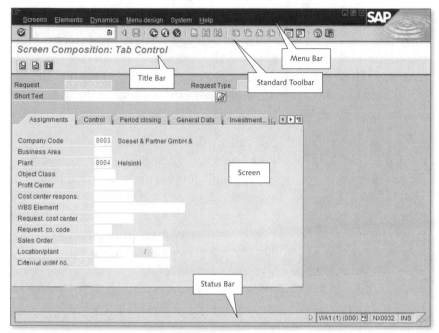

Figure 5.20 Components of a Window

▶ **Title Bar**

This contains a title that you can define as required. The title bar should always be set; otherwise, the predefined "SAP" title appears, which doesn't fully describe the uses of the current screen.

▶ **Application Toolbar**

The application toolbar contains user-defined pushbuttons. You also edit the application toolbar in the SAP Menu Painter and it is part of the GUI status.

▶ **Screen**

The actual program screen begins from here; you therefore have completely free reign over the design, for example, for creating tabs and distributing the required input and output fields on these tabs. You edit the screens using the SAP Screen Painter.

▶ **Status Bar**

Although you cannot influence the system display to the right of the screen, you can use the remaining space to output status messages per MESSAGE command.

When the screen is sent to the user's computer, data is transferred from the global variables of the relevant ABAP program to the screen interface elements of the same name. After a user action takes place, the data is transferred in the reverse direction. You can also control this basic procedure using a number of special screen flow logic commands.

Screen flow logic
commands

Screen flow logic doesn't contain any data declarations; it is exclusively limited to functions for calling screens, changing the properties of individual interface elements, transferring data between interface elements and the ABAP program, and handling error messages. The screen flow logic defines four events for this purpose, which are initiated using the PROCESS keyword and can each execute a small set of statements. All statements of the screen flow logic are contained together in a source code that belongs to one screen in each case. If you were to use these commands outside of this screen flow logic source code in an ABAP source code, this would result in syntax error messages.

▶ PROCESS—**Introducing event blocks of the screen flow logic**

There are a total of four events that you can use to access the screen flow logic of each screen. The PROCESS BEFORE OUTPUT (PBO) event is triggered before a screen is displayed; the PROCESS AFTER INPUT (PAI) event is initiated after a user action; the PROCESS ON HELP-REQUEST (POH) event is executed after the help for an interface element is called using the F1 key; and the PROCESS ON VALUE-REQUEST (POV) event is activated when input help is requested for an interface element (for instance, using the F4 key). While the first two events, PBO and PAI, should appear in every ABAP screen source code, the latter two events are rare. Because you used data elements as data types, you're usually automatically presented with these functions and don't have to worry about them yourself. The following is an example:

```
PROCESS BEFORE OUTPUT.
  MODULE POSITION_TABLE_INIT.
* ...
```

▶ `MODULE`—**Calling dialog modules**

The `MODULE` command establishes the connection between the screen flow logic and ABAP commands by enabling parts of the ABAP program that were programmed in this type of module to be called from the screen flow logic source code (that is, from one of the events mentioned). The syntax is

```
MODULE m.
```

The `m` here is the name of the module defined in the ABAP program. In ABAP, you must define a module using the keyword and provide it with one of the additions `INPUT` or `OUTPUT`, where the former may only be called from the PAI, POH, and POV events, and the latter may only be called from the PBO event. The following example shows how a module is called from an event:

```
PROCESS AFTER INPUT.
  MODULE user_exit_0100 AT EXIT-COMMAND.
```

▶ `FIELD`—**Controlling the transfer of data**

You can use the `FIELD` command in the PAI, POH, and POV event blocks to transfer the contents of interface elements to the global variables of an ABAP program. The syntax is

```
FIELD f [module].
```

The `f` here stands for the name of the screen interface element, the content of which is to be transferred into a global variable (of the same name) of the ABAP program. Optionally, you can use the `[module]` addition to specify the name of a module that is called directly after the transfer. This is generally done to perform additional checks on the value entered. If the check proves to be negative, a warning or an error message can be issued using the `MESSAGE` command, at which point the screen automatically switches all other interface elements to *not ready for input* until the user enters a correct value or exits the dialog box entirely. When data elements are used, many checks are performed automatically, which means that this situation primarily occurs if there are dependencies between the values of several interface elements. The following example shows the use of the `FIELD` command for transferring the content from an input field into a variable of the same name with an additional value check:

```
     FIELD G_POSITION_ITAB-MARK
     MODULE POSITION_TABLE_MARK ON REQUEST.
*    ...
```

▶ CHAIN ... ENDCHAIN—**Concatenating processing steps**

You can use the CHAIN and ENDCHAIN commands to concatenate screen flow logic statements such as FIELD to be able to check them together in a module call. If the check proves to be negative, a warning or an error message can be issued using the MESSAGE command. This causes the screen to automatically switch all other interface elements, which were not transferred within the current CHAIN ... ENDCHAIN processing, to *not ready for input*. The other interface elements can only be used as normal again after the user has corrected all values and the check has been completed successfully. The following example shows the transfer of *several* contents from an interface element into a global variable, whereby a check is called for these values at the end:

```
CHAIN.
   FIELD G_POSITION_ITAB-PR_ID.
   FIELD G_POSITION_ITAB-PSTYPE.
   FIELD G_POSITION_ITAB-WH_ID.
   FIELD G_POSITION_ITAB-AMOUNT.
   FIELD G_POSITION_ITAB-CURRENCY.
   FIELD G_POSITION_ITAB-QUANTITY.
   FIELD G_POSITION_ITAB-UNIT.
   FIELD G_POSITION_ITAB-MARK.
   MODULE POSITION_TABLE_MODIFY ON CHAIN-REQUEST.
ENDCHAIN.
```

▶ LOOP ... ENDLOOP—**Processing table controls**

Table controls (also called *table views*) are complex interface elements that contain several input and output fields for accepting and displaying values in tables. With table controls, the data is always transferred between the ABAP program and the interface element line by line within the LOOP ... ENDLOOP loop, which is similar to the one in the ABAP programs. You are permitted to use it only within the PBO and PAI events. The syntax is

```
LOOP AT itab WITH CONTROL tc.
```

Here, `itab` is the internal table and `tc` represents the name of the control. To ensure that the data is transferred, the fields of the structure for the internal table must have the same name as the individual input and output elements within the table control. The following example demonstrates how the values are transferred once to the table control:

```
LOOP AT   G_POSITION_TABLE_ITAB
     INTO G_POSITION_TABLE_WA
     WITH CONTROL POSITION_TABLE
     CURSOR POSITION_TABLE-CURRENT_LINE.
ENDLOOP.
```

▶ `CALL SUBSCREEN`—**Calling a subscreen**
Subscreens are screens that you can display in areas of another screen that have been provided for this purpose. You use this procedure to enable you to reuse parts of interfaces in several windows, and you also use it for windows with tabs. The `CALL SUBSCREEN` command can call screens from its own program as well as screens from other programs. The syntax is

```
CALL SUBSCREEN sub_area INCLUDING [program name] dynnr.
```

The following example shows how a screen is called from an external program:

```
CALL SUBSCREEN s1 INCLUDING zmyprogram 120.
```

Alternatively, however, you also have ABAP statements, which are provided for working with screens and are typically used within the modules that are called from the source code of the screen flow logic.

ABAP commands for processing screens

▶ `CALL SCREEN`—**Calling a screen directly**
This command is similar to the command for calling a selection screen (see Section 5.1, Simple Input and Output Interfaces—SELECTION SCREEN, SELECT-OPTIONS, CALL SELECTION SCREEN, SAP List Viewer) and has the following syntax

```
CALL SCRFEN dynnr [STARTING AT x1 y1 [ENDING AT x2 y2]]
```

It calls the `dynnr` screen, where the `STARTING AT` addition can also generate a new window on the `x1 y1` screen position. Optionally, the expansion of the window up to the x2 y2 screen position can also be determined using the ENDING AT addition. The following example shows a screen, once in the main menu and once in a separate window:

```
CALL SCREEN 0100.
CALL SCREEN 0100 STARTING AT 10 10.
```

▶ SET SCREEN—**Setting the next default screen**
Within the SAP Screen Painter, you can specify a follow-up screen that is automatically called as the next screen after processing has been successful. You can also change this specification at program runtime using the SET SCREEN command because, for example, certain conditions necessitate calling a different screen. The following example defines screen 100 as the follow-up screen:

```
SET SCREEN 0100.
```

▶ SET PF-STATUS—**Setting the GUI status of the window**
You use the SAP Menu Painter to create the GUI status. Initially, it doesn't depend on an individual screen. You use the SET PF-STATUS command to determine a GUI status for the screen and this status will apply for calling all windows until such time as you set a new GUI status. The syntax of the command is

```
SET PF-STATUS guistatus.
```

The guistatus is the name of a GUI status previously created using the SAP Menu Painter. The command is usually called in the PBO event of a screen to ensure that the correct menu is displayed and the pushbutton bar returns the required codes in a field that you define, called ok_code, for example. In the programming tasks, you can see where you must create this field in the Screen Painter to ensure that the codes provided in the Menu Painter for the buttons (such as BACK, CANCEL, or SAVE) are transferred to the Screen Painter for further processing. The following example demonstrates how you call the command:

```
SET PF-STATUS 'ZPTB00_OBJ_BTA_STD'.
```

▶ **GET PF-STATUS—Reading the GUI status of the window**
The GET PF-STATUS command returns the name of the active GUI status. The syntax is

```
GET PF-STATUS guistatus.
```

In this case, guistatus should be a character variable with 20 characters. This command is used very rarely and is usually only required as an additional aid in deciding how to respond to a certain code. The following example reads the name of the current GUI status into the l_gui_status variable:

```
DATA:
  l_gui_status TYPE string.
GET PF-STATUS l_gui_status.
```

▶ **SET TITLEBAR—Setting a new text in the title bar of the window**
Window titles are normal development objects (like data elements or source codes) and are created using a dialog box and stored under a name. The SET TITLEBAR command reads the TITLE previously created and assigns it to the current screen. The syntax is

```
SET TITLEBAR name.
```

Here, name is the name of the created title development object. A special feature of titles is that they can also contain placeholders in the form of &1, &2, and up to &9. You can replace these placeholders in the command using the WITH v1 .. vn addition, where v1 to vn are variables, constants, or parameters, whose content replaces the &1 to &9 placeholders.

```
SET TITLEBAR 'ZPTB00_OBJ_BTA_STD' WITH sy-uname.
```

▶ **LOOP AT SCREEN—Reading the field properties of the screen**
You can use this loop statement to read the properties of all screen elements of a screen. In each loop pass, the properties of each screen element are contained in the SCREEN system variable. This consists of a structure which, in addition to containing very important fields like name, required (required-entry field), input (ready for input), or output (display only), also uses the invisible field to provide information about the visibility, or the length field to inform you of the visible

length on the screen. The following example reads the properties of all interface elements of a screen into the internal `l_tab_screen` table:

```
DATA:
  l_tab_screen LIKE STANDARD TABLE OF screen.
LOOP AT SCREEN.
  APPEND screen TO l_tab_screen.
ENDLOOP.
```

▶ `MODIFY SCREEN`—**Modifying the field properties of the screen**
You can only use the `MODIFY SCREEN` command with the `LOOP AT SCREEN` command, which facilitates transferring the modified properties of interface elements to the screen (for instance, this enables the program to make input fields invisible, or to modify their input lengths). The syntax is

```
MODIFY SCREEN [FROM wa].
```

The content of the predefined `screen` system variable is usually transferred to the corresponding interface element here; when the `FROM wa` addition is used, the content of the variable defined in `wa` is transferred instead. The following example demonstrates how an interface element called `amount` is changed in an output field:

```
LOOP AT SCREEN.
  IF screen-name = amount.
    SCREEN-INPUT = ' '.
    SCREEN-OUTPUT = '1'.
    MODIFY SCREEN.
  ENDIF.
ENDLOOP.
```

▶ `SET CURSOR`—**Setting the screen cursor position**
The `SET CURSOR` command was already mentioned briefly in Section 3.1, Basic Commands and Fields—WRITE, PARAMETERS, MOVE, SY Fields. This command is also suitable for the interface elements of screens, but can only be used in the PBO event. The syntax of the command is as follows

```
SET CURSOR FIELD f.
```

Here, f is the name of an interface element that is to have the input focus below. You use this command very rarely because changing the input focus usually confuses the user. During the input check using the FIELD command, however, this SET CURSOR command is automatically set as soon as a warning or an error message is issued. The following example demonstrates how the input focus is set on an interface element called quantity:

```
SET CURSOR quantity.
```

▶ **GET CURSOR—Reading the screen cursor position**
In contrast, the name of the interface element that holds the current input focus can be read at any time. This information can be important if, for example, a particular response has to be made with an input field to a function key being pressed. The following example shows how the interface element that currently has the input focus is read:

```
GET CURSOR l_element.
```

▶ **CONTROLS—Declaring a control**
You can use the CONTROLS command to introduce a tabstrip or table view interface element that exists in the screen into ABAP. A tabstrip is also known as a *tab* and enables you to switch between several subscreens of a screen. A table view, which you've already gotten to know in the context of LOOP command from the screen flow logic, is a complex interface element for displaying and inputting data in tables. The syntax of the command for displaying data is

```
CONTROLS ts TYPE TABSTRIP.
```

In this case, ts must be the name of a control of the same type defined on the current screen. From here on, the properties of the interface element can be accessed using the name in the ABAP program. One of the most important properties is activetab, which can be used to determine the name of the tab currently displayed. The syntax of the command for entering data is

```
CONTROLS tv TYPE TABLEVIEW USING SCREEN scrnr.
```

Here, `tv` must be the name of a defined table control and `scrnr` the name of the screen or one of its subscreens. Here again, the properties of the interface element can also be accessed using this name from now on. One of the most important properties here is `current_line`, which specifies the line currently being edited by the user as an index. The following two examples demonstrate how the properties mentioned are accessed for a tab called `pagecontrol` and a table called `tablecontrol`:

```
CONTROLS:
  pagecontrol TYPE TABSTRIP,
  tablecontrol TYPE TABLEVIEW USING SCREEN '0100'.
MODULE dosomething_100 INPUT.
  IF pagecontrol-activetab = 'PAGE1'.
* do something
  ENDIF.
  IF tablecontrol-current_line = 1.
* do something
  ENDIF.
ENDMODULE.
```

▶ **REFRESH CONTROL**—**Initializing the control properties**
You can use the `REFRESH CONTROL` command to reset table views and tabstrips to the properties originally defined with the SAP Screen Painter. The syntax is

```
REFRESH CONTROL co FROM SCREEN scrnr.
```

Here `co` is replaced by the name of the control and `scrnr` with the name of the screen. You use this command very rarely, for example, if a subscreen is used several times consecutively in a program and the values of the previous inputs are not supposed to be displayed. The following example shows how a tabstrip called `pagecontrol` is refreshed:

```
CONTROLS:
  pagecontrol TYPE TABSTRIP.
MODULE dosomething_100 INPUT.
  IF pagecontrol-activetab = 'PAGE1'.
    REFRESH CONTROL pagecontrol FROM SCREEN '0100'.
  ENDIF.
```

▶ `SET HOLD DATA`—**Saving and displaying field contents of the screen**
Screens can retain user entries across several calls. The `SET HOLD DATA` command simply has to activate the "memory" for this in a module at the time of PBO event. You activate the memory using the `ON` addition and likewise deactivate it using the `OFF` addition. Through the System • User Defaults • Hold Data menu option, you can now take a snapshot of the current screen inputs, and these are subsequently displayed automatically as default values the next time you call data. The following example shows how the option for saving and displaying values is activated:

```
SET HOLD DATA ON.
```

▶ `SUPPRESS DIALOG`—**Suppressing the screen**
The `SUPPRESS DIALOG` command is only useful within modules that are called during the PBO event and suppresses the screen from being displayed. Instead, the PAI event is triggered immediately and the processing is continued there. You will find this command useful if the data that must be queried by a screen is already known elsewhere in the program and it is therefore unnecessary to output one of several successive windows. The following example shows this call:

```
SUPPRESS DIALOG.
```

▶ `LEAVE SCREEN`—**Exiting the current screen**
The `LEAVE SCREEN` command exits the current screen and calls the next screen. Alternatively, you can also call the command in the `LEAVE TO SCREEN scrnr` variant to be able to specify the required follow-up screen. The example in Table 5.1 demonstrates how you call screen 200:

LEAVE TO SCREEN '0200'.	
Command	**Description**
`CALL SCREEN`	Calls a screen directly
`SET SCREEN`	Sets the next default screen
`SET PF-STATUS`	Sets the GUI status of the window
`GET PF-STATUS`	Reads the GUI status of the window

Table 5.1 ABAP Statements for Screens

LEAVE TO SCREEN '0200'.	
Command	**Description**
SET TITLEBAR	Sets a new text in the title bar of the window
LOOP AT SCREEN	Reads the field properties of the screen
MODIFY SCREEN	Changes the field properties of the screen
SET CURSOR	Sets the screen cursor position
GET CURSOR	Reads the screen cursor position
CONTROLS	Declares a control
REFRESH CONTROL	Initializes the control properties
SET HOLD DATA	Saves and displays the field contents of the screen
SUPPRESS DIALOG	Suppresses the screen
LEAVE SCREEN	Exits the current screen

Table 5.1 ABAP Statements for Screens (Cont.)

After so many new commands, you now learn how everything falls into place and produces a functioning program interface. We will reuse the result of the following exercise in our training scenario in Chapter 7, Practice Scenario—Automated Accounting for Corporate Subsidiaries, which is why the programming guidelines (see Appendix A) are already taken into account now. This fact impacts the naming conventions of variables and functions in particular.

Exercise 5.2

Create the ZPTB00_BUSINESS_TRANSACTION program for inputting a business transaction. Use the screen technology to design an interface within the new ZPTB00_OBJ_BTA function group to be created and call this using a ZPTB00_OBJ_BTA_EDIT function declared there.

The interface should contain the following header information:

ID	Data element
Business partner ID	ZPTB00_DTE_BTA_BP_ID
Business transaction type	ZPTB00_DTE_BTA_BTTYPE
Business transaction date	ZPTB00_DTE_BTA_BTDATE

The position information must be received in a table displayed underneath:

ID	Data element
Product ID	ZPTB00_DTE_BTA_PR_ID
Position type	ZPTB00_DTE_BTA_PSTYPE
Storage location ID	ZPTB00_DTE_BTA_WH_ID
Amount	ZPTB00_DTE_BTA_AMOUNT
Currency	ZPTB00_DTE_BTA_CURRENCY
Quantity	ZPTB00_DTE_BTA_QUANTITY
Unit	ZPTB00_DTE_BTA_UNIT

Store the header information plus the field:

Booking	ZPTB00_DTE_BTA_BOOKED

after the input in a database table called ZPTB00_BTAHEADER and the position information relationally linked plus the field:

Selection	ZPTB00_DTE_BTA_MARK

in the ZPTB00_BTAITEM table. Each line in the tables should be identifiable by a unique key that contains the header information of the client and a header ID and additionally a position ID for the position information.

Use your own domains for all data elements that have "DOM" instead of "DTE" as the name component; some exceptions include the currency and unit, for which you use the standard WAERS and MEINS domains. Only use the ZPTB00_OBJ_BTA_SAVE function from the ZPTB00_DB_BTA function group to write data into the tables.

If you require messages, store these in the ZPTB00_BTA message class.

The following (elementary) business transaction types are to be allowed:

Business transaction type	Description
1000	Buy
2000	Sell
3000	Transfer
4000	Return
5000	Claim
6000	Scrapping

Only two item types are to be allowed:

> ▶ PRODUCT
>
> ▶ SERVICE
>
> For product ID, only allow 1000 = "Aspirin", 2000 = "Autan", and 3000 = "Consulting"; for storage location, only allow 0001 = "1st floor, 1st space", 1002 = "2nd floor, 2nd space", and 2003 = "3rd floor, 3rd space"; and for booking, only allow 1 = "unbooked", 2 = "booked", and 3 = "not relevant for booking".

Product IDs 1000, 2000, and 3000 are used here as an example of possible characteristic values of master data. In larger enterprises, products IDs are longer and are partially assigned manually and partially copied automatically by upstream systems.

Creating a domain   Because you want to use the data elements and tables in the program and the function modules, it makes sense to create these beforehand. You therefore require domains for this purpose, which you define first.

▷ In the context menu of the package or development class, select the CREATE • DDIC OBJECT • DOMAIN menu option.

A dialog box appears, where you must specify the name of the domain.

▷ Specify "ZPTB00_DOM_BTA_BTTYPE" as the name.

A window is displayed in the tools area of the SAP Object Navigator where you can maintain the domain properties (see Figure 5.21).

▷ Enter "Business transaction type" as the short text, "NUMC" as the data type, and "4" as the number of characters.

▷ Select the VALUE RANGE tab.

The setting options in the VALUE RANGE tab are displayed. There, use the setting options under SINGLE VALS to ensure that a check is automatically performed on the entered values afterwards.

▷ Under SINGLE VALS, enter the business transaction types with a short text, as mentioned in the exercise (see Figure 5.22).

▷ Click the SAVE button.

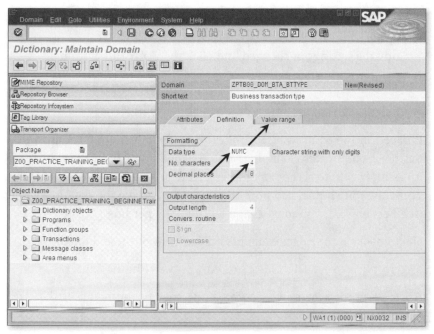

Figure 5.21 Maintaining Properties of the ZPTB00_DOM_BTA_BTTYPE Domain

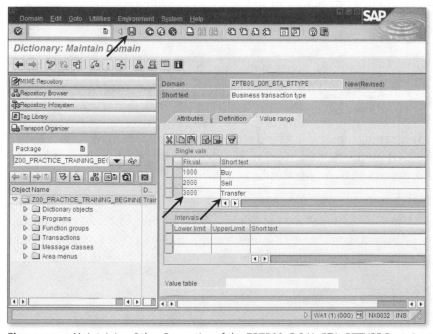

Figure 5.22 Maintaining Other Properties of the ZPTB00_DOM_BTA_BTTYPE Domain

The transport dialog box opens, where you must define the request for logging the domain.

▷ Copy the settings unchanged and click the CONTINUE button.

You can now check and activate the domain.

▷ Click the CHECK button, and then click ACTIVATE.

Creating other domains in the same way
Proceed in the same way with the other domains. Only the business partner alone in this example is not assigned any fixed values; instead, it is simply able to accept any input. Create all other fixed values for the domains. You should also note that in order to save the data in a table (see Section 4.2), you must assign a unique ID per line.

Creating a data element
Next you create the data elements on the basis of these domains.

▷ Select CREATE • DDIC OBJECT • DATA ELEMENT in the context menu.

A dialog box appears, where you must specify the name of the data element.

▷ Specify "ZPTB00_DTE_BTA_BTTYPE" as the name.

A window is displayed in the tools area of the SAP Object Navigator where you can maintain the properties of the data element (see Figure 5.23).

▷ Enter "Business transaction type" as the short text and "ZPTB00_DOM_BTA_BTTYPE" as the domain.

▷ Select the FIELD LABEL tab.

The setting options in the FIELD LABEL tab are displayed (see Figure 5.24). Specify field labels of varying lengths for the data element here in order to be able to use the data element in all possible input and output screens.

▷ Specify "BT type" for the SHORT label, "Business trans. Type" for the MEDIUM label, and "Business transaction type" for the LONG and HEADING labels. The dialog box fills the length information automatically.

▷ Click the SAVE button.

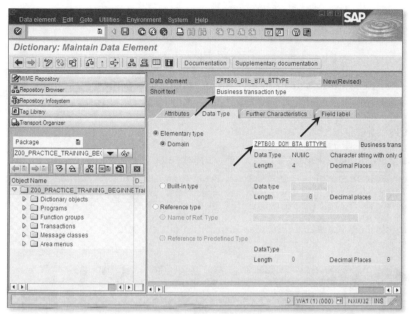

Figure 5.23 Maintaining Properties of the ZPTB00_DTE_BTA_BTTYPE Data Element

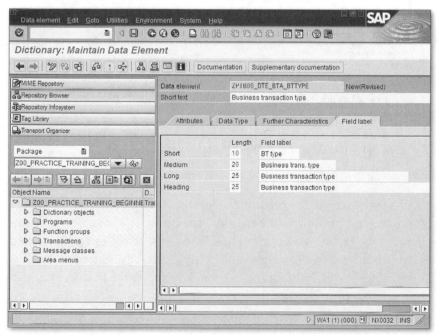

Figure 5.24 Maintaining Other Properties of the ZPTB00_DTE_BTA_BTTYPE Data Element

A transport dialog box opens, where you must define the request for logging the data element.

▷ Copy the settings unchanged and click the CONTINUE button.

You are now supposed to maintain the documentation for the data element to ensure that the user can call online help for this input field.

▷ Click the DOCUMENTATION button.

A new window appears, where you can enter the documentation for the data element.

▷ Copy the documentation from Figure 5.25.

▷ Click the SAVE ACTIVE button, and then click BACK.

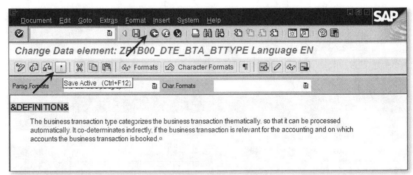

Figure 5.25 Maintaining Documentation for the ZPTB00_DTE_BTA_BTTYPE Data Element

You can now check and activate the data element.

▷ Select the CHECK button and then ACTIVATE.

Creating other data elements in the same way You can now create the other data elements in the same way. Enter the following text as the documentation: "The business transaction type categorizes the business transaction thematically, so that it can be processed automatically. It co-determines indirectly if the business transaction is relevant for the accounting and on which accounts the business transaction is booked."

Create all other documentation for the data elements yourself. Also bear in mind that, to save the data in a table, you must assign a unique ID per line (see Section 4.2), which should refer to a corresponding domain and records a GUID.

You can now define the tables based on the new data elements you've created. First, you need to create the table for the header information of the business transaction.

Creating a table

▷ In the context menu of the package or development class, select the CREATE • DDIC OBJECT • DATABASE TABLE menu option.

A dialog box subsequently opens, prompting you to enter the name of the database table that you want to create.

▷ Enter "ZPTB00_BTAHEADER" as the name of the table and confirm your entries by clicking OK.

In the tool area, a window is displayed where you can maintain all properties of the table (see Figure 5.26).

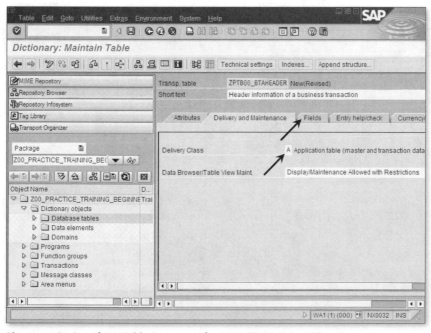

Figure 5.26 Specifying Table Properties for ZPTB00_BTAHEADER

▷ Enter "Header information of a business transaction" as the short text and "A" as the delivery class.

▷ Switch to the FIELDS tab.

Specify the names of all fields here that are supposed to appear as columns in the table (see Figure 5.27).

▷ Specify the fields CLIENT, HEADER_ID, BP_ID, BTTYPE, BTDATE, and BOOKED with the relevant data elements. Specify the predefined MANDT data element for the CLIENT field.

▷ Check the KEY checkbox for the CLIENT and HEADER_ID fields, and click the TECHNICAL SETTINGS button.

A dialog box opens, prompting you to confirm whether you want to save the table.

▷ Click YES to confirm the prompt.

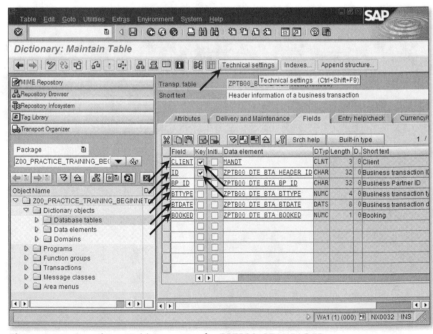

Figure 5.27 Specifying Field Properties for ZPTB00_BTAHEADER

You're now asked for the package to which you want to assign the database table.

▷ The package is already preset, so you can simply confirm your entries by clicking the SAVE button.

A dialog box now asks you for the transport request for the table.

▷ Copy the existing transport request unchanged, and confirm the prompt by clicking YES.

The technical settings must be specified before you activate the table and contain information about the data class and size category in particular (see Figure 5.28).

▷ Enter "APPL1" as the data class because this is data that is changed frequently.

▷ Enter "4" as the size category because hundreds of thousands of data records can accumulate in the table in live operations.

▷ Click the SAVE button, and then click BACK.

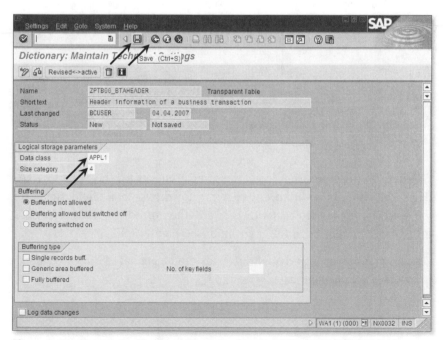

Figure 5.28 Maintaining Technical Properties for the ZPTB00_BTAHEADER Table

299

All necessary properties of the ZPTB00_BTAHEADER table have been set, and you can now activate them.

▷ Click BACK and then ACTIVATE.

Creating another
table in the
same way

You can now create the second table ZPTB00_BTAITEM in the same way. Use a foreign key to create the relation with the ZPTB00_BTAHEADER table. Figure 5.29 shows the complete table.

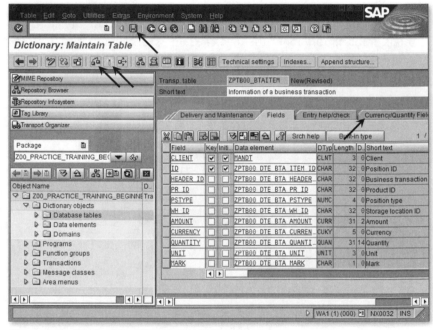

Figure 5.29 Fields of the ZPTB00_BTAITEM Table

The technical settings should get the same inputs as for the ZPTB00_BTA-HEADER table. In addition, the currency for the AMOUNT field must also be searched for in the CURRENCY field and the unit for the QUANTITY field must be searched for in the UNIT field (see Figure 5.30).

Tables with currency and quantity fields can be activated only after these particular details have been specified.

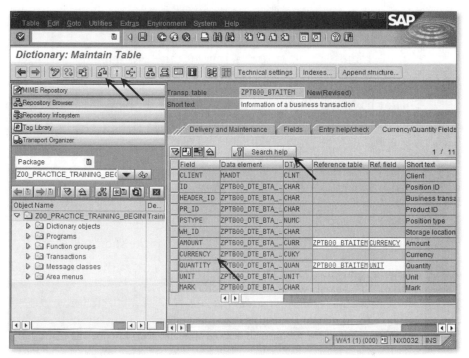

Figure 5.30 Currency and Quantity Specifications for the ZPTB00_BTAITEM Table

After these preparations, you can begin writing the program.

Creating a program

▷ Create a program called "ZPTB00_BUSINESS_TRANSACTION" and without a TOP include. The title should be "Enter a business transaction manually". The other settings and the transport request remain unchanged.

As usual, the SAP Object Navigator creates a program structure that you can now complete.

Before you begin creating the program, function groups, and functions, you create a table type and structure that will help you greatly when transferring the business transaction between the individual parts of the program. They will also make the communication between the screen and ABAP easier at a later stage. Lastly, this is how you integrate all the data that is communicating with the interface (screen) into a deep structure, which can be transferred using a single variable. Because a business

Creating a
table type

transaction can consist of several positions, you begin with defining a table type.

▷ In the context menu of the package or the development class, select CREATE • DDIC OBJECT • TABLE TYPE.

A dialog box subsequently appears, requesting the name of the function group.

▷ Enter "ZPTB00_TTY_BTA_ITEM" as the name of the function group, and confirm your entries by clicking OK.

A window is displayed in the tools area of the development environment where you can define the properties of the table type.

▷ Enter "Positions of a business transaction" as the short text.

▷ Enter the name of the ZPTB00_BTAITEM table as the line type, and click ACTIVATE (see Figure 5.31).

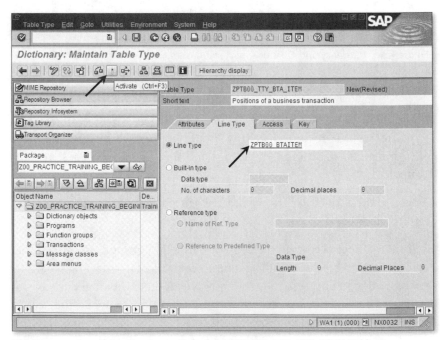

Figure 5.31 Specifying the Properties of the ZPTB00_TTY_BTA_ITEM Table Type

The SAP Object Navigator finally asks for the transport request.

▷ The number of the transport request used previously is set by default. Simply confirm it with the OK button.

You now integrate the header information of a business transaction with the table type already created to ensure that a deep structure is generated.

Creating a structure with all interface data

▷ In the context menu of the package or development class, select the CREATE • DDIC OBJECT • STRUCTURE menu option.

A dialog box opens, requesting the name of the structure.

▷ Enter "ZPTB00_STR_BTA" as the name of the structure, and confirm your entries by clicking OK.

A window is displayed in the tools area of the development environment where you can define the properties of the table type.

▷ Enter "Business transaction" as the short text and select the COMPONENTS tab (see Figure 5.32).

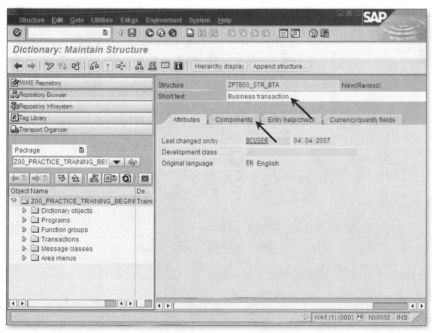

Figure 5.32 Specifying the Properties of the ZPTB00_STR_BTA Table Type

The structure of the ZPTB00_BTAHEADER table already created is now also copied, like the newly defined ZPTB00_TTY_BTA_ITEM table type, into the ZPTB00_STR_BTA structure.

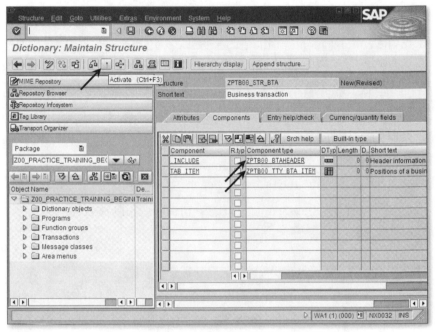

Figure 5.33 Specifying the Components of the ZPTB00_STR_BTA Structure

▷ In the first line, enter ".INCLUDE" as the component and "ZPTB00_BTAHEADER" as the component type.

▷ In the second line, enter "TAB_ITEM" as the component and "ZPTB00_TTY_BTA_ITEM" as the component type.

▷ Click the ACTIVATE button.

You can use this approach to group together almost any complex structures that keep data organized within ABAP programs.

The SAP Object Navigator finally asks for the transport request.

▷ The number of the transport request used previously is set by default. Simply confirm it with the OK button.

The include part of the structure is then expanded and displayed within the components (see Figure 5.34).

Figure 5.34 ZPTB00_STR_BTA Structure with Include Components Displayed

The next step involves creating the function group where you want to design the screen together with the title and status as well as store the function for calling the window. This enables you to make it easier to reuse the window than would be possible if you were to create the screen directly in the program.

Creating a function group

▷ Select the CREATE • FUNCTION GROUP menu option in the context menu of the package or development class.

A dialog box subsequently appears, requesting the name of the function group.

▷ Enter "ZPTB00_OBJ_BTA" as the name and "Process business transaction" as the short text. Then confirm your entries by clicking the SAVE button.

The SAP Object Navigator finally asks for the transport request.

▷ The number of the transport request already used before is set by default and you simply have to confirm it by clicking the OK button.

Creating a function module

You next find the function group in the object area list again and can now create a function in it, which is to encapsulate the actual user interface call for entering a business transaction.

▷ In the context menu of the ZPTB00_OBJ_BTA function group, select the CREATE • FUNCTION MODULE menu option.

A dialog box opens, requesting the name of the function module.

▷ Enter "ZPTB00_OBJ_BTA_EDIT" as the name and "Edit business transaction" as the short text.

▷ Confirm your entries with the SAVE button, and click the CHANGING tab.

As the interface, you simply need a changing parameter that you enter on the corresponding tab.

▷ Enter "C_STR_BTA" under PARAMETER NAME, "TYPE" under TYPING, and "ZPTB00_STR_BTA" under REFERENCE TYPE.

▷ Confirm your entries with the SAVE button.

Now create the ZPTB00_OBJ_BTA_SAVE function module in the same way. You should define the Import, Export, and Changing parameters as follows:

```
*"*"Local interface:
*"  IMPORTING
*"     REFERENCE(I_STR_BTA) TYPE  ZPTB00_STR_BTA
*"  EXCEPTIONS
*"     FAILED
```

Listing 5.2 Interface of ZPTB00_OBJ_BTA_SAVE Function Module

Creating text symbols

A typical screen includes confirmation prompts that are displayed in the global toolbar when you exit a window using the BACK, EXIT, or CANCEL buttons. Store these text symbols allocated to the ZPTB00_OBJ_BTA function group.

▷ In the object area, double-click one of the function modules within the ZPTB00_OBJ_BTA function group to display its source code in the tools area.

▷ Select the GOTO • TEXT ELEMENTS • TEXT SYMBOLS menu option.

The window where you define text symbols is displayed in the tools area.

▷ Enter the texts shown in Figure 5.35 and click the SAVE button.

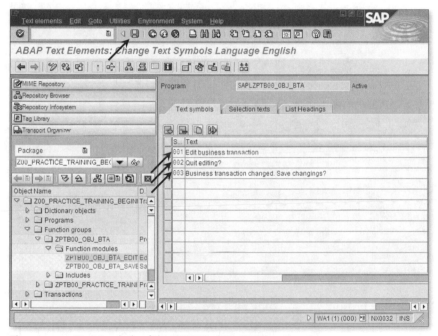

Figure 5.35 Text Symbols of the ZPTB00_OBJ_BTA Function Group

In the next step, you create a message class and define some messages in this class that are to be displayed during the program flow.

Creating a message class and defining messages

▷ Select the CREATE • OTHERS • MESSAGE CLASS menu option in the context menu of the package or development class.

A dialog box opens, requesting the name of the message class.

▷ Enter "ZPTB00_BTA" as the name for the message class and confirm your entries by clicking the OK button.

In the tools area, a window is displayed where you can maintain other properties of the message class and also define the individual messages in the MESSAGES tab (see Figure 5.36).

▷ Select the MESSAGES tab.

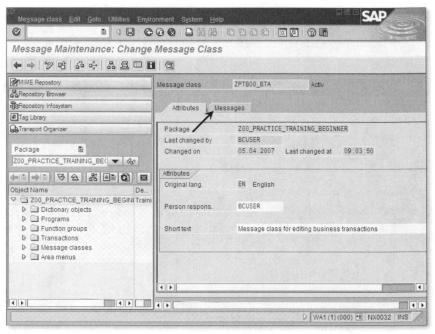

Figure 5.36 Properties of the ZPTB00_BTA Message Class

The usual prompt for the transport request appears.

▷ The number of the transport request used previously is set by default. Simply confirm it with the OK button.

The active tab then switches to MESSAGES and you can enter the required messages (see Figure 5.37).

▷ Enter the following message texts:

  ▷ Message 000: "Please insert product ID"

  ▷ Message 001: "Please insert transaction type"

  ▷ Message 002: "Please insert amount"

▷ Message 003: "Please insert currency"

▷ Message 004: "Please insert quantity"

▷ Message 005: "Please insert quantity unit"

▷ Message 006: "Please insert business partner ID"

▷ Message 007: "Please insert business transaction type"

▷ Message 008: "Please insert business transaction date"

▷ Click the SAVE button, and then click BACK to return to the source code.

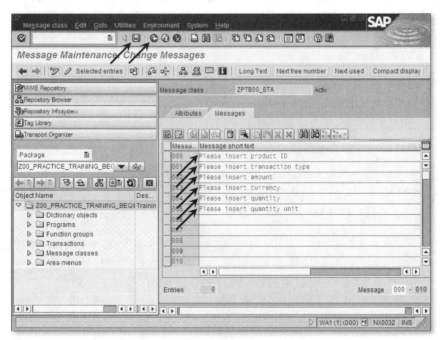

Figure 5.37 Creating Texts in the ZPTB00_BTA Message Class

You now require a GUI title to be able to assign a title to the screen window for the output in the toolbar.

Creating a GUI title

▷ In the context menu of the ZPTB00_OBJ_BTA function group, select the CREATE • GUI TITLE menu option.

309

The SAP Object Navigator displays a dialog box where, in addition to the title code for uniquely identifying the GUI title, you can also specify the title.

▷ Enter "ZPTB00_OBJ_BTA" as the title code and "Edit business transaction" as the title.

▷ Confirm your entries by clicking the Copy button.

The GUI title is now also created. You activate the title at a later stage together with the function group.

Creating a
GUI status

You also require a GUI status to add the toolbar with the Back, Exit, and Cancel buttons common to all SAP applications. Although you can also define your own menu options in the same way, this option is not used in this chapter.

▷ In the context menu of the ZPTB00_OBJ_BTA function group, select the Create • GUI Status menu option.

A dialog box opens, requesting the name of the GUI status and a short text.

▷ Enter "ZPTB00_OBJ_BTA_STD" as the name and "Edit standard GUI status business transaction" as the short text.

▷ Confirm your entries by clicking the Continue button.

A window is displayed in the tools area of the development environment where you can define the properties of the GUI status. Only the Function keys area is interesting for you; this is where you can define some function codes for the toolbar buttons. As soon as you click one of these buttons, the screen will automatically return the corresponding function code and you can then react to it accordingly.

▷ Click the button on the right-hand side next to Function keys. The symbols and key combinations that you can use are now displayed (see Figure 5.38).

▷ Specify the "SAVE" function code for the disk icon, "BACK" for the arrow pointing to the left on the green background, "QUIT" for the arrow pointing upward on the yellow background, "CANC" for the X on the red background, "FIRST" for the yellow double arrows pointing upward, "PREV" for the yellow arrow pointing upward, "NEXT" for the yellow arrow pointing downward, and "LAST" for the yellow double arrows pointing downward.

Figure 5.38 Specifying Properties of the GUI Status in the ZPTB00_OBJ_BTA Function Group

There are even more setting options for each function code:

▷ Select the PROPERTIES menu option in the context menu for the CANC function code.

You can now specify in a dialog box the function type that you can use to set the different special handling options. If the user inserts incorrect entries, the preferred "E" type also enables the screen processing to be canceled, whereby the processing for this function code is executed before all other checks are performed.

▷ Select "E" as the function type and confirm your settings with the OK button.

The GUI status is now created and can be used in the function group.

Creating a screen You now create a screen that includes the input elements for the business transaction header and the input table for the business transaction positions.

▷ To prepare for the next steps, you must first create the following variables in the LZPTB00_OBJ_BTATOP include:

```
TABLES:
        zptb00_btaheader.
DATA:
        g_position_tc_itab TYPE zptb00_tty_bta_item,
        g_position_tc_wa   TYPE zptb00_btaitem,
        g_str_bta TYPE zptb00_str_bta,
        g_data_copied TYPE c.
```

▷ In the context menu of the ZPTB00_OBJ_BTA function group, select the CREATE • SCREEN menu option.

A dialog box opens, requesting the name of the screen.

▷ Insert the number "100" and confirm your entry with the CONTINUE button.

A window is displayed in the tools area of the development environment where you can set a number of properties for the screen.

▷ Enter "Edit business transaction" as the short description, and then click the LAYOUT button to go to the graphical layout editor (see Figure 5.39).

After a short load time, the graphical layout editor appears with the available interface elements displayed in the left margin. The toolbar on the upper margin, however, is very similar to the typical SAP toolbar.

Creating interface elements The layout editor has automatically switched to edit mode, and you can immediately begin creating the interface elements. The following describes the easiest way (see Figure 5.40).

▷ Select the DICTIONARY/PROGRAM FIELDS WINDOW button.

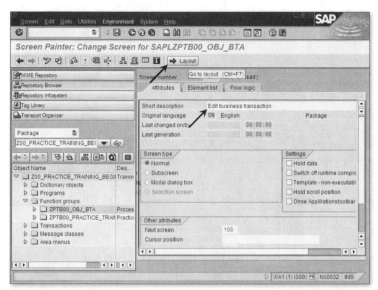

Figure 5.39 Specifying Properties of the Screen in the ZPTB00_OBJ_BTA Function Group

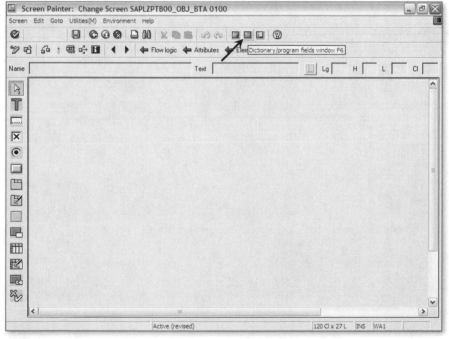

Figure 5.40 Editing the Layout of the Screen in the ZPTB00_OBJ_BTA Function Group

A dialog box is displayed where you must specify only the name of an existing structure. This will result in all fields being listed automatically for selection. The SAP Screen Painter then automatically suggests suitable interface elements (see Figure 5.41).

▷ Enter the name of the "ZPTB00_STR_BTA" database table as the table/ field name.

▷ Click the GET FROM DICT. button. The structure of the database table is then imported and the fields are displayed in the subordinate table.

▷ Use the buttons on the left margin to select the BP_ID, BTTYPE, and BTDATE fields, and confirm your selection with the OK button.

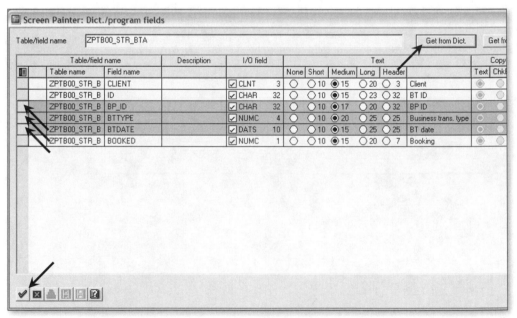

Figure 5.41 Specifying Fields for the Header Information Properties of the Screen in the ZPTB00_OBJ_BTA Function Group

You can now use the mouse to position the fields in a suitable place on the screen. As soon as you press the mouse button, the fields are created there.

▷ Place the mouse cursor on the second column and second line.

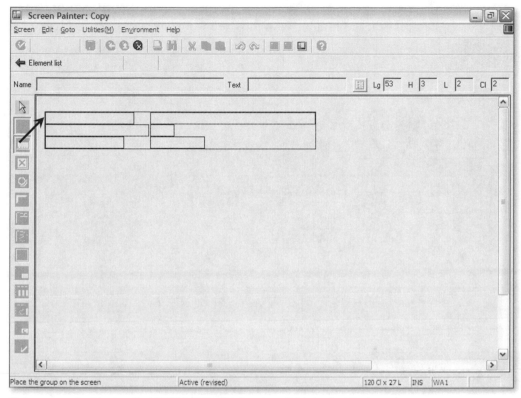

Figure 5.42   Positioning the ZPTB00_STR_BTA Database Table in the Window

As you can see, you can position the fields anywhere in the window, and the SAP Screen Painter automatically ensures that the input fields don't overlap in the right-hand margin.

▷ Press the left mouse button. The fields are created where the mouse cursor is positioned (see Figure 5.43).

The SAP Screen Painter has now automatically created three input fields with a title. You know from the second input field that the number of possible business transaction types is not large, and you therefore change the interface element from an input field into a listbox using the input help ([F4] help).

Changing an input field into a listbox

▷ Select the input field next to the BUSINESS TRANS. TYPE TITLE (see Figure 5.44). Drag it to the same width as the input field for the business partner ID (BP ID). You need this space because you also want to display the name along with the fixed value in the listbox.

▷ Click the ATTRIBUTE WINDOW button.

Figure 5.43 Creating Input Elements for the Fields of the ZPTB00_BTAHEADER Database Table

Figure 5.44 Increasing the Size of the Input Field for the Business Transaction Type

An additional window is displayed where you have full access to all properties of the selected interface element (see Figure 5.45).

▷ Select LISTBOX WITH KEY from the dropdown list.

▷ Switch to the PROGRAM tab, and choose the RECOMMENDED value in the INPUT field.

▷ Click the CLOSE button.

Figure 5.45 Setting the Attributes of the Input Field for the Business Transaction Type

The input field now appears as a listbox in the preview for your program window. Because a business transaction without a date makes no sense, also switch the property to INPUT RECOMMENDED. During the execution of the program, the input field is provided with the typical checkmark that indicates that an entry is required.

▷ Select the input field next to BT DATE TITLE (BUSINESS TRANSACTION DATE), and click the ATTRIBUTE WINDOW button.

You can implement the required setting in the ATTRIBUTE window.

▷ Switch to the PROGRAM tab.

▷ Select the RECOMMENDED value in the INPUT FIELD, and click the CLOSE button.

Creating complex table elements using the table control wizard

Next you attend to the input fields for the position information. As was already described in this exercise, table controls for several positions need to be implemented. This can be done using the table control wizard.

▷ Click the TABLE CONTROL (USING WIZARD) button on the left of the screen in the control bar.

▷ Click the upper right area of the window, and use the mouse to hold and drag the frame to the required size that is sufficient to include the buttons to be added in the next steps (you can also change this again at any time). See Figure 5.46.

▷ Release the mouse button to start the table control wizard.

A dialog window appears that leads you step by step to the interface for the table control (see Figure 5.47).

▷ Read the text, and then click the CONTINUE button.

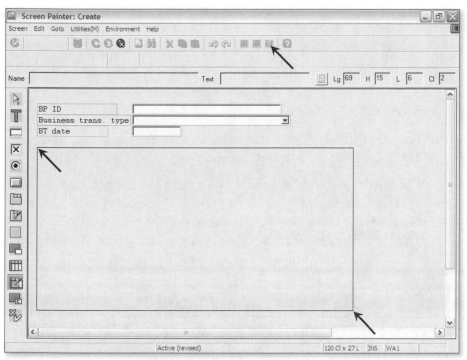

Figure 5.46 Expanding the Area for the Table Control

Figure 5.47 Initial Screen of the Table Control Wizard

Main tasks of
the wizard

As you can see, in addition to creating the interface element, one of the table control wizard's main tasks is to automatically program the screen flow logic that is required to transfer data, scroll page by page, and so on. It therefore saves you a lot of work.

▷ Enter "POSITION_TABLE" as the future name of the table control, and select CONTINUE.

The table control will be addressed from the screen flow logic under this POSITION_TABLE name from hereon out.

▷ Select the INTERNAL PROGRAM TABLE radio button, and enter the "G_POSITION_TC_ITAB" table as the name. The structure information for the columns to be displayed in the next step comes from this internal table. Select the TABLE WORK AREA button, and enter "G_POSITION_TC_WA" as the name (see Figure 5.48).

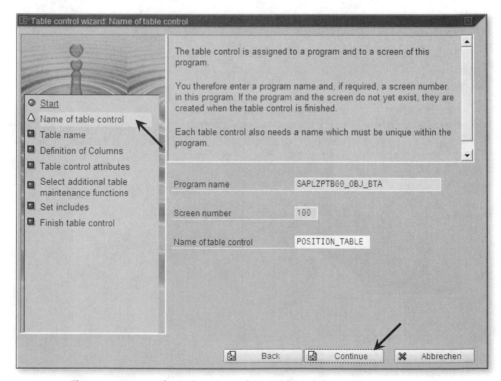

Figure 5.48 Specifying the Name of the Table and the Work Area

▷ Click the CONTINUE button.

The structure information of the table is read and displayed in a list. From this information, you now select the fields that you want to be displayed in the table control.

▷ Select the PR_ID, PSTYPE, WH_ID, AMOUNT, CURRENCY, QUANTITY, and UNIT columns and then click the CONTINUE button.

Some attributes of the table control that refer to the ready-for-input status of the selected columns are queried next (see Figure 5.49).

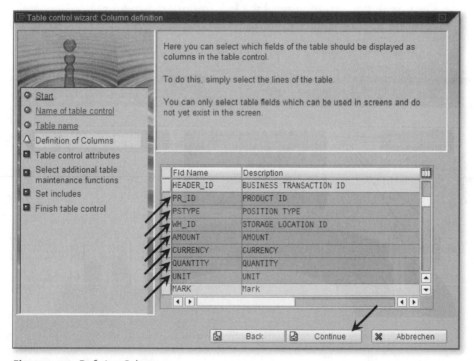

Figure 5.49 Defining Columns

▷ Select the INPUT radio button. Only then can the user enter his values in the lines.

▷ Check the WITH COLUMN HEADERS checkbox.

▷ Check the WITH SELECTION COLUMN checkbox. This enables you to select individual lines of the table control to then be able to delete or move them, for example.

▷ Select the MULTIPLE radio button, which enables you to select several lines.

▷ Depending on the version of the SAP NetWeaver Application Server, you can also enter the selection column directly here. Enter "MARK" in this case.

▷ Click the CONTINUE button.

Naturally, you want to use all the features offered and therefore check all the options available for selection in the next screen.

▷ Check the SCROLL, INSERT/DELETE LINE, and SELECT/DESELECT ALL checkboxes. Programming code is automatically generated at a later stage for all selected features.

▷ Click the CONTINUE button.

Inserting the include files

Next, insert the include files where you want to store the generated program code (see Figure 5.50). It is important that you always store the data (as suggested by the wizard) in the TOP include of the function group because this means that all functions can access it. This allows the screen and the ABAP program to communicate easily with one another. You can also store the program code for the PAI and PBO processing in a common include. However, use the wizard recommendations here.

▷ Leave the details for the individual include files unchanged, and select the CONTINUE button.

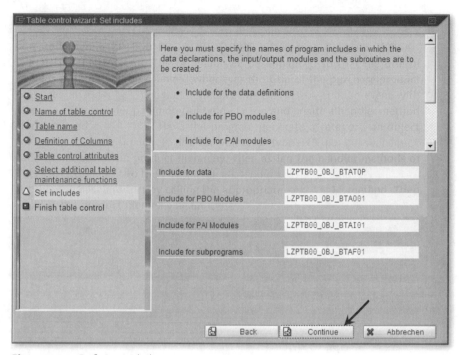

Figure 5.50 Defining Includes

All the required information has now been accepted and in the next step you're prompted to confirm whether you now want to create the table control with all its program code.

▷ Select the BACK button to start the generating process.

After a short wait time, during which the includes are being created, the table control appears on the interface of the program window that you designed yourself (see Figure 5.51). You now optimize the interface layout of the table a little. First, drag the individual fields to a width that corresponds to the quantity of data to be expected. For the fields that provide only a small amount of possible input data, use a listbox to make the input easier. This is somewhat faster to use than the standard $\boxed{\text{F4}}$ help, which is also suitable for very large amounts of data.

Optimizing the interface design

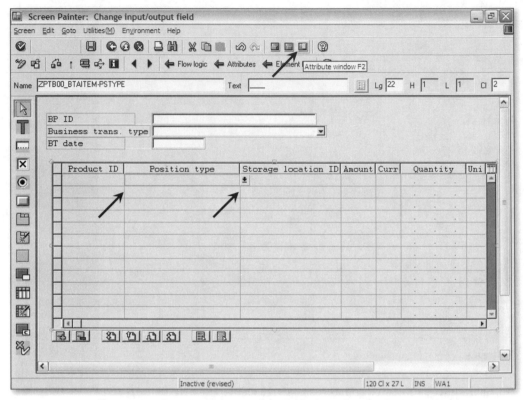

Figure 5.51 Dragging Columns of the Table Control to the Optimum Width

▷ Click a table column (not a column header) and then drag the margin via drag-and-drop to the required width.

▷ Click the POSITION TYPE table column (not the column header), and then select the ATTRIBUTES button.

The ATTRIBUTE window is displayed in the foreground.

▷ Select LISTBOX WITH KEY from the dropdown list.

▷ Click the PRODUCT ID column title without closing the ATTRIBUTES window, and enter LISTBOX WITH KEY in the dropdown field.

▷ Click the STORAGE LOCATION ID column title without closing the ATTRIBUTES window, and enter LISTBOX WITH KEY in the dropdown field.

▷ Click the CURRENCY column title without closing the ATTRIBUTES window, and enter "Curr" as the text in the ATTRIBUTES window.

▷ Click the UNIT column title without closing the ATTRIBUTES window, and enter "Uni" as the text in the ATTRIBUTES window.

▷ Select the table control. The best way to do this is by clicking the scrollbar on the right-hand margin.

Check whether the table control wizard has performed the following activities (see Figure 5.52):

▷ The MULTIPLE radio button is selected under the COLUMN SEL. header in the ATTRIBUTES window.

▷ The WITH COLUMN SEL. checkbox is selected.

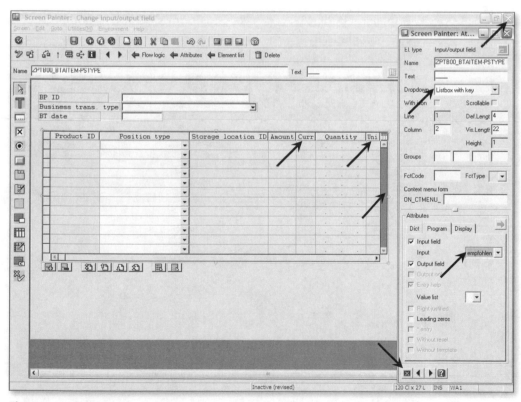

Figure 5.52 Adjusting the Columns and Headers of the Table Control Individually

▷ "G_POSITION_TC_WA-MARK" is entered as the name for the selection column.

▷ Close the ATTRIBUTES window by clicking the CLOSE button.

▷ Close the SAP Screen Painter by clicking the CLOSE button.

Adjusting the screen flow logic

Depending on the version of SAP NetWeaver Application Server you use, you must now manually adjust the selection column in the automatically generated source code because a syntax error otherwise will occur at activation time (see Figure 5.53).

▷ Switch to the FLOW LOGIC tab, and change line 30 to "FIELD G_POSITION_TC_WA-MARK."

▷ Remove the comment selection before the last MODULE USER_COMMAND_0100 line, and click SAVE.

▷ Double-click the USER_COMMAND_0100 term so that the module is created automatically.

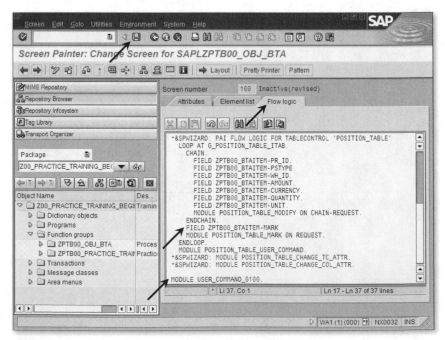

Figure 5.53 Adjusting the Screen Flow Logic

326

A dialog box opens, asking whether you want to create the module.

▷ Click YES.

Another dialog box opens, enabling you to modify the include in which the module is created.

▷ Select "LZPTB00_OBJ_BTAI01" as the include.

▷ Enter "USER_COMMAND_0100" as the short text and select the CON-TINUE button.

The empty module appears in the source code editor, and you can program it together with the other modules in the last step.

Next, you are supposed to intercept the CANCEL button. You need an additional module for this, which is only called at the time of the USER_EXIT.

▷ Enhance the source code MODULE USER_EXIT_0100 in the PAI flow logic of the screen as in Figure 5.54, and click the SAVE button.

Figure 5.54 Further Adjusting the Screen Flow Logic

327

▷ Double-click the USER_EXIT_0100 term so that the module is created automatically.

A dialog box opens, asking whether you want to create the module.

▷ Click YES.

Another dialog box opens, enabling you to modify the include in which the module is created.

▷ Select "LZPTB00_OBJ_BTAI01" as the include.

▷ Enter "USER_EXIT_0100" as the short text, and click the CONTINUE button.

Third module

This empty module is also supposed to be programmed together with the other modules in the last step. You first need a third module where you can set the GUI status and GUI title that you created. Of course, this only makes sense in the PBO block (that is, before the screen is output). In the same module, you can then also handle the transfer of the header data to the corresponding interface elements.

▷ Remove the comment asterisk before the last command in the PBO block MODULE STATUS_0100, and click the SAVE button.

▷ Double-click the STATUS_0100 term so that the module is created automatically.

A dialog box opens, asking whether you want to create the module.

▷ Click YES.

Another dialog box opens, enabling you to modify the include in which the module is created.

▷ Select "LZPTB00_OBJ_BTAO01" as the include.

▷ Enter "STATUS_0100" as the short text, and click the CONTINUE button.

You have now created all the modules in the screen flow logic that you require. All modules are within two includes, separated according to PBO and PAI logic. All modules are called from the screen flow logic, the source code of which you want to look at first.

▷ In the object list area, double-click screen 100 to display its properties in the tools area.

▷ Switch to the FLOW LOGIC tab, and complete the source code according to the following example:

```
PROCESS BEFORE OUTPUT.
*&SPWIZARD: PBO FLOW LOGIC FOR TABLECONTROL *&'POSITION_TABLE'
  MODULE POSITION_TABLE_CHANGE_TC_ATTR.
*&SPWIZARD: MODULE POSITION_TABLE_CHANGE_COL_ATTR.
  LOOP AT   G_POSITION_TC_ITAB
       INTO G_POSITION_TC_WA
       WITH CONTROL POSITION_TABLE
       CURSOR POSITION_TABLE-CURRENT_LINE.
*&SPWIZARD:   MODULE POSITION_TABLE_CHANGE_FIELD_ATTR
    MODULE POSITION_TABLE_GET_LINES.
  ENDLOOP.

  MODULE status_0100.

PROCESS AFTER INPUT.
  module user_exit_0100 at exit-command.
*&SPWIZARD: PAI FLOW LOGIC FOR TABLECONTROL
*'POSITION_TABLE'
  LOOP AT G_POSITION_TABLE_ITAB.
    CHAIN.
       FIELD G_POSITION_TC_WA-PR_ID.
       FIELD G_POSITION_TC_WA-PSTYPE.
       FIELD G_POSITION_TC_WA-WH_ID.
       FIELD G_POSITION_TC_WA-AMOUNT.
       FIELD G_POSITION_TC_WA-CURRENCY.
       FIELD G_POSITION_TC_WA-QUANTITY.
       FIELD G_POSITION_TC_WA-UNIT.
       FIELD G_POSITION_TC_WA-MARK
       MODULE POSITION_TABLE_MODIFY ON CHAIN-REQUEST.
    ENDCHAIN.
    FIELD G_POSITION_TC_WA-MARK
    MODULE POSITION_TABLE_MARK ON REQUEST.
  ENDLOOP.
  MODULE POSITION_TABLE_USER_COMMAND.
*&SPWIZARD: MODULE POSITION_TABLE_CHANGE_TC_ATTR.
*&SPWIZARD: MODULE POSITION_TABLE_CHANGE_COL_ATTR.
```

```
MODULE user_command_0100.
```

Listing 5.3 Source Code of Screen 0100 Flow Logic

Explanation of the source code of the screen flow logic

You have inserted only three lines in this source code. As the last command in the PBO block, you have arranged the `status_0100` module, where you set the GUI status and GUI title and transfer the header data to the corresponding interface element. The handling of the CANC function code was set in the `user_exit_0100` module. Thanks to the special distinction as function type "E," the function code can be processed by this module. The third module `user_command_0100` contains the processing of the remaining function codes for the SAVE, BACK, and EXIT buttons specifically.

The next step involves the logic for outputting the screen (PBO).

▷ Load the LZPTB00_OBJ_BTAO01 include, and enter the following source code:

```
*&------------------------------------------------------*
*&   Include           LZPTB00_OBJ_BTAO01
*&------------------------------------------------------*

*&SPWIZARD: OUTPUT MODULE FOR TC 'POSITION_TABLE'.
*DO NOT CHANGE THIS LI
*&SPWIZARD: UPDATE LINES FOR EQUIVALENT SCROLLBAR
MODULE position_table_change_tc_attr OUTPUT.
  DESCRIBE TABLE g_position_tc_itab LINES position_table-
lines.
ENDMODULE.                      "POSITION_TABLE_CHANGE_TC_ATTR
OUTPUT

*&SPWIZARD: OUTPUT MODULE FOR TC 'POSITION_TABLE'.
*DO NOT CHANGE THIS LI
*&SPWIZARD: GET LINES OF TABLECONTROL
MODULE POSITION_TABLE_GET_LINES OUTPUT.
  G_POSITION_TABLE_LINES = SY-LOOPC.
ENDMODULE.              "POSITION_TABLE_GET_LINES OUTPUT

*&------------------------------------------------------*
*&      Module  STATUS_0100  OUTPUT                      *
```

```
*&---------------------------------------------------------*
* Setting of GUI-Status, titlebar and initialization  *
* of header data.                                      *
*---------------------------------------------------------*
MODULE STATUS_0100 OUTPUT.

  SET PF-STATUS 'ZPTB00_OBJ_BTA_STD'.
  SET TITLEBAR 'ZPTB00_OBJ_BTA_STD'.

  IF g_data_copied IS INITIAL.
    FIELD-SYMBOLS:
      <g_str_item> TYPE zptb00_btaitem.
* assign header data to appropriate controls
    zptb00_btaheader-bp_id = g_str_bta-bp_id.
    zptb00_btaheader-bttype = g_str_bta-bttype.
    zptb00_btaheader-btdate = g_str_bta-btdate.
    LOOP AT g_str_bta-tab_item ASSIGNING <g_str_item>.
      MOVE-CORRESPONDING <g_str_item> TO g_position_tc_wa.
      APPEND g_position_tc_wa TO g_position_tc_itab.
    ENDLOOP.
    REFRESH CONTROL 'POSITION_TABLE' FROM SCREEN '0100'.
    g_data_copied = 'X'.
  ENDIF.
ENDMODULE.                    " STATUS_0100 OUTPUT
```

Listing 5.4 Source Code of the LZPTB00_OBJ_BTAO01 Include

The source code begins with the three generated modules that you nevertheless leave untouched. The first source code is part of the STA-TUS_0100 module. The first thing you need to do is set the GUI status and GUI title required. You also need to perform a first initialization of the header and position interface elements. The g_data_copied variable ensures that the execution is only performed once because it is immediately set to 'X' after being assigned, which means that the IF statement will not be run a second time.

Explanation of the source code of the LZPTB00_OBJ_BTAO0 include

Continue with the logic for outputting the screen (PAI).

▷ Load the LZPTB00_OBJ_BTAI01 include, and enter the following source code:

```
*&---------------------------------------------------------*
```

```
*&  Include            LZPTB00_OBJ_BTAI01              *
*&-----------------------------------------------------*


*&SPWIZARD: INPUT MODULE FOR TC 'POSITION_TABLE'.
*DO NOT CHANGE THIS LINE
*&SPWIZARD: MODIFY TABLE
MODULE POSITION_TABLE_MODIFY INPUT.
  MODIFY G_POSITION_TC_ITAB
    FROM G_POSITION_TC_WA
    INDEX POSITION_TABLE-CURRENT_LINE.
ENDMODULE.                   "POSITION_TABLE_MODIFY INPUT


*&SPWIZARD: INPUT MODULE FOR TC 'POSITION_TABLE'.
*DO NOT CHANGE THIS LIN
*&SPWIZARD: MARK TABLE
MODULE POSITION_TABLE_MARK INPUT.
  MODIFY G_POSITION_TC_ITAB
    FROM G_POSITION_TC_WA
    INDEX POSITION_TABLE-CURRENT_LINE
    TRANSPORTING MARK.
ENDMODULE.                   "POSITION_TABLE_MARK INPUT


*&SPWIZARD: INPUT MODULE FOR TC 'POSITION_TABLE'.
*DO NOT CHANGE THIS LIN
*&SPWIZARD: PROCESS USER COMMAND
MODULE POSITION_TABLE_USER_COMMAND INPUT.
  PERFORM USER_OK_TC USING    'POSITION_TABLE'
                              'G_POSITION_TC_ITAB'
                              'MARK'
                 CHANGING OK_CODE.
ENDMODULE.             "POSITION_TABLE_USER_COMMAND INPUT


*&-----------------------------------------------------*
*&      Module  USER_COMMAND_0100  INPUT               *
*&-----------------------------------------------------*
*       text                                           *
*------------------------------------------------------*
MODULE USER_COMMAND_0100 INPUT.
  DATA:
* Popup
    g_answer TYPE c,
* Position checking
```

```
       g_index TYPE sy-tabix,
       g_str_item TYPE zptb00_btaitem.
*    save_ok LIKE ok_code.
   FIELD-SYMBOLS:
* Position checking
       <position_str> TYPE zptb00_btaitem.

   IF  ok_code = 'BACK' OR ok_code = 'QUIT'.
      CALL FUNCTION 'POPUP_TO_CONFIRM_STEP'
         EXPORTING
*           DEFAULTOPTION         = 'Y'
            textline1             = text-003
*           TEXTLINE2             = ' '
            titel                 = text-001
*           START_COLUMN          = 25
*           START_ROW             = 6
*           CANCEL_DISPLAY        = 'X'
         IMPORTING
            ANSWER                = g_answer .
      IF g_answer = 'N'.
        CLEAR g_str_bta.
        LEAVE TO SCREEN 0.
      ELSEIF g_answer = 'J'.
        ok_code = 'SAVE'.
      ENDIF.
   ENDIF.
   IF ok_code = 'SAVE'.
* check header data
      IF ZPTB00_BTAHEADER-BP_ID IS INITIAL.
        MESSAGE i006(zptb00_bta).
        RETURN.
      ENDIF.
      IF ZPTB00_BTAHEADER-BTTYPE IS INITIAL.
        MESSAGE i007(zptb00_bta).
        RETURN.
      ENDIF.
      IF ZPTB00_BTAHEADER-btdate IS INITIAL.
        MESSAGE i008(zptb00_bta).
        RETURN.
      ENDIF.
* check position data
      LOOP AT G_POSITION_TC_ITAB ASSIGNING
```

```
         <position_str>.
           g_index = sy-tabix.
           IF <position_str>-pr_id IS INITIAL.
             MESSAGE i000(zptb00_bta) WITH g_index.
             RETURN.
           ENDIF.
           IF <position_str>-pstype IS INITIAL.
             MESSAGE i001(zptb00_bta) WITH g_index.
             RETURN.
           ENDIF.
           IF <position_str>-amount IS INITIAL.
             MESSAGE i002(zptb00_bta) WITH g_index.
             RETURN.
           ENDIF.
           IF <position_str>-currency IS INITIAL.
             MESSAGE i003(zptb00_bta) WITH g_index.
             RETURN.
           ENDIF.
           IF <position_str>-quantity IS INITIAL.
             MESSAGE i004(zptb00_bta) WITH g_index.
             RETURN.
           ENDIF.
           IF <position_str>-unit IS INITIAL.
             MESSAGE i005(zptb00_bta) WITH g_index.
             RETURN.
           ENDIF.
* put header data into communication structure
* g_str_bta
           IF g_str_bta-header_id IS INITIAL.
             CALL FUNCTION 'GUID_CREATE'
                 IMPORTING
*                EV_GUID_16      =
*                EV_GUID_22      =
                 ev_guid_32      = g_str_bta-header_id.
           ENDIF.
           g_str_bta-bp_id = ZPTB00_BTAHEADER-bp_id.
           g_str_bta-bttype = ZPTB00_BTAHEADER-bttype.
           g_str_bta-btdate = ZPTB00_BTAHEADER-btdate.

* put position data into communication structure
* g_str_bta
           READ TABLE g_str_bta-tab_item INDEX g_index INTO
```

```
        g_str_item.
        IF sy-subrc <> 0.
          MOVE-CORRESPONDING <position_str> TO g_str_item.
          CALL FUNCTION 'GUID_CREATE'
                IMPORTING
*                  EV_GUID_16        =
*                  EV_GUID_22        =
                   ev_guid_32        = g_str_item-item_id.
          g_str_item-HEADER_ID = g_str_bta-header_id.
          APPEND g_str_item TO g_str_bta-tab_item.
        ELSE.
          IF g_str_item-item_id IS INITIAL.
            MOVE-CORRESPONDING <position_str> TO g_str_item.
            CALL FUNCTION 'GUID_CREATE'
                  IMPORTING
*                    EV_GUID_16        =
*                    EV_GUID_22        =
                     ev_guid_32        = g_str_item item_id.
            g_str_item-HEADER_ID = g_str_bta-header_id.
          ENDIF.
          MODIFY g_str_bta-tab_item FROM g_str_item INDEX
          g_index.
        ENDIF.
      ENDLOOP.
      LEAVE TO SCREEN 0.
    ENDIF.
    CLEAR ok_code.
ENDMODULE.                    " USER_COMMAND_0100   INPUT
*&---------------------------------------------------------*
*&      Module   user_exit_0100   INPUT                    *
*&---------------------------------------------------------*
*       text                                               *
*---------------------------------------------------------*
MODULE user_exit_0100 INPUT.
* has the user typed in any data? ...
  IF sy-datar = 'X'.
* ... then we have to confirm the cancel process
    CALL FUNCTION 'POPUP_TO_CONFIRM_LOSS_OF_DATA'
      EXPORTING
        textline1             = text-002
*       TEXTLINE2             = ' '
        titel                 = text-001
*       START_COLUMN          = 25
```

```
*        START_ROW          = 6
*        DEFAULTOPTION      = 'N'
         IMPORTING
            answer                  = g_answer .
     ELSE.
*  ... otherwise we need no confirmation
        g_answer = 'J'.
     ENDIF.
     IF g_answer = 'J'.
        CLEAR g_str_bta.
        LEAVE TO SCREEN 0.
     ENDIF.

   ENDMODULE.                       " user_exit_0100   INPUT
```

Listing 5.5   Source Code of the LZPTB00_OBJ_BTAI01 Include

Explanation of the source code of the LZPTB00_OBJ_BTAI01 include

The source code begins with the three generated modules that you nevertheless leave untouched. The first source code is part of the USER_COMMAND_0100 module and mainly deals with checking user entries. When we created the GUI status, you already ensured that this module is always called when the user clicks the SAVE, BACK, or EXIT buttons.

You then find the corresponding function code in the ok_code variable and can diversify the other procedure into a simple IF statement. Use the POPUP_TO_CONFIRM_STEP function to execute a confirmation prompt for the BACK and QUIT function codes. The user can answer this prompt with YES (save before), NO (do not save), and CANCEL (do not exit the screen).

Depending on the user's answer, which is available in the g_answer variable, you delete the g_str_bta global variable—this is the standard procedure that you follow if the SAVE button was not clicked. Alternatively, set the programming of ok_code to SAVE so that the next IF statement is executed. The ok_code SAVE requires the user to have entered all the data correctly. Check this using different IF statements that issue error messages, if necessary.

You fill the displayed fields of the global g_str_bta structure as well as the remaining fields (not shown on the interface) only when all checks have been performed. In this case, pay particular attention to the fact that a new GUID can only be generated for the primary key of the header and the items if the user has also actually inserted the corresponding line again. Otherwise, copy the existing GUID, which will result in the existing data being overwritten on the database.

Finally, exit the screen using LEAVE TO SCREEN 0. As a result, the program execution is continued in the calling ZPTB00_OBJ_BTA_EDIT function.

Exiting the screen

The User_Exit_0100 module proceeds in exactly the same way; however, it's executed before all the checks and also contains only a confirmation prompt to see whether the user wants to exit the window despite the threat of loss of data.

▷ Enter the following source code for the ZPTB00_OBJ_BTA_EDIT function:

```
FUNCTION zptb00_obj_bta_edit.
*"----------------------------------------------------
*"*"Local interface:
*"  CHANGING
*"     REFERENCE(C_STR_BTA) TYPE  ZPTB00_STR_BTA
*"     OPTIONAL
*"----------------------------------------------------
DATA:
  l_str_item type ZPTB00_BTAITEM.

  IF c_str_bta IS INITIAL.
* Just add one line to the position by default
    APPEND l_str_item TO c_str_bta-tab_item.
  ENDIF.

* Make manual posting global for dynpro
  MOVE-CORRESPONDING c_str_bta TO g_str_bta.
* Call edit screen
  CALL SCREEN 0100.
* If the user pressed save and everthing is fine,
* then g_str_bta is filled with user input;
* Otherwise the structure is initial;
* Move edited data back to our interface variable
    MOVE-CORRESPONDING g_str_bta TO c_str_bta.
ENDFUNCTION.
```

Listing 5.6 Source Code of the ZPTB00_OBJ_BTA_EDIT Function

Explanation of the
source code for
the ZPTB00_OBJ_
BTA_EDIT function

As you can see, calling the screen this way is very easy. To be expedient, first add a line to the `tab_items`, provided the overall structure is initial. This saves the user from later having to click the INSERT button that was created by the table control wizard. After you've transferred the data to be displayed from the changing parameter into the global structure, call the screen using `CALL SCREEN 0100`. Then transfer the global data in `g_str_bta` back into the changing parameter.

The next step involves the source code of the ZPTB00_OBJ_BTA_SAVE function for saving the entered business transaction in the database.

▷ Enter the following source code for the ZPTB00_OBJ_BTA_SAVE function:

```
FUNCTION ZPTB00_OBJ_BTA_SAVE.
*"----------------------------------------------------------
*"*"Local interface:
*"  IMPORTING
*"    REFERENCE(I_STR_BTA) TYPE  ZPTB00_STR_BTA
*"  EXCEPTIONS
*"    FAILED
*"----------------------------------------------------------

  DATA:
* Structure like header and item table
    l_str_btaheader TYPE ZPTB00_BTAHEADER,
    l_tab_btaitem TYPE STANDARD TABLE OF
    ZPTB00_BTAITEM.

* Get header data and write to database table
  MOVE-CORRESPONDING i_str_bta TO l_str_btaheader.
  MODIFY ZPTB00_BTAHEADER FROM l_str_btaheader.
  IF sy-subrc <> 0.
    RAISE FAILED.
  ENDIF.

  DELETE FROM ZPTB00_BTAITEM WHERE HEADER_ID =
    l_str_btaheader-HEADER_ID.
  INSERT ZPTB00_BTAITEM FROM TABLE i_str_bta-tab_item.
  IF sy-subrc <> 0.
```

```
   RAISE FAILED.
  ENDIF.

ENDFUNCTION.
```

Listing 5.7   Source Code of the ZPTB00_OBJ_BTA_SAVE Function

This source code is also very short. It basically contains the call of the MODIFY database command for the header table. The MODIFY command first tries to insert the data record. If this doesn't work because a data record is already saved under the same ID, the command overwrites it.

Explanation of the source code for the ZPTB00_OBJ_BTA_SAVE function

A slightly different procedure was necessary for the item table because the data records which were deleted by the user in the interface should also be deleted in the database. You therefore first delete all data records belonging to the specified header. You can then be sure that the INSERT command stores the correct position lines on the database.

You only need to insert the following additional lines in this generated source code:

Explanation of the source code of the LZPTB00_OBJ_BTATOP TOP include

```
DATA:
  g_str_bta TYPE ZPTB00_STR_BTA
```

Lastly, you still require the source code for the ZPTB00_BUSINESS_TRANSACTION main program.

▷ Enter the following source code in the ZPTB00_BUSINESS_TRANS-ACTION program.

```
REPORT  ZPTB00_BUSINESS_TRANSACTION.
DATA:
  l_str_bta type ZPTB00_Str_BTA.

DO.
  CALL FUNCTION 'ZPTB00_OBJ_BTA_EDIT'
    CHANGING
      C_STR_BTA = l_str_bta.

  IF NOT l_str_bta IS INITIAL.
```

```
      CALL FUNCTION 'ZPTB00_OBJ_BTA_SAVE'
        EXPORTING
          I_STR_BTA = l_str_bta
        EXCEPTIONS
          FAILED    = 1
          OTHERS    = 2.
      CLEAR l_str_bta.
    ELSE.
      RETURN.
    ENDIF.
  ENDDO.
```

Listing 5.8 Source Code of the ZPTB00_BUSINESS_TRANSACTION Program

Explanation of the source code You place the call for the window in an endless loop as usual. This is only exited when the value of the l_str_bta structure is initial. Otherwise, the EDIT and SAVE functions are called consecutively. Because you always ensure within the screen PAI processing that the g_str_bta global variable there is returned as initial for all actions except SAVE, we can depend on there being a valid input to save here if the l_str_bta variable is filled.

Testing the program You can now test the functional efficiency of your source code in the running program.

▷ Click the ACTIVATE button, and then click DIRECT.

The program starts and shows the interface for inputting a business transaction (see Figure 5.55).

▷ Specify "Bayer" as the business partner, "PURCHASE Product" as the business transaction type, and "01.01.2014" as the business transaction date.

▷ Click the INSERT button to insert an initial position line in the table.

▷ In the position line, enter "Aspirin" as the product ID, "PRODUCT" as the position type, "1st floor, 1st space" as the storage location ID, "1000" as the amount, "EUR" as the currency, "10000" as the quantity, and "ST" as the unit.

▷ Click the SAVE button.

Figure 5.55 Inputting and Saving a Business Transaction

The program displays an empty input screen for inputting a new business transaction after the data record has been saved on the database.

In professional ABAP development, screens are usually created in function groups and the call is controlled using function modules. This practice makes it much easier to reuse the screens because the function module can be called directly from any other program.

The introduction of object-oriented programming triggered a real improvement in productivity for many programming languages, because such programming often involves new frameworks and component libraries that simplify the programming of interfaces and database programming.

6   Object-Oriented Language Elements

Object-oriented programming is one of the most important achievements of modern software development. The initial research occurred in the 1970s at research facilities like the Massachusetts Institute of Technology (MIT). Ever since the enhancement of the C programming language with object-oriented capabilities that became common in the 1990s and that was standardized by ISO as C++, the dominance of object-oriented programming has been unstoppable. In the meantime, most general programming languages like C++, Java, Delphi, and the latest version of Visual Basic, VB.NET, are equipped with object-oriented language enhancements. Even special-purpose programming languages—like COBOL for financial and mathematical purposes, PROLOG for software projects that involve artificial intelligence, and ABAP for business applications—have all been expanded to include object-oriented capabilities. In some cases, the enhancements improve flexibility so much that a special-purpose programming language can achieve the status of a general-purpose language.

Due to the pressure of increasingly larger and evermore complex software development projects, procedural programming has focused on the reusability of program parts (subprograms and functions). Object-orientation is the preliminary goal: It combines program parts and data into reusable units, or *objects*.

What is an object orientation?

Theoretically, you can meet all the requirements of software with procedural or object-oriented programming. No hard and fast rule exists as to when one approach should be used over the other, but the existing

Object-oriented and procedural programming

and new software solutions from SAP make one thing clear: The more that an application focuses on the mass processing of data, the greater the preference for procedural programming. The opposite also holds true. Applications with numerous user interfaces are often created with object-oriented programming. You must decide carefully which approach to use and consider the related modules.

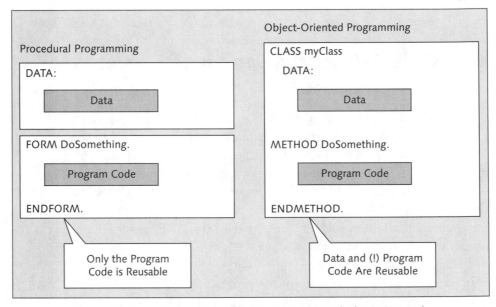

Figure 6.1 Comparison of Procedural Programming and Object-Oriented Programming

History of ABAP Objects As of SAP Basis 4.5, the ABAP programming language has supported the initial functionalities of a typical object-oriented programming language. With SAP Basis 4.6, the functions became mature and complete, so SAP changed the name of the language from ABAP/4 to ABAP Objects. The appearance of Release 6.10 showed some cosmetic improvements, such as simplified notation. For example, users can omit the CALL METHOD command when calling a method, as long as no opening parenthesis follows the name of the method. This syntax is similar to that of C++ and Java. Release 6.20 has no innovations in this area. By now, SAP NetWeaver Application Server supports ABAP Objects and Java equally.

Even if users of other common programming languages found procedural programming with ABAP odd and unusual, they feel completely at home with object-oriented programming. Users of other languages often prefer object-oriented programming, and beginners prefer procedural programming. Whichever programming method you prefer, you'll find support in both camps. However, it is essential that you become familiar with the language in order to work successfully in your projects.

Tips for those familiar with other programming languages

6.1 Classes and Objects—CLASS, CREATE OBJECT, METHOD

Classes and objects are key terms in object-oriented programming. But learning about object-oriented programming is not merely a matter of mastering new terms; it's also a whole new way of thinking. You should become familiar with this new way of thinking by using ABAP Objects but without ignoring its roots in procedural programming.

The design of object-oriented programming emerged against the background of procedural programming, so it can best be understood from that starting point. Let's look at the evolution of object-oriented programming (see Figure 6.2).

Basics

▶ **Structured Data and Program**
When programming language development first began, you could use only the main memory (hardware), a main processor (hardware), and the machine language (software) to define the interplay of the main memory and main processor in programs. When a program started, the machine language commands and the data defined in the commands were loaded into the main memory and stored in a structure. The main processor then worked through the machine language command step by step, which usually involved using the data for calculations and changing the data. After the last machine language command, the result was defined and could be output from main memory to a printer, for example.

▶ **Structured Data and Reusable Functions**
The procedural programming concept of high-level languages like C and Pascal required significant simplification to enable processing of

345

the structured data in the main memory by modular, reusable functions. Homemade or commercial function libraries simplified software development and freed programmers from the obligation to be an expert in every field.

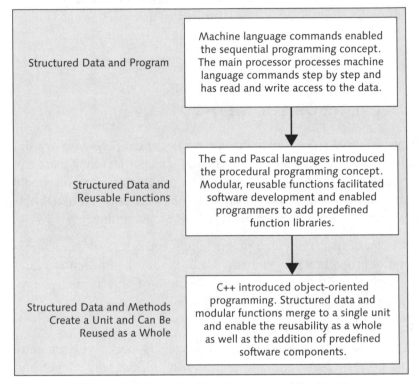

Structured Data and Program	Machine language commands enabled the sequential programming concept. The main processor processes machine language commands step by step and has read and write access to the data.
Structured Data and Reusable Functions	The C and Pascal languages introduced the procedural programming concept. Modular, reusable functions facilitated software development and enabled programmers to add predefined function libraries.
Structured Data and Methods Create a Unit and Can Be Reused as a Whole	C++ introduced object-oriented programming. Structured data and modular functions merge to a single unit and enable the reusability as a whole as well as the addition of predefined software components.

Figure 6.2 Evolution from Procedural to Object-Oriented Programming

▶ **Structured Data and Functions Create a Unit That Can Be Reused as a Whole**

Object-oriented represents that last great evolutionary step. It united the structured data in the main memory with the functions that process the data into a unit, which enabled reusability as a whole. A unit that consists of structured data and functions is referred to as an *object*; its definition is referred to as a *class*. For the most popular object-oriented languages like C++, Delphi, and Visual Basic.NET, a large market of software manufacturers has already formed, offering libraries of classes for almost any purpose, thereby forcing reusability across development projects and enterprises.

In ABAP Objects and other object-oriented programming languages, classes serve as templates for objects, much as data types act as templates and variables as reference variables. To continue the analogy with data types, classes are often called *object types*, which can make them easier to understand. Just as any number of variables (also called *data instances*) can be generated from one data type and used in a program, any number of objects (also called *object instances*) can be generated from a class and used in a program. The memory location of data instance is reserved exclusively and behaves in that manner with the data of an object.

Classes and objects

Along with a data definition, a class includes program code, also called *methods*, which is stored only once in memory and automatically supplied with data depending on the object instance. The primary task of a good object-oriented compiler or interpreter is to manage the instance-dependent data and shared program code of the objects with optimal performance, thereby ensuring that each object has unlimited access only to its data. The following section of code shows the definition and implementation of a class with the keywords CLASS and ENDCLASS, declaration of a reference variable of the class type, the generation of an object instance with the CREATE OBJECT command, and the use of a method. The following sections explain the background and rules of the commands used in this example.

Class definition and instantiation

```
REPORT  z_product_configurator.

* Class definition
CLASS lcl_product DEFINITION.
  PUBLIC SECTION.
    METHODS:
      set_price IMPORTING _price TYPE f.
    DATA:
      price TYPE f.
ENDCLASS.                     "lcl_product DEFINITION

*.Main program start ***
DATA:
  l_rcl_product TYPE REF TO lcl_product.
```

```
CREATE OBJECT l_rcl_product.
CALL METHOD l_rcl_product->set_price
  EXPORTING
    _price = '123'.
* Main program end ***

* Class implementation
CLASS lcl_product IMPLEMENTATION.
  METHOD set_price.
    price = _price.
  ENDMETHOD.                    "lcl_product
ENDCLASS.                       "lcl_product IMPLEMENTATION
```

Listing 6.1 Code Fragment for the Definition and Use of Classes and Objects

Class definition
and visibility
of attributes
and methods

Data (*attributes*) and functions (*methods*) can be defined within a class. The first is introduced with the keyword DATA; the second with METHODS. Various visibility sections ensure that the other parts of a program can access only selected attributes and methods of a class. The rest is invisible to them. ABAP has three visibility sections, each with its own keyword:

▶ PUBLIC SECTION

Other sections of a program can use all attributes and methods executed in the public section—to read the value of an attribute or call a method, for example. The following example shows the definition of a class with public methods and attributes:

```
CLASS lcl_product DEFINITION.
  PUBLIC SECTION.
    METHODS:
      set_price IMPORTING _price TYPE f.
    DATA:
      price TYPE f.
ENDCLASS.                       "lcl_product DEFINITION
```

▶ PROTECTED SECTION

Only "descendants" of a class can use all the attributes and methods from the protected sections. Section 6.2, Inheritance and Polymorphism—INHERITING FROM, REDEFINITION, explains the exact meaning here, but right now it will suffice to know that the other parts of a program (with a few exceptions) don't have access to attributes and methods. The following example shows the definition of a class with protected methods and attributes:

```
CLASS lcl_product DEFINITION.
  PROTECTED SECTION.
    METHODS:
      set_price IMPORTING _price TYPE f.
    DATA:
      price TYPE f.
ENDCLASS.                     "lcl_product DEFINITION
```

▶ **PRIVATE SECTION**

All attributes and methods from the private section of a class can be used only by its own methods (and those from the other two sections). They are invisible to all other parts of a program. (Private *friends* are an exception that this book does not deal with.) The following example shows the definition of a class with private methods and attributes:

```
CLASS lcl_product DEFINITION.
  PRIVATE SECTION.
    METHODS:
      set_price IMPORTING _price TYPE f.
    DATA:
      price TYPE f.
ENDCLASS.                     "lcl_product DEFINITION
```

You can use the visibility sections during programming to define exactly who can use given attributes and methods. This ability helps you create clear and unique interfaces, which has a positive effect on development in a team. ABAP doesn't support the visibility level familiar from Java, Package, for visibility within a packet of classes, or the level familiar from Delphi, published, for properties that should appear in the object inspector. Instead, the package concept described in Section 2.1, Getting Started with the SAP Object Navigator, covers visibility at the packet level. ABAP objects require specification of visibility. Unlike the case with most other programming languages, a class does not need to be introduced with the keyword TYPE for a type definition. Use of the keywords CLASS, ENDCLASS, and DEFINITION sufficiently identifies the definition.

The following code fragment shows the syntax to define a class with attributes and methods:

```
REPORT SimpleProgram.
CLASS lcl_category DEFINITION.
  PUBLIC SECTION.
    DATA:
      title TYPE string.
    CONSTANTS:
      vat TYPE f VALUE '0.16'.
ENDCLASS.                  "lcl_category DEFINITION

CLASS lcl_product DEFINITION.
  PUBLIC SECTION.
    METHODS:
      constructor IMPORTING _category TYPE REF TO
        lcl_category,
      get_price RETURNING value(_price) TYPE f,
      set_price IMPORTING _price TYPE f.
    DATA:
      title TYPE string,
      description TYPE string,
      category TYPE REF TO lcl_category,
      unit TYPE string.
  PROTECTED SECTION.
    DATA:
      price TYPE f.
ENDCLASS.                        "lcl_product DEFINITION
```

Listing 6.2 Overview of the Definition and Implementation of Classes with Attributes and Methods

In ABAP Objects, the keywords DATA and METHODS are normally given only once per SECTION with a colon (:). The methods are then listed one after the other according to attribute. Alternatively, you could insert the appropriate keyword separately in front of each piece of data and method, along with a closing period (.) at the end of the statement. Procedural programming with ABAP uses the keywords IMPORTING, EXPORTING, CHANGING, and RETURNING. The last keyword is similar to the return parameters of other languages: you must specify exactly one parameter as value transfer (with keyword VALUE). ABAP doesn't support *properties* that might be familiar to you from the development environment of other programming languages and that elegantly encapsulate read and write access to attributes.

Unlike the case with Java, but similar to the case with C++ and Delphi, definition of a class in ABAP is separate from its implementation. A code section like the following listing is always required to complete the class definition given for the object:

Class implementation

```
CLASS lcl_product IMPLEMENTATION.
* constructor IMPORTING _category TYPE REF TO
* lcl_category,
  METHOD constructor.
    super->constructor( ).
    IF _category IS BOUND.
      category = _category.
    ELSE.
      CREATE OBJECT category TYPE lcl_category.
    ENDIF.
    price = 10.
    title = 'Cherry G80 3000'.
    description = 'Fully featured computer keyboard
                  with click.'.
    unit = 'Piece'.
  ENDMETHOD.                     "Constructor
*     get_price RETURNING value(_price) TYPE f,
  METHOD get_price.
    _price = price.
  ENDMETHOD.                     "get_price
*     set_price IMPORTING _price TYPE f.
  METHOD set_price.
    price = _price.
  ENDMETHOD.                     "set_price
ENDCLASS.                        "lcl_product IMPLEMENTATION
```

Listing 6.3 Code Fragment to Implement Classes

Setting off the entire implementation of a class with CLASS and ENDCLASS after the keyword IMPLEMENTATION makes it superfluous to specify a class with a period before each method, as is typical in most other programming languages. The signatures of a method (the transfer parameters) may not be repeated in the implementation area, as is typical in most other object-oriented languages. That's why it's helpful to include extensive comments in the source code and avoid having to jump between definition and implementation. Repeated specification of visibility is not allowed, as is true in other languages.

Referencing objects

ABAP Objects generally references objects. Unlike pointers in C++ and Delphi, and like references in Java and VisualBasic.Net, no calculation operations can be executed to manipulate data. That fact limits the technical freedom of programmers but also reduces the number of possible sources of errors. The runtime environment includes a garbage collector that automatically releases main memory that is no longer needed and automatically counts the number of references to an object. If the number drops to 0, the object is removed from main memory, without any special instructions from the programmer. In the example given above, the attribute `category` from class `cl_product` is such a reference. Each class has two predefined references that always exist and that the garbage collector ignores: the pseudo-reference SUPER to the superior class (see Section 6.2, Inheritance and Polymorphism—INHERITING FROM, REDEFINITION) and ME as a reference to the object itself.

Creating objects

The keyword CREATE OBJECT is available to create objects. With this keyword, you create the instance of a class, that is, an object, via program controls. The specification of the class after TYPE is optional, as long as the variable is completely typed, as shown in the following example. A generic REF TO OBJECT is not permitted. You can also create objects dynamically within a program by specifying a paired parameter after TYPE.

```
DATA:
  category TYPE REF TO lcl_category,
  classname TYPE string.
  CREATE OBJECT category. " Use type of variable
                          " category
  CREATE OBJECT category TYPE lcl_category. " Use type
                          " classname = 'lcl_category'.
  CREATE OBJECT category TYPE (classname). " Use type
                          " in variable classname
```

Listing 6.4 Creating Objects in Different Ways

All three commands given have exactly the same effect. It's easy to imagine that the value in `classname` can be looked up ahead of time in a database table. If no class with this name exists, the program ends after the `CREATE OBJECT` command.

Dereferencing an object for access to the attributes and methods available in it occurs with the pointer operator -> (as in C++), not with a period as in Java, Delphi, and VisualBasic.Net, because a period is already used to end a statement. Unlike other programming languages, ABAP Objects has strict restrictions on multiple instances of dereferencing in a statement.

Dereferencing objects

```
DATA:
  product TYPE REF TO lcl_product,
  category TYPE REF TO lcl_category.
CREATE OBJECT product.
product->category->title = 'Keyboard'.
```

Listing 6.5 Dereferencing Objects and Access to Attributes

The last statement in this example assumes that all references to the left of the equals sign (=) involve the attributes of objects, which is rarely the case in the real world and with good encapsulation of read and write access methods. If one or more methods appears in between, the object must first be assigned to an intermediate variable before you can define the next dereference, and so on. The following code excerpt demonstrates that kind of access:

Access to attributes and methods

```
DATA:
  Items TYPE REF TO cl_Memo,
  Lines TYPE REF TO cl_StringList,
  Item TYPE REF TO cl_Item.
  Lines = Items->Get_Lines( ).
  CALL METHOD Lines->Get_FirstItem
    RETURNING
      _FirstItem = Item.
  Item->Set_AsString( IMPORTING _AsString = 'Hallo' ).
```

Listing 6.6 Dereferencing Objects and Access to Methods

This characteristic of ABAP Objects requires the definition of many more variables than in other object-oriented programming languages, which lengthens the code. Because the variables must be completely typed, looking up the return types is indispensable. The increased amount of code is due to the additional variable declarations and dereference statements. Luckily, the ABAP editor features forward navigation, so you can double-click a method to arrive at its definition, where you can read all the related information. Note that this example features two ways to call methods, both of which have been available as of SAP Web AS 6.10. The method call in the middle uses CALL METHOD, which has been supported since Release 4.6 and is still used with the SAMPLE button to create source code statements automatically. As of Release 6.10, you can use parentheses, so that writing code here is very similar to other common programming languages like C++ and Java.

Instance constructors

One special element of classes is the ability to define an *instance constructor*. This is a method that is called automatically during the creation of an object and that can initialize data sections or generate other objects. In accordance with other object-oriented programming languages, the method must be named CONSTRUCTOR. ABAP Objects doesn't support several alternative instance constructors per class, as does C++ (each has the same name but different transfer parameters) or the ability to select a constructor ID at will, as does Delphi. Implementation occurs just as it does for a normal method.

```
CLASS lcl_staticclass DEFINITION.
  PUBLIC SECTION.
    METHODS:
      constructor,
    CLASS-DATA:
      initvalue TYPE i.
ENDCLASS.                    "lcl_staticclass DEFINITION
```

Listing 6.7 Definition of Instance Constructors

Static constructors

Static constructors are defined in ABAP Objects with the keyword CLASS_CONSTRUCTOR. They are called automatically by the runtime system a single time during the first access to the class or a class derived from it (see Section 6.2) to execute the program. Static constructors differ from instance constructors: They may call and use only static methods and static attributes (that is, methods and attributes that function without the creation of an object instance).

```
CLASS lcl_staticclass DEFINITION.
```

```
PUBLIC SECTION.
  CLASS-METHODS:
   class_constructor,
   initsomething IMPORTING _value TYPE i.
  CLASS-DATA:
   initvalue TYPE i.
ENDCLASS.                  "lcl_staticclass DEFINITION

CLASS lcl_staticclass IMPLEMENTATION.
  METHOD class_constructor.
    initsomething( EXPORTING _value = 1 ).
  ENDMETHOD.                "class_constructor
  METHOD initsomething.
    initvalue = _value.
  ENDMETHOD.              "initsomething
ENDCLASS.                 "lcl_staticclass IMPLEMENTATION
```

Listing 6.8 Definition and Implementation of Static Constructors, Data, and Methods

As is the case with other common programming languages, parameter interfaces are not permitted for static constructors but are permitted for the methods called from there. The keyword REDEFINITION (see Section 6.2) is obsolete. The runtime environment automatically calls the static constructor of the parent class. An explicit call in the program code is impossible: you must trust the ABAP runtime environment completely in this regard.

ABAP Objects provides keywords CLASS-DATA and CLASS-METHODS to define attributes and methods that can be used without instancing an object—comparable to functions and global variables. Note that in the implementation, keyword METHOD must be given to introduce a method and not, as might be expected, CLASS-METHOD. Otherwise, the implementation would make it difficult to tell whether a static method is involved. For access to static attributes and methods, ABAP Objects provides the => operator, which makes it easy to recognize special access in the source code, just as in C++ and Java.

Static attributes and methods

```
* attribute
  Staticclass=>initvalue = 23.
* method
```

```
Staticclass=>initmethod( _value = 23 ).
```

Listing 6.9 Accessing Static Attributes and Methods

Static methods—
useless or
important?

The opinions of developers and experts differ the most when it comes to the question of using static methods and attributes. One group sees them as being a sign of bad software design, a stopgap, or as being completely useless. The other group swears by the enhanced object-oriented options they provide and uses them intensively for customizing and configuration. In fact, however, they are an element of the ISO standardization of C++. Our opinion? The use of static attributes and static methods to configure frameworks and component libraries has its greatest advantages in very generic and extendable SAP applications. If you look beyond the SAP development platform toward Java and its comprehensive frameworks, Microsoft.NET, and the CLX component library from Borland, you can see that the use of static attributes and static methods there is limited to issues regarding runtime type information and object streaming (the storage and loading of objects). It would appear the market outside of ABAP Objects has already made up its mind as far as static methods are concerned and that any extended use of these methods or attributes would be unusual for most developers.

Global and local classes

Object-oriented ABAP programming uses local and global classes, which are similar to subprograms and function modules. Subprograms and function modules are declared and implemented directly and completely in the source code, as is the case with other common programming languages. The SAP Object Navigator offers a user-friendly interface for local and global classes.

You can use the interface to specify all attributes, methods, and transfer parameters from dialogs. You can manage local and global classes in internal tables and query information via class names, methods, attributes, and so on at runtime.

Runtime type identification

For some time, even procedural ABAP contained the DESCRIBE FIELD command to define the technical properties of a variable at runtime. But it applied only to elementary types, flat structures, and standard internal tables without table keys. The following code excerpt demonstrates reading the type, the length, and the number of decimal places of a transfer parameter:

```
DATA:
  l_dec(11) TYPE p DECIMALS 3.
PERFORM describe_field USING l_dec.
FORM describe_field USING i_number TYPE any.
  DATA:
    l_type TYPE c,
    l_length TYPE i,
    l_decimals TYPE i.
  DESCRIBE FIELD i_number TYPE l_type LENGTH l_length
    IN BYTE MODE DECIMALS l_decimals.
  WRITE: / 'Type:', l_type, 'Length:', l_length,
    'Decimals', l_decimals.
ENDFORM.                          "describe_field
```

Listing 6.10   Access to Technical Properties via DESCRIBE FIELD

The introduction of reference variables, complex structures, and object-oriented enhancements into the language pushed the command to its limits. That's the reason for the introduction of *runtime type identification* (RTTI) along with that of the ABAP Objects language. The concept is familiar from other programming languages. It can be used to define all technical properties of a variable, constant, or field symbol at runtime. The following classes are available for this purpose:

| CL_ABAP_TYPEDESCR |
| CL_ABAP_DATADESCR |
| CL_ABAP_ELEMDESCR |
| CL_ABAP_COMPLEXDESCR |
| CL_ABAP_STRUCTDESCR |
| CL_ABAP_TABLEDESCR |
| CL_ABAP_REFDESCR |
| CL_ABAP_OBJECTDESCR |
| CL_ABAP_CLASSDESCR |
| CL_ABAP_INTFDESCR |

Table 6.1   Classes for RTTI

You can use RTTI to examine all simple and complex data types. For example, RTTI can set the name of a class at runtime and execute additional actions based on the name. Listing 6.11 demonstrates this feature.

```
DATA:
  l_str_bta TYPE zptb00_str_bta.
PERFORM dosomething USING l_str_bta.

FORM dosomething USING i_structure TYPE any.
  DATA:
    l_rcl_abap_typedescr TYPE REF TO
       cl_abap_typedescr,
    l_string TYPE string.
  l_rcl_abap_typedescr ?=
    cl_abap_typedescr=>describe_by_data( i_structure ).
  WRITE:/ l_rcl_abap_typedescr->absolute_name.
* In Release 6.20 the relative name is also provided
*  CALL METHOD l_rcl_abap_typedescr->get_relative_name
*     RECEIVING
*        p_relative_name = l_string.
ENDFORM.                        "dosomething
```

Listing 6.11 Accessing the Name of a Structure with RTTI

The static attribute ABSOLUTE_NAME stores the complete name of the structure, including a prefix, /TYPE=. As of Release 6.20, you can call method get_relative_name to query the structure name without this prefix.

Type casting The casting of data objects with the ASSIGN var TO <fieldsymbol> CASTING statement is familiar from procedural ABAP: Any memory area can ultimately be examined by assuming a specific type. *Type casting* also applies to objects: it is programmed with assignment operator ?=. The following code excerpt demonstrates its use.

```
DATA:
  l_tab_childs TYPE STANDARD TABLE OF REF TO object,
  l_rcl_product   TYPE REF TO lcl_product.
FIELD-SYMBOLS:
  <l_object> TYPE REF TO object.

* create object and append to table
  CREATE OBJECT l_rcl_product.
  APPEND l_rcl_product TO l_tab_childs.
```

```
    CLEAR l_rcl_product.
* later on get object out of table ...
    LOOP AT l_tab_childs ASSIGNING <l_object>.
      l_rcl_product ?= <l_object>.
```

Listing 6.12 Accessing the Name of a Structure with RTTI

You can easily manage objects of different classes in tables that contain the generic type `REF TO OBJECT`. The generic class, `OBJECT`, is the basis of all other classes. In other words, all other classes are derived from it (see Section 6.2 for more information). Therefore, assignments of other objects to variables of type `OBJECT` always work. You can use type casting, a special form of assignment, during an assignment to force ABAP Objects to reassign an object previously managed as an `OBJECT` to a variable of the type of the original class. The last statement in the present example forces the ABAP runtime environment to treat the object references with the symbol field, as if they were of the type of variable `l_rcl_product`, and it can assign them accordingly.

You can learn about working with classes and objects in more detail based on an actual example.

Exercise 6.1

Create program ZPTB00_PRODUCT_CONFIGURATOR. Implement two local classes: `lcl_category` to manage product categories and `lcl_product` to record product information. The `lcl_category` class should manage information on the "higher category," "lower category," "sales tax," "title," and "description." The `lcl_product` class should manage information on the "higher category," "title," "description," and "individual net price." For the sake of simplicity, use data type `f` without a data element for the individual net price.

For example, combine three products and two categories into a hierarchy. Summarize all categories under a root category named "All Products."

For `lcl_product`, write a method that returns the gross price upon entry of the number of items, based on the individual price entered during object creation. Write another method that displays the title and gross price on the screen.

For `lcl_category`, write a method that outputs all the categories, products (with title), and gross price (if available) contained in it to the screen. As an example, call this method for the root category.

▷ Create a new program, ZPTB00_PRODUCT_CONFIGURATOR, without a TOP include. The title should be "Product Configurator." Leave the default settings in place for the other properties and the transport request.

Now complete the program structure to calculate the gross and net costs for sales from the entries for starting price and selling price.

▷ Type the following source code beneath the comment lines:

```
REPORT  zptb00_product_configurator.

CLASS lcl_category DEFINITION.
  PUBLIC SECTION.
    METHODS:
      constructor
        IMPORTING
          i_rcl_parent TYPE REF TO lcl_category
            OPTIONAL
          i_title TYPE string,
      write_to_screen
        IMPORTING
          i_column TYPE i DEFAULT 0.
    DATA:
     parent TYPE REF TO lcl_category,
     childs TYPE STANDARD TABLE OF REF TO object,
     title TYPE string,
     description TYPE string,
     vat TYPE f VALUE '0.16'.
  ENDCLASS.                       "lcl_category DEFINITION

CLASS lcl_product DEFINITION.
  PUBLIC SECTION.
    METHODS:
      constructor
        IMPORTING
          i_rcl_parent TYPE REF TO lcl_category
          i_title TYPE string
          i_net_price TYPE f,
      write_to_screen
        IMPORTING
          i_column TYPE i DEFAULT 0,
```

```
      get_gross_price
        RETURNING
          value(r_price) TYPE f.
    DATA:
      title TYPE string,
      description TYPE string,
      parent TYPE REF TO lcl_category,
      net_price TYPE f.
ENDCLASS.                      "lcl_product DEFINITION

* Main program ***
DATA:
  l_category_root TYPE REF TO lcl_category,
  l_category TYPE REF TO lcl_category,
  l_product TYPE REF TO lcl_product.

CREATE OBJECT l_category_root
  EXPORTING
    i_title        = 'Products'.
CREATE OBJECT l_category
  EXPORTING
    i_rcl_parent = l_category_root
    i_title        = 'Hardware'.
CREATE OBJECT l_product
  EXPORTING
    i_rcl_parent = l_category
    i_title        = 'Toshiba Satellite 430s'
    i_net_price  = '1500'.
CREATE OBJECT l_product
  EXPORTING
    i_rcl_parent = l_category
    i_title        = 'IBM Thinkpad 30p'
    i_net_price  = '1650'.
CREATE OBJECT l_category
  EXPORTING
    i_rcl_parent = l_category_root
    i_title        = 'Software'.
CREATE OBJECT l_product
  EXPORTING
    i_rcl_parent = l_category
    i_title        = 'Microsoft Office SBE'
    i_net_price  = '600'.
```

```
l_category_root->write_to_screen( ).
* End of main program ***

CLASS lcl_category IMPLEMENTATION.
  METHOD constructor.
*    super->constructor( ).
    IF i_rcl_parent IS BOUND.
* This is my daddy
      parent = i_rcl_parent.
* Hi daddy, i am your child
      APPEND me TO parent->childs.
    ENDIF.
    title = i_title.
  ENDMETHOD.                      "Constructor
  METHOD write_to_screen.
    DATA:
      l_rcl_category  TYPE REF TO lcl_category,
      l_rcl_product   TYPE REF TO lcl_product,
      l_rcl_descr     TYPE REF TO cl_abap_typedescr,
      l_classname     TYPE string,
      l_column        TYPE i.
    FIELD-SYMBOLS:
      <l_object> TYPE REF TO object.
    WRITE: AT /i_column 'Title :', title.
    l_column = i_column + 2.
    LOOP AT childs ASSIGNING <l_object>.
      l_rcl_descr =
        cl_abap_typedescr=>describe_by_object_ref(
          <l_object> ).
      l_classname = l_rcl_descr->absolute_name.
      FIND 'CL_CATEGORY' IN l_classname.
      IF sy-subrc = 0.
        l_rcl_category ?= <l_object>.
        l_rcl_category->write_to_screen( l_column ).
      ELSE.
        l_rcl_product ?= <l_object>.
        l_rcl_product->write_to_screen( l_column ).
      ENDIF.
    ENDLOOP.
  ENDMETHOD.                "write_to_screen
ENDCLASS.                   "lcl_category IMPLEMENTATION
```

```
CLASS lcl_product IMPLEMENTATION.
  METHOD constructor.
* Initialize attributes
*     super->constructor( ).
    IF i_rcl_parent IS BOUND.
* This is my daddy
      parent = i_rcl_parent.
* Hi daddy, i am your child
      APPEND me TO parent->childs.
    ENDIF.
    title = i_title.
    net_price = i_net_price.
  ENDMETHOD.                    "Constructor
  METHOD write_to_screen.
    DATA:
      l_gross_price TYPE p DECIMALS 2.
    l_gross_price = me->get_gross_price( ).
    WRITE: AT /i_column 'Title :', title, '. Gross
      Price :', (10) l_gross_price.
  ENDMETHOD.                    "lcl_product
  METHOD get_gross_price.
    r_price = net_price + net_price * parent->vat.
  ENDMETHOD.                    "get_price
ENDCLASS.                       "lcl_product IMPLEMENTATION
```

Listing 6.13 Source Code of Program ZPTB00_Product_Configurator

The source code begins with the definition of classes `lcl_category` and `lcl_product` with the default attributes and methods. In both cases, the `constructor` method contains `i_rcl_parent` and `i_title` as transfer parameters because they are important to the end user for organizing the product hierarchy and identifying an individual object. The constructor of the `lcl_product` class also contains the `i_net_price` transfer parameter because a product without a defined price cannot be instanced as an object. Both classes also include a method, `write_to_screen`: the product object must be able to output only its title and price, but the category object must loop through all its children (lower categories and products). To visualize the object hierarchy, transfer the column number from which output occurs to the `write_to_screen` method. The column number should increase by two when a lower object is called.

Explanation of
the source code

The main program consists of five constructor calls to set up a product hierarchy. Output is triggered from the root node by calling the `WRITE_TO_SCREEN` method.

Implementation of the two classes follows the main program. The constructors with `APPEND me TO parent ->childs` contain a direct call of the `childs` attribute of the higher categories so that the object also learns about its new, lower object. The `write_to_screen` method of the `lcl_product` class calculates only the gross price and then displays it on the screen along with the title of the product. The `write_to_screen` method of the `lcl_category` class is more interesting. The `LOOP` statement runs through all the registered objects in the `Childs` table; their class names are revealed with RTTI. If it involves a category object, its `write_to_screen` method is called after type casting. In the other case, it must involve a product object: its `write_to_screen` method is called after type casting.

Testing the program

Take a look at the program during execution.

▷ Save, check, activate, and start the program directly.

The program now displays all the products and categories on the screen, according to your hierarchy (see Figure 6.3).

Figure 6.3   Result of Program ZPTB00_Product_Configurator

As you would expect, you can also use all the features of object-oriented ABAP programming with global classes.

Exercise 6.2

Create program ZPTB00_PRODUCT_CONFIGURATOR_GL. Implement the exact same functionality, but use global classes for categories and products. Use `ZPTB00_CL_CATEGORY` and `ZPTB00_CL_PRODUCT` as the class names. You can use the content of the methods from the previous exercise.

To prepare for the definition of the global classes, you must examine all the planned typing of transfer parameters and attributes to see whether they implicitly use structures or tables. Of course, you also have to define them globally. The only candidate here is the definition `childs TYPE STANDARD TABLE OF REF TO object`.

Defining global table types

Therefore, start with the definition of an appropriate table type that you need to define a class.

▷ In the context menu of the package or the development class, select CREATE • DDIC OBJECT • TABLE TYPE.

▷ A dialog then asks for the name of the planned table type. Enter "ZPTB00_TTY_CHILDS" and confirm the entry with the CONTINUE button (see Figure 6.4).

Figure 6.4 Entering the Name of Table Type ZPTB00_TTY_CHILDS

You can maintain additional properties of the table type in the tool area (see Figure 6.5).

▷ Enter "Subsidiary objects of the hierarchy" as the short description.

▷ As the row type, select the radio buttons REFERENCE TYPE and NAME OF REF. TYPE and then enter the predefined ABAP "OBJECT" type.

▷ Click the SAVE button.

The familiar dialog that asks about the transport request appears.

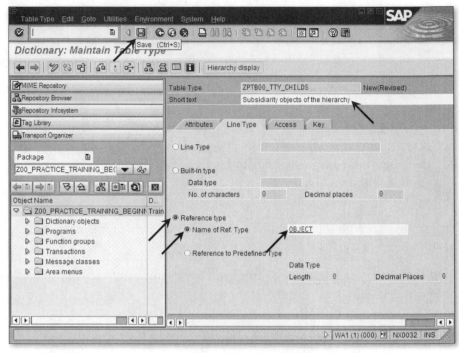

Figure 6.5 Maintaining Properties of Table Type ZPTB00_TTY_CHILDS

▷ The number of the transport request used previously is set by default. Simply confirm it with the OK button.

You can now activate the table type (see Figure 6.6).

▷ Click the ACTIVATE button.

Creating a global class   You have now fulfilled all the preliminary steps to start defining global class ZPTB00_CL_CATEGORY (see Figure 6.7).

▷ In the context menu of the package or the development class, SELECT CREATE • CLASS LIBRARY • CLASS.

▷ Enter ZPTB00_CL_CATEGORY as the class and uncheck the FINAL checkbox: you want to inherit from the class in the next section.

▷ Confirm your entries with the SAVE button.

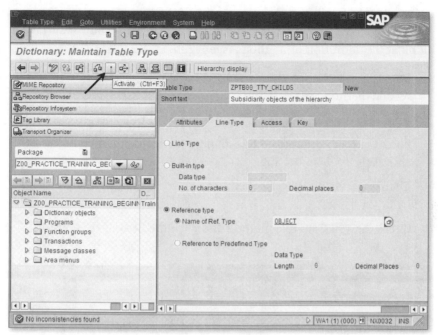

Figure 6.6 Activating Table Type ZPTB00_TTY_CHILDS

Figure 6.7 Creating Class ZPTB00_CL_CATEGORY

The SAP Object Navigator asks for the transport request.

▷ The number of the transport request used previously is set by default. Simply confirm it with the OK button.

Defining methods of a global class

A window opens in the tool area of the SAP Object Navigator. You can complete the development of the class in the window. But, first, take a look at the definition of methods (see Figure 6.8).

▷ Enter `CONSTRUCTOR` as the first method and `write_to_screen` as the second method.

▷ Apply the texts "Constructor" and "Output of title and gross price."

▷ Press the Enter key. The SAP Object Navigator then completes the entries for type and visibility.

▷ Change the visibility of the methods to `Public` because it will be called by other classes.

▷ Check the `CONSTRUCTOR` method and click the PARAMETERS button.

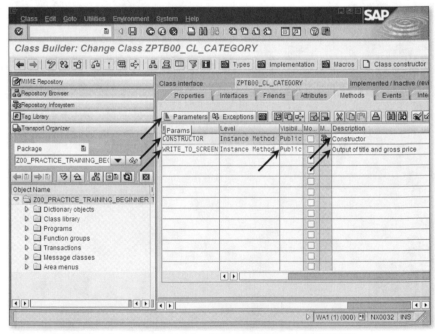

Figure 6.8 Maintaining the Methods of Class ZPTB00_CL_CATEGORY

Transfer parameters of a method

The display in the tool area switches to the transfer parameters of the `CONSTRUCTOR` method.

▷ Enter the transfer parameters shown in Figure 6.9. Note the checkbox set as OPTIONAL for `i_rcl_parent`, and go to `Type Ref to` in the typing column. Also note the type, which in this case is always `importing`.

▷ Click the METHODS button to return to the method view.

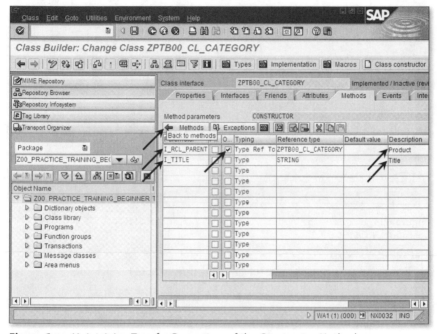

Figure 6.9 Maintaining Transfer Parameters of the Constructor Method

The process here is similar to the one for the `WRITE_TO_SCREEN` method, which should also have the required transfer parameters (see Figure 6.10).

▷ Check the row with the `WRITE_TO_SCREEN` method.

▷ Click the PARAMETERS button.

You can now enter the desired transfer parameters.

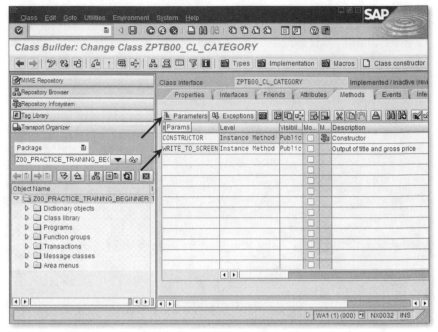

Figure 6.10 Checking the WRITE_TO_SCREEN Method of Class ZPTB00_CL_CATEGORY

▷ Enter the transfer parameter shown in Figure 6.11.

▷ Click the METHODS button to return to the method view.

Defining the attributes of a global class

A user-friendly input dialog also exists for the attributes of the class on the ATTRIBUTES tab.

▷ Select the ATTRIBUTES tab.

You can maintain the names and properties of the attributes here.

▷ Enter the attribute as you do source code, and as shown in Figure 6.12.

▷ Only the description for the defined table type is transferred automatically. You must enter the other attributes yourself: "PARENT", "CHILDS", "TITLE", and "VAT".

▷ Click the SAVE button.

▷ Return to the METHODS tab.

Figure 6.11 Maintaining the Transfer Parameters of the write_to_screen Method

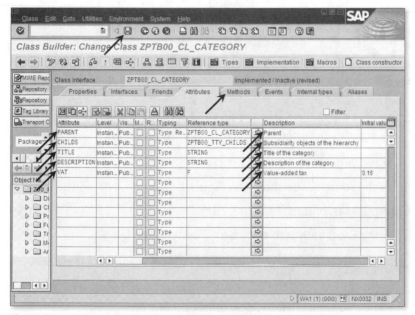

Figure 6.12 Maintaining Attributes of Class ZPTB00_CL_CATEGORY

Source code of the constructor method

Now that all the preparations are complete, you can create the source code for the individual methods.

▷ Double-click the CONSTRUCTOR method. You could also click the method and then click the SOURCE CODE button (see Figure 6.13).

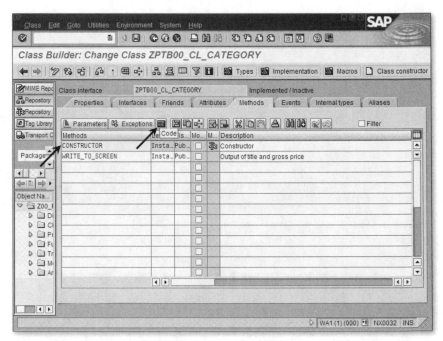

Figure 6.13 Move to the CONSTRUCTOR Method in the Source Code

Source code is managed for each method for global classes. You can display the transfer parameters (signatures) of the method.

▷ Click the SIGNATURE button.

▷ Enter the source code shown in Figure 6.14.

▷ Click the SAVE button, and then click CHECK.

▷ Click the BACK button to return to the METHODS tab.

Source Code of the write_to_ screen method

Entering the source code for the write_to_screen method is similar.

▷ Double-click the write_to_screen method. You could also click the method, and then click the SOURCE CODE button.

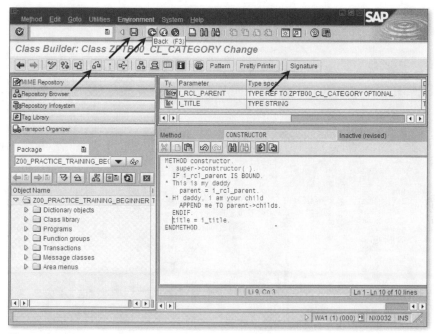

Figure 6.14 Entering the Source Code of the CONSTRUCTOR Method

This method contains the logic to call the subordinate objects.

▷ Enter the source code shown in Figure 6.15.

▷ Click the SAVE button.

▷ Click the BACK button to return to the METHODS tab.

Please note that the method has not yet been successfully checked and that it cannot be activated because you have not yet created global class ZPTB00_CL_Product.

You can create the second class, ZPTB00_CL_Product, in the same way (see Listing 6.13). Figure 6.16 illustrates the completed definition of the method.

Creating additional global classes in the same manner

Figure 6.15 Source Code of the write_to_screen Method

Figure 6.16 Method of Global Class ZPTB00_CL_PRODUCT

The entries for the attributes are very similar to the ZPTB00_CL_Category class (see Figure 6.17).

Figure 6.17 Attributes of Global Class ZPTB00_CL_PRODUCT

Both global classes can be activated only after creation of class ZPTB00_ CL_PRODUCT is complete: Each one uses the other.

You can now write the main program.

▷ Create a new program, ZPTB00_PRODUCT_CONFIGURATOR_GL, without a TOP include. The title should be "Product Configurator Global". Leave the default settings in place for the other properties and the transport request.

Now complete the program structure by taking the source code from program ZPTB00_Product_Configurator and adjusting the names of the classes that it uses.

Creating the main program

▷ Type the following source code beneath the comment lines:

```
REPORT   zptb00_product_configurator_gl.
DATA:
  l_category_root TYPE REF TO ZPTB00_cl_category,
  l_category TYPE REF TO ZPTB00_cl_category,
  l_product TYPE REF TO ZPTB00_cl_product.

CREATE OBJECT l_category_root
  EXPORTING
    i_title      = 'Products'.
CREATE OBJECT l_category
  EXPORTING
    i_rcl_parent = l_category_root
    i_title      = 'Hardware'.
CREATE OBJECT l_product
  EXPORTING
    i_rcl_parent = l_category
    i_title      = 'Toshiba Satellite 430s'
    i_net_price  = '1500'.
CREATE OBJECT l_product
  EXPORTING
    i_rcl_parent = l_category
    i_title      = 'IBM Thinkpad 30p'
    i_net_price  = '1650'.
CREATE OBJECT l_category
  EXPORTING
    i_rcl_parent = l_category_root
    i_title      = 'Software'.
CREATE OBJECT l_product
  EXPORTING
    i_rcl_parent = l_category
    i_title      = 'Microsoft Office SBE'
    i_net_price  = '600'.
l_category_root->write_to_screen( ).
```

Listing 6.14 Source Code of Program ZPTB00_Product_Configurator_GL

Testing program ZPTB00_Product_Configurator_GL returns the exact same results as before, when it was implemented with local classes (see Figure 6.18).

Figure 6.18   Program ZPTB00_Product_Configurator_GL During Execution

Professional ABAP developers usually prefer global classes to local classes. The advantages in terms of the ability to create documentation and reusability in other projects without linking include files, and simple external addressability by RFC, web services, and similar protocols (as of Release 6.20) are the same as those of using function modules instead of subprograms and outweigh the effort needed to enter them.

6.2   Inheritance and Polymorphism— INHERITING FROM, REDEFINITION

The combination of data and program code in a reusable class creates a number of advantages during the implementation of a software project. But object-oriented programming truly becomes exciting with the use of two additional features: inheritance and polymorphism. These features ensure that you can change and enhance the behavior of classes without touching the source code of the original class.

The ability of one class to inherit the attributes and methods of another class is an important feature of every object-oriented programming language. The inheriting class can use almost all the attributes and methods as though they were its own, and even replace inappropriate methods with new ones. This kind of flexibility is a prerequisite for the reuse of program code and data in a *class hierarchy*, often called a *framework* or *component library*, or simply a *library*. Starting from a common ancestor with a series of basic attributes and methods, ever more specialized and enhanced descendants are created in a class hierarchy. Object-oriented programming languages have hundreds of examples. The most familiar

Basics

377

include the CLX Library from Borland, the Java Development Kit from Sun, and the Microsoft.NET Framework.

Inheritance Unlike C++ and like Java, ABAP Objects supports the mechanism of simple inheritance. Each class can inherit from only one other class, but each class can act as the parent class of any number of inheriting classes. Over time, several terms have been used to describe this relationship between two classes: Parent class and child class, ancestor and descendant, original class and derived class, and so on. But all the terms express the same idea.

Figure 6.19 illustrates the context graphically. Note that in ABAP Objects, every class is directly or indirectly derived from the `Object` class. The `Object` class is predefined in the ABAP runtime environment and is always the basic class.

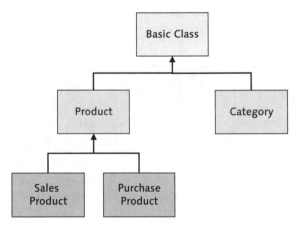

Figure 6.19 Class Hierarchies and Inheritance

Derivation of one class from another occurs with an addition to the `CLASS` command: `INHERITING FROM`. See the example in the following source code:

```
CLASS lcl_product DEFINITION.
  PUBLIC SECTION.
    METHODS:
      Constructor
        IMPORTING
```

```
        i_rcl_parent TYPE REF TO lcl_category
        i_title TYPE string
        i_net_price TYPE f,
      write_to_screen
        IMPORTING
          i_column TYPE i DEFAULT 0,
      get_gross_price
        RETURNING
          value(r_price) TYPE f.
    DATA:
      title TYPE string,
      description TYPE string,
      parent TYPE REF TO lcl_category,
      net_price TYPE f.
ENDCLASS.                    "lcl_product DEFINITION


CLASS lcl_salesproduct DEFINITION INHERITING FROM lcl_product.
  PUBLIC SECTION.
    METHODS:
      get_gross_price REDEFINITION.
  PROTECTED SECTION.
    DATA:
      margin TYPE f VALUE '0.2'.
ENDCLASS.                    "lcl_salesproduct DEFINITION
```

Listing 6.15 Inheritance and Polymorphism: Sample Source Code

In this example, the `lcl_salesproduct` class is derived from `lcl_prod-`
`uct`. You can see the derivation in keyword `INHERITING FROM` of the
`lcl_salesproduct` class. As in other programming languages, all the
attributes and methods of the parent class are inherited, but those from
the `PRIVATE SECTION` of the parent class are invisible from within the
derived class. New methods and attributes can be inserted without
problems.

You can also replace inherited methods if you want to enhance, rewrite,
or correct the functionality there, for example. All calls are automatically
processed by the new, rewritten method instead of the original method.
The new method is also called a *redefined method*. The keyword `REDEFI-`
`NITION` in the definition area of a method indicates that the method is
being rewritten in the implementation area (see Figure 6.20). In larger

Method
redefinition
(polymorphism)

class hierarchies, it is certainly possible for one method to be redefined several times.

Figure 6.20 Class Hierarchies and Redefinition

Unlike the situation in most other object-oriented programming languages, the parent class in ABAP Objects does require an explicit release for the redefinition option. ABAP Objects sees every method as capable of being redefined. Relisting the transfer parameters is not permitted, which illuminates how things work. The interface of a redefined method cannot differ from the original. Otherwise, it might no longer be called correctly by the other methods of the parent class. A redefined method in the derived class overshadows the original method in the parent class, but it can call pseudoreference SUPER to include the inherited functionality.

Redefinition of instance constructors
The definition of the Constructor instance constructor does not involve an explicit entry of keyword REDEFINITION even though it is always involved. The system sets it implicitly. You must always redefine the transfer parameters of instance constructors because they may differ from the parent class. The constructors of the higher class use the SUPER pseudoreference, which must be explicitly entered in the coding. Unlike C++ and Delphi, object creation in ABAP Objects cannot be separated from

the call of the constructor. You must always specify the transfer parameters of the constructor methods with the CREATE OBJECT statement.

The redefinition of static constructors is similar to that of object constructors. In this case, however, the explicit call of the static constructor of the parents is prohibited because the runtime environment automatically handles the call of all static constructors in the correct sequence when a class is called for the first time.

Redefinition of static constructors

In summary, we can say that inheritance and polymorphism are indispensable for the setup of class hierarchies. They enable optimal control of the reuse of classes and follow-up enhancement of the available functionality.

Exercise 6.3

Create program ZPTB00_PRODUCT_ENHANCER by copying program ZPTB00_PRODUCT_CONFIGURATOR. Derive two new classes, lcl_sales_product and lcl_purchase_product, from lcl_product and redefine the get_gross_price method. The first class calculates a margin of 20% on the net price. The second class calculates a cash discount of 3% of the gross price. In the main program, exchange the objects of type lcl_product with objects of type lcl_salesproduct and lcl_purchaseproduct and observe the effects on the price during output of the product hierarchy.

▷ In the context menu of program ZPTB00_PRODUCT_CONFIGURATOR, select COPY.

▷ Enter ZPTB00_PRODUCT_ENHANCER as the name of the target program, and confirm your entry with the COPY button (see Figure 6.21).

Figure 6.21 Copying Program ZPTB00_PRODUCT_CONFIGURATOR

The next dialog asks which information on the program should be copied in detail. Because you have not created dynpros, documentation, or other elements in program ZPTB00_PRODUCT_CONFIGURATOR, you can accept the default settings.

▷ Leave the default settings as they are and confirm with the COPY button. The transport request also remains the same (see Figure 6.22).

Figure 6.22 Selecting Copying Details on Program ZPTB00_PRODUCT_CONFIGURATOR

The program is now copied, and you can double-click the name of the program to display it in the object list area.

▷ Double-click the name of program ZPTB00_Product_Enhancer.

You now enhance this program by defining and implementing two new classes.

▷ Enter the following source code.

```
REPORT   zptb00_product_enhancer.
*----------------------------------------------------*
*        CLASS lcl_category DEFINITION
*----------------------------------------------------*
*
*----------------------------------------------------*
CLASS lcl_category DEFINITION.
  PUBLIC SECTION.
```

```
      METHODS:
        constructor
          IMPORTING
            i_rcl_parent TYPE REF TO lcl_category
              OPTIONAL
            i_title TYPE string,
        write_to_screen
          IMPORTING
            i_column TYPE i DEFAULT 0.
      DATA:
        parent TYPE REF TO lcl_category,
        childs TYPE STANDARD TABLE OF REF TO object,
        title TYPE string,
        description TYPE string,
        vat TYPE f VALUE '0.16'.
ENDCLASS.                   "lcl_category DEFINITION
*-----------------------------------------------------*
*       CLASS lcl_product DEFINITION
*-----------------------------------------------------*
*
*-----------------------------------------------------*
CLASS lcl_product DEFINITION.
  PUBLIC SECTION.
    METHODS:
      constructor
        IMPORTING
          i_rcl_parent TYPE REF TO lcl_category
          i_title TYPE string
          i_net_price TYPE f,
      write_to_screen
        IMPORTING
          i_column TYPE i DEFAULT 0,
      get_gross_price
        RETURNING
          value(r_price) TYPE f.
    DATA:
      title TYPE string,
      description TYPE string,
      parent TYPE REF TO lcl_category,
      net_price TYPE f.
ENDCLASS.                   "lcl_product DEFINITION
```

```
*------------------------------------------------------*
*         CLASS lcl_salesproduct DEFINITION
*------------------------------------------------------*
*
*------------------------------------------------------*
CLASS lcl_salesproduct DEFINITION INHERITING FROM lcl_
product.
  PUBLIC SECTION.
    METHODS:
      get_gross_price REDEFINITION.
  PROTECTED SECTION.
    DATA:
      margin TYPE f VALUE '0.2'.
ENDCLASS.                "lcl_salesproduct DEFINITION


*------------------------------------------------------*
*         CLASS lcl_purchaseproduct DEFINITION
*------------------------------------------------------*
*
*------------------------------------------------------*
CLASS lcl_purchaseproduct DEFINITION INHERITING FROM lcl_
product.
  PUBLIC SECTION.
    METHODS:
      get_gross_price REDEFINITION.
  PROTECTED SECTION.
    DATA:
      discount TYPE f VALUE '0.03'.
ENDCLASS.                "lcl_purchaseproduct DEFINITION

* Main program ***
DATA:
  l_category_root TYPE REF TO lcl_category,
  l_category TYPE REF TO lcl_category,
  l_salesproduct TYPE REF TO lcl_salesproduct,
  l_purchaseproduct TYPE REF TO lcl_purchaseproduct.

CREATE OBJECT l_category_root
  EXPORTING
    i_title      = 'Products'.
CREATE OBJECT l_category
  EXPORTING
```

```
      i_rcl_parent = l_category_root
      i_title       = 'Hardware'.
  CREATE OBJECT l_purchaseproduct
    EXPORTING
      i_rcl_parent = l_category
      i_title       = 'Toshiba Satellite 430s'
      i_net_price  = '1500'.
  CREATE OBJECT l_salesproduct
    EXPORTING
      i_rcl_parent = l_category
      i_title       = 'Toshiba Satellite 430s'
      i_net_price  = '1500'.
  CREATE OBJECT l_purchaseproduct
    EXPORTING
      i_rcl_parent = l_category
      i_title       = 'IBM Thinkpad 30p'
      i_net_price  = '1650'.
  CREATE OBJECT l_salesproduct
    EXPORTING
      i_rcl_parent = l_category
      i_title       = 'IBM Thinkpad 30p'
      i_net_price  = '1650'.
  CREATE OBJECT l_category
    EXPORTING
      i_rcl_parent = l_category_root
      i_title       = 'Software'.
  CREATE OBJECT l_purchaseproduct
    EXPORTING
      i_rcl_parent = l_category
      i_title       = 'Microsoft Office SBE'
      i_net_price  = '600'.
  CREATE OBJECT l_salesproduct
    EXPORTING
      i_rcl_parent = l_category
      i_title       = 'Microsoft Office SBE'
      i_net_price  = '600'.
  l_category_root->write_to_screen( ).
* End of main program ***

CLASS lcl_category IMPLEMENTATION.
  METHOD constructor.
    super->constructor( ).
```

```
      IF i_rcl_parent IS BOUND.
* This is my daddy
      parent = i_rcl_parent.
* Hi daddy, I am your child
      APPEND me TO parent->childs.
    ENDIF.
    title = i_title.
  ENDMETHOD.                    "Constructor
  METHOD write_to_screen.
    DATA:
      l_rcl_category  TYPE REF TO lcl_category,
      l_rcl_product   TYPE REF TO lcl_product,
      l_rcl_descr     TYPE REF TO cl_abap_typedescr,
      l_classname     TYPE string,
      l_column        TYPE i.
    FIELD-SYMBOLS:
      <l_object> TYPE REF TO object.
    WRITE: AT /i_column 'Title :', title.
    l_column = i_column + 2.
    LOOP AT childs ASSIGNING <l_object>.
      l_rcl_descr = cl_abap_typedescr=>describe_by_
        object_ref( <l_object> ).
      l_classname = l_rcl_descr->absolute_name.
      FIND 'CL_CATEGORY' IN l_classname.
      IF sy-subrc = 0.
        l_rcl_category ?= <l_object>.
        l_rcl_category->write_to_screen( l_column ).
      ELSE.
        l_rcl_product ?= <l_object>.
        l_rcl_product->write_to_screen( l_column ).
      ENDIF.
    ENDLOOP.
  ENDMETHOD.          "write_to_screen
ENDCLASS.             "lcl_category IMPLEMENTATION


*------------------------------------------------------*
*        CLASS lcl_product IMPLEMENTATION
*------------------------------------------------------*
*
*------------------------------------------------------*
CLASS lcl_product IMPLEMENTATION.
  METHOD constructor.
```

```
* Initialize attributes
*     super->constructor( ).
    IF i_rcl_parent IS BOUND.
* This is my daddy
      parent = i_rcl_parent.
* Hi daddy, i am your child
      APPEND me TO parent->childs.
    ENDIF.
    title = i_title.
    net_price = i_net_price.
  ENDMETHOD.                    "Constructor
  METHOD write_to_screen.
    DATA:
      l_gross_price TYPE p DECIMALS 2.
    l_gross_price = me->get_gross_price( ).
    WRITE: AT /i_column 'Title :', title, '. Gross Price
      :', (10) l_gross_price.
  ENDMETHOD.                    "lcl_product
  METHOD get_gross_price.
    r_price = net_price + net_price * parent->vat.
  ENDMETHOD.                    "get_price
ENDCLASS.                    "lcl_product IMPLEMENTATION


*-------------------------------------------------------*
*       CLASS lcl_salesproduct IMPLEMENTATION
*-------------------------------------------------------*


*
*-------------------------------------------------------*
CLASS lcl_salesproduct IMPLEMENTATION.
  METHOD get_gross_price.
    DATA:
      l_margin_net_price TYPE f.
    l_margin_net_price = net_price + net_price *
                         margin.
    r_price =   l_margin_net_price +
                l_margin_net_price * parent->vat.
  ENDMETHOD.              "lcl_salesproduct
ENDCLASS.                 "lcl_salesproduct IMPLEMENTATION


*-------------------------------------------------------*
*       CLASS lcl_purchaseproduct IMPLEMENTATION
```

```
*-----------------------------------------------------*
*
*-----------------------------------------------------*
CLASS lcl_purchaseproduct IMPLEMENTATION.
  METHOD get_gross_price.
    DATA:
      l_gross_price TYPE f.
      l_gross_price = super->get_gross_price( ).
      r_price = l_gross_price - l_gross_price * discount.
  ENDMETHOD.          "lcl_purchaseproduct
ENDCLASS.            "lcl_purchaseproduct IMPLEMENTATION
```

Listing 6.16 Source Code of Program ZPTB00_Product_Enhancer

Explanation of the source code

The source code begins with the definition of classes `lcl_category` and `lcl_product` with the default attributes and methods. New coding added to program ZPTB00_Product_Configurator includes the definition of classes, `lcl_salesproduct` and `lcl_purchaseproduct`, which redefine the inherited method `get_gross_price`. In the protected area, you also have attributes to store the current margin or the current discount.

The reimplementation of each method accesses these attributes. The sales price is calculated by an intermediate calculation of a 20 percent margin on the net price and then by adding the sales tax. For the sales product, however, you can use the original method, `get_gross_price`, from class `lcl_product`. A discount of 3 percent is then calculated for the net price and the result is returned as the gross price. The call of the inherited method occurs with the new form `super->get_gross_price( )`.

The main program now consists of nine constructor calls to set up a product hierarchy that lists every product as a purchase product and as a sales product. Output is triggered from the root node by calling the `write_to_screen` method.

Testing the program

Take a look at the program during execution.

▷ Save, check, activate, and start the program directly.

The program starts and displays all the products and categories on the screen, according to your hierarchy (see Figure 6.23).

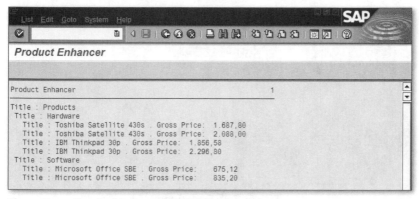

Figure 6.23   Result of Program ZPTB00_Product_Enhancer

Exercise 6.4

Create program ZPTB00_PRODUCT_ENHANCER_GL. Implement the exact same functionality, but use global classes for categories and products. Use ZPTB00_CL_PURCHASEPRODUCT as the class name for sales product ZPTB00_CL_SALESPRODUCT and purchase product ZPTB00_CL_PURCHASEPRODUCT. Implement the new functionality there. Copy the main program from ZPTB00_PRODUCT_ENHANCER, and adjust the names of the classes being used.

Note the different prices for the same product: The sales product has a higher price.

As you would expect, you can also use inheritance with global classes.

Let's start with the definition of global class ZPTB00_CL_SALESPRODUCT (see Figure 6.24).

Creating global class

▷ In the context menu of the package or the development class, SELECT CREATE • CLASS LIBRARY • CLASS.

▷ Enter "ZPTB00_CL_SALESPRODUCT" as the class.

▷ Click the CREATE INHERITANCE button, which displays an additional entry row, SUPERCLASS.

▷ Enter class "ZPTB00_CL_PRODUCT" in the SUPERCLASS field.

▷ Enter "Sales product" as the description.

▷ Deactivate the FINAL checkbox so that you can implement derivations from this class later on.

▷ Confirm your entries with the SAVE button.

Figure 6.24 Creating the ZPTB00_CL_SalesProduct Class

▷ The number of the transport request used previously is set by default. Simply confirm it with the OK button.

A window opens in the tool area of the SAP Object Navigator. You can complete the development of the class in the window.

Defining the attributes of a global class

Begin with the definition of the additional attribute, `Margin`.

▷ Select the ATTRIBUTES tab.

Here you can maintain the name and the properties of the new attribute (see Figure 6.25).

▷ Enter "Margin" as the name of the attribute, "Instance Attribute" as the level, "Protected" as visibility, "F" as reference type, and "Margin" as the description.

▷ Set the MARGIN attribute in the "Initial Value" column to "0.2".

▷ Click the SAVE button, and return to the METHODS tab.

Redefining the methods of a global class

Now deal with the redefinition of the `get_gross_price` method (see Figure 6.26).

▷ Go to the METHODS tab in the tool area.

▷ Check the `get_gross_price` method, and click the REDEFINE button.

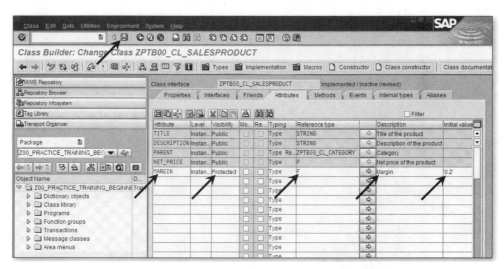

Figure 6.25 Maintaining Attributes of Class ZPTB00_CL_SALESPRODUCT

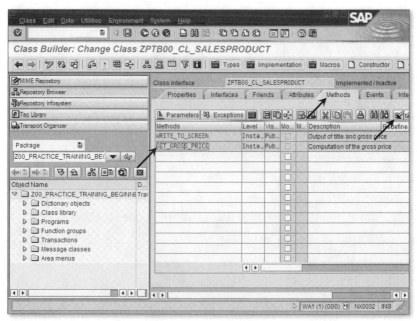

Figure 6.26 Redefining the get_gross_price Method of Class ZPTB00_CL_SALESPRODUCT

391

The current view in the tool area changes to display the source code of the method.

Enter the source code shown in Figure 6.27. Click the SAVE button and then ACTIVATE.

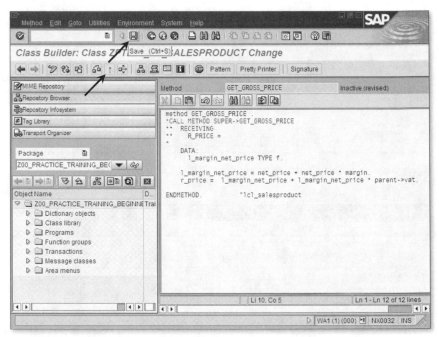

Figure 6.27 Saving Redefined Method get_gross_price of Class ZPTB00_CL_SALESPRODUCT

The font color for the `get_gross_price` method in the list of methods changes from blue (inherited) to black (self-implemented).

Creating additional global classes in the same manner

You can now create the second class in the same manner. Figure 6.28 illustrates the completed definition of the method.

The source code of the `WRITE_TO_SCREEN` method is similar to the code implementation in the local class, and the entries for the attribute are similar to those of class `ZPTB00_CL_SalesProduct` (see Figure 6.29).

Both global classes can be activated only after creation of class `ZPTB00_CL_Product` is complete: Each one uses the other.

Figure 6.28 Methods of Global Class ZPTB00_CL_PURCHASEPRODUCT

Figure 6.29 Attributes of Global Class ZPTB00_CL_PURCHASEPRODUCT

Creating the
main program
You can now write the main program.

▷ Create a new program, ZPTB00_PRODUCT_ENHANCER_GL without a TOP include. Enter "Product Enhancer Global" as the title. The remaining properties and the transport request remain unchanged.

Now complete the program structure by taking the source code of program ZPTB00_PRODUCT_ENHANCER and adjusting the names of the classes in use as needed.

▷ Type the following source code beneath the comment lines:

```
REPORT  zptb00_product_enhancer_gl.

DATA:
  l_category_root TYPE REF TO zptb00_cl_category,
  l_category TYPE REF TO zptb00_cl_category,
  l_salesproduct TYPE REF TO zptb00_cl_salesproduct,
  l_purchaseproduct TYPE REF TO
                    zptb00_cl_purchaseproduct.

CREATE OBJECT l_category_root
  EXPORTING
    i_title      = 'Products'.
CREATE OBJECT l_category
  EXPORTING
    i_rcl_parent = l_category_root
    i_title      = 'Hardware'.
CREATE OBJECT l_purchaseproduct
  EXPORTING
    i_rcl_parent = l_category
    i_title      = 'Toshiba Satellite 430s'
    i_net_price  = '1500'.
CREATE OBJECT l_salesproduct
  EXPORTING
    i_rcl_parent = l_category
    i_title      = 'Toshiba Satellite 430s'
    i_net_price  = '1500'.
CREATE OBJECT l_purchaseproduct
  EXPORTING
    i_rcl_parent = l_category
    i_title      = 'IBM Thinkpad 30p'
```

```
    i_net_price  = '1650'.
  CREATE OBJECT l_salesproduct
    EXPORTING
      i_rcl_parent = l_category
      i_title      = 'IBM Thinkpad 30p'
      i_net_price  = '1650'.
  CREATE OBJECT l_category
    EXPORTING
      i_rcl_parent = l_category_root
      i_title      = 'Software'.
  CREATE OBJECT l_purchaseproduct
    EXPORTING
      i_rcl_parent = l_category
      i_title      = 'Microsoft Office SBE'
      i_net_price  = '600'.
  CREATE OBJECT l_salesproduct
    EXPORTING
      i_rcl_parent = l_category
      i_title      = 'Microsoft Office SBE'
      i_net_price  = '600'.
  l_category_root->write_to_screen( ).
```

Listing 6.17 Source Code of Program ZPTB00_PRODUCT_ENHANCER_GL

As expected, when you test program ZPTB00_PRODUCT_ENHANCER_ GL, you get the same results as during the implementation with local classes (see Figure 6.30).

Testing the program

Figure 6.30 Program ZPTB00_PRODUCT_ENHANCER_GL During Execution

Redefinition of methods during inheritance of classes is one of the most important elements of object-oriented programming because it enables follow-up enhancement without changing the original functionality. That's why many professional object-oriented programmers design class hierarchies with an eye to follow-up enhancement.

6.3 EVENTS

Communication of classes
Classes and inheritance mechanisms are designed for the creation and enhancement of functionality; events are required for communication between classes and for combining individual parts into a large whole. Events convert the modular principle into a reality, so they have a high value in modern class hierarchies.

Basics
When working with modern class libraries, you might have the impression that object-oriented software development has reached the end of the road. Instead of deriving each class from another class and adjusting the functionality to meet your own needs, you simply instance the classes without change and adjust a couple attributes here and there to meet your actual requirements. You then use events and homegrown lines of program code (also known as *glue logic*) to create a completed application. All rapid application development tools (RAD tools) like Delphi, Visual Basic.NET, and so on work according to this principle and allow programmers to create software in a modular procedure (see Figure 6.31). Of course, something like this works only when the classes of the class hierarchy have a great deal of functionality and can be set flexibly so that they meet the needs of programmers without requiring any additional work.

While it works well for the development of interfaces, database connections, and network communications, this scenario is not as well suited for complex business tasks. You cannot resent SAP and its ABAP Objects programming language for not having a comprehensive class hierarchy to solve business tasks that include sales, productions, and accounting. Nonetheless, SAP is, of course, developing such frameworks.

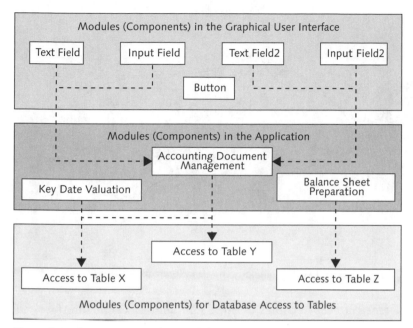

Figure 6.31 Programming with a Modular Procedure

Events are the technical basis for creating software in a modular man- **Events** ner. Events are interfaces to a class that are called at specific points or in specific circumstances. If you use such classes in a program and connect some methods with event interfaces, the program code contained in them is included in the flow of the class and called automatically. What might well sound complicated in theory becomes informative in actual practice. You would append the CLICK event to a button class to provide information when a user clicks the button. You would append the FAILED_DOCUMENTS event to an accounting class to inform users about an accounting document that contains errors.

Note the basic distinction between two types of concepts to realize events in object-oriented programming languages. The first is the *listener concept* (also called *publish and subscribe*) used in ABAP Objects and Java. The second is the *method pointer concept* used in languages like C++, Delphi, and VB.NET.

Figure 6.32 Events Help with Communication and Interconnectivity

Listener concept

The listener concept enables a 1:n assignment of event interfaces to event-handler methods. It does so with a list in which you can enter any number of event-hander methods that you can then call when the object triggers the event. The following code excerpt shows the syntax for the definition of events and event-handler methods (also called *handler methods*) and the connection created by the registration of the handler.

```
CLASS lcl_product DEFINITION.
  PUBLIC SECTION.
    EVENTS:
      on_title_change
        EXPORTING
          value(i_title) TYPE string.
    METHODS:
      set_title FOR EVENT on_title_change OF
        lcl_product
        IMPORTING
          i_title.
    DATA:
      title TYPE string.
ENDCLASS.                      "lcl_product DEFINITION

DATA:
```

```
l_product1 TYPE REF TO lcl_product,
l_product2 TYPE REF to lcl_product.

CREATE OBJECT l_product1.
CREATE OBJECT l_product2.
* Connect handle of product1 with event of product2
SET HANDLER l_product1->set_title FOR l_product2.
```

Listing 6.18 Defining Events and Event Handlers

Events are declared in classes with the keyword EVENTS name EXPORT-ING parameters and define the name of the event and the transfer parameter that will be transferred when the event is called later on. Classes that have events are also called *triggering classes*. You can also use the CLASS-EVENTS statement to define static events that you can use without instancing an object with CREATE OBJECT (in this context, see the material on static methods in Section 6.1, Classes and Objects—CLASS, CREATE OBJECT, METHOD). This section limits itself to the declaration of instance events.

Declaring events

You can compare events to "distributor lists" in which you can enter "prospective" methods to receive information whenever the event is triggered (see Figure 6.33).

In every class, you can define event-handler methods for the events of other classes or, as in this example, in your own class. Event-handler methods are declared with statements METHODS name FOR EVENT evt OF class or CLASS-METHODS name FOR EVENT evt for class, where name is the name of the method, evt is the name of the event, and class is the name of the class in which the event is declared. The name of the handler method can differ from the name of the event. The parameter interface of an event-handler method is limited to an Importing parameter, which was defined as an Exporting parameter with the same name during the declaration of the event. The handler method doesn't have to accept all the parameters. You don't have to type the Importing parameter; you can accept the typing of the Exporting parameter of the event. The ABAP runtime environment also always makes the SENDER parameter available as an implicit parameter. When triggered, it always contains a reference to the triggering object. If you have connected a handler method to several events, you can uniquely define the triggering object. Classes with handler methods are also called *handler classes*.

Declaring handler methods

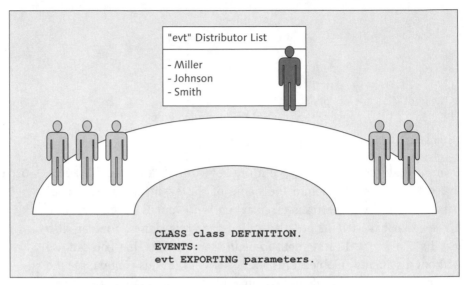

Figure 6.33 ABAP Objects Events as Distributor Lists

You can think of a handler method as a prospect that can become part of a distributor list (see Figure 6.34).

Figure 6.34 Handler Methods as Prospects

To ensure that a handler method is actually called when an event is triggered, you must register all the desired events. Call the SET HAN-DLER ref_handler FOR ref_sender [ACTIVATION act] command, where ref_handler is a reference variable for the handler method and ref_sender is a reference variable for the object in which the event is declared. As long as ACTIVATION act is not appended or act has a value of "X," registration of the handler method is active: it will be called automatically whenever the event is triggered. You can deactivate the call of a handler method by setting " " as the value for act.

Alternatively, you can also perform a mass activation or deactivation for all the objects in memory that trigger an event by adding FOR ALL INSTANCES.

You can think of the registration and deregistration of a handler method as adding or removing an entry to a distributor list (see Figure 6.35).

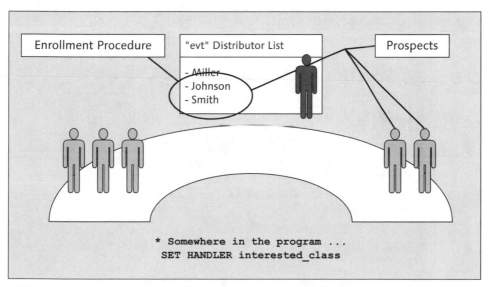

Figure 6.35 Registering Handler Methods as an Enrollment Procedure

To trigger an event and call all the registered handler methods, use the RAISE EVENT evt EXPORTING parameters statement, where evt is the name of the triggering event. You must assign the values of the event to the declared EXPORTING parameters in PARAMETERS. This statement interrupts the execution of methods at this precise location, and the runtime environment executes all the handler methods registered for the event. The triggering method is then continued after the statement. The RAISE EVENT statement is called in the triggering class itself.

You can think of the triggering of an event as follows (see Figure 6.36): All the prospects listed in the distributor list are called one after the other and informed of the value of the transfer parameters.

Figure 6.36 Triggering an Event as the Call of a Prospect on the Distributor List—RAISE EVENT

Take a closer look at this interplay and see how it works in the real world.

Create program ZPTB00_PRODUCT_EVENT by copying program ZPTB00_PRODUCT_ENHANCER. The program will be enhanced so that the title of a sales product will be changed whenever the title of the purchase product changes. In class `lcl_product`, enhance the `on_title_change` event with the `i_title` transfer parameter of type `string` and create a handler method for it named `set_title`. Have the program generate a category, an object of type `lcl_salesproduct`, and an object of type `lcl_purchaseproduct` and then output the product hierarchy. Then assign the handler methods of `lcl_salesproduct` to the `lcl_purchaseproduct` event and change the text of the purchase product by calling the appropriate `set_title` method. Then output the product hierarchy again.

▷ In the context menu of program ZPTB00_PRODUCT_ENHANCER, click COPY.

▷ Enter "ZPTB00_PRODUCT_EVENT" as the name of the target program and confirm your entries with the COPY button.

The next dialog asks which information on the program should be copied in detail. Because you have not created dynpros, documentation, or other elements in program ZPTB00_PRODUCT_ENHANCER, you can accept the default settings.

▷ Leave the default settings as they are, and confirm with the COPY button. The transport request also remains unchanged.

The program is now copied, and you can double-click the name of the program to display it in the object list area.

▷ Double-click the name of program ZPTB00_PRODUCT_EVENT.

You now enhance this program by defining and implementing two new classes.

▷ Enter the following source code:

```
REPORT  zptb00_product_event.
*---------------------------------------------------------*
*       CLASS lcl_category DEFINITION
```

```
*------------------------------------------------------*
*
*------------------------------------------------------*
CLASS lcl_category DEFINITION.
  PUBLIC SECTION.
    METHODS:
      constructor
        IMPORTING
          i_rcl_parent TYPE REF TO lcl_category
            OPTIONAL
          i_title TYPE string,
        write_to_screen
          IMPORTING
            i_column TYPE i DEFAULT 0.
    DATA:
      parent TYPE REF TO lcl_category,
      childs TYPE STANDARD TABLE OF REF TO object,
      title TYPE string,
      description TYPE string,
      vat TYPE f VALUE '0.16'.
ENDCLASS.                    "lcl_category DEFINITION
*------------------------------------------------------*
*      CLASS lcl_product DEFINITION
*------------------------------------------------------*
*
*------------------------------------------------------*
CLASS lcl_product DEFINITION.
  PUBLIC SECTION.
    EVENTS:
      on_title_change
        EXPORTING
          value(i_title) TYPE string.
    METHODS:
      constructor
        IMPORTING
          i_rcl_parent TYPE REF TO lcl_category
          i_title TYPE string
          i_net_price TYPE f,
        write_to_screen
          IMPORTING
```

```
              i_column TYPE i DEFAULT 0,
        get_gross_price
          RETURNING
            value(r_price) TYPE f,
        set_title FOR EVENT on_title_change OF
          lcl_product
          IMPORTING
            i_title.
    DATA:
      title TYPE string,
      description TYPE string,
      parent TYPE REF TO lcl_category,
      net_price TYPE f.
ENDCLASS.                  "lcl_product DEFINITION


*-------------------------------------------------------*
*       CLASS lcl_salesproduct DEFINITION
*-------------------------------------------------------*
*
*-------------------------------------------------------*
CLASS lcl_salesproduct DEFINITION INHERITING FROM lcl_
product.
  PUBLIC SECTION.
    METHODS:
      get_gross_price REDEFINITION.
  PROTECTED SECTION.
    DATA:
      margin TYPE f VALUE '0.2'.
ENDCLASS.                  "lcl_salesproduct DEFINITION


*-------------------------------------------------------*
*       CLASS lcl_purchaseproduct DEFINITION
*-------------------------------------------------------*
*
*-------------------------------------------------------*
CLASS lcl_purchaseproduct DEFINITION INHERITING FROM lcl_
product.
  PUBLIC SECTION.
    METHODS:
      get_gross_price REDEFINITION.
```

```
         PROTECTED SECTION.
           DATA:
             discount TYPE f VALUE '0.03'.
       ENDCLASS.              "lcl_purchaseproduct DEFINITION

       * Main program ***
       DATA:
         l_category_root TYPE REF TO lcl_category,
         l_category TYPE REF TO lcl_category,
         l_salesproduct TYPE REF TO lcl_salesproduct,
         l_purchaseproduct TYPE REF TO lcl_purchaseproduct.

       CREATE OBJECT l_category_root
         EXPORTING
           i_title      = 'Products'.
       CREATE OBJECT l_category
         EXPORTING
           i_rcl_parent = l_category_root
           i_title      = 'Hardware'.
       CREATE OBJECT l_purchaseproduct
         EXPORTING
           i_rcl_parent = l_category
           i_title      = 'Toshiba Satellite 430s'
           i_net_price  = '1500'.
       CREATE OBJECT l_salesproduct
         EXPORTING
           i_rcl_parent = l_category
           i_title      = 'Toshiba Satellite 430s'
           i_net_price  = '1500'.
       l_category_root->write_to_screen( ).
       * connect l_purchaseproduct to event of
       * l_salesproduct, so we get noticed in
       * l_purchaseproduct
       SET HANDLER l_salesproduct->set_title FOR l_purchaseproduct.
       CALL METHOD l_purchaseproduct->set_title
         EXPORTING
           i_title = 'Toshiba Portege 120s'.
       l_category_root->write_to_screen( ).
       * End of main program ***
```

```
*------------------------------------------------------*
*        CLASS lcl_category IMPLEMENTATION
*------------------------------------------------------*
*
*------------------------------------------------------*
CLASS lcl_category IMPLEMENTATION.
  METHOD constructor.
    super->constructor( ).
    IF i_rcl_parent IS BOUND.
* This is my daddy
      parent = i_rcl_parent.
* Hi daddy, I am your child
      APPEND me TO parent->childs.
    ENDIF.
    title = i_title.
  ENDMETHOD.                        "Constructor
  METHOD write_to_screen.
    DATA:
      l_rcl_category   TYPE REF TO lcl_category,
      l_rcl_product    TYPE REF TO lcl_product,
      l_rcl_descr      TYPE REF TO cl_abap_typedescr,
      l_classname      TYPE string,
      l_column         TYPE i.
    FIELD-SYMBOLS:
      <l_object> TYPE REF TO object.
    WRITE: AT /i_column 'Title :', title.
    l_column = i_column + 2.
    LOOP AT childs ASSIGNING <l_object>.
      l_rcl_descr =
        cl_abap_typedescr=>describe_by_object_ref(
          <l_object> ).
      l_classname = l_rcl_descr->absolute_name.
      FIND 'CL_CATEGORY' IN l_classname.
      IF sy-subrc = 0.
        l_rcl_category ?= <l_object>.
        l_rcl_category->write_to_screen( l_column ).
      ELSE.
        l_rcl_product ?= <l_object>.
        l_rcl_product->write_to_screen( l_column ).
      ENDIF.
```

```
      ENDLOOP.
    ENDMETHOD.              "write_to_screen
  ENDCLASS.                 "lcl_category IMPLEMENTATION


*------------------------------------------------------*
*       CLASS lcl_product IMPLEMENTATION
*------------------------------------------------------*
*
*------------------------------------------------------*
CLASS lcl_product IMPLEMENTATION.
  METHOD constructor.
* Initialize attributes
*     super->constructor( ).
    IF i_rcl_parent IS BOUND.
* This is my daddy
      parent = i_rcl_parent.
* Hi daddy, I am your child
      APPEND me TO parent->childs.
    ENDIF.
    title = i_title.
    net_price = i_net_price.
  ENDMETHOD.                     "Constructor
  METHOD write_to_screen.
    DATA:
      l_gross_price TYPE p DECIMALS 2.
    l_gross_price = me->get_gross_price( ).
    WRITE: AT /i_column 'Title :', title, '. Gross
      Price :', (10) l_gross_price.
  ENDMETHOD.                     "lcl_product
  METHOD get_gross_price.
    r_price = net_price + net_price * parent->vat.
  ENDMETHOD.                     "get_price
  METHOD set_title.
    RAISE EVENT on_title_change
      EXPORTING
        i_title = i_title.
    title = i_title.
  ENDMETHOD.                "lcl_product
ENDCLASS.                   "lcl_product IMPLEMENTATION
```

```
*---------------------------------------------------*
*         CLASS lcl_salesproduct IMPLEMENTATION
*---------------------------------------------------*
*
*---------------------------------------------------*
CLASS lcl_salesproduct IMPLEMENTATION.
  METHOD get_gross_price.
    DATA:
     l_margin_net_price TYPE f.
     l_margin_net_price = net_price + net_price *
       margin.
     r_price =  l_margin_net_price +
                l_margin_net_price * parent->vat.
  ENDMETHOD.            "lcl_salesproduct
ENDCLASS.              "lcl_salesproduct IMPLEMENTATION




*---------------------------------------------------*
*         CLASS lcl_purchaseproduct IMPLEMENTATION
*---------------------------------------------------*
*
*---------------------------------------------------*
CLASS lcl_purchaseproduct IMPLEMENTATION.
  METHOD get_gross_price.
    DATA:
     l_gross_price TYPE f.
     l_gross_price = super->get_gross_price( ).
     r_price = l_gross_price - l_gross_price *
       discount.
  ENDMETHOD.           "lcl_purchaseproduct
ENDCLASS.             "lcl_purchaseproduct IMPLEMENTATION
```

Listing 6.19 Source Code of Program ZPTB00_PRODUCT_EVENT

The existing source code is enhanced in the lcl_product class with the declaration of an event named on_title_change, whose only export parameter, i_title, is of type String. The parameter can later be used to inform a handler method of the new title of a product as soon as it changes.

Explanation of the source code

Handler method `set_title` is declared in the same class and explicitly defined as an event handler for the `on_title_change` event.

To keep things manageable, all products were removed from the main program except one sales and one purchase product. Use the SET HAN-DLER statement to assign the `set_title` event-handler method of the sales product to the related event of the purchase product. The following calls of the `set_title` methods of the sales product then trigger the event.

Implement the `set_title` method in the `lcl_product` class. It sets its own title and calls the `on_title_change` event with the RAISE EVENT statement. The runtime environment automatically ensures that all the handler methods affiliated by a SET HANDLER statement are called and contain the value of transfer parameter `i_title`. In the present case, the handler method is linked to the sales product, so the title is changed there as well.

Testing the program

Take a look at the program during execution.

▷ Save, check, activate, and start the program directly.

The program starts and displays all the products and categories twice on the screen, according to your hierarchy (see Figure 6.37).

You can clearly see the changed title of both products during the first and second output.

As you would expect, you can also use events with global classes.

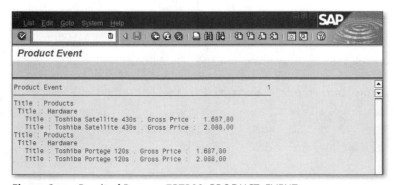

Figure 6.37 Result of Program ZPTB00_PRODUCT_EVENT

Exercise 6.6

Create program ZPTB00_PRODUCT_EVENT_GL. Implement the exact same functionality, but use global classes for categories and products. Copy the main program from ZPTB00_PRODUCT_ENHANCER, and adjust the names of the classes being used.

Start with the definition of the `on_title_change` event.

Declaring an event in a global class

▷ In the object list area, select the `ZPTB00_CL_PRODUCT` class, and double-click to load its declaration into the tool area (see Figure 6.38).

▷ Select the EVENTS tab.

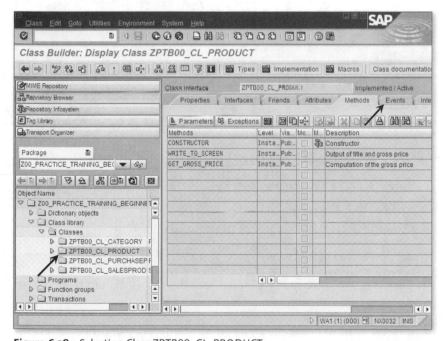

Figure 6.38 Selecting Class ZPTB00_CL_PRODUCT

Declare the event on the new page.

▷ Enter "ON_TITLE_CHANGE" as the event, select "Instance event" as the type, and select "Public" for visibility. Enter "Event when changing the title" as the description (see Figure 6.39).

▷ Click the PARAMETERS button.

Figure 6.39 Entering the on_title_change Event of Class ZPTB00_CL_PRODUCT

You can declare the parameters of the event in this window.

▷ Enter "I_TITLE" as the parameter and "STRING" as the reference type (see Figure 6.40).

▷ Click the EVENTS button to return to the events view.

To access the event in its own class, you must first save it.

▷ Click the SAVE button, and then select the METHODS tab to return to the list of methods.

Defining event-handler methods
The result is now declared, and you can define the appropriate event-handler methods.

▷ Enter "set_title" as the name of the new method, "Instance Method" as the type, "Public" as visibility, and "Set title" as the description (see Figure 6.41).

▷ Select the DETAIL VIEW button.

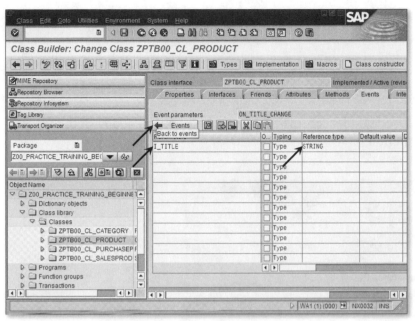

Figure 6.40 Entering the Parameter for on_title_change

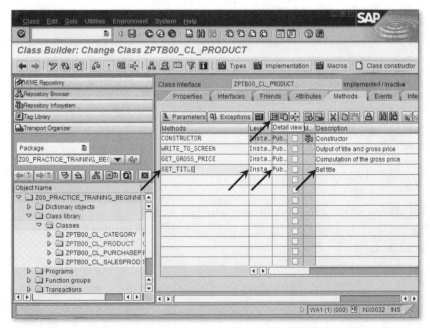

Figure 6.41 Defining the set_title Event-Handler Method of Class ZPTB00_CL_PRODUCT

The method is still missing a specification that it's a handler for a specific event. We can take care of this setting in the detailed view.

▷ Activate the EVENT HANDLER FOR checkbox; which opens the fields below it for input (see Figure 6.42).

▷ Enter "ZPTB00_CL_PRODUCT" as the CLASS/INTERFACE.

▷ Use F4 to select the on_title_change event, and click the CHANGE button.

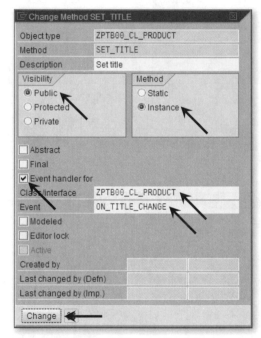

Figure 6.42 Defining the Details of the set_title Event-Handler Method of Class ZPTB00_CL_PRODUCT

The dialog closes, and a new icon appears as the method type next to the set_title method. The icon indicates that the method is an event-handler method.

Now you have to tell the method which parameters you want to accept.

▷ Click the PARAMETERS button (see Figure 6.43).

Figure 6.43 Changing to the Parameter List of the set_title Event-Handler Method

An empty list of parameters displays because the development environment did not accept the parameters immediately. This happens only in response to an explicit command.

▷ Click the COPY EVENT PARAMETERS button.

▷ Click the METHODS button to return to the method list (see Figure 6.44).

You can now write the source code for the set_title method.

▷ Click the set_title method.

▷ Click the SAVE button and then SOURCE CODE (see Figure 6.45).

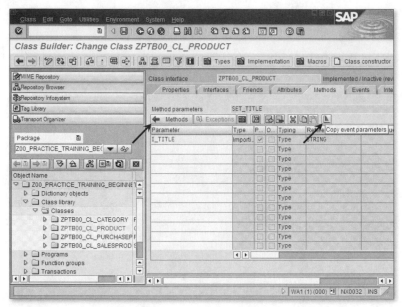

Figure 6.44 Adjusting the Parameters of the set_title Event-Handler Method of Class ZPTB00_CL_PRODUCT

Figure 6.45 Changing to the Source Code of the set_title Event-Handler Method of Class ZPTB00_CL_PRODUCT

Because this method is both an event-handler method and the trigger of an event, add the `RAISE EVENT` statement next to the obligatory assignment of the new title.

▷ Enter the source code shown in Figure 6.46.

▷ Click the SAVE button, and then click BACK.

Figure 6.46 Defining the Source Code of the set_title Event-Handler Method of Class ZPTB00_CL_PRODUCT

The enhancement of the `ZPTB00_CL_Product` class is now complete.

You can now write the main program.

Creating the main program

▷ In the context menu of program ZPTB00_PRODUCT_EVENT, click COPY.

Enter "ZPTB00_PRODUCT_EVENT_GL" as the name of the program, and confirm your entries with the COPY button.

The next dialog asks which additional information should be copied along with the source code and the text elements.

▷ Leave the default settings in place, and confirm with the COPY button.

▷ The number of the transport request used previously is set by default. Simply confirm it with the OK button.

You can now load the program with the object list area and display the source code (see Figure 6.47).

▷ Double-click the name of program ZPTB00_PRODUCT_EVENT_GL in the object list area to display the source code.

▷ Change to editing mode with Ctrl + F1.

Figure 6.47 Copied Source Code for Program ZPTB00_PRODUCT_EVENT_GL

Now you are supposed to adjust this program.

▷ Type the following source code beneath the comment lines:

```
REPORT  zptb00_product_event.

* Main program ***
```

```
DATA:
  l_category_root TYPE REF TO ZPTB00_cl_category,
  l_category TYPE REF TO ZPTB00_cl_category,
  l_salesproduct TYPE REF TO ZPTB00_cl_salesproduct,
  l_purchaseproduct TYPE REF TO
    ZPTB00_cl_purchaseproduct.

CREATE OBJECT l_category_root
  EXPORTING
    i_title      = 'Products'.
CREATE OBJECT l_category
  EXPORTING
    i_rcl_parent = l_category_root
    i_title      = 'Hardware'.
CREATE OBJECT l_purchaseproduct
  EXPORTING
    i_rcl_parent = l_category
    i_title      = 'Toshiba Satellite 430s'
    i_net_price  - '1500'.
CREATE OBJECT l_salesproduct
  EXPORTING
    i_rcl_parent = l_category
    i_title      = 'Toshiba Satellite 430s'
    i_net_price  = '1500'.
l_category_root->write_to_screen( ).
* connect l_purchaseproduct to event of
* l_salesproduct, so we get noticed in
* l_purchaseproduct
SET HANDLER l_salesproduct->set_title FOR l_purchaseproduct.
CALL METHOD l_purchaseproduct->set_title
  EXPORTING
    i_title = 'Toshiba Portege 120s'.
l_category_root->write_to_screen( ).
* End of main program ***
```

Listing 6.20 Source Code of Program ZPTB00_PRODUCT_EVENT_GL

As in the example in the previous section, you simply have to exchange the name of the local class with that of the related global class in the data declaration.

Testing the program

As expected, when you test program ZPTB00_PRODUCT_EVENT_GL, you get the same results as during the implementation with local classes (see Figure 6.48).

Figure 6.48 Program ZPTB00_PRODUCT_EVENT_GL During Execution

The use of the ABAP event concept in global classes doesn't play a secondary role when compared to its use in local classes. On the contrary, its user-friendliness and dialog-driven approach help users avoid oversights common among beginners. The development environment for global classes always ensures consistency and improves manageability. That's why we particularly recommend the use of events along with global classes.

Not only does this book use many examples to introduce you to the basics of ABAP Objects; it also has a comprehensive real-life scenario, which is implemented using the information provided in the previous chapters. Based on this practice scenario, you learn the typical means used in professional ABAP development — even how it is done at SAP — and you develop a substantial application: the automated accounting for the subsidiaries of a trading enterprise.

7 Practice Scenario—Automated Accounting for Corporate Subsidiaries

The information provided in the previous chapters enables you to create small- to medium-sized ABAP applications and represents a solid basis if you want to get to know the details of SAP applications and solutions. The real-life scenario described in the following sections doesn't really bridge any knowledge gap; instead, it gives you the required information and necessary experience that you will gain when implementing software projects in the SAP environment.

Practice Scenario

The practice scenario is set in the *Pharma Trades Corporation*, a globally operating pharmaceutical enterprise. The application to be developed should be a solution that enables automated accounting in the enterprise's subsidiaries. The name of the application is PHARMA-TRANSACT.

As a developer at Pharma Trades Corporation, you will be responsible for providing some essential core functions of PHARMA-TRANSACT. The following sections guide you step by step through the different stages of this project. You will perform important development tasks and learn a lot about how to use ABAP Objects efficiently.

> During the kick-off meeting for the PHARMA-TRANSACT project, your project manager tells you which stages of the software development project have already been completed successfully. These stages are:
>
> 1. Defining the requirements and creating a list of functions in collaboration with the specialist department.
> 2. Providing the architecture and design of individual software components.

7.1 Defining the Requirements and a List of Functions for the Application

The definition of the requirements, also referred to as the *specification*, describes the requirements of the software to be created at a purely content-related level (in this case, it's the accounting level). The specification represents the first stage of any software project and is created and maintained in written form by the management team of the development project (that is, the project manager, software architect, and product manager) and the customer. In this case, the customer is represented by members of the involved specialist departments in the subsidiaries and headquarters of Pharma Trades Corporation. You should regard everything described here as being an "integral part of the contract."

Overview of functions

Pharma Trades Corporation is a wholesaler of drugs and has more than 100 subsidiaries worldwide. These subsidiaries are supposed to be integrated with the corporate network via the Internet using a *virtual private network* (VPN). This way, all subsidiaries can transfer all business transactions from their POS and warehousing systems to the centrally installed PHARMA-TRANSACT system. In this way, each sales transaction to a customer, each replenishment for a subsidiary's warehouse, and each disposal of drugs whose best-before date has passed are to be recorded in PHARMA-TRANSACT in real time, automatically (that is, without any manual interaction by an accounting employee) converted into a corresponding posting document, and saved. Only for emergency cases do you want to implement a user interface that provides employees with the option to enter business transactions manually.

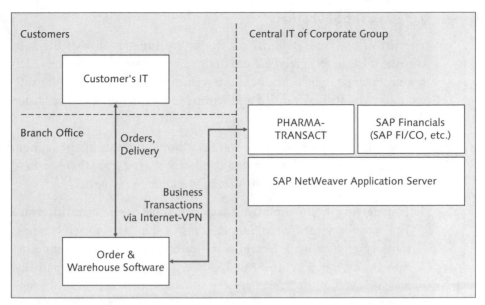

Figure 7.1 PHARMA-TRANSACT in the Environment of Pharma Trades Corporation

A special logic within PHARMA-TRANSACT is responsible for generating correct posting documents, which are based on the different business transactions and are in compliance with the rules of proper double-entry accounting as well as with the accounting principles applied in the enterprise (for instance, IAS or US-GAAP), and for storing these documents in the database. The advantages over manual accounting are readily apparent. Unlike a department of accountants, the software can post identical business transactions much faster, always in the same way (that is, to the same accounts), and without error.

The posted documents are then made available to a wide range of software solutions. In the case of Pharma Trades Corporation, these solutions include the enterprise's accounting and controlling system (SAP FI/CO), a solution for planning and optimizing inventory and purchasing processes (SAP APO), and a solution for strategic enterprise analysis and planning (SAP SEM). Of course, almost any other external application will also benefit from the result.

7.1.1 List of Functions

The list of functions summarizes the entire functionality of the software as it has been agreed on and defined by the involved parties. Each requirement contained in this list describes a core function of the software, which must be verified and approved by the individual specialist departments.

From business transaction to posting document

The path from entering a business transaction in the subsidiary's system to storing the posting document in the database, and from there onward to any external application, consists of the following steps:

1. **Transferring the business transaction through the inbound interface**
   The subsidiary uses a program to transfer the data of each business transaction from its POS and warehousing software to an inbound interface of the new PHARMA-TRANSACT application. Alternatively, an employee of the subsidiary can enter the data manually through a user interface of the new application. A typical example of a business transaction consists of transferring the data of an invoice that has been created by the subsidiary and sent to a drugstore. For emergency cases, another user interface is provided that enables users to enter business transactions manually.

2. **Checking the business transaction for accuracy**
   In order to avoid making the new application unusable by entering inconsistent data, each business transaction must be checked for accuracy (validation) before it can be processed. For example, products must always be entered along with an indication of the quantity (such as 10 packages) and a price (such as a sales or purchase price).

3. **Converting the business transaction to a posting document and saving it in the database**
   Each business transaction must be documented in the form of one or several posting documents, just as an accountant would do manually. Nevertheless, in this respect, the rules of proper double-entry accounting must be adhered to. A business transaction always consists of a header and one or more items. The header data provides comprehensive information about the type of the business transaction (for instance, purchase, sale, and so on), the customer's address, the date, and payment terms. The item data, on the other hand, contains infor-

mation on the item type (for instance, purchase of a product, sale of a service, and so on), products, associated quantities, and amounts. The conversion to a posting document is generally carried out in such a way that for each business transaction header, you must generate exactly one document header, and for each business transaction item, you must generate two document items (credits and debits). The posting logic contained in PHARMA-TRANSACT determines the entire process flow. The posting documents that are generated are stored in the database and are therefore always available. They represent the final output of the application.

4. **Reading posting documents**
To enable other third-party and SAP applications to further process the accounting documents, a specific interface is defined that provides us with read access to the final result, that is, to all data stored in the database. This way, you can flexibly search for specific data by using search criteria. In addition, an accounting document display is provided, which meets simple reporting requirements and enables you to view a selection of stored accounting documents in a table on your screen. You can transfer documents from this table manually to other programs via copy and paste.

The entire project team, that is, all team members with a technical focus as well as those from the specialist departments in the corporation, is responsible for developing the new application and for customizing existing software systems both in the subsidiaries and the headquarters in such a way that these systems can communicate with the new application. Because the scope of the project is quite considerable, we'll use a formal development approach that includes the creation of the specification and list of functions, the description of the software architecture and design, as well as change requests, if necessary.

The job of the project team

7.1.2 Selection List

While the list of functions describes what the software must be able to do, the selection list describes what it is not (yet) able to do, and therefore what must be handled by either other software systems in the landscape or carried out manually.

Among other things, the selection list regularly deals with the "glue logic," which is responsible for connecting existing software systems with the system that is to be created, for instance, via additional middleware tools such as SAP NetWeaver Process Integration or through transfer programs that are to be developed simultaneously. These transfer programs are also referred to as the *transformation layer*; they are responsible for the data conversion and data exchange between the software systems. Furthermore, the selection list also describes functions that might become necessary in the long term but cannot be included in the current software release due to organizational reasons.

1. **Integrating upstream and downstream systems**
   The PHARMA-TRANSACT application provides remote-enabled function modules for entering business transactions and reading posting documents. These function modules can be called from a wide range of different systems and platforms (Windows, Java, Web services). However, it doesn't directly integrate the upstream systems. Instead, the software lets the upstream and downstream systems or an appropriate middleware call the interfaces and the associated delivery and reception of data in the right format.

2. **Fixed logic for converting business transactions into accounting documents**
   The program code of PHARMA-TRANSACT supports the automatic creation of posting documents from business transactions. For the current release, it is not planned to allow the posting logic to be manipulated via customizing. In a future release, it will probably be possible to configure in customizing which credit and debit accounts can be posted to for each business transaction type and item type.

3. **Cancellation of business transactions**
   In the current release, you cannot process cancellations of business transactions or enter them. Instead, the software allows the other software systems to deliver an identical business transaction with reverse quantities and amounts. If cancellations of business transactions will be permitted in a future release, then it will probably be in such a way that a separate inbound interface is provided that is responsible for receiving these cancellations.

4. **Financial statement**

The creation of a financial statement—including a profit and loss statement and appendices that consist of the accounting documents—is
not supported by PHARMA-TRANSACT. A future release might contain a component for calculating the balances for an individual item
type, as well as for converting foreign currencies to the balance-sheet
currency and for assigning the balances to the financial statement
items, which, in turn, could be read and displayed by SAP NetWeaver
Business Intelligence.

7.2   Software Architecture

The technical structure and functionality of software is described by the
software architecture and the software design, both of which are created
on the basis of the specification (see Section 7.1, Defining the Requirements and a List of Functions for the Application). In this context, a
top-down approach is typically used in which you fine-tune the individual components down to the level of ABAP packages, ABAP function
groups, and ABAP classes. To do this, you normally use an overview
of the software architecture provided by the project managers. Then
the responsible project team members who are appointed afterwards
create the software design and its validation in review meetings with
coworkers, down to the level of individual functions and methods to be
implemented.

With regard to the complexity of modern business software, the design   Introduction
of an appropriate software architecture and the associated separation and
reuse of components are very important. Concerning PHARMA-TRANS-
ACT, the project team decided on a modular concept, which is described
in the programming guidelines in Appendix A. The central aspect of
these guidelines is the use of a layer model in which each layer has to
perform a specific task.

1. **MAPI layer—Communication with upstream and downstream
   systems**
   The communication with upstream and downstream systems is carried out by function modules that have been designed for this specific

purpose. These function modules can be called remotely (MAPI layer) and can internally call function modules from the API layer.

2. **API layer—Communication between the software components**
   The individual software components of PHARMA-TRANSACT communicate with each other through function modules that are specifically designed for this purpose (API layer). Direct access to the business logic or even database tables of other software components is not permitted.

3. **OBJ layer—Processing logic within a software component**
   The actual business logic of each software component is implemented in function modules of the object layer. This is where the main part of the coding is stored during the implementation.

4. **DB layer—Access to the database**
   Access to a software component's own database tables can be separated from the business logic, if necessary. You can do this by using function modules, which are specifically designed for this purpose and are referred to as the DB layer. With regard to more complex database accesses, you can increase the reusability of accesses in this way. Access to database tables of other software components is permitted only if you use function modules of the API layer of the software component in question.

This separation into layers enables large project teams to define and integrate interfaces (for calling function modules using transfer parameters) long before the complete source code is implemented within the function modules.

Architectural concept

The software architecture of PHARMA-TRANSACT is based on the layer model and defines several function groups for each software component. These function groups represent the individual layers (see Figure 7.2).

Standardized implementation of software components

Each software component of PHARMA-TRANSACT consists of at least the API layer for communicating with other software components, and the OBJ layer for implementing the business logic. Optionally, the MAPI layer for communicating with upstream and downstream systems and the DB layer for encapsulating database accesses can be included as well.

Each of the four items in the list of functions in the layer model represents a separate software component and is implemented via several function groups.

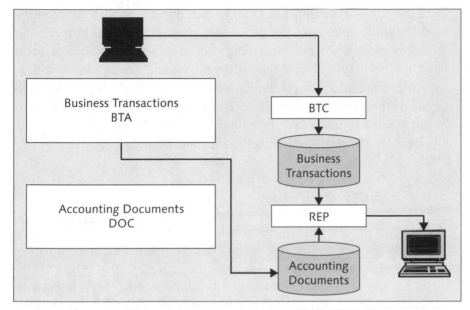

Figure 7.2 Overview of the Architecture of PHARMA-TRANSACT

Within the team, a discussion was held with regard to combining the validation of business transactions with the reception and storage of business transactions. The advantage of separating these processes is that validations can be extended at a later stage (even by other project teams that define new business transaction and item types) without affecting the reception and storage of business transactions.

The functionality of PHARMA-TRANSACT is implemented in three processes that can be started and used independently of each other:

1. Reception, validation, and storage of business transactions
2. Conversion of business transactions into accounting documents and storage of these documents
3. Outputting the accounting documents

429

The separation of the reception and processing of business transactions enables the distribution of the server load to different periods. For example, business transactions can be loaded to the database quickly and without any complex processing steps in the evenings. The processing of these business transactions into posting documents then starts during the night. Furthermore, the business transactions are thus brought into a chronological sequence according to the posting data and independent of the delivery time and the upstream system. This sequence is then adhered to during the posting process. The output of accounting documents through a display interface or an outbound interface can occur at any time and irrespective of the other processes. At daytime, Controlling can access the processed data efficiently and without restriction.

7.3   Software Design

The software design fine-tunes the software components of PHARMA-TRANSACT down to the level of individual function modules, which are arranged in function groups. The procedure is very formal and standardized. It focuses on the rapid availability of information that is relevant to the implementation. Because of the use of the layer model, some of the functionality descriptions apply to several functions.

Integrating the components in the overall architecture
The objects of this design are the software components, which have been described in the specification:

1. ZPTB00_***_BTA—Receive and save business transactions

2. ZPTB00_***_BTC—Validate business transactions

3. ZPTB00_***_DOC—Convert business transactions to accounting documents

4. ZPTB00_***_REP—Read accounting documents

These processes represent the core processes of PHARMA-TRANSACT. All other processes that must be implemented in order to integrate the subsidiaries with the software system of the headquarters are not relevant to this software project.

7.3.1 Rough Design

The rough design is more detailed than the architectural concept. It describes the names of external and internal interfaces and explains the important processes.

Interdependencies between the software components described here and other software systems do not exist because all inbound and outbound interfaces within this software project are predefined. For this reason, we don't need to describe any interdependencies at this point.

Interdependencies

The programming interfaces listed below are available to other software systems. They have been implemented as function modules that can be called remotely. This results primarily in the restriction that all transfer parameters must be transferred as value parameters and not as references.

External programming interfaces

▶ ZPTB00_MAP_BTA_SET
Receive and save business transaction

▶ ZPTB00_MAP_REP_GET
Read accounting documents

The following programming interfaces are available to other software systems within the project. They have been implemented as function modules and were included in the package interface of the Z00_PRAC-TICE_TRAINING_BEGINNER package:

Internal programming interfaces

▶ ZPTB00_API_BTA_SET
Receive and save business transaction

▶ ZPTB00_API_BTA_EDIT
Edit business transaction manually

▶ ZPTB00_API_BTC_CHECK
Check business transaction

▶ ZPTB00_API_DOC_RUN
Generate accounting documents from business transactions

▶ ZPTB00_API_REP_GET
Read accounting documents

▶ ZPTB00_API_REP_DISPLAY
Display accounting documents

User interfaces and programs

The manual entry of business transactions is divided into an entry option for the business transaction header and a table that allows you to enter the individual business transaction items (see Figure 7.3). This user interface was already created in Section 5.2, Complex Input and Output Interfaces—Dynpros.

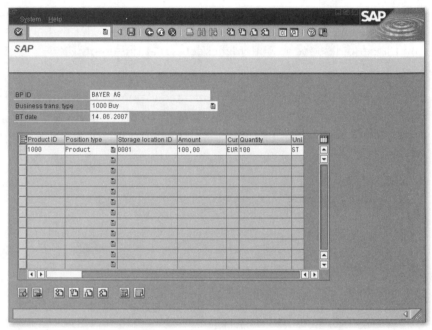

Figure 7.3 Manual Entry of Business Transactions

Another program interface is used to start the conversion of business transactions into accounting documents, and allows the selection of data according to business transaction type and posting date (see Figure 7.4). The result of this selection is then processed exclusively, while all other business transactions remain untouched.

Figure 7.4 Converting Business Transactions to Accounting Documents

The manual evaluation of accounting documents is enabled by two screens. First, a selection screen appears that enables you to limit the documents to be displayed according to business transaction type and posting date. Next, a full screen ALV displays the selection result (see Figure 7.5).

Figure 7.5 Displaying Accounting Documents

Figure 7.6 shows the names of all function groups to be implemented, including their function modules.

Chart overview

Figure 7.6 Overview of all Function Groups of the Project

In an object-oriented design, the designed classes would be shown along with their methods and attributes.

Important flow charts Figure 7.7 illustrates the steps that are carried out once a business transaction has been received.

Figure 7.7 Flow Chart "Reception, Validation, and Storage of Business Transactions"

Figure 7.8 illustrates the steps that are carried out once the conversion of business transactions into accounting documents has been started and the accounting documents have been saved.

Figure 7.9 illustrates the steps involved in reading an accounting document either for outputting the document on the screen or for transferring it through the outbound interface of the system.

Figure 7.8 Flow Chart "Converting Business Transactions to Accounting Documents"

Figure 7.9 Flow Chart "Reading and Displaying Accounting Documents"

7.3.2 Detailed Design

The detailed design contains the interface of each individual function or method to be implemented. Thus, a software design that is created in a joint collaboration of several persons allows for the synchronization of interfaces and data requirements within the individual software components.

Function group
ZPTB00_MAP_BTA The ZPTB00_MAP_BTA function group (business transaction) contains the external interface for receiving, validating, and saving business transactions that have been delivered by other systems. All function modules contained in this function group are marked as remote-enabled and they transfer parameters as values.

In an input structure, the ZPTB00_API_BTA_SET function module receives a business transaction including header and item data and passes the business transaction on to other function modules in order to validate and save it. If this process does not complete successfully, an exception will be triggered.

```
FUNCTION zptb00_map_bta_set.
*"----------------------------------------------------------
*"*"Local interface:
*"  IMPORTING
*"      VALUE(I_STR_BTA) TYPE  ZPTB00_STR_BTA
*"  EXCEPTIONS
*"      FAILED
*"----------------------------------------------------------
```

Function group
ZPTB00_MAP_REP The ZPTB00_MAP_REP function group (reporting) contains the external interface for reading and further processing accounting documents. All function modules contained in this function group are marked as remote-enabled and they transfer parameters as values.

In an input structure, the ZPTB00_MAP_REP_GET function module receives a range of posting dates and uses this information to read the accounting documents whose posting dates lie within this range. After that, the accounting documents are returned to the caller.

```
FUNCTION zptb00_map_rep_get.
*"----------------------------------------------------------
*"*"Local interface:
*"  IMPORTING
*"      VALUE(I_TAB_BOOKING_DATE) TYPE  DDTRANGE
*"  EXPORTING
*"      VALUE(E_TAB_DOC) TYPE  ZPTB00_TTY_DOC
```

```
*"    EXCEPTIONS
*"        FAILED
*"----------------------------------------------------------
```

The ZPTB00_API_BTA function group (business transaction) contains the internal interface for receiving, reading, and modifying business transactions. The function modules contained in this function group are called by other software components of the project in order to process information about business transactions.

Function group
ZPTB00_API_BTA

The ZPTB00_API_BTA_LOAD function module loads business transactions and returns them in a hierarchical table including header and item information. As an input parameter, this function module expects information as to whether it is supposed to read only non-posted or only posted business transactions.

```
FUNCTION zptb00_api_bta_load.
*"----------------------------------------------------------
*"*"Local interface:
*"  IMPORTING
*"    REFERENCE(I_BOOKED) TYPE  ZPTB00_DTE_BTA_BOOKED
*"        DEFAULT '1'
*"  EXPORTING
*"    REFERENCE(E_TAB_BTA) TYPE  ZPTB00_TTY_BTA
*"  EXCEPTIONS
*"        FAILED
*"----------------------------------------------------------
```

The ZPTB00_API_BTA_MARK_AS_BOOKED function module modifies the business transactions that have been transferred via input parameters to the database in such a way that the BOOKED field is assigned the value '2', that is, posted. Therefore, these business transactions differ from those business transactions that haven't been posted and whose BOOKED field is assigned the value '1'. Ultimately, this method avoids the duplicate processing of accounting documents.

```
FUNCTION zptb00_api_bta_mark_as_booked.
*"----------------------------------------------------------
*"*"Local interface:
*"  IMPORTING
*"    REFERENCE(I_TAB_BTA) TYPE  ZPTB00_TTY_BTA
```

```
*"    EXCEPTIONS
*"        FAILED
*"------------------------------------------------------
```

In an input structure, the ZPTB00_API_BTA_SET function module receives a business transaction including header and item data and passes the business transaction on to other function modules in order to validate and save it. If this process does not complete successfully, an exception will be triggered.

```
FUNCTION zptb00_api_bta_set.
*"------------------------------------------------------
*"*"Local interface:
*"  IMPORTING
*"      REFERENCE(I_STR_BTA) TYPE  ZPTB00_STR_BTA
*"  EXCEPTIONS
*"      FAILED
*"------------------------------------------------------
```

Function group ZPTB00_API_BTC

The ZPTB00_API_BTC function group (business transaction check) contains the internal interface for receiving and checking business transactions. The function modules contained in this function group are called by other software components of the project in order to check the validity of business transactions.

In an input structure, the ZPTB00_API_BTC_CHECK function module receives a business transaction including header and item data and checks the validity of its fields. For this purpose, the function module passes the business transaction on to the corresponding object layer.

```
FUNCTION zptb00_api_btc_check.
*"------------------------------------------------------
*"*"Local interface:
*"  IMPORTING
*"      REFERENCE(I_STR_BTA) TYPE  ZPTB00_STR_BTA
*"  EXCEPTIONS
*"      FAILED
*"------------------------------------------------------
```

Function group ZPTB00_API_DOC

The ZPTB00_API_DOC function group (accounting documents) contains the internal interface for the automatic conversion of business transactions to accounting documents. The function modules contained in this function group are called by other software components of the project.

In an input structure, the ZPTB00_API_DOC_LOAD function module receives a range of posting dates and uses this information to read the accounting documents whose posting dates lie within this range. Then, the respective accounting documents are returned to the caller in a hierarchical table, including header and item information. For this purpose, the function module passes the input parameter on to the corresponding object layer and receives the returned accounting documents.

```
FUNCTION zptb00_api_doc_load.
*"----------------------------------------------------
*"*"Local interface:
*"       IMPORTING
*"            REFERENCE(I_TAB_BOOKING_DATE) TYPE
*"                 DDTRANGE
*"       EXPORTING
*"            REFERENCE(E_TAB_DOC) TYPE  ZPTB00_TTY_DOC
*"       EXCEPTIONS
*"            FAILED
*"----------------------------------------------------
```

The ZPTB00_API_DOC_RUN function module processes the non-posted business transactions in such a way that it first reads them and then transforms them into accounting documents. Then it saves the accounting documents and finally marks the processed business transactions as posted. This function module doesn't require any transfer parameters.

```
FUNCTION zptb00_api_doc_run.
*"----------------------------------------------------
*"*"Local interface:
*"  EXCEPTIONS
*"      FAILED
*"----------------------------------------------------
```

The ZPTB00_API_REP function group (reporting) contains the internal interface for displaying accounting documents on the screen. The function modules contained in this function group are called by other software components of the project.

Function group
ZPTB00_API_REP

In an input structure, the ZPTB00_API_REP_DISPLAY function module receives a range of posting dates and uses this information to read the accounting documents whose posting dates lie within this range. These accounting documents are then combined into a flat table whose header and item information is located next to each other in a structure, then passed on to an ALV grid display, and output on the screen. For this purpose, the function module passes the input parameter on to the corresponding object layer and receives the returned accounting documents.

```
FUNCTION zptb00_api_rep_display.
*"----------------------------------------------------
*"*"Local interface:
*"  IMPORTING
*"     REFERENCE(I_TAB_BOOKING_DATE) TYPE  DDTRANGE
*"  EXCEPTIONS
*"       FAILED
*"----------------------------------------------------
```

Function group ZPTB00_OBJ_BTA

The ZPTB00_OBJ_BTA function group (business transactions) contains the business logic for receiving and saving business transactions. The function modules contained in this function group are called either exclusively in the same layer or by the higher API layer because they're not intended to be used in other software components.

The ZPTB00_OBJ_BTA_EDIT function module was already implemented in Section 5.2, Complex Input and Output Interfaces—Dynpros. In an input structure, this function module either receives an existing business transaction for editing or allows the entry of a new business transaction, if the structure was left initial. Once the correct entry has been made, the complete business transaction structure is returned to the caller for further processing. Internally, this function makes extensive use of the dynpro technology in order to present and control the input interface.

```
FUNCTION zptb00_obj_bta_edit.
*"----------------------------------------------------
*"*"Local interface:
*"  CHANGING
*"     REFERENCE(C_STR_BTA) TYPE  ZPTB00_STR_BTA OPTIONAL
*"----------------------------------------------------
```

The ZPTB00_OBJ_BTA_ENRICH function module was complemented by the information that is needed for saving purposes, such as the primary and foreign keys. This was specifically done to enrich business transactions that have not been entered manually. The required input parameter is the business transaction to be enriched, which is returned after the enrichment.

```
FUNCTION zptb00_obj_bta_enrich.
*"----------------------------------------------------
*"*"Local interface:
*"  CHANGING
*"     REFERENCE(C_STR_BTA) TYPE  ZPTB00_STR_BTA
*"  EXCEPTIONS
*"      FAILED
*"----------------------------------------------------
```

In an input structure, the ZPTB00_OBJ_DOC_LOAD function module receives a range of posting dates and uses this information to read the accounting documents whose posting dates lie within this range. Then the respective accounting documents are returned to the caller in a hierarchical table, including header and item information.

```
FUNCTION zptb00_obj_bta_load.
*"----------------------------------------------------
*"*"Local interface:
*"  IMPORTING
*"     REFERENCE(I_BOOKED) TYPE  ZPTB00_DTE_BTA_BOOKED
*"        DEFAULT '1'
*"  EXPORTING
*"     REFERENCE(E_TAB_BTA) TYPE  ZPTB00_TTY_BTA
*"  EXCEPTIONS
*"      FAILED
*"----------------------------------------------------
```

The ZPTB00_OBJ_BTA_MARK_AS_BOOKED function module modifies the business transactions that have been transferred via input parameters to the database in such a way that the BOOKED field is assigned the value '2', that is, posted. Therefore, these business transactions differ from those business transactions that haven't been posted and whose BOOKED field is assigned the value '1'. Ultimately, this method avoids the duplicate processing of accounting documents.

```
FUNCTION zptb00_obj_bta_mark_as_booked.
*"----------------------------------------------------------
*"*"Local interface:
*"      IMPORTING
*"            REFERENCE(I_TAB_BTA) TYPE  ZPTB00_TTY_BTA
*"      EXCEPTIONS
*"              FAILED
*"----------------------------------------------------------
```

The ZPTB00_OBJ_BTA_SAVE function module was already implemented in Section 5.2. Here it will be used in an input structure in order to receive either a business transaction structure or several business transactions in a table, and to save these objects in a database table. If an error occurs during the save process, an exception will be triggered.

```
FUNCTION zptb00_obj_bta_save.
*"----------------------------------------------------------
*"*"Local interface:
*"  IMPORTING
*"     REFERENCE(I_STR_BTA) TYPE  ZPTB00_STR_BTA
*"        OPTIONAL
*"     REFERENCE(I_TAB_BTA) TYPE  ZPTB00_TTY_BTA
*"        OPTIONAL
*"  EXCEPTIONS
*"        FAILED
*"----------------------------------------------------------
```

Function group ZPTB00_OBJ_BTC

The ZPTB00_OBJ_BTC function group (business transaction check) contains the necessary function for checking business transactions. The function modules contained in this function group are called either exclusively in the same layer or by the higher API layer because they're not intended to be used in other software components.

In an input structure, the ZPTB00_OBJ_BTC_CHECK function module receives a business transaction including header and item data and checks the validity of its fields. To do this, it should internally use the basic function, DD_DOMVALUES_GET, for reading fixed values against which the check is supposed to be carried out. To check the currencies and units, an appropriate Select statement should be used to access the corresponding master data tables, TCURC and T006 respectively.

```
FUNCTION zptb00_obj_btc_check.
*"-----------------------------------------------------
*"*"Local interface:
*"      IMPORTING
^"          REFERENCE(I_STR_BTA) TYPE  ZPTB00_STR_BTA
*"      EXCEPTIONS
*"          FAILED
*"-----------------------------------------------------
```

The ZPTB00_OBJ_DOC function group (accounting documents) contains the necessary function for loading and saving accounting documents as well as for posting business transactions. The function modules contained in this function group are called either exclusively in the same layer or by the higher API layer because they're not intended to be used in other software components.

Function group ZPTB00_OBJ_DOC

The ZPTB00_OBJ_DOC_BOOK function module contains the core of the PHARMA-TRANSACT application. This function module receives the business transactions that haven't been posted yet as input parameters, and converts them into accounting documents. In this process, the business transaction header is left unchanged, while two posting items (credit and debit) are generated for each business transaction item and then are assigned the corresponding account information. Finally, the generated accounting documents are returned to the caller as return parameters.

```
FUNCTION zptb00_obj_doc_book.
*"-----------------------------------------------------
*"*"Local interface:
*"   IMPORTING
*"      REFERENCE(I_TAB_BTA) TYPE  ZPTB00_TTY_BTA
*"   EXPORTING
*"      REFERENCE(E_TAB_DOC) TYPE  ZPTB00_TTY_DOC
*"   EXCEPTIONS
*"      FAILED
*"-----------------------------------------------------
```

In an input structure, the ZPTB00_OBJ_DOC_LOAD function module receives a range of posting dates and uses this information to read the accounting documents whose posting dates lie within this range. Then the respective accounting documents are returned to the caller in a hierarchical table, including header and item information.

```
FUNCTION zptb00_obj_doc_load.
*"----------------------------------------------------
*"*"Local interface:
*"  IMPORTING
*"     REFERENCE(I_TAB_BOOKING_DATE) TYPE  DDTRANGE
*"  EXPORTING
*"     REFERENCE(E_TAB_DOC) TYPE  ZPTB00_TTY_DOC
*"  EXCEPTIONS
*"      FAILED
*"----------------------------------------------------
```

The ZPTB00_OBJ_DOC_SAVE function module is implemented like the ZPTB00_OBJ_BTA_SAVE function module. In an input structure, this function module receives either an accounting document structure or several accounting documents in a table and saves these objects in a database table. If an error occurs during the save process, an exception will be triggered.

```
FUNCTION zptb00_obj_doc_save.
*"----------------------------------------------------
*"*"Local interface:
*"  IMPORTING
*"     REFERENCE(I_STR_DOC) TYPE  ZPTB00_STR_DOC
*"        OPTIONAL
*"     REFERENCE(I_TAB_DOC) TYPE  ZPTB00_TTY_DOC
*"        OPTIONAL
*"  EXCEPTIONS
*"      FAILED
*"----------------------------------------------------
```

In an input structure, the ZPTB00_OBJ_REP_SHOW function module receives the accounting documents to be displayed. These accounting documents are then combined into a flat table whose header and item information are located next to each other in a structure, then passed on to an ALV grid display, and output on the screen.

```
FUNCTION zptb00_obj_rep_show.
*"----------------------------------------------------
*"*"Local interface:
*"  IMPORTING
*"     REFERENCE(I_TAB_DOC) TYPE  ZPTB00_TTY_DOC
```

```
*"  EXCEPTIONS
*"      FAILED
*"- - - - - - - - - - - - - - - - - - - - - - - - - - - - - - - - - - - - - - -
```

7.4   Implementation

In the implementation phase, the software design, which has been described in a document, is converted into program code. For this purpose, each development object described must be created in the SAP Object Navigator and the source code must be completed according to the description. In actual projects, it sometimes happens that smaller or bigger change requests occur when certain sections of the software design turn out to be inefficient, less than optimal, or can't be implemented, which would be the worst-case scenario. Depending on how extensive the deviations are, project management or the customer—in this case, the specialist departments—must consent to the change in written form; the impact of the change on the project schedule and budget must be calculated as well.

Convert into code

> **Tip**
>
> Check it out by yourself! If you can use the information regarding technology and content provided in Section 7.1 to implement a functioning prototype, you're ready to execute your first professional project. Of course, the implementation outlined in the following sections represents only one of many possible solution concepts and is intended to provide you with a commonly used method of implementing the project. If you get stuck at a certain stage, you can reproduce the details of the sample implementation in this section. The descriptions of development objects deliberately weren't repeated because the documents introduced in the previous sections represent the official documentation in a real-life project.

7.4.1   Dictionary Objects

This section contains the most important information about all Dictionary objects used in this practice scenario, with the exception of the data elements and domains that were extensively described in Section 5.2.

Database Tables

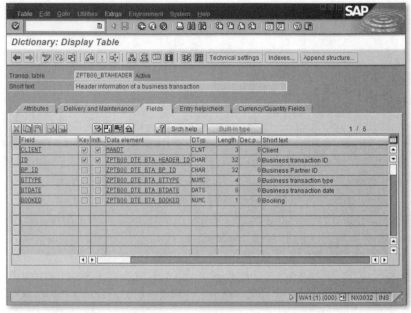

Figure 7.10   ZPTB00_BTAHEADER—Header Information of a Business Transaction

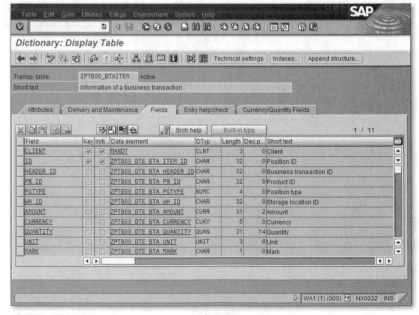

Figure 7.11   ZPTB00_BTAITEM—Item Information of a Business Transaction

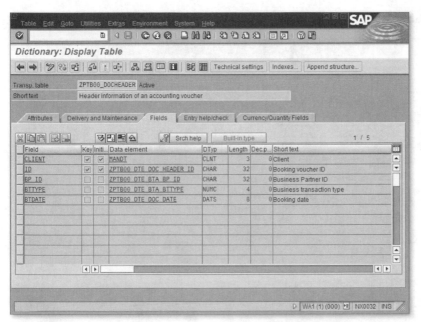

Figure 7.12 ZPTB00_DOCHEADER—Header Information of Accounting Documents

Figure 7.13 ZPTB00_DOCITEM—Item Information of Accounting Documents

Table Types

Figure 7.14 ZPTB00_TTY_BTA—Table of Business Transactions

Figure 7.15 ZPTB00_TTY_BTA_ITEM—Items of Business Transactions

Figure 7.16 ZPTB00_TTY_DOC—Accounting Documents

Figure 7.17 ZPTB00_TTY_DOC_ITEM—Items of Accounting Documents

Structures

Figure 7.18 ZPTB00_STR_BTA—Business Transaction

Figure 7.19 ZPTB00_STR_DOC—Accounting Document

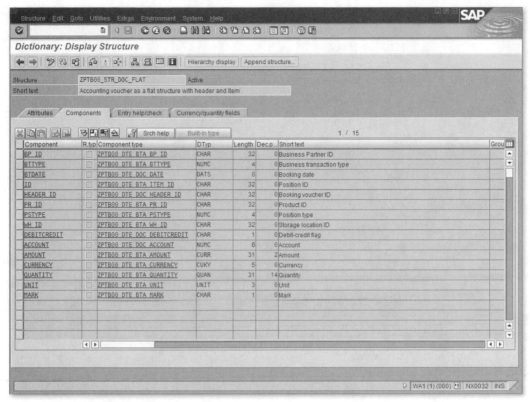

Figure 7.20 ZPTB00_STR_DOC_FLAT—Accounting Document as a Flat Structure with Header and Item

7.4.2 Programs

This section contains the complete source code for the programs in this practice scenario.

```
REPORT  zptb00_business_transaction.

DATA:
  l_str_bta TYPE zptb00_str_bta.

DO.
  CALL FUNCTION 'ZPTB00_OBJ_BTA_EDIT'
    CHANGING
      c_str_bta = l_str_bta.
```

```
      IF NOT l_str_bta IS INITIAL.
        CALL FUNCTION 'ZPTB00_OBJ_BTA_SAVE'
          EXPORTING
            i_str_bta = l_str_bta
*           i_tab_bta =
          EXCEPTIONS
            failed    = 1
            OTHERS    = 2.
        IF sy-subrc <> 0.
          MESSAGE e008(ZPTB00_BTA).
        ENDIF.
        CLEAR l_str_bta.
      ELSE.
        RETURN.
      ENDIF.

ENDDO.
```

Listing 7.1 ZPTB00_BUSINESS_TRANSACTION—Enter Business Transaction Manually

```
REPORT   zptb00_document_booking.

PARAMETERS:
  p_book TYPE boolean.

CALL FUNCTION 'ZPTB00_API_DOC_RUN'
  EXCEPTIONS
    failed = 1
    OTHERS = 2.
IF sy-subrc <> 0.
  message e000(ZPTB00_DOC).
ENDIF.
```

Listing 7.2 ZPTB00_DOCUMENT_BOOKING—Process Business Transactions

```
REPORT   zptb00_document_viewer.

DATA:
  l_btdate TYPE zptb00_dte_bta_btdate,
  l_tab_btdate TYPE ddtrange,
  l_str_btdate TYPE ddrange.
FIELD-SYMBOLS:
```

```
  <l_str_btdate> TYPE ANY.

* Input new reservation as selection screen
SELECTION-SCREEN BEGIN OF SCREEN 110.
SELECTION-SCREEN BEGIN OF BLOCK b110 WITH FRAME TITLE text-005.
SELECT-OPTIONS:
  p_btdate FOR l_btdate.
SELECTION-SCREEN END OF BLOCK b110.
SELECTION-SCREEN END OF SCREEN 110.

* Main program
DO.
  CALL SELECTION-SCREEN 110.
  IF sy-subrc <> 0.
    EXIT.
  ELSE.
    LOOP AT p_btdate ASSIGNING <l_str_btdate>.
      MOVE-CORRESPONDING <l_str btdate> TO l_str_bt.date.
    ENDLOOP.
    CALL FUNCTION 'ZPTB00_API_REP_DISPLAY'
      EXPORTING
        i_tab_booking_date = l_tab_btdate
      EXCEPTIONS
        failed             = 1
        OTHERS             = 2.
    IF sy subrc <> 0.
      message e000(ZPTB00_REP).
    ENDIF.

  ENDIF.
ENDDO.
```

Listing 7.3 ZPTB00_DOCUMENT_VIEWER—Show Accounting Documents

7.4.3 Function Groups

This section contains the complete source code for all function modules. The screen flow logic and the associated modules of the editing function for business transactions were already described in detail in Section 5.2.

ZPTB00_API_BTA—Receive and Save Business Transactions

```
FUNCTION zptb00_api_bta_load.
*"----------------------------------------------------
*"*"Local interface:
*"  IMPORTING
*"     REFERENCE(I_BOOKED) TYPE  ZPTB00_DTE_BTA_BOOKED
*"        DEFAULT '1'
*"  EXPORTING
*"     REFERENCE(E_TAB_BTA) TYPE  ZPTB00_TTY_BTA
*"  EXCEPTIONS
*"      FAILED
*"----------------------------------------------------


  CALL FUNCTION 'ZPTB00_OBJ_BTA_LOAD'
*    EXPORTING
*      I_BOOKED        = '1'
     IMPORTING
       e_tab_bta       = e_tab_bta
     EXCEPTIONS
       failed          = 1
       OTHERS          = 2.
   IF sy-subrc <> 0.
     RAISE failed.
   ENDIF.

ENDFUNCTION.
```

Listing 7.4 ZPTB00_API_BTA_LOAD—Load Business Transactions

```
FUNCTION zptb00_api_bta_mark_as_booked.
*"----------------------------------------------------
*"*"Local interface:
*"  IMPORTING
*"     REFERENCE(I_TAB_BTA) TYPE  ZPTB00_TTY_BTA
*"  EXCEPTIONS
*"      FAILED
*"----------------------------------------------------


  CALL FUNCTION 'ZPTB00_OBJ_BTA_MARK_AS_BOOKED'
    EXPORTING
      i_tab_bta = i_tab_bta
```

```
        EXCEPTIONS
          failed    = 1
          OTHERS    = 2.
      IF sy-subrc <> 0.
        RAISE failed.
      ENDIF.


ENDFUNCTION.
```

Listing 7.5 ZPTB00_API_BTA_MARK_AS_BOOKED—Mark Business Transactions as Posted

```
FUNCTION zptb00_api_bta_set.
*"----------------------------------------------------
*"*"Local interface:
*"  IMPORTING
*"     REFERENCE(I_STR_BTA) TYPE  ZPTB00_STR_BTA
*"  EXCEPTIONS
*"      FAILED
*"----------------------------------------------------
  DATA:
    l_str_bta TYPE zptb00_str_bta.

* assign to local variable, because we want to enrich
* the structure
  l_str_bta = i_str_bta.

* Enrich the structure by technical fields
  CALL FUNCTION 'ZPTB00_OBJ_BTA_ENRICH'
    CHANGING
      c_str_bta = l_str_bta
    EXCEPTIONS
      failed    = 1
      OTHERS    = 2.
  IF sy-subrc <> 0.
    RAISE failed.
  ENDIF.

* Check the structure
  CALL FUNCTION 'ZPTB00_API_BTC_CHECK'
    EXPORTING
      i_str_bta = l_str_bta
```

```
        EXCEPTIONS
          failed    = 1
          OTHERS    = 2.
     IF sy-subrc <> 0.
       RAISE failed.
     ENDIF.


*  Save the structure in the database table
     CALL FUNCTION 'ZPTB00_OBJ_BTA_SAVE'
       EXPORTING
         i_str_bta = l_str_bta
*        l_tab_bta =
       EXCEPTIONS
         failed    = 1
         OTHERS    = 2.
     IF sy-subrc <> 0.
       RAISE failed.
     ENDIF.


ENDFUNCTION.
```

Listing 7.6 ZPTB00_API_BTA_SET—Receive and Save Business Transaction

ZPTB00_API_BTC—Check Business Transaction

```
FUNCTION zptb00_api_btc_check.
*"----------------------------------------------------
*"*"Local interface:
*"  IMPORTING
*"     REFERENCE(I_STR_BTA) TYPE  ZPTB00_STR_BTA
*"  EXCEPTIONS
*"      FAILED
*"----------------------------------------------------

  CALL FUNCTION 'ZPTB00_OBJ_BTC_CHECK'
    EXPORTING
      i_str_bta = i_str_bta
    EXCEPTIONS
      failed    = 1
      OTHERS    = 2.
  IF sy-subrc <> 0.
    RAISE failed.
```

```
   ENDIF.

ENDFUNCTION.
```

Listing 7.7   ZPTB00_API_BTC_CHECK—Check Business Transaction

ZPTB00_API_DOC—Generate Accounting Documents

```
FUNCTION zptb00_api_doc_load.
*"----------------------------------------------------
*"*"Local interface:
*"      IMPORTING
*"             REFERENCE(I_TAB_BOOKING_DATE) TYPE   DDTRANGE
*"      EXPORTING
*"             REFERENCE(E_TAB_DOC) TYPE   ZPTB00_TTY_DOC
*"      EXCEPTIONS
*"             FAILED
*"----------------------------------------------------

  CALL FUNCTION 'ZPTB00_OBJ_DOC_LOAD'
    EXPORTING
      i_tab_booking_date = i_tab_booking_date
    IMPORTING
      e_tab_doc          = e_tab_doc
    EXCEPTIONS
      failed             = 1
      OTHERS             = 2.
  IF sy-subrc <> 0.
    RAISE failed.
  ENDIF.

ENDFUNCTION.
```

Listing 7.8   ZPTB00_API_DOC_LOAD—Load Business Transactions

```
FUNCTION zptb00_api_doc_run.
*"----------------------------------------------------
*"*"Local interface:
*"   EXCEPTIONS
*"      FAILED
*"----------------------------------------------------
```

```
DATA:
  l_tab_bta TYPE zptb00_tty_bta,
  l_tab_doc TYPE zptb00_tty_doc.

CALL FUNCTION 'ZPTB00_API_BTA_LOAD'
*   EXPORTING
*     I_BOOKED       = '1'
    IMPORTING
      e_tab_bta      = l_tab_bta
    EXCEPTIONS
      failed         = 1
      OTHERS         = 2.
  IF sy-subrc <> 0.
    RAISE failed.
  ENDIF.

CALL FUNCTION 'ZPTB00_OBJ_DOC_BOOK'
    EXPORTING
      i_tab_bta = l_tab_bta
    IMPORTING
      e_tab_doc = l_tab_doc
    EXCEPTIONS
      failed    = 1
      OTHERS    = 2.
  IF sy-subrc <> 0.
    RAISE failed.
  ENDIF.

CALL FUNCTION 'ZPTB00_OBJ_DOC_SAVE'
    EXPORTING
*     i_str_doc =
      i_tab_doc = l_tab_doc
    EXCEPTIONS
      failed    = 1
      OTHERS    = 2.
  IF sy-subrc <> 0.
    RAISE failed.
  ENDIF.

CALL FUNCTION 'ZPTB00_API_BTA_MARK_AS_BOOKED'
    EXPORTING
      i_tab_bta = l_tab_bta
```

```
      EXCEPTIONS
        failed   = 1
        OTHERS   = 2.
    IF sy-subrc <> 0.
      RAISE failed.
    ENDIF.


  ENDFUNCTION.
```

Listing 7.9 ZPTB00_API_DOC_RUN—Process Non-Posted Business Transactions

ZPTB00_API_REP—Report Accounting Documents

```
FUNCTION ZPTB00_API_REP_DISPLAY.
*"----------------------------------------------------------
*"*"Local interface:
*"  IMPORTING
*"     REFERENCE(I_TAB_BOOKING_DATE) TYPE  DDTRANGE
*"  EXCEPTIONS
*"      FAILED
*"----------------------------------------------------------
DATA:
  l_tab_doc type zptb00_tty_doc.

  CALL FUNCTION 'ZPTB00_OBJ_DOC_LOAD'
    EXPORTING
      i_tab_booking_date      = i_tab_booking_date
    IMPORTING
      E_TAB_DOC               = l_tab_doc
    EXCEPTIONS
      FAILED                  = 1
      OTHERS                  = 2.
  IF sy-subrc <> 0.
    raise failed.
  ENDIF.

  CALL FUNCTION 'ZPTB00_OBJ_REP_SHOW'
    EXPORTING
      i_tab_doc     = l_tab_doc
    EXCEPTIONS
      FAILED        = 1
      OTHERS        = 2.
```

```
    IF sy-subrc <> 0.
      RAISE failed.
    ENDIF.


ENDFUNCTION.
```

Listing 7.10 ZPTB00_API_REP_DISPLAY—Display Accounting Documents

ZPTB00_MAP_BTA—Receive and Save Business Transactions

```
FUNCTION zptb00_map_bta_set.
*"----------------------------------------------------
*"*"Local interface:
*"  IMPORTING
*"     VALUE(I_STR_BTA) TYPE  ZPTB00_STR_BTA
*"  EXCEPTIONS
*"      FAILED
*"----------------------------------------------------


  CALL FUNCTION 'ZPTB00_API_BTA_SET'
    EXPORTING
      i_str_bta = i_str_bta
    EXCEPTIONS
      failed    = 1
      OTHERS    = 2.
  IF sy-subrc <> 0.
    RAISE failed.
  ENDIF.


ENDFUNCTION.
```

Listing 7.11 ZPTB00_MAP_BTA_SET—Receive and Save Business Transaction

ZPTB00_MAP_REP—Report Accounting Documents

```
FUNCTION zptb00_map_rep_get.
*"----------------------------------------------------
*"*"Local interface:
*"  IMPORTING
*"     VALUE(I_TAB_BOOKING_DATE) TYPE  DDTRANGE
*"  EXPORTING
*"     VALUE(E_TAB_DOC) TYPE  ZPTB00_TTY_DOC
```

```
*"  EXCEPTIONS
*"      FAILED
*"------------------------------------------------------

  CALL FUNCTION 'ZPTB00_API_DOC_LOAD'
    EXPORTING
      i_tab_booking_date = i_tab_booking_date
    IMPORTING
      e_tab_doc           = e_tab_doc
    EXCEPTIONS
      failed              = 1
      OTHERS              = 2.
  IF sy-subrc <> 0.
    RAISE failed.
  ENDIF.

ENDFUNCTION.
```

Listing 7.12 ZPTB00_MAP_REP_GET—Display Accounting Documents

ZPTB00_OBJ_BTA—Receive and Save Business Transactions

```
FUNCTION zptb00_obj_bta_edit.
*"------------------------------------------------------
*"*"Local interface:
*"  CHANGING
*"    REFERENCE(C_STR_BTA) TYPE  ZPTB00_STR_BTA
*"      OPTIONAL
*"------------------------------------------------------
DATA:
  l_str_item type ZPTB00_BTAITEM.

  IF c_str_bta IS INITIAL.
* Just add one line to the position by default
    APPEND l_str_item TO c_str_bta-tab_item.
  ENDIF.

* Make manual posting global for dynpro
  MOVE-CORRESPONDING c_str_bta TO g_str_bta.
* Call edit screen
  CALL SCREEN 0100.
* If the user pressed save and everthing is fine,
```

461

```
* then g_str_bta is filled with user input
* otherwise the structure is initial
* move edited data back to our interface variable
    MOVE-CORRESPONDING g_str_bta TO c_str_bta.
ENDFUNCTION.
```

Listing 7.13 ZPTB00_OBJ_BTA_EDIT—Edit Business Transaction

```
FUNCTION zptb00_obj_bta_enrich.
*"----------------------------------------------------
*"*"Local interface:
*"  CHANGING
*"     REFERENCE(C_STR_BTA) TYPE  ZPTB00_STR_BTA
*"  EXCEPTIONS
*"       FAILED
*"----------------------------------------------------
  FIELD-SYMBOLS:
    <l_str_item> TYPE zptb00_btaitem.

* enrich header
  c_str_bta-client = sy-mandt.
  CALL FUNCTION 'GUID_CREATE'
      IMPORTING
*       EV_GUID_16      =
*       EV_GUID_22      =
        ev_guid_32      = c_str_bta-id.
  c_str_bta-booked = '1'.

* enrich items
  LOOP AT c_str_bta-tab_item ASSIGNING <l_str_item>.
    <l_str_item>-client = sy-mandt.
    CALL FUNCTION 'GUID_CREATE'
        IMPORTING
*         EV_GUID_16       =
*         EV_GUID_22       =
          ev_guid_32       = <l_str_item>-id.
    <l_str_item>-header_id = c_str_bta-id.
    <l_str_item>-mark = ' '.
  ENDLOOP.
ENDFUNCTION.
```

Listing 7.14 ZPTB00_OBJ_BTA_ENRICH—Enrich Business Transaction with Technical
Information

```
FUNCTION zptb00_obj_bta_load.
*"----------------------------------------------------
*"*"Local interface:
*"  IMPORTING
*"     REFERENCE(I_BOOKED) TYPE  ZPTB00_DTE_BTA_BOOKED
*"         DEFAULT '1'
*"  EXPORTING
*"     REFERENCE(E_TAB_BTA) TYPE  ZPTB00_TTY_BTA
*"  EXCEPTIONS
*"       FAILED
*"----------------------------------------------------
  DATA:
* db
    l_tab_bta_header   TYPE STANDARD TABLE OF
      zptb00_btaheader,
    l_tab_bta_item     TYPE STANDARD TABLE OF
      zptb00_btaitem,
* local
    l_str_bta TYPE zptb00_str_bta.
  FIELD-SYMBOLS:
* db
    <l_str_bta_header> TYPE zptb00_btaheader,
    <l_str_bta_item>   TYPE zptb00_btaitem.


* read the header data
  SELECT * FROM zptb00_btaheader INTO TABLE
    l_tab_bta_header
  WHERE booked = i_booked.
  IF sy-dbcnt = 0.
    RAISE failed.
  ENDIF.


* read the item data
* abap statement "for all entries" only works up to ca.
* 1700 entries so we better loop
  LOOP AT l_tab_bta_header ASSIGNING
   <l_str_bta_header>.
    MOVE-CORRESPONDING <l_str_bta_header> TO l_str_bta.
    SELECT * FROM  zptb00_btaitem INTO TABLE
   l_tab_bta_item
    WHERE header_id = <l_str_bta_header>-id.
    l_str_bta-tab_item = l_tab_bta_item.
```

```
    APPEND l_str_bta TO e_tab_bta.
  ENDLOOP.
  IF sy-dbcnt = 0.
    RAISE failed.
  ENDIF.

ENDFUNCTION.
```

Listing 7.15 ZPTB00_OBJ_BTA_LOAD—Load Business Transactions

```
FUNCTION zptb00_obj_bta_mark_as_booked.
*"----------------------------------------------------
*"*"Local interface:
*"        IMPORTING
*"            REFERENCE(I_TAB_BTA) TYPE
*"              ZPTB00_TTY_BTA
*"        EXCEPTIONS
*"            FAILED
*"----------------------------------------------------
  FIELD-SYMBOLS:
    <l_str_bta> TYPE zptb00_str_bta.

  LOOP AT i_tab_bta ASSIGNING <l_str_bta>.
    UPDATE zptb00_btaheader SET booked = '2'
    WHERE id = <l_str_bta>-id.
  ENDLOOP.

ENDFUNCTION.
```

Listing 7.16 ZPTB00_OBJ_BTA_MARK_AS_BOOKED—Mark Business Transactions as Posted

```
FUNCTION zptb00_obj_bta_save.
*"----------------------------------------------------
*"*"Local interface:
*"  IMPORTING
*"    REFERENCE(I_STR_BTA) TYPE   ZPTB00_STR_BTA
*"      OPTIONAL
*"    REFERENCE(I_TAB_BTA) TYPE   ZPTB00_TTY_BTA
*"      OPTIONAL
*"  EXCEPTIONS
*"      FAILED
```

```
*"---------------------------------------------------------
  DATA:
* Structure like header and item table
     l_tab_bta       TYPE zptb00_tty_bta,
     l_str_btaheader TYPE zptb00_btaheader.
  FIELD-SYMBOLS:
     <l_str_bta>     TYPE zptb00_str_bta.

  l_tab_bta = i_tab_bta.
  IF NOT i_str_bta IS INITIAL.
    APPEND i_str_bta TO l_tab_bta.
  ENDIF.


* loop through all the data for saving
  LOOP AT i_tab_bta ASSIGNING <l_str_bta>.
* Get header data and write to database table
    MOVE-CORRESPONDING <l_str_bta> TO l_str_btaheader.
    MODIFY zptb00_btaheader FROM l_str_btaheader.
    IF sy-subrc <> 0.
      RAISE failed.
    ENDIF.

    DELETE FROM zptb00_btaitem WHERE header_id =
      l_str_btaheader-id.
    MODIFY zptb00_btaitem FROM TABLE
      <l_str_bta>-tab_item.
    IF sy-subrc <> 0.
      RAISE failed.
    ENDIF.
  ENDLOOP.

ENDFUNCTION.
```

Listing 7.17   ZPTB00_OBJ_BTA_SAVE—Save Business Transaction

ZPTB00_OBJ_BTC—Check Business Transactions

```
FUNCTION zptb00_obj_btc_check.
*"---------------------------------------------------------
*"*"Local interface:
*"       IMPORTING
*"               REFERENCE(I_STR_BTA) TYPE
```

```
*"                    ZPTB00_STR_BTA
*"          EXCEPTIONS
*"                    FAILED
*"----------------------------------------------------
  DATA:
    l_tab_dd07v LIKE STANDARD TABLE OF dd07v,
    l_str_currency TYPE tcurc,
    l_str_quantity TYPE t006.
  FIELD-SYMBOLS:
    <l_str_item> TYPE zptb00_btaitem.

************* check header
* check bp_id
  IF i_str_bta-bp_id IS INITIAL.
    RAISE failed.
  ENDIF.

* check bttype
  CALL FUNCTION 'DD_DOMVALUES_GET'
    EXPORTING
      domname            = 'ZPTB00_DOM_BTA_BTTYPE'
*         TEXT               = ' '
*         LANGU              = ' '
*         BYPASS_BUFFER      = ' '
*     IMPORTING
*         RC                 =
    TABLES
      dd07v_tab          = l_tab_dd07v
    EXCEPTIONS
      wrong_textflag     = 1
      OTHERS             = 2.
  IF sy-subrc <> 0.
    RAISE failed.
  ENDIF.
  READ TABLE l_tab_dd07v WITH KEY domvalue_l =
    i_str_bta-bttype TRANSPORTING NO FIELDS.
  IF sy-subrc <> 0.
    RAISE failed.
  ENDIF.

* check btdate
  IF i_str_bta-btdate IS INITIAL.
```

```
       RAISE failed.
     ENDIF.

************* check item
* check tab_item
   IF i_str_bta-tab_item IS INITIAL.
     RAISE failed.
   ENDIF.
   LOOP AT i_str_bta-tab_item ASSIGNING <l_str_item>.

* check pr_id
     CALL FUNCTION 'DD_DOMVALUES_GET'
       EXPORTING
         domname              = 'ZPTB00_DOM_BTA_PR_ID'
*          TEXT               = ' '
*          LANGU              = ' '
*          BYPASS_BUFFER      = ' '
*       IMPORTING
*          RC                 =
       TABLES
         dd07v_tab            = l_tab_dd07v
       EXCEPTIONS
         wrong_textflag       = 1
         OTHERS               = 2.
     IF sy-subrc <> 0.
       RAISE failed.
     ENDIF.
     READ TABLE l_tab_dd07v WITH KEY domvalue_l =
       <l_str_item>-pr_id TRANSPORTING NO FIELDS.
     IF sy-subrc <> 0.
       RAISE failed.
     ENDIF.

* check pstype
     CALL FUNCTION 'DD_DOMVALUES_GET'
       EXPORTING
         domname              = 'ZPTB00_DOM_BTA_PSTYPE'
*          TEXT               = ' '
*          LANGU              = ' '
*          BYPASS_BUFFER      = ' '
*       IMPORTING
*          RC                 =
```

467

```
            TABLES
              dd07v_tab              = l_tab_dd07v
            EXCEPTIONS
              wrong_textflag       = 1
              OTHERS               = 2.
          IF sy-subrc <> 0.
            RAISE failed.
          ENDIF.
          READ TABLE l_tab_dd07v WITH KEY domvalue_l =
            <l_str_item>-pstype TRANSPORTING NO FIELDS.
          IF sy-subrc <> 0.
            RAISE failed.
          ENDIF.

* check wh_id
          CALL FUNCTION 'DD_DOMVALUES_GET'
            EXPORTING
              domname                = 'ZPTB00_DOM_BTA_WH_ID'
*             TEXT                   = ' '
*             LANGU                  = ' '
*             BYPASS_BUFFER          = ' '
*           IMPORTING
*             RC                     =
            TABLES
              dd07v_tab              = l_tab_dd07v
            EXCEPTIONS
              wrong_textflag       = 1
              OTHERS               = 2.
          IF sy-subrc <> 0.
            RAISE failed.
          ENDIF.
          READ TABLE l_tab_dd07v WITH KEY domvalue_l =
            <l_str_item>-wh_id TRANSPORTING NO FIELDS.
          IF sy-subrc <> 0.
            RAISE failed.
          ENDIF.

* check currency
          SELECT SINGLE * FROM tcurc INTO l_str_currency
            WHERE waers = <l_str_item>-currency.
          IF sy-subrc <> 0.
            RAISE failed.
```

```
      ENDIF.

* check unit
      SELECT SINGLE * FROM t006 INTO l_str_quantity WHERE
        msehi = <l_str_item>-unit.
      IF sy-subrc <> 0.
        RAISE failed.
      ENDIF.
    ENDLOOP.


ENDFUNCTION.
```

Listing 7.18 ZPTB00_OBJ_BTC_CHECK—Check Business Transaction

ZPTB00_OBJ_DOC—Generate Accounting Documents

```
FUNCTION zptb00_obj_doc_book.
*"----------------------------------------------------
*"*"Local interface:
*"  IMPORTING
*"     REFERENCE(I_TAB_BTA) TYPE   ZPTB00_TTY_BTA
*"  EXPORTING
*"     REFERENCE(E_TAB_DOC) TYPE   ZPTB00_TTY_DOC
*"  EXCEPTIONS
*"      FAILED
*"----------------------------------------------------
  DATA:
* accounting document
    l_str_doc               TYPE zptb00_str_doc,
    l_str_doc_item          TYPE zptb00_docitem,
* business transaction
    l_str_bta               TYPE zptb00_btaheader.
  FIELD-SYMBOLS:
* business transaction
    <l_str_bta>             TYPE zptb00_str_bta,
    <l_str_bta_item>        TYPE zptb00_btaitem.
  CONSTANTS:
* business transaction field constants
    con_bta_bttype_purchase TYPE zptb00_dte_bta_bttype
      VALUE 'PURCHASE',
    con_bta_bttype_sale     TYPE zptb00_dte_bta_bttype
      VALUE 'SALE',
```

```
        con_bta_pstype_service  TYPE zptb00_dte_bta_pstype
          VALUE 'SERVICE',
        con_bta_pstype_product  TYPE zptb00_dte_bta_pstype
          VALUE 'PRODUCT',
* document field constants
        con_doc_debit  TYPE zptb00_dte_doc_debitcredit
          VALUE 'D',
        con_doc_credit  TYPE zptb00_dte_doc_debitcredit
          VALUE 'C',
        con_doc_account_BGA  TYPE zptb00_dte_doc_account
          VALUE '001000',
        con_doc_account_cash    TYPE zptb00_dte_doc_account
          VALUE '002000'.


* loop through every business transaction
  LOOP AT i_tab_bta ASSIGNING <l_str_bta>.
* direct move-corresponding <l_str_bta> TO l_str_doc
* not possible, so use intermediate structure
    MOVE-CORRESPONDING <l_str_bta> TO l_str_bta.
    MOVE-CORRESPONDING l_str_bta TO l_str_doc.
* loop through every business transaction position
    LOOP AT <l_str_bta>-tab_item ASSIGNING
      <l_str_bta_item>.
      MOVE-CORRESPONDING <l_str_bta_item> TO
        l_str_doc_item.
* this is the accounting brain
* book every business transaction as an accounting
* document
      IF <l_str_bta>-bttype = con_bta_bttype_purchase.
        IF <l_str_bta_item>-pstype =
          con_bta_pstype_service.
        ELSEIF <l_str_bta_item>-pstype =
          con_bta_pstype_product.
* For our project we implement only one example, but
* more to come
          l_str_doc_item-debitcredit = con_doc_debit.
          l_str_doc_item-account = con_doc_account_BGA.
          APPEND l_str_doc_item TO l_str_doc-tab_item.
          CALL FUNCTION 'GUID_CREATE'
            IMPORTING
*             EV_GUID_16       =
*             EV_GUID_22       =
```

```
            ev_guid_32       = l_str_doc_item-id.
         l_str_doc_item-debitcredit = con_doc_credit.
         l_str_doc_item-account =
             con_doc_account_cash.
          APPEND l_str_doc_item TO l_str_doc-tab_item.
       ENDIF.
     ENDIF.
   ENDLOOP.
   APPEND l_str_doc TO e_tab_doc.
 ENDLOOP.

ENDFUNCTION.
```

Listing 7.19 ZPTB00_OBJ_DOC_BOOK—Post Business Transactions

```
FUNCTION zptb00_obj_doc_load.
*"----------------------------------------------------
*"*"Local interface:
*"  IMPORTING
*"     REFERENCE(I_TAB_BOOKING_DATE) TYPE  DDTRANGE
*"  EXPORTING
*"     REFERENCE(E_TAB_DOC) TYPE  ZPTB00_TTY_DOC
*"  EXCEPTIONS
*"       FAILED
*"----------------------------------------------------
  DATA:
* db
    l_tab_doc_header    TYPE STANDARD TABLE OF
      zptb00_docheader,
    l_tab_doc_item      TYPE STANDARD TABLE OF
      zptb00_docitem,
* local
    l_str_doc TYPE zptb00_str_doc.
  FIELD-SYMBOLS:
* db
    <l_str_doc_header> TYPE zptb00_docheader,
    <l_str_doc_item>   TYPE zptb00_docitem.

* read the header data
  SELECT * FROM zptb00_docheader INTO TABLE
    l_tab_doc_header
  WHERE btdate IN i_tab_booking_date.
```

```
      IF sy-dbcnt = 0.
        RAISE failed.
      ENDIF.


* read the item data
* abap statement "for all entries" only works up to ca.
* 1700 entries so we better loop
      LOOP AT l_tab_doc_header ASSIGNING
        <l_str_doc_header>.
        MOVE-CORRESPONDING <l_str_doc_header> TO l_str_doc.
        SELECT * FROM  zptb00_docitem INTO TABLE
          l_tab_doc_item
        WHERE header_id = <l_str_doc_header>-id.
        l_str_doc-tab_item = l_tab_doc_item.
        APPEND l_str_doc TO e_tab_doc.
      ENDLOOP.
      IF sy-dbcnt = 0.
        RAISE failed.
      ENDIF.


ENDFUNCTION.
```

Listing 7.20 ZPTB00_OBJ_DOC_LOAD—Load Business Transactions

```
FUNCTION zptb00_obj_doc_save.
*"----------------------------------------------------
*"*"Local interface:
*"  IMPORTING
*"     REFERENCE(I_STR_DOC) TYPE  ZPTB00_STR_DOC
*"        OPTIONAL
*"     REFERENCE(I_TAB_DOC) TYPE  ZPTB00_TTY_DOC
*"        OPTIONAL
*"  EXCEPTIONS
*"      FAILED
*"----------------------------------------------------


  DATA:
* Structure like header and item table
    l_tab_doc TYPE zptb00_tty_doc,
    l_str_docheader TYPE zptb00_docheader.
  FIELD-SYMBOLS:
    <l_str_doc>      TYPE zptb00_str_doc.
```

```
    l_tab_doc = i_tab_doc.
    IF NOT i_str_doc IS INITIAL.
      APPEND i_str_doc TO l_tab_doc.
    ENDIF.

* loop through all the data for saving
    LOOP AT i_tab_doc ASSIGNING <l_str_doc>.
* Get header data and write to database table
      MOVE-CORRESPONDING <l_str_doc> TO l_str_docheader.
      MODIFY zptb00_docheader FROM l_str_docheader.
      IF sy-subrc <> 0.
        RAISE failed.
      ENDIF.

      DELETE FROM zptb00_docitem WHERE header_id =
        l_str_docheader-id.
      MODIFY zptb00_docitem FROM TABLE
        <l_str_doc>-tab_item.
      IF sy-subrc <> 0.
        RAISE failed.
      ENDIF.
    ENDLOOP.

ENDFUNCTION.
```

Listing 7.21 ZPTB00_OBJ_DOC_SAVE—Save Posting Documents

ZPTB00_OBJ_REP—Report Accounting Documents

```
FUNCTION zptb00_obj_rep_show.
*"----------------------------------------------------------
*"*"Local interface:
*"  IMPORTING
*"     REFERENCE(I_TAB_DOC) TYPE  ZPTB00_TTY_DOC
*"  EXCEPTIONS
*"     FAILED
*"----------------------------------------------------------
* Contains ALV-Grid structures, needed for variables
  TYPE-POOLS slis .

  DATA:
```

```
* for data handling
    l_str_doc_flat     TYPE zptb00_str_doc_flat,
    l_tab_doc_flat     TYPE STANDARD TABLE OF
      zptb00_str_doc_flat,
* for ALV-Grid display
    l_dis              TYPE disvariant,
    l_rda_table        TYPE REF TO data,
    l_str_layout       TYPE slis_layout_alv.
  FIELD-SYMBOLS:
* for data handling
    <l_str_doc>        TYPE zptb00_str_doc,
    <l_str_doc_item>   TYPE zptb00_docitem.


* convert data to flat structure
  LOOP AT i_tab_doc ASSIGNING <l_str_doc>.
    MOVE-CORRESPONDING <l_str_doc> TO l_str_doc_flat.
    LOOP AT <l_str_doc>-tab_item ASSIGNING
      <l_str_doc_item>.
      MOVE-CORRESPONDING <l_str_doc_item> TO
        l_str_doc_flat.
      APPEND l_str_doc_flat TO l_tab_doc_flat.
    ENDLOOP.
  ENDLOOP.


* Make column width as small as possible
  l_str_layout-colwidth_optimize = 'X'.
* This text should be displayed as the window title
  l_str_layout-window_titlebar = text-001.
* Give the name of our report, so that the user can
* save individual configurations of the ALV-Grid
* display. You could also provide another text here, if
* you want separate configuration of the show and
* deletion display
  l_dis-report = sy-repid.


* Call the ALV-Grid display function
  CALL FUNCTION 'REUSE_ALV_GRID_DISPLAY'
    EXPORTING
*     I_INTERFACE_CHECK                = ' '
*     I_BYPASSING_BUFFER               = ' '
*     I_BUFFER_ACTIVE                  = ' '
*     I_CALLBACK_PROGRAM               = ' '
```

```
*        I_CALLBACK_PF_STATUS_SET          = ' '
*        I_CALLBACK_USER_COMMAND           = ' '
*        I_CALLBACK_TOP_OF_PAGE            = ' '
*        I_CALLBACK_HTML_TOP_OF_PAGE       = ' '
*        I_CALLBACK_HTML_END_OF_LIST       = ' '
         i_structure_name                 =
            'ZPTB00_STR_DOC_FLAT'
*        I_BACKGROUND_ID                   = ' '
*        I_GRID_TITLE                      =
*        I_GRID_SETTINGS                   =
         is_layout                        = l_str_layout
*        IT_FIELDCAT                       =
*        IT_EXCLUDING                      =
*        IT_SPECIAL_GROUPS                 =
*        IT_SORT                           =
*        IT_FILTER                         =
*        IS_SEL_HIDE                       =
*        I_DEFAULT                         = 'X'
         i_save                           = 'A'
         is_variant                       = l_dis
*        IT_EVENTS                         =
*        IT_EVENT_EXIT                     =
*        IS_PRINT                          =
*        IS_REPREP_ID                      =
*        I_SCREEN_START_COLUMN             = 0
*        I_SCREEN_START_LINE               = 0
*        I_SCREEN_END_COLUMN               = 0
*        I_SCREEN_END_LINE                 = 0
*        IT_ALV_GRAPHICS                   =
*        IT_HYPERLINK                      =
*        IT_ADD_FIELDCAT                   =
*     IMPORTING
*        E_EXIT_CAUSED_BY_CALLER           =
*        ES_EXIT_CAUSED_BY_USER            =
      TABLES
         t_outtab                         =
            l_tab_doc_flat
      EXCEPTIONS
         program_error                    = 1
         OTHERS                           = 2.
   IF sy-subrc <> 0.
* Error? -> Show to the user what happened
```

475

```
        MESSAGE ID sy-msgid TYPE sy-msgty NUMBER sy-msgno
                WITH sy-msgv1 sy-msgv2 sy-msgv3 sy-msgv4.
    ENDIF.

ENDFUNCTION.
```

Listing 7.22 ZPTB00_OBJ_REP_SHOW—Show Accounting Documents

Appendices

A   **Programming Guidelines and Tools** 479

B   **Glossary** 491

C   **Sources and Literature Recommendations** 495

D   **The Authors** 497

This appendix provides a brief, easy-to-understand overview of selected basic principles and technical concepts used in this book.

A   Programming Guidelines and Tools

A.1   Programming Guidelines

Programming guidelines are indispensable in large software development projects because they are used to standardize source code structures and development objects, and therefore improve both the readability and comprehensibility of developments in ABAP.

In professional software development, strict programming guidelines are an important prerequisite. They provide the following advantages:

Advantages of strict programming guidelines

▶ **Good Readability of Custom Programs**
Even in the simplest case, that is, with regard to the use of meaningful names with a reference to their type, programs are much more readable than if they had short names consisting of numbers or letters in alphabetical order such as i1, i2, a, b, and so on.

▶ **Easy Orientation in External Programs**
For example, if you generally adhere to the layer model regarding functions, external developers will find it much easier to understand the program structure.

▶ **Simple Modification and Maintenance of Programs**
If, for instance, you use factory methods and interfaces to generate classes, it is very easy to implement completely new customer-specific classes, which can be used by the remaining program code as well because they use the same interface.

▶ **Good Quality due to the Avoidance of Errors**
A standardized, tried-and-tested software development procedure

cannot prevent you from making severe errors in your concept, but it can help you avoid small errors that are difficult to find at a later stage.

For the comprehensive and complex SAP applications, which, to a large extent, are designed as generic applications that can be customized and must even allow for being modified and extended since they are delivered in source code, adherence to programming guidelines is essential. As an ABAP developer, you should use uniform programming guidelines wherever possible to produce development objects and source code that can be reproduced and compared in all respects.

Scientific in nature
At SAP, programming guidelines are regarded as being a little scientific in nature, and several teams are permanently optimizing them in both industry-specific and general areas. As soon as new technologies or tools are available, they're included in this process. Of course, this means that the guidelines change over the years, which becomes obvious when you compare the source code of older developments such as SAP Financials with that of new developments like SAP E-Business Accounting (FIN-eAcc), for example.

The following descriptions are based on the programming guidelines of SAP IBU Financial Services where the SAP Bank Analyzer was produced. In addition to specifications about the naming convention, the guidelines also contain instructions regarding procedural and object-oriented software development. The following programming guidelines are used consistently in Chapter 7, Practice Scenario—Automated Accounting for Corporate Subsidiaries.

A.1.1 General Naming Conventions

The following naming conventions apply to all development objects:

▶ Development objects must have an English name.
▶ All names must be meaningful.
▶ Compound names must contain an underscore character.

- ▸ Instead of inventing new names, you must use commonly used names.

- ▸ Comments in the source code must be written in English.

These guidelines improve readability, especially since the ABAP language and all globally declared development objects (with the exception of BOR object types) are not case-sensitive, and the source code as well as all development objects must be read and understood by international team members.

Namespaces

Partner enterprises and customers should have SAP reserve a prefix for them of the type "/<partnerprefix>/". The setup of partner namespaces is described in SAP Note 72843.

New SAP development projects must reserve a namespace for themselves (for instance, the namespace "/BA1/" was reserved for the SAP Bank Analyzer software).

Variables and Parameters

Variables and parameters are declared in such a way that their names directly indicate their visibility (prefix1, for instance, "l" for local or "g" for global) and their type (prefix2, for instance, "str" for structure or "tab" for table). The names of variables and parameters are structured according to the following pattern:

```
<Prefix1>_[<Prefix2>_]<name>
```

Guidelines for indicating the visibility and structure of variables and parameters are shown in Table A.1 and Table A.2, respectively.

Prefix1	Description
G	Global variable
L	Local variable
S	Static variable
I	Import parameter in a function module

Table A.1 Guidelines for Indicating the Visibility of Variables and Parameters

Prefix1	Description
E	Export parameter in a function module
C	Changing parameter in a function module or in a form
U	Using parameter in a form
P	Parameter of a report
O	Selection options of a report

Table A.1 Guidelines for Indicating the Visibility of Variables and Parameters (Cont.)

Prefix2	Description
FLG	Flag
CNT	Counter
SAV	Variable for saving data to the clipboard
STR	Structure
TAB	Internal table
TAH	Internal hashed table
TAS	Internal sorted table
TTY	Table type if you don't want to further subdivide
RNG	"Ranges" table
WRK	Structure, which is used as the work area of an internal table
RCD	Return code
RDA	Ref to Data
RIF	Ref to Interface
RCL	Ref to Class

Table A.2 Guidelines for Indicating the Structure of Variables and Parameters

The TABLES parameter must no longer be used; instead, you must create dictionary table types. Nonetheless, if you do use TABLES, you must use the prefix I, C, E, or U.

Prefix2 Prefix2 must be used to identify variables and parameters, and it sometimes provides information about the semantics.

Prefix2 is optional because elementary data types such as an integer variable don't contain any Prefix2; only structured data types contain this prefix. Internal tables must always be used without headers. This method is outdated and can be found in only a few old function modules.

Examples:

Local flag: `L_FLG_FLOW_POSTED`

Global internal table: `G_TAB_ITEMS`

Guidelines for naming internal tables as parameters are shown in Table A.3.

In Function Modules	In Forms
I_TAB_ITEMS	U_TAB_ITEMS
E_TAB_ITEMS	C_TAB_ITEMS
C_TAB_ITEMS	

Table A.3 Guidelines for Naming Internal Tables as Parameters

Constants

Constants are used to standardize the usage of values in different source codes and therefore don't need to be marked as being global. Instead, they always contain the prefix "CON". Because ABAP doesn't allow structured constants to be used, you can only use elementary constants, which means you cannot use Prefix2. The names of constants are structured as follows:

`CON_<name>`

The following two rules apply:

Rules

► Literals can only be used in exceptional cases in source code. Instead of literals, you must generally use constants, such as `IF L_FLG_FLOW_POSTED = CON_TRUE`.

► Message IDs must not be defined as constants and should be specified as completely qualified so that the where-used list functions properly. Example: `MESSAGE e018(/BA1/EACC_CONFIG)`.

Constants are defined via includes. The choice of the appropriate include depends on the type of the constant. Constants of different types must not be defined in the same include. Each package or development class usually contains one or several "public" and "private" includes with constants, which accordingly can be used by other packages or only within one package. The includes shouldn't be too big. We recommend creating a separate include for each topic.

Program-Local Data Types

Only in exceptional cases

Program-local data types, that is, data types that are defined in the source code, should be used only in exceptional cases. In general, you should use global data types because of the preferable documentation options they provide. Otherwise, program-local data types are subject to the same rules as variables and parameters, the only difference being that Prefix1 is set to "TYP."

Dictionary-Data Types

Generally, you should use Dictionary data types over program-local data types because they're much easier to document and you can control how they are used in other packages via the package interfaces. The most important Dictionary data types must contain a three-character prefix so that you can recognize the type at first sight when looking at the declaration within the source code. If a reserved namespace is available, you must, of course, use it as well. Guidelines for Dictionary data types are shown in Table A.4. The names are structured as shown in the following example:

```
<Namespace>_<Prefix>_<Name>
```

Prefix	Description
TAB	Database table if the number of available characters is sufficient. Example: /BA1/TAB_TOTAL
TTY	Table type, Example: /BA1/B1_TTY_TOTALS
STR	Structure, Example: /BA1/B1_STR_TOTALS
DTE	Data element, Example: /BA1/B1_DTE_TOTALS_ID
DOM	Domain, Example: /BA1/B1_DOM_TOTALS_ID

Table A.4 Guidelines for Dictionary Data Types such as Database Tables, Structures, or Data Elements

Data elements must refer to domains that define the technical properties. You cannot directly specify built-in data types for data elements. By using the `Include` statement, you can maximize the reusability of structures, database tables, and table types (see, for example, structure ZPTB00_STR_BTA in Section 5.2, Complex Input and Output Interfaces—Dynpros). For tables with delivery class "S" and "E", you must create table documentation (see technical properties of tables in Section 4.2, Defining and Processing Database Tables—SELECT, INSERT, UPDATE, DELETE).

Function Groups

The naming conventions for function groups comprise the namespace, a prefix, and the actual group name. Guidelines for function groups are shown in Table A.5

```
<Namespace>_<Prefix>_<Groupname>
```

Prefix	Description
MAP	MAPI layer (Message API); function modules contained are provided for calls from external systems, such as /BA1/ B1_MAP_BTA.
API	API layer (Application Programming Interface); function modules contained are provided for calls from other software parts, such as /BA1/B1_API_BTA.
OBJ	OBJ layer (Object); function modules contained are provided for calls from other function modules of the OBJ layer and of the API layer of the same software part, such as /BA1/ B1_OBJ_BTA.
DB	DB layer (Database); function modules contained are provided for calls from function modules of the OBJ layer of the same software part, such as /BA1/B1_DB_BTA.

Table A.5 Guidelines for Function Groups

One function group can contain up to 99 function modules. Make sure that the function groups don't become too large (think of the system performance when loading the function group as well as of the memory requirement). A function group can only contain function modules of one layer (MAPI, API, Object, or Database layer).

Function Modules

In general, the same naming conventions and rules apply to function modules as to the function groups that contain the modules. The only difference is that the name of the function module is added to the end of the function group name. In this respect, you must adhere to certain rules, because names should be uniform to ensure clarity, irrespective of the data to be processed. If possible, you should use the names listed in Table A.6:

```
<Namespace>_<Prefix>_<Groupname>_<Name>
```

Name	Description
OPEN	Initializing a function group. Example: /BA1/B1_API_FPT_OPEN
CHECK	Performing a data check. Example: /BA1/B1_API_FPT_CHECK
SET	Copying and checking data. Example: /BA1/B1_API_FPT_SET
GET	Reading data. Example: /BA1/B1_API_FPT_GET
SAVE	Saving data in the database. Example: /BA1/B1_API_FPT_SAVE
CLOSE	"Closing" a function group and releasing memory. Example: /BA1/B1_API_FPT_CLOSE
UPDATE	Performing a data update. Example: /BA1/B1_API_FPT_UPDATE
INSERT	Inserting data. Example: /BA1/B1_API_FPT_INSERT
DELETE	Deleting data. Example: /BA1/B1_API_FPT_DELETE
MODIFY	Modifying data. Example: /BA1/B1_API_FPT_MODIFY

Table A.6 Guidelines for Naming Function Modules

You must create documentation for the function modules of the MAPI and API layers. This documentation should describe the following topics: functionality of the function module, prerequisites for calling the function module, possible side effects when using the function module, and interface parameters. Function modules should not be too large or complex. Moreover, they should contain only one function, and the interfaces should be as small as possible. Regarding the function modules of the database layer, you should ensure that they don't contain any application logic. In particular, you should ensure that checks and database changes aren't performed in the same function module.

Forms—Subprograms

Because subprograms cannot be documented as easily as function modules, you shouldn't use them. However, there are still a few old tools that require the use of subprograms for callback calls.

Message Classes

Message classes contain the namespace as well as the group name, which specifies the function group or class to which the message classes belong:

```
<Namespace>_<Groupname>
```

Messages

In many cases, objects contain a text and an ID, such as "Transaction type 4711 = 'Eurocheque.'" End users are usually only interested in the text. However, there are also users who are interested in the ID as well because they need the ID for customizing and interfaces. For this reason, you should proceed as follows:

▶ The short text of the message displays only the text. For example, "Transaction type Eurocheque is not allowed."

▶ The long text of the message contains the text as well as the ID in parentheses. For example, "Transaction type Eurocheque (4711) is not allowed."

Error Messages

Error messages should comply with the following guidelines:

▶ You should ensure that their tone is friendly and courteous.

- You cannot use a period at the end of the short text.
- You should describe the problem in the "Diagnosis" section of the long text.
- In the "Procedure" section of the long text, you should describe what the end user can do to solve the problem.

Example 1: The user has entered an incorrect value. In this case, you should explain how the user can find the permitted values.

Example 2: The program has detected an error in the customizing settings. Because end users are generally not allowed to make any customizing settings, the message should output the text, "Please contact the system administrator."

Warnings

In the "System activities" section of the long text, warnings describe what happens if the user presses Enter or CANCEL.

Modules

You must not enter any data definitions in Process Before Output (PBO) and Process After Input (PAI) modules, because definitions in these modules are always global. Instead, a FORM or function module is called in a MODULE and the required dynpro fields are transferred as parameters. In this way, you can often avoid duplication of code in similar modules of different dynpros.

Screens

You must never define screen fields with variables that don't have a Dictionary reference. You should always use meaningful names for field labels of data elements you use (also for headings) so that the user can see the complete text in lists and table controls.

Readability of Programs

You should adhere to the following guidelines to ensure the readability of programs:

- Use the Pretty Printer function of the ABAP Editor.

- Use only one statement per line.

- Delete all coding that has been commented out and variable definitions that are no longer needed. In exceptional cases (for instance, if the coding will actually remain commented out if not deleted), you should use the following comments: "to be deleted by...", "not yet deleted because...", "Do not delete! ", and so on.

Miscellaneous

The following guidelines pertain to aspects of programming that would normally be assumed, but are often forgotten due to time constraints:

Matter of course

- After a database operation, the reading of internal tables, and returning from a function module, SY-SUBRC must be queried.

- Your "ToDos" in the program should be indicated by a specific flag so that you find these action items easily when needed. You could use the flag, *ToDo, for example.

A.2   Program Check Tools

Over the years, comprehensive tools have been created for ABAP development, which enable you to check the programs as well as development objects and database accesscs.

Comprehensive tools

This section contains a selection of the most important tools. You can obtain a complete list of all program check tools by viewing the individual applications in the application menu (SAP Easy Access) under the TOOLS menu item.

Extended Program Check

Performing the extended program check prior to transporting the program into the test and consolidation system is mandatory. You can access the extended program check in the program editor via the context menu of a program or function module and by selecting CHECK • EXT. PROGRAM CHECK.

Checkman Checks

Provided your administrator has implemented a regular check of code parts, you can use Transaction CHECKMAN to search across multiple programs for notes, earnings, or error messages of different severity levels that you yourself have created. In addition to information about the source code, the CHECKMAN also provides tips and suggestions for improvement for all other ABAP development objects, such as transactions, authorization objects, screens, and so on.

Runtime Analysis

Transaction SE30 (Runtime Analysis) provides detailed information about the runtime of individual components of an application down to the level of individual source code fragments such as function modules and database accesses. In addition, the TIPS & TRICKS menu of this transaction contains many useful hints regarding the performance optimization of ABAP programs.

B   Glossary

This glossary contains an overview of the most important technical terms used in this book.

ABAP Dictionary/DDIC   A storage location for data types like database tables, data elements, and domains. You can define the data types with Transaction SE80.

ABAP runtime environment   A program that can compile and execute ABAP source code on various operating systems and hardware platforms.

ABAP Workbench   A collection of more than 100 programs that enables the creation and testing of ABAP programs. Newer releases of SAP software provide it in the SAP Object Navigator development environment (Transaction SE80).

Adapter   A module that simplifies linking existing applications with other applications or another infrastructure. An adapter provides both the technical connection and the required business logic.

Advanced Business Application Programming (ABAP)   Along with Java/J2EE, ABAP is the object-oriented programming language and environment for the development and use of SAP software applications.

Application   A logically related set of functions or Web services (for accounting, for example) that is delivered as a total package and that a user can employ over a user interface.

Application Programming Interface (API)   A logically and closely related set of functions or Web services (for price calculation,

for example) that is intended for use by programmers.

Business Application Programming Interface (BAPI)   An open interface standard from SAP (Business Application Programming Interface) via which all SAP solutions provide their functions to each other and to applications of other manufacturers. All BAPIs can be addressed as a Web service.

Business process   A logically related execution of one or more functions from one or more applications, which supports the activities of an enterprise or the activities between enterprises.

Business scenario   A business scenario that consists of one or more topically related business processes and, as software, supports the activities of a business area or the activities between entire business areas.

Business Server Pages   A special SAP technology for creating Web-based user interfaces.

C   A procedural programming language that is used widely in operating systems and applications but is primarily used in scientific contexts. C++ and Java have increasingly supplanted C as part of the wide spread of object-oriented programming.

Class   In object-oriented programming, a class is a generalization of the properties of an object. In a class, you define the data that the objects in the class (instances) receive and the methods that can be applied to the data.

Client   A closed accounting unit with an SAP system. Client numbers are usually assigned to the group and to each subsidiary and must be entered when logging on to the SAP system. This approach logically differentiates the application data of the subsidiaries and that of the group. One subsidiary cannot change the data of another subsidiary.

Compiler   A program that converts the commands of a specific programming language into code or a machine language that a computer's processor understands and can execute. The code of interpreted programming languages is processed at runtime, but programs in compiler languages must be transformed before the program can run.

Component   Like applications, components are a collection of topically related functions and Web services. Components can be delivered independently of other parts of an application and have their own development cycle.

Data Dictionary   → ABAP Dictionary

Database   A collection of structured information that can be accessed (for reading and writing) with the help of a special language. Most of today's databases are organized in relational tables.

DDIC   → ABAP Dictionary

Directory   A directory is used to store common digital information.

Dynpro   Dynamic program. It is a component of an executable program and contains a graphical user interface for operation.

Dynpro flow logic   Part of a dynpro that is programmed with the help of a procedural language similar to ABAP.

Engine   The term "engine" describes the core of a large software package, much like the motor is the core of an automobile.

Enterprise Resource Planning (ERP)
ERP describes the software-supported organization of the essential business processes of an enterprise. ERP software provides applications for all important areas of enterprise: Accounting, HR, and materials management, for example. The applications standardize and simplify the related processes.

Field Symbol   Symbolic name of a data object. A field symbol points to a data object, so it initially does not occupy any storage space. Assignment to memory areas occurs during the program's runtime.

GUI   Graphical User Interface of an application.

GUID   Global Unique Identifier. System-wide, unambiguous key to access data.

Inheritance   In object-oriented programming, inheritance refers to passing on the definitions of a class (parent) to its subclasses (children).

Internet Standards   General and open standards used for communication and integration over the Internet. Examples include HTTP, XML, and WSDL.

Interpreter   A program that converts the commands of a programming language (an interpreter language like Perl) in machine-readable code at runtime. Unlike compiler languages like C, interpreter languages don't require compilation before the programs can run.

Java Platform, Enterprise Edition (JEE)
Defines the standard for the development of multilevel, Java-based enterprise applications. The standard was defined by an open initiative (with the participation of SAP) and developed by Sun Microsystems. For more information, go to java.sun.com.

Method In object-oriented programming, this term describes a logical sequence with which an object can be manipulated. A method is always an element of a class.

Microsoft.NET A platform developed by Microsoft for XML Web services. It consists of functions for the development and use of Internet-supported applications. For more information, go to www.microsoft.com/net.

Native SQL In ABAP source code, you can use the complete Structured Query Language (SQL) of the underlying database (for instance, from IBM or Oracle). SAP calls this type of database access Native SQL, but warns that Native SQL commands have to run on all databases. It differs from Open SQL, whose commands do run on all databases.

Object Objects are the matter of object-oriented programming. Each object belongs to a class or, more accurately, is the instance of a class in which you define the specific properties of an object (data, methods, and so on).

Object-oriented programming A new concept in application programming that began to spread in the mid-1990s. In early concepts (procedural programming), a program was seen as a logical process that generated output by manipulating the data that had been entered. The challenge lay in the optimal implementation of the manipulation logic. Object-oriented programming, however, begins with the objects that are to be manipulated (for instance, the windows and buttons on a screen). The manipulation logic is part of the object: each object already contains specifications about the possible data and about the actions (methods) that can be applied to the object. This information is stored in the classes, of which the individual objects are instances.

Open SQL In ABAP source code, a subset of Structured Query Language (SQL)) can be used directly by databases. SAP calls this subset Open SQL.

Release SAP calls the versions of its software releases.

Remote Function Call (RFC) RFC is a proprietary SAP protocol that can call the functions and BAPIs of applications from other computers. SAP provides the protocol as APIs for many operating systems and programming languages.

Repository Metadata and information (for instance, about development objects) is stored and made accessible in repositories. In the context of application development, the repository is primarily used for information during the configuration period.

SAP Business Suite The SAP Business Suite applications consist of the complete set of business applications from SAP. The obsolete name, mySAP.com, covered both business solutions and the underlying technology. The current differentiation between SAP Business Suite (applications) and SAP NetWeaver (platform and technology) clarifies the new strategic direction of SAP as a provider of solutions and technology.

SAP Easy Access   Menu with all the applications that are available to a user within an SAP system.

SAP GUI   Software that must be installed on an end user's computer so that the user can work with an SAP system. In the SAP GUI, user interfaces of ABAP programs are output, user entries are accepted, and entries are redirected to the ABAP program.

SAP NetWeaver   The name of the platform that is the foundation of new SAP system landscapes. SAP NetWeaver includes three important components: SAP NetWeaver Portal, SAP NetWeaver Application Server, and SAP NetWeaver Process Integration.

SAP R/3   Realtime System 3. A product from SAP that was the enterprise's global breakthrough in the market for business applications in the 1990s. SAP R/3 is based on a revolutionary three-layer architecture that separates the frontend, application server, and database from each other.

SAP system   An SAP system consists of three logical layers: SAP GUI, SAP NetWeaver Application Server, and the database. All three layers can physically reside on one computer.

Single Sign-on (SSO)   Mechanism that doesn't require users to enter a password for each system they log on to. With SSO, users identify themselves only to the front end. They can then log on to all the systems that are part of the single sign-on environment.

Web Dynpro   Technique for creating user interfaces for Java and ABAP programs. It is executed under SAP software, but it can be displayed and operated in the end user's Web browser.

Web service   Independent, modular functions that can be published, searched, and made accessible over a network with the help of open standards. They represent the implementation of an interface by a component. A Web service is a closed, executable unit. For the calling and transmitting unit, a service is a type of black box that requests an entry and delivers a result. Web services provide services for integration within an enterprise and across enterprises, regardless of the communications technology (synchronous or asynchronous) and of the format.

C   Sources and Literature Recommendations

Sources

- Färber, Günther; Kirchner, Julia: *mySAP Technology. Einführung in die neue Technologie-Plattform der SAP*. Galileo Press, Bonn 2002. (German only)

- Keller, Horst: *The Official ABAP Reference*. SAP PRESS, Boston 2005.

- Keller, Horst; Krüger, Sascha: *ABAP Objects. ABAP Programming in SAP NetWeaver*. 2nd edition, SAP PRESS, Boston 2007.

- Online help of the SAP system

- SAP Knowledge Warehouse

Literature Recommendations

- Heinemann, Frédéric; Rau, Christian: *Web Programming with the SAP Web Application Server*. SAP PRESS, Boston 2005.

- Kessler, Karl, et al.: *Java Programming with SAP NetWeaver*. SAP PRESS, Boston 2008.

D   The Authors

Günther Färber is a partner at NEXONTIS IT GmbH in Düsseldorf, Germany. He runs the development and consulting departments for insurance and banking.

During and after his IT studies, his reputation as a successful IT author helped to propel his career as an IT consultant and developer in numerous large projects at renowned enterprises and service providers. He began work in a startup company in 1997. In 2001, he and Julia Kirchner founded NEXONTIS IT GmbH.

Julia Kirchner is a managing partner at NEXONTIS IT GmbH in Düsseldorf, Germany. She runs the corporates and organization departments.

During and after her IT studies, she worked as a developer in several projects at renowned banks and service providers. She began work in a management position in a startup company in 1999. In 2001, she and Günther Färber founded NEXONTIS IT GmbH.

NEXONTIS

NEXONTIS is a highly specialized financials and technology consultancy firm that focuses on the support related to strategically significant, new requirements in the banking, insurance, and industry segments as well as their implementation using modern software technologies and applications in the SAP®, Microsoft®, and Oracle® environments. This focus involves the entire lifecycle of a project from the business/functional preliminary study, to the planning and design, to the implementation, training, and maintenance. For five years now, NEXONTIS has combined its industry expertise, which is evidenced by numerous publications and projects, with comprehensive management, process, and technology know-how and thus has contributed to the sustainable success of its customers.

Business Consulting

We have the necessary business experience to turn ideas into innovations and ultimately into successfully completed projects in the banking, insurance, and industry segments. Furthermore, we have the current know-how to implement the latest legal requirements in the areas of accounting, controlling, consolidation, publication, and registration in the corresponding processes within and across the enterprise.

Consulting for SAP

Close development cooperation with SAP over many years in the financial services and financials areas, including Strategic Enterprise Management, ensure that our employees receive first-hand SAP® know-how and pass it on to our customers. Moreover, as project coaches and SpeedUp consultants we ensure—often on behalf of SAP—an implementation phase that is optimized with regard to time and costs, and as troubleshooters we provide help in case of critical problems.

IT Consulting

Our technology is based on state-of-the-art fundamentals, such as SAP NetWeaver, Microsoft BackOffice Server, and Oracle, to be able to ensure the openness of the solutions created and their trouble-free integration with enterprise-internal and enterprise-external systems. Our employees can plan, set up, and maintain such heterogeneous system landscapes.

Software Development

With the help of our employees and focused on customer-specific developments and extensions on the basis of ABAP Objects, Java, and Microsoft.NET, we plan and implement requirements that an enterprise cannot implement using standard software. The ultimate goal here is the seamless integration with the other business processes and minimum adaptation of the existing standard software.

NEXONTIS Software

Over the course of the past several years, our employees utilized their experience to create the high-performance NEXONTIS Toolkit, which provides numerous tools to accelerate project implementation in the SAP financial service environment in the areas of interface connection, test automation, and business methods.

Publications

Our employees' numerous publications in trade journals, at conferences, and in books demonstrates our outstanding demand for quality, which sets us apart from competitors.

Index

1:1 relation, 225
3GL language, 117
4GL language, 117

A

AB, 17
ABAP, 20, 119, 491
  debugger, 87
  Dictionary, 491
  Editor, 52, 85
  Objects, 13, 24, 344
  runtime environment, 24, 491
  Workbench, 27, 60, 62, 491
ABAP/4, 22
Adapter, 491
ALV, 251
Ancestor, 378
ANY TABLE, 156
API (Application Programming
Interface), 491
  layer, 428
APPEND, 157
Application, 491
application base, 17
Application menu, 95
Application toolbar, 279
Area menu
  create, 95
Array, 117
AS CHECKBOX, 130
Assignment, 121
Attribute, 348
Authentication, 36
Avoiding redundancy, 164

B

Back end, 25, 27
Backward navigation, 51
BAdI, 32

BAPI (Business Application
Programming Interface), 31, 491
BEGIN OF, 152
BEGIN OF BLOCK, 246
BEGIN OF SCREEN, 246
Branching instruction, 184
Browser area, 60
Build, decentralized, 57
Business module, 21
Business process, 491
Business scenario, 491
Business Server Page, 60, 491

C

Call by Reference, 169
Call by Value, 170
CALL METHOD, 354
CALL SCREEN, 283
CALL SELECTION-SCREEN, 249
CALL SUBSCREEN, 283
CASE ... WHEN, 192
Casting, 130
CHAIN ... ENDCHAIN, 282
CHANGING, 168
Changing parameter, 167
Character, 131
Checklist for Programmers, 27
Checkman check, 490
Child class, 378
Class, 346, 347
  attribute, 355
  create, 366
  definition, 348
  hierarchy, 377
  implementation, 351
  method, 355
  redefine method, 390
CLASS_CONSTRUCTOR, 354
CLASS-DATA, 355
CLASS-EVENTS, 399
CLASS-METHODS, 355

Client, 21, 29, 37, 492
CLOSE CURSOR, 231
COLLECT, 157
Command line, 41
Comment, 30
Comment language, 30
Comparison operator
   IS SUPPLIED, 190
   BETWEEN, 186
   CA, 187
   CN, 187
   CO, 187
   CP, 188
   CS, 188
   EQ, 185
   GE, 186
   GT, 185
   IS ASSIGNED, 189
   IS BOUND, 189
   IS INITIAL, 190
   IS REQUESTED, 190
   IS SUPPLIED, 190
   LE, 185
   NA, 187
   NE, 186
   NP, 189
   NS, 188
Component, 492
Constant, 129
Constraint, 210
CONSTRUCTOR, 354
   static, 354
CONTINUE, 199
Control example, 60
CONTROLS , 287
Counting loop, 199
CREATE DATA, 128, 136
CREATE OBJECT, 347, 352

D

Data, 127, 348
Database design , 205
Database table, 225
   fields, 225

Data element, 207
   create, 213, 233, 294
   define, 210
   edit documentation, 216
   tables, 225
Data instances, 347
Data transfer, 227
Data type, 131
   any, 149
   Boolean, 135
   c, 131
   d, 134
   f, 133
   i, 132
   n, 132
   p, 133
   string, 135
   t, 134
   x, 133
   xstring, 135
DB layer, 428
Debugging, 56, 86
Declaration, 127
DEFINITION, 349
DELETE, 155, 159, 230
Derived class , 378
Descendent, 378
DESCRIBE FIELD, 356
Descriptive properties, 210
DESTINATION , 166
Developer key, 25, 27
Development class, 68
   create, 75
Development language, 30
Development object, 55
Development system, 29
Dictionary data type, 207, 484
   built-in, 209, 210
   select, 209
Directory, 492
DNS address, 35
DO ... ENDDO, 198
Domain, 210
   create, 292
Drag-and-Drop, 32
DUPLICATES, 159

Dynamic data, 128, 136
Dynpro, 278, 492
  flow logic, 119, 330

E

ENDFORM , 164
ENDING AT, 249
END OF, 152, 246
END OF BLOCK, 246
Engine, 492
Enhancement ID, 100
EnjoySAP, 251
ERP (Enterprise Resource Planning), 21
Event, 396, 397
  declare, 399
  trigger, 401
Exception, 167, 168
EXIT, 199
EXPORTING, 168, 169, 350

F

F1 help, 61
F4 help, *65*
FETCH, 231
FIELD, 281
FIELD-SYMBOLS, 130
Flat structure, 153
Floating point number, 133
Font convention, 16
Foreign key, 224
FORM, 164
Forward navigation, 51
Framework, 377
Front end, 25, 27
  integration, 33
Function, 163, 165, 348
Function group, 165
  create, 305
Function module, 165
  create, 306

G

Garbage collector, 136, 352
General report-formatting processor, 20
GET, 120
GET CURSOR, 121, 287
GET PF-STATUS, 285
GET PROPERTY OF, 120
GET REFERENCE OF, 121, 128
GET TIME, 120
Global class
  create, 389
  declare an event, 411
  define a method, 368
  define attributes, 370
  define event-handler methods, 412
  defining attributes, 390
Global table types, 365
Glue-Logic, 396
GUID (Globally Unique Identifier), 17
GUI (Graphical User Interface), 492
GUI status, 254, 256, 278
  create, 310
GUI title
  create, 309

H

Handler class, 399
Handler method, 398
  declare, 399
  register, 401
Hardware, 26
Hash algorithm, 156
HASHED TABLE, 156
help.sap.com, 105
Hexadecimal, 133
Hierarchical database, 20

I

IF ... ELSE, 192
IMPLEMENTATION, 351
IMPORTING, 168, 169, 350

IN, 248
INCLUDE, 79, 165
INDEX TABLE, 156
Inheritance, 378
INHERITING FROM, 378
Input elements, 129
Input interface, 246
Input parameter, 167
INSERT, 155, 157, 228
Instance constructor, 354
Integer, 132
Interface, 31, 166
Interface element
    create, 312
Interface parameter, 164, 166
Internal table, 151
Internal table types
    generic, 156
Internet standard, 492
Internet technology, 18

J

Java, 18
JEE (Java Platform, Enterprise Edition),
493
Just-In-Time Compiler, 52

K

Key, 224
Knowledge warehouse, 109

L

Layer model, 427
LEAVE SCREEN, 289
Library, 377
License renewal, 27
List, 78
Listener concept, 397
List header, 138
List of functions, 424

Local Class, 356
Local language, 211
Logical expression, 184
Logon, 32
Logon transaction, 36
Loop, 158, 198
LOOP AT SCREEN, 285
LOOP ... ENDLOOP, 282

M

m:n relation, 225
Main memory, 127
Main package , 69
MAPI layer, 427
Mapping, 209
Massachusetts Institute of Technology
(MIT), 343
Mass data, 151
Master data check, 210
MDI window, 32
Menu bar, 278
Menu system, 40
Message, 249
    create, 260
    define, 307
    output, 249
Message class, 250
    create, 260, 307
Message server, 36
Metadata, 136, 211
Method, 345, 347, 348, 355, 399
    define transfer parameters, 369
Method pointer concept, 397
Method redefinition, 379
Microsoft, 19
Microsoft.NET, 493
MODIFY, 155, 158, 230
MODIFY SCREEN, 286
Modularization, 164
MODULE, 281
Module pool, 78
MOVE, 121
MOVE-CORRESPONDING, 153

N

n:1 relation, 224
Name conflict, 72
Namespace, 31, 72
  customer, 481
Name
  technical, 44
Naming convention
  constants, 483
  Dictionary data types, 484
  error messages, 487
  function groups, 485
  function modules, 486
  general, 480
  message classes, 487
  messages, 487
  modules, 488
  program-local data types, 484
  screens, 488
  subprograms, 487
  variables and parameters, 481
  warnings, 488
Native SQL, 231, 493
Nested structure, 152
NON-UNIQUE KEY, 156
Notation rule, 119
Numeric, 132

O

Object, 343, 346, 347
  create, 352
  dereferencing, 353
  instance, 347
  list area, 60
  orientation, 343
  referencing, 352
  type, 347
OBJ layer, 428
OBLIGATORY, 130
Offset, 121
Online help, 105, 106
OPEN CURSOR, 231
Open SQL, 227, 493

Operator, 185
  AND, 191
  NOT, 191
  OR, 191
Oracle, 19
Original class, 378
Original language, 30
Output parameter, 167

P

Package, 68
Packed, 133
PARAMETERS, 86, 120, 129, 246, 248
Parent class, 378
passed data, 166
passed parameter, 166
passed variable, 166
Password, 37
pattern, 180
PERFORM, 165
Performance example, 61
Polymorphism, 377, 379
Pretty Printer, 85
PRIVATE SECTION, 349
Procedure, 163
PROCESS, 280
  AFTER INPUT, 280
  BEFORE OUTPUT, 280
  ON HELP-REQUEST, 280
  ON VALUE-REQUEST, 280
Production system, 29
Program, 78, 80
  copy, 145
  create, 82
  enter transport request, 83
Program check
  extended, 489
  tools, 489
Programming
  guideline, 31, 479
  object-oriented, 344
  procedural, 163, 344
Programming model, declarative, 117
Program start, 48
Property, 350

PROTECTED SECTION, 348
PUBLIC SECTION, 348
Publish and subscribe, 397

R

R/1, 19
R/2, 20
R/3, 21
RAD tools, 396
RAISE EVENT, 401
RAISING, 165, 168
RAM, 127
Rapid application development, 396
READ, 155, 158
Record, 151, 222
REDEFINITION, 379
    class constructors, 381
    instance constructors, 380
    methods, 379
REDEFINITION, 355
Reference variable, 128, 136
REFRESH CONTROL, 288
REF TO, 130
    OBJECT, 352
Relational database design, 224
Relational type, 224
Release, 493
Report, 78, 79, 89
Repository, 493
Repository info system, 62
RETURNING, 350
Return value, 121
REUSE_ALV_GRID_DISPLAY, 252
REUSE_ALV_GRID_LAYOUT_INFO_
rGET, 253
REUSE_ALV_GRID_LAYOUT_INFO_
rSET, 254
RFC (Remote Function Call), 493
RTTI, 357

S

SAP, 13
SAP access

setup, 24
SAP Basis, 20
SAP Basis system, 22
SAP Business Suite, 23
SAP Customer Relationship
Management, 13
SAP Easy Access, 39, 494
SAP ERP, 13
SAP GUI, 36, 494
SAP Help Portal, 105, 108
SAP Library, 110
SAP List Viewer, 243, 251
SAP Menu Painter, 278
SAP NetWeaver, 22
SAP NetWeaver Application Server, 17,
22
SAP NetWeaver Process Integration, 426
SAP Notes, 106, 113
SAP Object Navigator, 55
    browser area, 60
    getting started, 59
    object list area, 60
    tool area, 60
SAP screen painter, 25, 278
SAP Service Marketplace, 106, 112
SAP Supply Chain Management, 13
SAP system, 494
    back end, 25
    front end, 25
    hardware, 25
    Linux, 26
SAP Web Application Server, 17, 24
Save, 41
Screen, 279
    components, 278
    create, 312
    flow logic, 278, 280, 326
SELECT, 228
Selection help, 65
Selection list, 425
SELECTION-SCREEN, 246
SELECTION-SCREEN COMMENT, 246
SELECTION-SCREEN PUSHBUTTON, 246
SELECTION-SCREEN ULINE, 246
Selection text, 138
    edit, 217
SELECT-OPTIONS, 247

Server cluster, 35
Session, 42
  new, 49
SET, 121
  CURSOR, 286
  EXTENDED CHECK ON/OFF, 121
  HANDLER, 401
  HOLD DATA, 289
  PARAMETER, 121
  PF-STATUS, 284
  SCREEN, 284
  TITLEBAR, 285
Signature, 166
Single server, 35
SORTED TABLE, 155
Specification, 422
SSO (Single Sign-on), 38, 494
Stack list, 88
Standard software, business, 13
STANDARD TABLE, 155
Standard toolbar, 40, 278
STARTING AT, 249
Static attribute, 354
Static method, 354
Static variable, 128
Status bar, 280
Status line, 42
Stop transaction, 40
Structure, 151, 152
  create, 303
  deep, 153
Structure package, 69
Subprogram, 163
subprogram return code, 122
SUPPRESS DIALOG, 289
SY, 121
  sy-dbcnt, 122
  sy-host, 122
  sy-index, 122, 199, 200
  sy-subrc, 121, 168
  sy-tabix, 122
  sy-uname, 122
System
  field, 121
  information, 42
  requirement, 17
  setup, 32
  status, 46

T

Table
  create, 233, 297
  internal, 154
Table control, 282
Table control wizard, 318
Table key, 156
TABLE OF, 155
TABLES, 168
Table type
  create, 301
  global, 242
  internal, 155
Table view , 282
Technical property, 210
Test system, 29
Text element, 137
Text symbol, 138
  create, 306
TIME ZONE, 126
Title bar, 279
Tool area, 60
Top-down approach, 427
Transaction, 44, 64, 92, 93
  SE80, 490
Transformation layer, 426
TRANSPORTING, 158
Transport management system, 67
Transport Organizer, 67
Transport request, 76
Transport system, 58
TYPE, 128
Type casting, 358
Type checking, 211
TYPE REF TO, 128
TYPES, 152
Type safety, 211

U

Unicode, 17
UNIQUE KEY, 156

UPDATE, 229
Usage explanation, 207
User name, 37
USING, 168

V

VALUE, 128, 350
Value help, 65
Variable, 127
Visibility, 348

W

Web Dynpro, 34, 119, 244, 494
Web service, 494
WHERE, 228
WHILE ... ENDWHILE, 199
Workplace computer, 21
WRITE, 83, 120

Z

ZPTB00_BUSINESS_TRANSACTION, 290
ZPTB00_HELLO_WORLD, 81
ZPTB00_HOTEL_RESERVATION, 232
ZPTB00_HOTEL_RESERVATION_COOL, 254
ZPTB00_INTERNAL_TABLE_JUGGLER, 159
ZPTB00_PERFORMANCE_TESTER, 171
ZPTB00_PRODUCT_CONFIGURATOR_ GLOBAL, 365
ZPTB00_PRODUCT_ENHANCER_GL, 389
ZPTB00_PRODUCT_EVENT_GL, 411
ZPTB00_PROVISION_CALCULATOR, 193
ZPTB00_ROOM_CHECKER, 212
ZPTB00_SALES_ORDER, 138
ZPTB00_SALES_ORDER_DYNAMIC, 144
ZPTB00_SAVINGS_CALCULATOR, 200
ZPTB00_SYSTEM_INFORMATION, 123

Presents the most recent ABAP technologies and tools through the eyes of a developer

Includes new topics like syntax enhancements, ABAP Test Cockpit, AJAX, SAP BusinessObjects integration, XML processing, Rich Islands, NWBC 3.0, and many more

Rich Heilman, Thomas Jung

Next Generation ABAP Development

After reading this book, you will be able to assess and employ the new tools and features of ABAP within SAP NetWeaver 7.0 to 7.0 EHP2. The updated and revised second edition assumes a scenario where a fictive university has just converted from SAP R/3 4.6C to SAP NetWeaver 7.0 (SAP Business Suite 7.0), this time with the default installation option of EHP2. Readers will experience the entire development process of applications – design, development and testing of all areas – through the eyes of a developer, and will walk away with a firm understanding of many of the newer technologies or design techniques that were not previously available in ABAP.

approx. 695 pp., 2. edition, with CD, 69,95 Euro / US$ 69.95
ISBN 978-1-59229-352-0, Dec 2010

>> www.sap-press.com

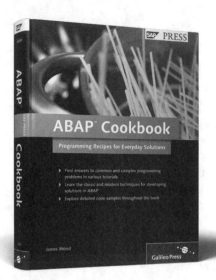

Find answers to common and
complex programming problems in
various tutorials

Learn the classic and modern
techniques for developing solutions
in ABAP

Explore detailed code samples
throughout the book

James Wood

ABAP Cookbook

Programming Recipes for Everyday Solutions

This book is intended to quickly provide answers to typical ABAP development
problems or tasks: persistence programming, interface programming, security
and tracing techniques, etc. You'll discover best practices in developing
solutions, and you can use this book to broaden your skills and see how to apply
ABAP to solve various types of problems. The complexity of the "recipes" ranges
from the simple starter plates to the complex main courses – and some sweet
deserts, of course! Each chapter is a short tutorial in itself, all organized and
consolidated into an easy-to-read format. Many code samples, screenshots, and
different icons will help you to follow the best practices provided. Enjoy your
ABAP meal!

548 pp., 2010, 69,95 Euro / US$ 69.95
ISBN 978-1-59229-326-1

>> www.sap-press.com

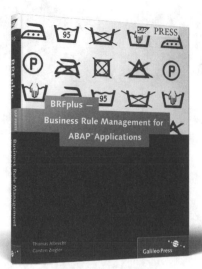

Discover the brand-new ABAP Rules Engine

Find out about functionality, content management, and Expression and Action Types

Benefit from extensive code tutorials

Thomas Albrecht, Carsten Ziegler

BRFplus – Business Rule Management for ABAP Applications

In modern architectures, business rules are modeled and maintained in central engines. BRFplus is the tool of choice for developing business rules in ABAP. This book introduces BRFplus in all its aspects. It explains the tool's architecture and how its rules are structured. You will learn how to modify and develop rules, how to incorporate them into your own landscape, and how to extend BRFplus. Including extensive examples and tutorials, this book is a one-stop resource for developers as well as business analysts.

approx. 420 pp., 69,95 Euro / US$ 69.95
ISBN 978-1-59229-293-6, Nov 2010

>> www.sap-press.com